Lecture Notes in Computer Science 15500

Founding Editors

Gerhard Goos
Juris Hartmanis

The series Lecture Notes in Computer Science (LNCS), including its subseries Lecture Notes in Artificial Intelligence (LNAI) and Lecture Notes in Bioinformatics (LNBI), has established itself as a medium for the publication of new developments in computer science and information technology research, teaching, and education.

LNCS enjoys close cooperation with the computer science R & D community, the series counts many renowned academics among its volume editors and paper authors, and collaborates with prestigious societies. Its mission is to serve this international community by providing an invaluable service, mainly focused on the publication of conference and workshop proceedings and postproceedings. LNCS commenced publication in 1973.

Dominic Orchard · Tomas Petricek ·
Jeremy Singer
Editors

Languages, Compilers, Analysis - From Beautiful Theory to Useful Practice

Essays Dedicated to Alan Mycroft on the Occasion of His Retirement

Springer

Editors
Dominic Orchard
University of Cambridge and University of Kent
Cambridge, UK

Tomas Petricek
Charles University
Prague, Czech Republic

Jeremy Singer
University of Glasgow
Glasgow, UK

ISSN 0302-9743 ISSN 1611-3349 (electronic)
Lecture Notes in Computer Science
ISBN 978-3-032-08186-5 ISBN 978-3-032-08187-2 (eBook)
https://doi.org/10.1007/978-3-032-08187-2

This Springer imprint is published by the registered company Springer Nature Switzerland AG
The registered company address is: Gewerbestrasse 11, 6330 Cham, Switzerland

Preface

If "academia is a pie eating contest where the prize is more pie", then what better way to celebrate the distinguished career of a retiring professor than by giving talks and writing papers! Thus, in Autumn 2023, with Professor Alan Mycroft formally retiring from the University of Cambridge, after almost 40 years, we thought it fitting to celebrate his career with a one-day research symposium and a formal festschrift—this special volume in LNCS.

This festschrift comprises original papers focussing on (a subset of!) the topics covered by Alan's illustrious career. Alan is well-known for pioneering contributions to programming language theory and applications, covering both design and implementation. His work ranges from compilation and optimization techniques, through semantics, static analysis, and type systems, to parallel, concurrent, and dataflow programming. A broad and deep career indeed!

Following a BA in Mathematics at the University of Cambridge (1977) (as a student at King's College), Alan completed the Diploma in Computer Science (1978). He then moved to Edinburgh for a PhD on the topic of "Abstract Interpretation and Optimising Transformations for Applicative Programs" which was completed in 1981 under the supervision of Rod Burstall and Robin Milner. After an EPSRC post-doctoral fellowship at Edinburgh from 1981–83 and a stint as a *Forskarassistent* ('Research Assistant') at Chalmers in Gothenburg, Sweden, Alan returned to the Computer Laboratory at the University of Cambridge in 1984. He remained there until his retirement in 2023, metamorphosing from Lecturer to Senior Lecturer, then Reader in Programming Language Implementation[1], before becoming Professor of Computing in 2004[2]. Since 1987 he has also been a fellow at Robinson College.

Along the way Alan co-created the Norcroft C compiler with Arthur Norman, co-authored the book *Java 8 in Action: Lambdas, Streams, and Functional-Style Programming*, and co-founded the Raspberry Pi Foundation, helping to "put the fun back into learning computing" and encouraging programming in the homes of families worldwide.

As well as being well-known for his many research contributions, Alan is also known as an enthusiastic collaborator and inspiring advisor. Alan has supervised over 30 PhD students and post-doctoral researchers. Many of his former students and post-docs went on to have academic careers of their own (including the festschrift editors), in turn sharing Alan's wisdom and enthusiasm for computer science with their own students. Compiling a complete list of Alan's PhD students, post-doctoral researchers, and co-authors is a task we leave for future historians, but the initial list collected for the purpose of the symposium contained over 100 names.

To those who have worked with Alan, or have been taught by him, he is renowned for his unstoppable enthusiasm for any challenging problem related to programming and computers, making him an inspiring teacher, mentor, and collaborator. The impact of his

---

[1] https://www.admin.cam.ac.uk/reporter/2001-02/weekly/5877/5.html.

[2] https://www.admin.cam.ac.uk/reporter/2004-05/weekly/5992/12.html.

work is reflected in the diversity of talks presented at his retirement symposium and in the papers of this collection. We chose the title of this festschrift, *Languages, Compilers, Analysis—From Beautiful Theory to Useful Practice*, as an attempt to span Alan's many interests as well as the breadth of his activities in both theory and practice.

In the rest of this introduction, we briefly report on the activities of the symposium, particularly as the intersection of the 16 symposium talks and the 12 festschrift papers is a strict subset of both sets.

Details of the Symposium

A one-day symposium was held in honour of Alan on Friday 1st December 2023 at the Department of Computer Science and Technology (formally known officially, and still known informally, as the 'Computer Laboratory'). The day comprised 16 talks alongside an introductory address from the current Head of Department, Prof. Alastair Beresford (who had been supervised by Alan earlier in his career). Dr. Ken Moody also gave a lively and entertaining account of Alan's time as an undergraduate at Cambridge in the 1970s, during which time Ken was Alan's Director of Studies in Mathematics (at King's College).
The following collects the titles and abstracts of these talks, some of which grew to be full papers contained in this volume[3].

On the Norcroft Compiler

Jeremy Singer, University of Glasgow

> Back in the mid 1980s, a "couple of academics wearing startup-company hats" were developing a retargetable C compiler. The most prolific target for this compiler was the Arm processor, newly designed by Acorn. In this talk, we will review 1980s compiler technology and see how the Norcroft compiler significantly advanced the state of the art, particularly highlighting the friendly error messages and graph-colouring register allocation. We will conclude by considering the legacy of the Norcroft compiler.

Static Analysis for Hardware Design

Mads Rosendahl, Roskilde University
Maja Kirkeby, Roskilde University

> Implementing algorithms in hardware can be a substantial engineering challenge. Hardware accelerators for some algorithms may be a way to achieve better time and energy efficiency of the computational problems. We explore some possible

[3] For those papers appearing in this volume but with an associated talk, the abstracts reported here may differ to the abstracts given with the final papers.

applications of static analysis in the design phase of construction hardware design for algorithms targeting field-programmable gate arrays (FPGA).

Drawing inspiration from Alan Mycroft's 2007 invited talk on static analysis and subsequent articles discussing the connection between hardware evolution, language design, and static analysis, we explore the usage of static analysis as a tool to facilitate the realization of hardware accelerators for algorithms. We examine methodologies for analyzing communication and data flows within the hardware design, thereby enhancing our understanding of these aspects in the pursuit of efficient FPGA-based algorithm implementations.

When Obfuscations Preserve Constant-Time

Matteo Busi, Ca' Foscari University of Venice
Pierpaolo Degano, Dipartimento di Informatica, Universita' di Pisa
Letterio Galletta, IMT School for Advanced Studies Lucca

Obfuscating compilers are designed to protect a program by obscuring its meaning and impeding the reconstruction of its original source code. Usually, the main concern with such compilers is their robustness against reverse engineering. On the contrary, little attention is paid to ensure that obfuscation introduces no attacks in the transformed program that were not present in the original one—in the style of secure compilation. We are interested in checking whether a given obfuscation technique preserves the constant-time property. Cryptographic libraries often resort to this property to guarantee that no attackers can learn any secret values by monitoring and analysing program execution time.

Here, we propose a sufficient condition to check if a given obfuscation preserves constant-time. Checking this condition amounts to a simple and efficient static analysis that can be easily implemented.

We consider several obfuscating transformations implemented in popular obfuscating compilers (e.g. the Tigress C compiler and O-MVLL).

By relying on our condition we prove that some of them preserve constant-time, while others do not. When a transformation breaks constant-time, we propose a translation validation that applies our condition case by case.

No Need to Imply Anything

Paulo Torrens, University of Kent

The need to reason about source programs has led to the development of intermediate representation languages whose semantics are well-suited for analysis and optimization techniques employed within compilers. The monadic nature of such languages traces back to the double-negation translation found in logic, where the use of continuations not only exposes details about a program's control flow, but it also allows for a very natural imperative interpretation of functional programs by dropping the basic notion of a function, seeing lambda terms through the lenses of labels and jumps. In this presentation we aim to cover some ground in this imperative interpretation of functional calculi, such as the case of Thielecke's CPS-calculus, arising both from practical interest within compiler development and from a theoretical viewpoint, as these languages correspond to systems of logic that reject implication as a primitive and take negation as a more basic notion instead.

The Contributions of Alan Mycroft to Abstract Interpretation

Patrick Cousot, Courant Institute of Mathematical Sciences, New York University

We briefly summarize the contributions of Alan Mycroft to abstract interpretation which he pioneered by inventing strictness analysis of higher-order functional programming languages in the early 1980s. His work originated a lot of research on strictness analysis and more generally the static analysis of functional programs, a crucial contribution to the theory, diffusion, and application of abstract interpretation.

Comonadic Notions of Computation Revisited

Tarmo Uustalu, Reykjavik University

Comonadic and graded comonadic notions of computation became the subject of the work of Alan and his students on static analysis with type-and-coeffect systems.

I want to revisit the issue that it only makes good sense to pair contextual values (like values with their pasts in dataflow computation) if they are of the same shape. How to control shapes? We considered one solution in our CMCS 2008 paper. What can we say in 2023?

How to Construct Graded Monads

Dylan McDermott, Reykjavik University

Models of computational effects based on graded monads are a useful tool for reasoning about programs. Each grade can be viewed as an abstraction of a set of computations that we can reason about, a perspective that is not available for models based on (ungraded) monads. Given this perspective, it is natural to wonder whether we can construct graded monads from monads by choosing sets of computations for grades to represent. We show that this is usually the case. If the chosen sets of computations satisfy some closure conditions, we can extract a graded monad almost for free. It turns out that many of the graded monads appearing in the literature can be seen as instances of this construction. We obtain a technique for constructing graded models from ungraded models, in such a way that the graded model can actually be used for program reasoning.

A Tale of Two Graded Calculi: The Marriage of Coeffects and Graded Comonads

Vilem Liepelt, University of Kent
Danielle Marshall, University of Kent
Dominic Orchard, University of Kent and University of Cambridge

The notion of graded types is an overarching paradigm for type systems that embed additional information for reasoning about the underlying structure of programs. Examples include a wide range of effect systems and coeffect systems, which capture respectively how a program changes its context or depends upon it. In the literature, two styles of coeffect system have emerged in the last decade: those in which coeffects annotations are pervasive (requiring annotations on function types), and those in which coeffects are added by way of a graded modal type operator atop some existing base language. In this work, we show how the two styles of coeffect systems relate and in what circumstances they have equivalent power. This parallels the two styles of effect reasoning in the literature: effect systems or (graded) monads, which have also been studied and found to be equivalent. Our work thus serves to unify the literature on coeffect systems to enable transfer of results and ideas in the future.

Linearity, Uniqueness, Ownership: An Entente Cordiale

Danielle Marshall, University of Kent

Ten years ago, Mycroft and Voigt surveyed notions of aliasing and ownership in programming languages, and argued for the view that many existing forms of aliasing control represent limited facets of the higher-level structured view corresponding to ownership. More recently, concepts of ownership and borrowing have become relevant to practical programmers as well as researchers through the medium of Rust, which aims to enforce safe memory management while bringing some of the guarantees offered by pure functional programming into the realm of performant systems code. Models like RustBelt and Oxide aim to formalise Rust's ownership system in detail, but there is less of a focus on integrating the basic ideas directly into more traditional functional type systems. We explain Granule's approach towards this, which builds on existing mechanisms for linearity and uniqueness through a form of grading akin to Boyland's fractional permissions, and discuss how this mechanism fits in to the framework presented by Mycroft and Voigt. We then look to the future, and briefly consider how a graded setting such as Granule's type system might be well suited for a more unified theory such as the one they hoped to uncover.

Sustainable Software Development—New Challenges for Programming, Language Design and Program Analysis

Bent Thomsen, Aalborg University
Lone Leth Thomsen, Aalborg University
Thomas Bøgholm, Aalborg University

Energy consumption and the associated CO2 footprint of Information and Communication Technology (ICT) has become a major concern. Some estimates suggest that 4–6% of global energy consumption in 2020 was spent on ICT and, although the ICT industry is very good at using green energy, CO2 emissions from ICT are at par with CO2 emissions from Aviation. Pessimistic forecasts suggest that energy consumption from ICT may rise to 20% in 2030.

Clearly software as such does not emit CO2, but software is executed on hardware, and hardware consumes energy when executing software. In recent years there has been a huge effort in understanding the relationship between software and energy consumption of the underlying hardware. There is now evidence that the structure of the software, the program constructs used in the software and even the programming languages and compilers used for developing the software influence the energy consumption when the software is executed. There is a huge global effort on raising awareness of sustainable software development and there is a growing body of knowledge of many aspects.

However, the literature on how programming language design and analysis can impact energy consumption of the underlying hardware is sparse.

In a seminal presentation at SAS 2007 Alan gave an overview of the changes going on in hardware and outlined his view on the implications of this on programming language design and analysis research. In this paper we will try to follow in Alan's footsteps and outline our view on the implications of energy consumption on programming language design and analysis research.

A Symbolic Computing Perspective on Software Systems

Arthur Norman, Trinity College Cambridge
Stephen Watt, University of Waterloo

Symbolic mathematical computing systems have served as a canary in the coal mine of software systems for more than sixty years. They have introduced or have been early adopters of programming language ideas such as dynamic memory management, arbitrary precision arithmetic and dependent types. These systems have the feature of being highly complex while at the same time operating in a domain where results are well-defined and clearly verifiable. These software systems span multiple layers of abstraction with concerns ranging from instruction scheduling and cache pressure up to algorithmic complexity of constructions in algebraic geometry. All of the major symbolic mathematical computing systems include low-level code for arithmetic, memory management and other primitives, a compiler or interpreter for a bespoke programming language, a library of high level mathematical algorithms, and some form of user interface. Each of these parts invokes multiple deep issues.

We present some lessons learned from this environment and free flowing opinions on topics including:

- Portability of software across architectures and decades,
- Infrastructure to embrace and infrastructure to avoid,
- Choosing base abstractions upon which to build,
- How to get the most out of a small code base,
- How developments in compilers both to optimise and to validate code have always been and remain of critical importance, with plenty of remaining challenges,
- The way in which individuals like Alan Mycroft, who has been able to span from hand-crafting Z80 machine code up to the most abstruse high level code analysis techniques, are needed, and
- Why it is important to teach full-stack thinking to the next generation.

Programming Systems Deserve a Theory Too!

Tomas Petricek, Charles University
Joel Jakubovic, University of Kent

Making programming easier and more accessible to non-experts has been a dream since the dawn of computing. In 1957, a catchy advertising brochure for FLOW-MATIC promised that the system will "virtually eliminate your coding load". We have certainly learned how to build more complex and reliable systems since then, but programming largely remains accessible only to experts and even a simple change requires navigating through hundreds of thousands of lines of code.

What would it take to make programming simpler and more accessible? In this somewhat philosophical talk, we will reflect on a number of issues that we encountered along the way when thinking about the problem. What would the notation for a simple programming system have to look like? Have visions around Free Software or Smalltalk taken us closer to this aim? And can we overcome Fred Brooks' tenet that "there is no silver bullet"?

The starting point for our investigation is the belief that we need to think less about programming languages, in which textual programs are written, and start to think about programming systems, interactive and stateful environments with which we interact when creating and using programs.

Air Quality Big Data Analytics Using Low-Cost Sensors

Eleftheria Katsiri, Democritus University of Thrace, Department of Electrical and Computer Engineering

Air pollution is the fourth most important risk of death factor in the world with a proven burden of disease that includes billions of deaths and thousands of disability-adjusted life years. Furthermore, 4000 industries and 3000 diagnostic labs, in Greece only, are required by law to monitor air quality. Recently, both the Covid-19 pandemic and climate change are changing current legislation worldwide, strengthening the need to monitor air quality.

On the other hand, the emergence of low-cost sensor technology has changed the pollution monitoring paradigm, by enabling the monitoring of pollutants close to the source, with high temporal and spatial granularity. This makes it possible to answer new questions about the underlying causes of poor air quality, ensure more accurate modelling and prediction at local scales, improve the ability to identify the links between air quality and human health or environmental degradation, identify potential air pollution "hot spots", enhance the ability to quantify the impacts of pollutant mitigation techniques and promote savings through on-demand ventilation. However, the exploitation of low-cost sensors requires in-depth knowledge of sensing principles, low-noise electronics, calibration in the lab and in the field, real-time edge processing and device-cloud communication, analytics and AI. Our team has been engaged in the development of reliable air quality sensing devices using low-cost sensors, custom sensor boards, embedded software and cloud services. The SibaIoT PM device used in this work measures ambient particulate matter concentrations in ug/m3 of three classes of particles, namely PM1.0, PM2.5, PM10, humidity and temperature. The device has very good accuracy, response time and sensitivity in indoor pollution levels.

With respect to the methodology, we have conducted a pilot application in a state-of-the art industrial space that is sensitive to infection caused by particulate matter such as dust. Fifteen PM devices were installed in three different production areas with varying air quality sensitivity. Indicative visual analytics are presented in the paper such as descriptive analytics, histograms, density, delay and line plots, as well as outcomes from the application of analytic functions such as Pearson correlation, k-means clustering, classification and aggregated exposure to pollution on the sensor data. More specifically, both Production-Area analytics, i.e., analysis of multiple time-series generated by multiple devices deployed at a specific production area, and Intra-Area analytics, i.e., analysis of multiple time-series generated by multiple devices deployed at logically connected production areas, are discussed. For example, we have calculated annual max, min, average values per day-of-the-week, shift, day-of-the-month, hour-of-the-day, poor, good and fair quality clusters.

Preliminary results show that the above analytics are promising in providing useful insights on both the level of pollution and the intensity of industrial activity in a dairy plant. For example we have found that air quality is aggravated indoors during weekdays, and that annual average particulate matter concentration follows humidity and temperature with a fixed lag.

Parallel Multiprecision Arithmetic the Easy Way

Cosmin Oancea, University of Copenhagen
Stephen Watt, University of Waterloo

In today's world, computation on multiple precision integers is a cornerstone of privacy and other applications. At the same time, every device, from telephones to desktop computers, has a GPU, often underutilized. Programming these using vendor libraries or low-level APIs is tedious and error prone and not at all suitable for writing high-level mathematical code.

We look at applying a functional data parallel language aimed at GPU computation to building big integer functions. These functions can be expressed in terms of natural arithmetic operations that compose just as those using primitive types. We examine how functional primitives can be used to give elegant and efficient GPU arithmetic for multiple precision integers of the sizes needed for practical applications.

Computational thinking bridging the conceptual gap between idiosyncratic architectures and high-level abstractions is one of the hallmarks of Alan Mycroft's work from which we have taken inspiration.

axs: a Workflow Automation Language for Omni-Benchmarking and Optimization

Anton Lokhmotov, KRAI
Leo Gordon, KRAI
Alastair Donaldson, Imperial College London

We present axs (pronounced "access"), a workflow automation language developed at KRAI with the primary purpose of benchmarking and optimization of Computer Systems for Machine Learning applications. We discuss the most salient features of the language in the context of preparing highly competitive and fully compliant submissions to MLPerf, an industry competition often referred to as "The Olympics of ML Benchmarking". axs has enabled hundreds of such submissions from KRAI's partners including Qualcomm, HPE, Dell and Lenovo, sometimes helping them to win "Gold" and "Silver" medals against the entrenched competition represented by NVIDIA.

Triemaps That Match

Simon Peyton Jones, Epic Games
Sebastian Graf, Karlsruhe Institute of Technology

The trie data structure is a good choice for finite maps whose keys are data structures (trees) rather than atomic values. But what if we want the keys to be *patterns*, each of which matches many lookup keys? Efficient matching of this kind is well studied in the theorem prover community, but much less so in the context of statically typed functional programming. Doing so yields an interesting new viewpoint—and a practically useful design pattern, with good runtime performance.

This paper grew out of work on compilers and functional programming, both of which are among Alan's long term interests.

And so Onto this Volume...

After the symposium, a call for formal submissions to this festschrift was announced, the accepted papers of which comprise this collection following a round of single-blind peer review in standard fashion. Each paper received three reviews and we accepted all 12 submissions. The scope and extent of Alan's career is reflected in the breadth of topics covered by these original contributions—a fitting tribute to Alan and the influence of his contributions through a large number of collaborators, students, and their descendants.

Thank you Alan for your enthusiasm, encouragement, and much scribbled feedback in red pen; a fabricated sample of typical Alan-esque annotations is depicted in Fig. 1. We hope you enjoy your retirement!

Dominic Orchard
Tomas Petricek
Jeremy Singer

Introduction to this Festschrift Volume Celebrating the Career of Prof. Alan Mycroft

Dominic Orchard[1,2][0000-0002-7058-7842], Tomas Petricek[3][0000-0002-7242-2208], and Jeremy Singer[4][0000-0001-9462-6802]

[1] University of Cambridge, Cambridge, UK
dominic.orchard@cl.cam.ac.uk
[2] University of Kent, Canterbury, UK
[3] Charles University, Prague, Czech Republic
[4] University of Glasgow, Glasgow, UK

Abstract. We briefly summarise the career of Prof. Alan Mycroft, to whom this festschrift volume is dedicated on the occasion of his retirement. Alan is well-known for pioneering contributions to programming language theory and applications, covering both design and implementation. His work ranges from compilation and optimization techniques, through semantics, static analysis, and type systems, to parallel, concurrent, and dataflow programming. The breadth and depth of his career, as well as the extent of his impact on the field, is reflected in the contributions comprising this volume, to which we give a brief introduction. We also report on the associated retirement symposium held in Cambridge at the end of 2023, including the titles and abstracts of contributed talks.

1 Introduction

If "academia is a pie eating contest where the prize is more pie", then what better way to celebrate the distinguished career of a retiring professor than by giving talks and writing papers! Thus, in Autumn 2023, with Professor Alan Mycroft formally retiring from the University of Cambridge, after almost 40 years, we thought it fitting to celebrate his career with a one-day symposium and a formal festschrift—this special issue of LNCS.

This festschrift volume comprises original papers focussing on (a subset of?) the topics covered by Alan's illustrious career. Alan is well-known for pioneering contributions to programming language theory and applications, covering both design and implementation. His work ranges from compilation and optimization techniques, through semantics, static analysis, and type systems, to parallel, concurrent, and dataflow programming. A broad and deep career indeed!

Following a BA in Mathematics at the University of Cambridge (1977) (as a student at King's College), Alan completed the Diploma in Computer Science (1978). He then moved to Edinburgh for a PhD on the topic of "Abstract Interpretation and Optimising Transformations for Applicative Programs" [1] which

Fig. 1. A copy of an early draft of the first page of this document is annotated with entirely fictional variations on Alan's paper comments that all his PhD students, including the authors of this introduction, remember fondly.

Organization

Organizing Committee

Dominic Orchard	University of Kent, UK & University of Cambridge, UK
Tomas Petricek	Charles University, Prague, Czech Republic
Jeremy Singer	University of Glasgow, UK

Review Committee

Shreya Banerjee	University of New Orleans, USA
Olaf Chitil	University of Kent, UK
Richard Gabriel	Dream Songs, USA
James Geddes	Alan Turing Institute, UK
Chung-Kil Hur	Seoul National University, Republic of Korea
Dejice Jacob	University of Glasgow, UK
Paul Keir	University of the West of Scotland, UK
Stephen Kell	King's College London, UK
Uday Khedker	IIT Bombay, India
Andy King	University of Kent, UK
James Noble	Creative Research & Programming, New Zealand
Chris Okasaki	United States Military Academy, USA
Santiago Olmos	Max Planck Institute for Security and Privacy, Germany
Olalekan Popoola	University of Cambridge, UK
Chris Preist	University of Bristol, UK
Vineet Rajani	University of Kent, UK
Abhiroop Sarkar	ETH Zurich, Switzerland
Vít Šefl	Charles University, Prague, Czech Republic
Robert Stewart	Heriot-Watt University, UK
J. Ryan Stinnett	King's College London, UK
Cristian Urlea	University of Glasgow, UK
Yizhou Zhang	University of Waterloo, Canada

Contents

Software

Compilers and Code Generators

The Norcroft Compiler at Arm

Jeremy Singer[1(✉)] and Lee Smith[2]

[1] University of Glasgow, Glasgow, UK
jeremy.singer@glasgow.ac.uk
[2] Formerly of Arm, Cambridge, UK
lee.d.smith@cantab.net

Abstract. In the mid 1980 s, a 'couple of academics wearing startup-company hats' were developing a retargetable C compiler. The most prolific target for this compiler was the ARM processor, a novel RISC architecture initially designed by Acorn and subsequently developed by Arm with input from its partners. In this paper, we will review 1980 s compiler technology and see how the Norcroft compiler significantly advanced the state of the art, particularly highlighting the friendly error messages, flexible intermediate representation and graph-colouring register allocation. We will review the reach and legacy of the Norcroft compiler over the past four decades.

1 Introduction

In this paper, we document the origins, development and use of the Norcroft compiler, particularly with respect to the backend targetting the 32-bit ARM[1] instruction set architecture (ISA). This material was originally presented at Alan Mycroft's festschrift event, convened at Cambridge in December 2023. The first author was one of Alan Mycroft's PhD students in the early 2000 s; as such he learned all about compilers from Alan's lecture courses and conversational anecdotes in the Computer Lab common room. The second author ran Acorn's Programming Languages Group from 1987 to 1990. He was responsible for selecting the NorCroft compiler (from a field of four) in late 1986. He then ran the Software Group in Arm which became the Compiler Group in 2000. He moved on from compilers in the early 2000 s but remained closely involved until he retired at the end of 2022.

The word 'Norcroft' is a portmanteau, composed of the first syllable of Arthur Norman's surname and the second syllable of Alan Mycroft's surname. It is unclear whether the word should be written in Camel Case, i.e. NorCroft [11], or in initial caps only, i.e. Norcroft [21]: the latter variant seems to be more prominent in general usage online.

[1] Although the acronym 'ARM' has changed its meaning over time, and the company 'Arm' has changed its capitalization, throughout this paper we endeavour to refer consistently to 'ARM' when we mean the historic processors, and to 'Arm' when we mean the company.

D. Orchard et al. (Eds.): Alan Mycroft Festschrift, LNCS 15500, pp. 3–13, 2026.
https://doi.org/10.1007/978-3-032-08187-2_1

Norman was the project supervisor for Mycroft's diploma project at the Cambridge Computer Laboratory in 1978. Mycroft completed his PhD at Edinburgh in 1981 [17], and later returned to Cambridge to take up a lecturing position in 1984. It was around this time that the two academics[2] started collaborating on an industrial strength C compiler, written from scratch and self-hosting.

The compiler was adopted by Acorn Computers Limited for their new Acorn RISC Machine (ARM) processor, in 1987. Acorn had trialled several compilers, including an internal port of the portable C compiler (PCC) [13,14]. After evaluating several options, Acorn chose Norcroft based on its performance, licence flexibility, and the opportunity to further develop the compiler collaboratively.

In this paper, we review the background context in which the Norcroft compiler was initially developed (Sect. 2); then we consider particularly innovative features of this compiler (Sect. 3); we explore the adoption of the compiler toolchain (Sect. 4) and the enduring legacy of Norcroft (Sect. 5); finally Sect. 6 concludes.

2 Background

This section reviews the context in which the Norcroft compiler was developed, in terms of both the technological and commercial settings.

2.1 Computer Architecture

Through the 1970 s and early 1980 s, complex instruction set computers (CISC) had dominated the design of computer architecture. The Digital Equipment Corporation PDP machines, on which the C programming language was originally designed and implemented, were classic CISC specimens. However, the new design philosophy of reduced instruction set computers (RISC) was emerging in the early 1980 s. RISC devices were characterized by simple load/store architectures, simplified addressing modes, large general purpose register files and simple instructions with fixed-size encodings. The novel RISC approach was pioneered in the USA by Patterson [22], Hennessy [9], and others with remarkable early performance results. This innovation was soon spun out into companies, with processors families like SPARC and MIPS.

In the UK, Furber and Wilson were designing a new processor for their next-generation BBC Micro machine. Influenced by the RISC ideas from across the Atlantic, they developed a load-store architecture featuring per-instruction conditional execution and a barrel-shifting functional unit supporting a huge variety of shift operations. This was the ARM1, which was initially emulated in an 808-line BBC BASIC program [28]. The simple instructions of the ARM processor enabled pipelined execution, simplified decode, fetch and execute. There was a uniform instruction encoding and a register file with 16 32-bit registers. The prototype hardware for the ARM1 processor was fabricated in 1985. Early ARM

[2] John Fitch became involved at a later stage.

chips were released as coprocessors for the existing BBC Micro computer in 1986, with users expected to develop in machine code [3].

Acorn built 100 ARM1 workstations for internal use and to support development of Archimedes and associated operating systems (OSs). These machines had 4 MB of DRAM and 10 MB or 20 MB Winchester disks. Later on, the ARM processors were embedded in Acorn 'Archimedes' machines running RISC OS, a new graphical operating system developed in-house. ARM processors were also used in Acorn machines running a Unix variant known as RISCiX.

A key premise of RISC approach was that the compiler needed to be 'sufficiently smart', since the simplicity of the hardware placed a greater burden on the code generator to schedule instructions appropriately. However, it seems like the majority of early programs targeting ARM were written directly in assembly language. Was the ARM C compiler largely an afterthought?

2.2 Compiler Technology

Unlike the present time, when large open-source compilers like GCC and LLVM are widely available, back in the 1980 s compilers were much more esoteric. The first release of GCC was in 1987, and LLVM development commenced in 2000.

Much of the received wisdom regarding compilation was collated in the 'Dragon' textbook. The first edition (also known as the 'Green Dragon' book) was published in 1977 [2]. This textbook advocates syntax-directed translation into three-address code, bitvector-style data-flow analysis, and tree-based pattern-matching code generation with heuristic register allocation. This state-of-the-art approach is largely the model adopted by the Norcroft compiler. Note the second edition ('Red Dragon') book was not published until 1988 [1].

The 'standard' C compiler, if there was such as thing in the mid 1980 s, was the Portable C Compiler (PCC) from Unix [13]. Acorn did have an in-house project to adapt PCC for the ARM processor. However, PCC was inferior in performance relative to the Norcroft compiler, in terms of time and space for target generated code. For this reason, PCC development was abandoned in favour of adopting Norcroft.[3] Another complication involved legal issues: it was unclear whether PCC could be shipped as a RISC OS (i.e. non-Unix) compiler without Acorn entering into complex licence negotiations with AT&T.

While there were several C compilers available for Acorn's earlier BBC Micro computers [7], these were mostly front-ends that generated intermediate portable bytecode, which was then executed via an interpreter on the BBC's 6502 processor.

One of the key risks associated with C compiler development in the 1980 s was the evolving nature of the C language. The original syntax was specified *de facto* by Kernighan and Ritchie in 1978 [15,24]. Throughout the 1980 s there were standardization efforts led by ANSI committee X3J11, resulting in a number of intermediate draft standards before publication of the official ANSI C standard

[3] Information personally communicated to the first author by Sophie Wilson, but see expanded discussion in Sect. 4.

(ANSI X3.159-1989) in 1989. C compiler front-ends and libraries developed during this period needed to adapt constantly to the changing ANSI draft standards [23].

2.3 Commercial Background

Much of Acorn's early commercial success was derived from their partnership with the BBC Computer Programme, also known as the Computer Literacy Project. Around 1 million BBC-badged Acorn computers were sold through the 1980 s [12], based on the 6502 processor. Early versions of the Acorn 'Archimedes' computer with the ARM processor were also branded as BBC machines, although this was brought to a halt by complaints about unfair marketing from Acorn's industrial competitors.[4]

Many of the early Acorn applications (including OS components) were written directly in ARM assembly. A few programs and components were written in C, including the OS-bundled applications !Draw, !Edit and !Paint. These components would have been compiled with the Norcroft compiler.

The crucial point is that a commercially viable platform requires a strong software development ecosystem, including a C compiler toolchain. Norcroft provided the foundations for this ecosystem to Acorn in 1987, and continued to do so for at least a decade (see later sections).

3 Compiler Novelty

In a Usenet post to the `comp.lang.c` newsgroup [18] Mycroft describes the Norcroft developers as 'a couple of academics wearing startup-company hats' and the compiler as 'a re-targetable, optimising ANSI (draft) C compiler, oriented at the many new risc machines (e.g. register colouring etc.)'. He goes on to post a promotional announcement about the Norcroft compiler, reproduced in full in Fig. 1.

3.1 Front-End

The front-end of Norcroft, for the C language, is a hand-crafted recursive descent parser. This design decision was made in the interests of efficiency. The Norcroft parser is notably different from the PCC parser, which is a synthesized table-driven parser based on a yacc specification of the C grammar.

One key feature of the Norcroft parser is its user-friendly, actionable error messages, which is noticeably different from other toolchains of the same era [4]. Examples of such error messages are shown in Fig. 2.

The front-end featured support for the evolving C language definition. The ANSI C standard (including the C standard libraries) was effectively being developed concurrently with the Norcroft compiler. The Norcroft parser featured a

[4] https://nosher.net/archives/computers/micro_user_1989-08_001.

```
The NorCroft C compiler is a significantly optimising re-targetable
C compiler to the ANSI draft standard. It includes many 'lint'-like
features and warnings for common errors (e.g. printf format/argument
checks, '=' and '==' confused, /* inside comment, etc.).

The optimiser includes register allocation by colouring, loop invariant
optimisation and tail-recursion removal. Rapid re-targetability is
encouraged by the use of a machine (parameterised, but otherwise)
independent code which easily translates into many register-oriented
target architectures including many RISC machines. Ports to CISC
machines (e.g. NS32000) use peephole optimisation to map a load-store
architecture onto all of the CISC addressing modes while preserving
the ability to freely allocate temporaries and variables into
machine registers.

Standard NorCroft compilers can produce both assembler- and object-form
output. The compiler itself is written in C and includes many self-
checks.

NorCroft has holds and/or has licensed the machine independent
parts to various organisations for back-ends for
Acorn ARM, Inmos Transputer, IBM 370, AMD 29000, Clipper,
Motorola 68000-series, National Semiconductor 32000-series
and various proprietory CPU's.

A port (re-target) generally takes several weeks to the compiler being
able to bootstrap itself (of course exploiting every machine idiom takes
longer). In addition a small minority of our clients have been involved
in producing stack-oriented machine code directly from the optimised
parse tree instead of using the general register-oriented optimiser.

Various rights are for sale, including source code.
```

Fig. 1. Norcroft marketing collateral, as posted on Usenet in 1988

```
* Digit 8 or 9 found in octal number
* Missing hex digit(s) after \x
* \<space> and \<tab> are invalid escape sequences
* Wrong number of parameters to <function>
* Questionable use of '=' (not '==') in condition context.
* Dangling 'else' indicates possible error
* 'break' not in loop or switch - ignored
```

Fig. 2. Sample error messages and warnings

`-fussy` flag that promised to 'be extra strict about enforcing conformance to ANSI standard'.

Arm's in-house C++ was developed 1993–1997. To support C++, Arm first ensured that its Norcroft-derived C compiler could accept the output of CFront, an AT&T source-to-source translator lowering C++ to C. Arm then added C++ language support (but not templates or exceptions, since these were largely unused by embedded software in the 1990 s) based on Stroustrup's 'brown book' specification of C++ [25], finally licensing the Edison Design Group (EDG) C++ front-end when that became available in the second half of the 1990 s.

3.2 Middle-End

After lexical and syntax analysis, the parser produced a conventional tree representation and some canonicalization and optimization was performed prior to first-level code generation, at which stage the program was transformed into an abstract, three-address intermediate code with an unlimited set of virtual registers, This was an ideal abstraction, similar to Lattner's LLVM but predating it by more than a decade [16]. This abstract instruction set is referred to as JOP-code or jopcode.[5] There are standard jopcodes for loading/storing 8-bit bytes and 32-bit words from/to memory. There are also standard jopcodes for performing integer and floating point arithmetic. Instructions have variants for operands that are constants, in-memory variables or register values, with opcode typing for integers, floats and doubles. Low-level control flow is supported, including procedure calls and returns, also branching. Effectively, jopcode resembles the ARM ISA but with unlimited registers.

Peephole-style optimizations were performed on the intermediate representation, mostly to improve the code for halfword and signed byte loads. ARM7 later added proper support for 8-, 16-, and 32-bit signed and unsigned data types. The barrel shifter isn't really visible at the ISA level. It just manifests as signed and unsigned shifts of all lengths, 0-31 bits, and the rotate operation for which there is no C-language denotation, although there is a popular idiom. Rotating right by `N` is equivalent to shifting left by `32-N` bitwise ORRed with the same value shifted right by `N`. The compiler was taught to recognize `(x` $\ll$ `(32-N)) | (x` $\gg$ `N)` as `N`-bit right rotation of X, with a dual version for left rotation. Effectively this is pattern-matching on the expression tree.

Higher-level optimizations were largely standard. The most significant ones were common subexpression elimination and colouring register allocation. Flow-graph flattening was well constructed and supported tail call elimination, a simple high-level optimization from functional programming. There was a lot of very careful local code generation for function prologues and epilogues. Implementation details are sketched out in a set of lecture notes presented by Norman and Mycroft at the 1992 edition of the SOFSEM conference (an annual winter sem-

[5] Why JOP? It stands for Intermediate Operation Code, but IOP is not easy to pronounce so JOP (jay-OP or JOP) was chosen by Norman and Mycroft.

inar for computer scientists and software engineers in former Czechoslovakia) [19].[6]

A novel form of *faint variables analysis* was implemented in the Norcroft compiler. The available documentation [10] credits Giegerich et al. [8] for faint variables analysis in 1981, predating the Norcroft compiler. However, the fact remains that faint variable analysis was independently invented in Norcroft. Arthur Norman, who implemented this analysis, thought that it was 'the obvious thing to do'.[7]

3.3 Back-End

The most innovative feature of the code generation phase in the Norcroft compiler was its register allocation algorithm. This was based on register allocation by graph colouring, similar (but not identical) to the published technique of Chaitin from IBM [5]. Details of the Norcroft algorithm for register allocation are presented in the SOFSEM lecture notes [19]. The key benefit of the ARM architecture is its relatively large (for the time) register file with 15 general-purpose integer registers. A post-allocation peepholer was added at Acorn but it was never reliable.

4 Toolchain Reception

Acorn started to evaluate its C compiler options for ARM in late 1986.[8] The candidates were:

- SVr4's Portable C Compiler (PCC): compatible with Unix SVr4 source code;
- Lattice Logic's multi-source, multi-target C compiler;
- a from-scratch partial code generator written in-house by a couple of Acorn engineers working part time, to be attached to PCC's front-end;
- Norcroft; and
- Green Hills C compiler, not ideal due to prohibitive licensing costs, the requirement for an ongoing maintenance contract, and the difficulties of 1980 s transatlantic communication.

The most important action was to make a decision and terminate the others so they stopped consuming time and money. After a fairly brief evaluation, Acorn chose to back Norcroft and a joint development project began. Legal formalities were concluded in early 1987. The Acorn compiler team set about adding PCC compatibility to Norcroft and after a few months, it was possible to build SVr4 Unix for ARM.

The compiler was incorporated into Acorn's C Development Environment, which was the standard software development kit for RISC OS (Fig. 3). This

---

[6] https://www.sofsem.cz.

[7] Confirmed by personal communication from Alan Mycroft via Uday Khedker.

[8] The second author was asked to run the exercise, which was primarily a pragmatic business evaluation of candidate 'spec-ware'.

compiler was used for many projects, internally at Acorn and externally by third party developers. For instance, the developer David Pilling says, 'through my RISC OS career I only ever used Norcroft C'.[9]

5 Norcroft Legacy

The Norcroft compiler was relicensed into Arm when the company was spun out from Acorn as a separate legal entity in 1990. At this time, Arm had its own internal software tools division with four employees (33% of the initial workforce) of whom two were compiler engineers. By the end of 1994 the software tools group was around a dozen employees. The Norcroft compiler was used to generate code for the new Apple Newton device, a forerunner of the modern Arm-based Apple products.

Fig. 3. Front cover of the Acorn C Development Environment

The Norcroft-derived compiler remained as Arm's main proprietary compiler until a derivative of LLVM took over in the 2010s. However, the ARM fork of Norcroft started to diverge in 1995 as a result of trying to incorporate a new C++ front-end. The last successful merge was towards the end of 1995. Further, the back-end code generator also diverged because of the need to support the new 16-bit Thumb compressed instructions for memory-constrained embedded targets, such as cellphones. The first processor to support Thumb was the ARM7TDMI, released in 1994.

The in-house C++ front-end was replaced with the EDG front-end around 2000, providing support for templates. An optimization component from Crescent Bay Software[10] was included in 2004 to handle loop optimization and reshaping. In effect, very little of the original Norcroft codebase remained by the 2000 s.

The ARM backend for GCC was supported in-house from summer 1993 onwards. Customer demand meant Arm became more engaged with GCC from 1997 onwards, but the licensing terms of the GPL proved to be an obstacle for some commercial customers. By 2010, when AArch64 was under development, the Arm internal compiler group recognized the need to support both GCC and LLVM—which remains the state of affairs today.

In addition to the ARM backend, the Norcroft compiler also targeted a range of platforms including the Inmos Transputer [27] and the Cambridge Consultants

9 https://www.davidpilling.com/wiki/index.php/SoftwareBuild.
10 http://www.crescentbaysoftware.com/.

Extensible Application Processor (XAP). The compiler's amenability for retargeting derived largely from its flexible intermediate representation.

The Codemist Limited company was incorporated in 1987 and wound down in 2016 [6]. This was the commercial vehicle for Norcroft and other toolchains; on its website, the company was described as 'a software provider, dedicated to the creation of high quality software in the areas of compilers and symbolic computation'. Financial records filed with the UK Companies House database show that the Codemist annual turnover was generally in the tens of thousands of pounds, presumably the majority of this income was derived from Norcroft compiler licensing.

6 Conclusions

While the Norcroft compiler toolchain is now little more than a historical footnote, it was an important contributor to the success of the Arm ecosystem (particularly in the period 1991-2005) and Arm's Norcroft-derived compiler was not fully displaced by an LLVM-derived compiler until late in the 2010 s. Additionally, the development experience of the Norcroft compiler served to furnish case studies for compiler construction lecture series over several decades at the University of Cambridge Computer Laboratory [20].

As we have surveyed, there were several features that characterized the Norcroft compiler. Its front-end was an efficient, hand-crafted recursive descent parser for the evolving ANSI C standard. The Norcroft compiler was able to bootstrap itself in under 4 MB of memory. There was attention to detail in optimizing the tree representation, generating intermediate code, flattening the flowgraph, and final code generation (including crafting prologues and epilogues very carefully). Graph-colouring register allocation was critical to performance of the generated code.

While modern compilers may use radically different techniques for parsing (such as synthetic parsers generated from high-level grammar specifications) and register allocation (including exotic techniques such as integer linear programming) the Norcroft compiler was renowned for its reasonable compile times and target code efficiency.

In a small but meaningful way, the Norcroft compiler has contributed to the success of the Arm ecosystem, which is now practically ubiquitous, with around 280 billion ARM chips shipped cumulatively, in 2024 [26].

References

1. Aho, A., Sethi, R., Ullman, J.: Compilers: Principles. McGraw Hill, Techniques and Tools (1988)
2. Aho, A., Ullman, J.: Principles of Compiler Design. Addison-Wesley (1977)
3. Antell, B.: Acorn Computers Limited - Press Release (1986). http://chrisacorns.computinghistory.org.uk/docs/Acorn/PR/Acorn_announces_the_ARM_Evaluation_kit.pdf

4. Burke, M.G., Fisher, G.A.: A practical method for LR and LL syntactic error diagnosis and recovery. ACM Trans. Program. Lang. Syst. **9**(2), 164–197 (1987). https://doi.org/10.1145/22719.22720
5. Chaitin, G.J.: Register allocation & spilling via graph coloring. In: Proceedings of the 1982 SIGPLAN Symposium on Compiler Construction, pp. 98–105 (1982). https://doi.org/10.1145/800230.806984
6. Companies House: Codemist limited (2024). https://find-and-update.company-information.service.gov.uk/company/02197915
7. Denning, A.: To C or not to C. Acorn User **1**(65), 149–153 (1987). https://archive.org/details/AcornUser065-Dec87/page/n150/mode/1up
8. Giegerich, R., Möncke, U., Wilhelm, R.: Invariance of approximative semantics with respect to program transformations. In: Proceedings of the Third Conference of the European Co-operation in Informatics, pp. 1–10. Springer (1981). https://doi.org/10.1007/978-3-662-01089-1_1
9. Hennessy, J., et al.: MIPS: a microprocessor architecture. SIGMICRO Newsl. **13**(4), 17–22 (1982). https://doi.org/10.1145/1014194.800930
10. Horwitz, S., Demers, A., Teitelbaum, T.: An efficient general iterative algorithm for dataflow analysis. Acta Informatica **24**, 679–694 (1987). https://doi.org/10.1007/BF00282621
11. Howe, D., et al.: Free online dictionary of computing: Norcroft (1994). https://foldoc.org/NorCroft
12. Jarman, N.: BBC microcomputer - how many? (2024). https://bbcmicro.computer/how-many-made
13. Johnson, S.C.: A portable compiler: theory and practice. In: Proceedings of the 5th ACM SIGACT-SIGPLAN Symposium on Principles of Programming Languages, pp. 97–104 (1978). https://doi.org/10.1145/512760.512771
14. Johnson, S.: A tour through the portable C compiler (1981). http://maibriz.de/unix/ultrix/_root/porttour.pdf
15. Kernighan, B.W., Ritchie, D.M.: The C Programming Language. Prentice Hall (1978)
16. Lattner, C., Adve, V.: LLVM: a compilation framework for lifelong program analysis & transformation. In: International Symposium on Code Generation and Optimization, pp. 75–86. IEEE (2004). https://doi.org/10.1109/CGO.2004.1281665
17. Mycroft, A.: Abstract interpretation and optimising transformations for applicative programs. Ph. D. thesis, University of Edinburgh (1982). http://hdl.handle.net/1842/6602
18. Mycroft, A.: Query about C compilers on IBM 370s (1988). https://groups.google.com/g/comp.lang.c/c/Vdr-swuohZY/m/kc4laj-Hq2kJ
19. Mycroft, A., Norman, A.: Optimising compilation. Tech. Rep. UCAM-CL-TR-269, University of Cambridge, Computer Laboratory (1992). https://doi.org/10.48456/tr-269
20. Mycroft, A., et al.: Optimising compilers (2021). https://www.cl.cam.ac.uk/teaching/2021/OptComp/
21. Norman, A., Fitch, J., Mycroft, A.: Codemist Compilers / Norcroft (2017). https://foldoc.org/NorCroft
22. Patterson, D.A., Ditzel, D.R.: The case for the reduced instruction set computer. ACM SIGARCH Comput. Archit. News **8**(6), 25–33 (1980). https://doi.org/10.1145/641914.641917
23. Ritchie, D.M.: The development of the C language. In: The Second ACM SIGPLAN Conference on History of Programming Languages, pp. 201–208 (1993). https://doi.org/10.1145/154766.155580

24. Ritchie, D.M., Johnson, S.C., Lesk, M., Kernighan, B., et al.: The C programming language. Bell Sys. Tech. J **57**(6), 1991–2019 (1978)
25. Stroustrup, B.: The C++ Programming Language. Addison-Wesley (1985)
26. Thornton, I.: Arm holdings plc Q3 FYE24 results (2024). https://investors.arm.com/static-files/187d293b-42eb-48b0-b82f-e78bce4da9e4
27. Whitby-Strevens, C.: The transputer. In: Proceedings of the 12th Annual International Symposium on Computer Architecture, pp. 292–300 (1985). https://doi.org/10.1145/327070.327269
28. Wilson, S.: ARM development (2009). https://en.wikipedia.org/wiki/Sophie_Wilson#/media/File:ARM_development.jpg

When Obfuscations Preserve Constant-Time

Matteo Busi[1](✉), Pierpaolo Degano[2,3], and Letterio Galletta[3]

[1] DAIS, Ca' Foscari Università di Venezia, Venezia, Italy
matteo.busi@unive.it

[2] Computer Science Department, Università di Pisa, Pisa, Italy
pierpaolo.degano@unipi.it

[3] IMT School for Advanced Studies Lucca, Lucca, Italy
letterio.galletta@imtlucca.it

Abstract. Obfuscating compilers are designed to protect a program by obscuring its meaning and impeding the reconstruction of its original source code. Usually, the main concern with such compilers is their correctness and their robustness against reverse engineering. On the contrary, little attention is paid to ensure that obfuscation introduces no attacks in the transformed program that where not present in the original one. Cryptographic libraries often resort to the so-called cryptographic constant-time property to guarantee that no attackers can learn any secret values by monitoring and analyzing program execution time.

Here, we propose a sufficient condition to check if a given obfuscation preserves the constant-time property. Checking this condition amounts to a simple and efficient static analysis that can be easily implemented. We consider several obfuscating transformations implemented in popular obfuscating compilers (e.g. the `Tigress` C compiler and `O-MVLL`). By relying on our condition we prove that some of them preserve constant-time, while others do not. For the last case we propose a translation validation procedure that applies our condition to the given program and verify whether instead the constant-time property is kept.

Keywords: Secure compilation · Hyperproperty preservation · Secure translation validation

Although Alan and I had met at various conferences before, I had the rare pleasure to start cooperating with him only in 1993 within LOMAPS, a four-years ESPRIT Basic Research Project, founded by the EU Commission.
Since we met in Aarhus at the kick-off of that project, Alan established a special connection (even!) with me, maybe because of a sympathetic mutual understanding, a rather informal way of phrasing our comments, sometimes a little too sarcastic, but never unrespectful.

D. Orchard et al. (Eds.): Alan Mycroft Festschrift, LNCS 15500, pp. 14–32, 2026.
https://doi.org/10.1007/978-3-032-08187-2_2

That's why I consider Alan a great friend of mine, and I wish we will have more chances to meet and to share good bottles of wine—well, beer or rye will also do.
It was indeed easy for me to talk my young co-authors into writing this little
note, to express our gratitude for Alan's friendly and generous nature and for his impressive scientific contributions: Grazie Alan!
Pierpaolo

1 Introduction

The goal of an obfuscating compiler is to generate code that hides the purpose and the logic of the original program, as well as the confidential values embedded in it. In this way, the security of a piece of software gets enhanced against an attacker who can physically access, inspect, modify, and run it (*man-at-the-end attacks* [12]). Indeed, obfuscations protect secrets, are typically robust against compiler optimizations, make tampering difficult, and hinder reverse engineering, both for humans and for automated tools. The literature reports on many obfuscation techniques, among which are control flow flattening [19], opaque predicates [21], and mixed boolean-arithmetic transformations [31]. Also several commercial and open source tools [23,29] implement them. Usually, the main concern with such techniques is their robustness against reverse engineering and their correctness, i.e., whether they preserve program semantics. On the contrary, little attention has been paid to ensure that an obfuscation introduces no attacks that where not present in the original program.

We here aim to contribute to this little-studied line of research. In particular, we are interested in checking whether a given obfuscation technique preserves a well-studied security property, namely, *the (cryptographic) constant-time policy*. This property is particularly relevant for cryptographic libraries, because it prevents timing attacks, i.e., it ensures that an adversary cannot learn about secret values of programs by monitoring and analyzing their execution time (no secrets are leaked). Verification of the constant-time property has been investigated to a great extent in the literature [3–5]. To our knowledge, less research efforts have instead been devoted to study the interplay between obfuscation and constant-time [11]. Obfuscation may decrease the performance of a cryptographic program, but this price is worth paying when secrecy is a major concern. As an application case, consider the so-called white-box cryptography, where the cryptographic keys are embedded in the software, which the attacker fully controls, thus requiring the keys to be to heavily protected.

To reduce this gap, we place ourselves in the comfortable pure linguistic setting of Jasmin [15], a programming language for high-assurance and high-speed cryptography, and we follow Barthe's et al. [4] intuition: a program is constant-time if (*i*) it never branches on secrets and (*ii*) it never performs secret-dependent memory accesses. As expected, the constant-time property amounts to a form of observational non-interference: an attacker cannot distinguish any two runs of a program when executed on equivalent states, i.e., roughly speaking, that only differ in their private parts. Checking the preservation of constant-time means that the obfuscation transformation introduces no leaks of secret values that were not already present in the original program.

To achieve that, we propose a sufficient condition that guarantees that a given obfuscation preserves constant-time. This condition intuitively requires proving, for all programs, that the obfuscation introduces no new code that might reveal secrets, which for Jasmine are the values stored in the memory. When a given obfuscation meets our condition it means that *all* the programs will be constant-time once transformed. The validity and adequacy of our proposal are vindicated by Theorem 1 and Corollary 1.

To assess the efficacy and the applicability of our condition, we consider several transformations implemented in popular obfuscating compilers (e.g. the `Tigress` C [29] and `O-MVLL` [23]). Some of them pass the check of Theorem 1 and also that of Corollary 1, and thus these validated transformations can be freely and safely applied to all programs. In particular, this is the case for the techniques that apply Mixed Boolean Arithmetic transformations to obfuscate expressions. However, other popular techniques, e.g., the anti-taint analysis transformation of `Tigress` C, fail to meet the condition of Corollary 1, meaning that *some* obfuscated programs leak secrets. But this unfortunate situation does not prevent other obfuscated programs from enjoying the constant-time property. In this case, we exploit our condition to devise a static analysis (*a field where Alan contributed a lot!*) and implement a translation validation algorithm.[1] Furthermore, by inspecting these cases one may devise a way to constrain the obfuscations that do not preserve the constant-time property in general and make them constant-time preserving. This is typically the case for the obfuscations that alter the control flow, e.g., those based on opaque predicate transformations.

Our analysis operates on both the original and the obfuscated version of the program. It essentially inspects and compares the abstract syntax trees of both versions in order to verify that the obfuscation introduces no new branches which depend on values stored in the memory (private data). Needless to say, our static analysis is sound, but not complete and false positives may thus arise. In the last case, the programmer needs to check or to suitably tune the obfuscation to be sure that the no violation occurs in the resulting program.

In summary, the main contributions of this paper are:

- a sufficient condition that predicts whether a given obfuscation preserves the constant-time property;
- a screening of some popular obfuscations assessing those that preserve the constant-time property for all programs and those that do not;

[1] In brief, translation validation is a standard technique [25] to automatically check the correctness of the compilation of a *single* program, rather than proving the compiler correct for them all. Instead of correctness, our proposal focuses on the constant-time policy and guarantees that a given obfuscation preserves it on a case by case basis.

- for the obfuscations in the second class above, a translation validation procedure for proving on a case by case basis that an obfuscated program enjoys the constant-time property.

In the rest of the paper, we proceed as follows. Section 2 briefly sets up the framework and provides the relevant background. The conditions that guarantees constant-time preservation and the translation validation algorithm are in Sect. 3. Section 4 shows a few obfuscations and verifies if they preserve constant-time. Related work is surveyed in Sect. 5. We draw some conclusions in Sect. 6. The details of our formal development are in the Sect. A.

2 Background

Here, we introduce the security property we want to preserve and our linguistic framework based on Jasmin.

2.1 Cryptographic Constant-Time Policy

Nowadays, side-channels are among the most dangerous sources of attacks as they allow an adversary to extract confidential information from a system by observing its behavior. The idea is that the attacker measures some physical quantity about system execution, e.g., power consumption and time. Based on this information, the attacker can then infer some pieces of confidential data or can get indications on which parts are worth her cracking efforts. These attacks can be exploited remotely, and have been used to intrude into implementation of cryptographic protocols [1,2,30] and to break hardware isolation mechanisms [9, 10].

As a typical case of timing-based side channel vulnerability [18] consider a program that branches on a secret, e.g., the value of a cryptographic key. In this case, the attacker can measure and compare the execution times of the two branches. When the times differ, the attacker can understand which branch was taken and restrict the set of secret values to guess. A toy example follows (in a sugared syntax), where a user digits her pin that the program then checks against the stored one character by character.

```
pin := read_secret();
current_char := 1;
while (current_char ≤ stored_pin_length and
         current_char ≤ pin_length and
         pin(current_char) = stored_pin(current_char))
    current_char := current_char+1;

if (current_char = stored_pin_length+1) then
    print("OK!");
else
    print("KO!");
```

The above program is vulnerable because checking a correct pin takes longer than a wrong one.

Many mitigations to timing-based attacks have been proposed, both hardware and software. The *program counter* [20] and the *constant-time* [5] policies are software-based countermeasures, giving rise to the *constant-time programming* discipline. This discipline ensures that the variation in execution time is independent of secret information. This is achieved by requiring that neither the control-flow of programs nor the sequence of memory accesses depend on secrets, like the value of `pin` in our example. Imposing that branching instructions do not depend on secrets ensures that an attacker obtains no information. Making memory accesses independent of secrets means that no cache attack can be used.

Usually, the constant-time policy is formalized as a form of non-interference, with respect to an instrumented semantics that records information leakage, e.g., the timing of the executed instructions. Intuitively, this policy requires that two executions starting in equivalent states (from an attacker's point of view) reach equivalent states and yield equivalent leakage, which represents the attacker observations. Therefore, any two such runs are *indistinguishable* to the attacker. In Definition 1 below, we formalize this policy for the Jasmin language.

2.2 Jasmin and the Constant-Time Property

Below, we briefly survey the Jasmin language that is a verification-friendly programming language, whose description we borrow from [28], with very minor adjustments. Its syntax is defined in Table 1, where we assume that x ranges over scalar variables, a ranges over array variables, The instrumented semantics of Jasmin is in Fig. 3. It has the form of a standard big-step semantics of an imperative language with arrays and pointers, with additional information about *leakage*, i.e., on what an attacker can observe while a program is running. The execution of a program i from a state s to the final state s_f is represented as $i : s \Downarrow_\ell s_f$ where ℓ is the leakage (see Table 2). A *leakage* is a sequence of observable actions including (i) the number of operations the program executed, (ii) the sequence of memory operations, and (iii) the sequence of control-flow choices. Actually, the attacker can observe the addresses in memory that the program accessed, but not their contents, and only the overall result of the conditions evaluated. The leakage is structured in the sense that a term of the syntax carries information about the expression or the statement that generated it. For example, the term $while_f(\ell_e)$ represents the leakage of a while statement whose guard evaluates to false (recorded by $while_f$) and whose body produces the leakage ℓ_e.

Following [28] we assume memory to be private and scalars to be public, so here we say that two states s and s' are (low-)*equivalent*, $s =_L s'$, if and only if s coincides with s' on scalar variables x. This equivalence is the basis for defining the constant-time property.

Definition 1. *([4]). The program i enjoys the* constant-time property *if and only if $\forall s, s'. s =_L s'$ it holds that $(i : s \Downarrow_\ell s_f \wedge i : s' \Downarrow_{\ell'} s'_f) \Rightarrow \ell = \ell'$.*

Note that the definition above is a special form of observational non-interference in which the focus is on the timing aspects of programs, represented by the leakage that the attacker can observe.

$e \in \mathit{Expr} ::=$	x	*scalar variable*
	$\mid c$	*constant*
	$\mid a[e]$	*array access*
	$\mid [e]$	*memory load*
	$\mid op(e, \ldots, e)$	*operator*
$d \in \mathit{Lval} ::=$	x	*variable*
	$\mid a[e]$	*array store*
	$\mid [e]$	*memory store*
$i \in \mathit{Prog} ::=$	skip	*empty*
	$\mid d := e$	*assignment*
	$\mid \mathrm{if}\ e\ \mathrm{then}\ i\ \mathrm{else}\ i$	*conditional*
	$\mid \mathrm{while}\ e\ \mathrm{do}\ i$	*loop*
	$\mid i; i$	*sequencing*

Fig. 1. Jasmin syntax.

$\ell_e ::= \bullet$	*empty*		$\ell ::= \ell_e := \ell_e$	
$\mid [z]$	*index*		$\mid \mathit{if}_b(\ell_e, \ell)$	*conditional*
$\mid *p$	*address*		$\mid \mathit{while}_t(\ell_e, \ell, \ell)$	*iteration*
$\mid (\ell_e, \ldots, \ell_e)$	*sub-leakage*		$\mid \mathit{while}_f(\ell_e)$	*loop-end*
			$\mid \ell; \ell$	*sequence*

Fig. 2. Leakage for expressions (left) and programs (right).

3 Statically Checking Constant-Time Property Preservation

In this section we define our sufficient condition for when an obfuscating transformation $\mathcal{O}$ preserves the constant-time property. However, we first make explicit our assumptions on the obfuscation $\mathcal{O}$.

$$\frac{}{c \downarrow^{s}_{\bullet} c} \qquad \frac{v = s(x)}{x \downarrow^{s}_{\bullet} v} \qquad \frac{e_i \downarrow^{s}_{\ell_i} v_i,\ v = op(v_1, \dots, v_n)}{op(e_1, \dots, e_n) \downarrow^{s}_{\ell_1, \dots, \ell_n} v} \qquad \frac{e \downarrow^{s}_{\ell_e} z,\ s(a) = t}{a[e] \downarrow^{s}_{(\ell_e, [z])} t[z]} \qquad \frac{e \downarrow^{s}_{\ell_e} p}{[e] \downarrow^{s}_{(\ell_e, *p)} s[p]}$$

$$\frac{}{x := v \downarrow^{s}_{\bullet} s\{x \leftarrow v\}} \qquad \frac{e \downarrow^{s}_{\ell_e} z,\ s(a) = t,\ t' = t\{z \leftarrow v\}}{a[e] := v \downarrow^{s}_{(\ell_e, [z])} s\{a \leftarrow t'\}} \qquad \frac{e \downarrow^{s}_{\ell_e} p}{[e] \downarrow^{s}_{(\ell_e, *p)} s\{p \leftarrow v\}]}$$

$$\frac{}{skip : s \Downarrow_{\{\}} s} \qquad \frac{i : s \Downarrow_{\ell_i} s_1,\ i' : s_1 \Downarrow_{\ell_{i'}} s_2}{i; i' : s \Downarrow_{\ell_i; \ell_{i'}} s_2} \qquad \frac{e \downarrow^{s}_{\ell_e} v,\ d := v \downarrow^{s}_{\ell_d} s'}{d := e : s \Downarrow_{\ell_d := \ell_e} s'}$$

$$\frac{e \downarrow^{s}_{\ell_e} b,\ i_b : s \Downarrow_{\ell_i} s'}{\mathit{if}\ e\ \mathit{then}\ i_{tt}\ \mathit{else}\ i_{ff} : s \Downarrow_{\mathit{if}_b(\ell_e, \ell_{i_b})} s'}$$

$$\frac{e \downarrow^{s}_{\ell_e} ff}{\mathit{while}\ e\ \mathit{do}\ i : s \Downarrow_{\mathit{while}_f(\ell_e)} s} \qquad \frac{e \downarrow^{s}_{\ell_e} tt,\ i : s \Downarrow_{\ell_i} s_1,\ \mathit{while}\ e\ \mathit{do}\ i : s_1 \Downarrow_{\ell_w} s_2}{\mathit{while}\ e\ \mathit{do}\ i : s \Downarrow_{\mathit{while}_t(\ell_e, \ell_i, \ell_w)} s_2}$$

Fig. 3. Instrumented semantics. In the first line the rules for expressions; in the second line the rules for assignment; the remaining six rules are for the other instructions.

3.1 Obfuscations

We consider obfuscations that are defined by structural induction on the program syntax. More in detail, we take into account the following actions that modify the abstract syntax tree (AST for short) of the original program i, whose nodes we assume labelled by $\alpha, \alpha_0, \dots$:

1. introducing a new instruction represented by the node (labelled) β in the AST of the obfuscated program $[\![i]\!]_{\mathcal{O}}$, possibly with existing instructions as subtrees;
2. transforming an instruction, which amounts to leave unchanged the corresponding node (labelled) α in the AST of i, but possibly changing the subtrees rooted in it, typically after semantic-preserving changes of expressions;
3. duplicating an existing instruction, with corresponding node (labelled) α.

Essentially, our obfuscations permit to embed (modified) portions of the original AST into the AST of the obfuscated program.

Technically, through a function f we will link the portions of $[\![i]\!]_{\mathcal{O}}$ (actually their labels) to those in original program i they come from. Our sufficient condition roughly amounts then to verify that (i) the instructions introduced by the obfuscation involve no array or memory read/write accesses; that (ii) any array or memory store access in a modified instruction in $[\![i]\!]_{\mathcal{O}}$ is also present in the corresponding instruction of i it is linked to by f; and that (iii) the control flow is preserved.

Without loss of generality, from now onwards we assume that programs have neither uninitialized variables nor dead code.

3.2 Preservation Condition

Following the common practice [22], we assume that (the AST of) a program is uniquely labelled through an injective function λ mapping its instructions to an element of $\Lambda = \{\alpha, \alpha_1, \dots\}$, and we write as usual i^α when $\alpha = \lambda(i)$; the labelling function of an obfuscated program is denoted by $\lambda_\mathcal{O}$, with labels in $\Lambda_\mathcal{O} = \{\beta, \beta_1 \dots\}$. Since the labels uniquely identify the nodes in an AST, we feel free to write i^α when the label α identifies the node of the AST corresponding to the instruction i of the original program; similarly for j^β when j is an instruction of the obfuscated program.

Before formally defining our condition, we introduce the function f that links the (labels of) the instructions of the obfuscated program with those of the original one, if any. This function is not injective, rather it links the labels of the duplicated instructions with the original instruction, as well as those of the transformed instructions. Note that such function is easily computed along with the application of the obfuscation $\mathcal{O}$, while inducting on the program syntax—needless to say, the same holds for the labelling functions.

Definition 2. (Correspondence Function). *Let i be a program with labelling function λ; let $[\![i]\!]_\mathcal{O}$ be its obfuscated version under the obfuscation $\mathcal{O}$ with labelling function $\lambda_\mathcal{O}$ and nodes j^β.*
We define the correspondence function $f\colon \Lambda_\mathcal{O} \to \Lambda \uplus \Lambda_\mathcal{O}$ *as follows*

$$f(\beta) = \begin{cases} \beta \notin \Lambda & \textit{if } \mathcal{O} \textit{ introduces } j^\beta; \\ \alpha \in \Lambda & \textit{if } j^\beta \textit{ is a transformation or a duplication of } i^\alpha. \end{cases}$$

Example 1. Suppose to have the following instruction:

$$\big((a[3]{:=}42)^{\alpha_0}; ((x{:=}1)^{\alpha_1}; ([y+1]{:=}a[3]+x)^{\alpha_2})^{\alpha_3}\big)^{\alpha_4}$$

obfuscated as:

$$\begin{aligned} \big(&(\textit{if } x-7>0 \textit{ then } (a[3]{:=}42)^{\beta_0} \textit{ else } ((a[3]{:=}42)^{\beta_1}; (x{:=}1)^{\beta_2})^{\beta_3})^{\beta_4}; \\ &(\textit{if } 2+x>9 \textit{ then}((x{:=}1)^{\beta_5}; ([y+1]{:=}a[3]+x)^{\beta_6})^{\beta_7} \\ &\qquad\qquad \textit{else } ([y+1]{:=}a[3]+x)^{\beta_8})^{\beta_9}\big)^{\beta_{10}} \end{aligned}$$

Now the correspondence function is the identity on $\beta_3, \beta_4, \beta_9$ and maps the other labels as follows

$$\begin{array}{lll} f(\beta_0) = f(\beta_1) = \alpha_0 & f(\beta_2) = f(\beta_5) = \alpha_1 & \\ f(\beta_6) = f(\beta_8) = \alpha_2 & f(\beta_7) = \alpha_3 & f(\beta_{10}) = \alpha_4 \end{array}$$

Also, we define a partial order on the labels of a program i that essentially reflects the structure of its AST. We will show in Lemma 1 that this partial order statically represents the order in which the instructions of i are executed at run-time.

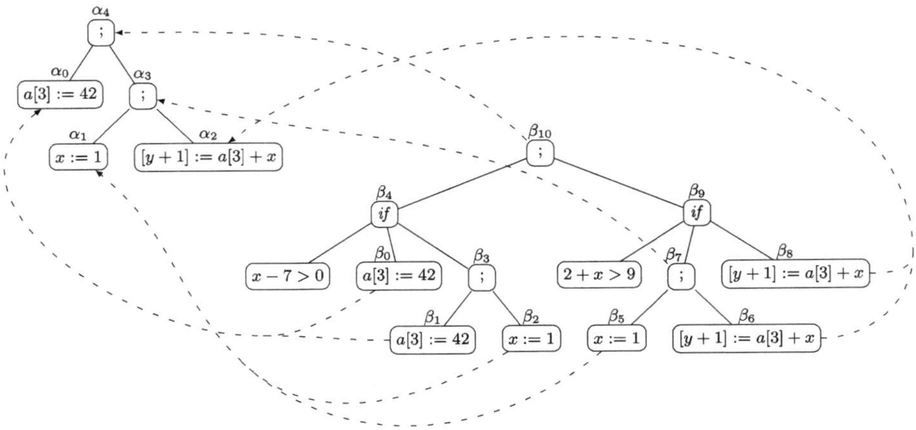

Fig. 4. The (simplified) labelled ASTs of the original instruction of Example 1 (left) and its obfuscated version (right). The dashed arrows between the nodes depict the correspondence function f, where it differs from the identity.

Definition 3. (Strict Partial Order of Program Labels). *Given a program i, we order the set of its labels by structural induction on the syntax of i as follows*

$$\begin{aligned} \alpha \sqsubset \alpha_1, \alpha_2 \textbf{ iff } i &= (\mathit{if}\ e\ \mathit{then}\ i_1^{\alpha_1}\ \mathit{else}\ i_2^{\alpha_2})^{\alpha} \\ \alpha \sqsubset \alpha_1 \textbf{ iff } i &= (\mathit{while}\ e\ \mathit{do}\ i^{\alpha_1})^{\alpha} \\ \alpha \sqsubset \alpha_0 \sqsubset \alpha_1 \textbf{ iff } i &= (\{i_0^{\alpha_0}; i_1^{\alpha_1}\})^{\alpha} \end{aligned}$$

The transitive closure $\sqsubset^+$ of $\sqsubset$ induces a strict partial order over the labels of i.

Back to Example 1, we have that $\beta_{10} \sqsubset^+ \beta_4 \sqsubset^+ \beta_0, \beta_3$, just to look at a small fragment of the AST of the obfuscated program (see the right part of Fig. 4).

Our last auxiliary definition extracts from instructions the relevant memory operations, e.g., those that appear in the guards of conditionals or in the expressions to evaluate.

Definition 4 (Memory operations). *The set of memory operations of a program i to be checked, check_ops, is defined as follows:*

$$\begin{aligned} &\mathit{check\_ops}(\mathit{skip}) = \emptyset \\ &\mathit{check\_ops}(x{:=}e) = \mathit{mem\_ops}(e) \\ &\mathit{check\_ops}(a[e']{:=}e) = \mathit{mem\_ops}(e) \cup \{a[e']\} \cup \mathit{mem\_ops}(e') \\ &\mathit{check\_ops}(\mathit{if}\ e\ \mathit{then}\ i_1\ \mathit{else}\ i_2) = \mathit{mem\_ops}(e) \\ &\mathit{check\_ops}(\mathit{while}\ e\ \mathit{do}\ i) = \mathit{mem\_ops}(e) \\ &\mathit{check\_ops}(i_1; i_2) = \emptyset \end{aligned}$$

where the memory operations mem_ops of the expression e is as follows:

$$
\begin{aligned}
&mem\_ops(x) = mem\_ops(c) = \emptyset\\
&mem\_ops(a[e]) = mem\_ops(e) \cup \{a[e]\}\\
&mem\_ops([e]) = mem\_ops(e) \cup \{[e]\}\\
&mem\_ops(op(e_1, \ldots, e_n)) = mem\_ops(e_1) \cup \cdots \cup mem\_ops(e_n)
\end{aligned}
$$

We now formally state the three conditions intuitively presented at the beginning of this section: the condition (1) below requires checking if the obfuscation introduces no memory reads/writes; the condition (2) says that when an instruction i is untouched or is transformed, the memory accesses of i are preserved by the obfuscation; and finally the condition (3) makes sure that the partial order on the labels of i coincides with the one on those of $[\![i]\!]_{\mathcal{O}}$ that are related by the correspondence function f. We will then prove an obfuscation that respects them all preserves the constant-time property.

Definition 5. (Preservation Check). *Let $\mathcal{O}$ be an obfuscation; let i be a program and $[\![i]\!]_{\mathcal{O}}$ its obfuscated version; and let Λ and $\Lambda_{\mathcal{O}}$ be their labels partially ordered by $\sqsubset^{+}$ and $\sqsubset^{+}_{\mathcal{O}}$, respectively.*
The program i passes the preservation check *under $\mathcal{O}$, denoted by $\mathcal{O} \boxtimes i$, if and only if the following conditions hold:*

(1) $\forall \beta \in \Lambda_{\mathcal{O}}.\, f(\beta) \in \Lambda_{\mathcal{O}}$ *implies* $check\_ops(v^{\beta}) = \emptyset$;

(2) $\forall \beta \in \Lambda_{\mathcal{O}}.\, f(\beta) = \alpha \in \Lambda$ *implies* $check\_ops(v^{\beta}) = check\_ops(t^{\alpha})$;

(3) $\forall \beta, \beta' \in \Lambda_{\mathcal{O}}.\, f(\beta) = \alpha, f(\beta') = \alpha'.\, \alpha \sqsubset^{+} \alpha'$ *if and only if* $\beta \sqsubset^{+}_{\mathcal{O}} \beta'$

The following theorem ensures that if a constant-time program and an obfuscation pass our check, then the obfuscated program is still constant-time.

Theorem 1. *Let $\mathcal{O}$ be a semantic preserving obfuscation and let i be a program enjoying the constant-time property.*
If $\mathcal{O} \boxtimes i$ then $[\![i]\!]_{\mathcal{O}}$ enjoys the constant-time property.

We can now lift the preservation check to a whole obfuscation technique in the obvious way, by requiring that the relation $\mathcal{O} \boxtimes i$ holds for all programs i, so ensuring that *all* the programs will be constant-time once transformed.

Corollary 1. *The obfuscation $\mathcal{O}$ preserves the constant-time property if $\forall i.\, \mathcal{O} \boxtimes i$.*

A further syntactic analysis on the form of $\mathcal{O}$ and on the conditions for its applicability often suffices to check that the relation $\mathcal{O} \boxtimes i$ holds for all programs i. A couple of obfuscations that pass this check are in Sect. 4.

As expected, there are several popular obfuscations that do not satisfy the condition of Corollary 1. In other words, some programs under a certain obfuscation leak secrets, and do not pass the preservation check. It may well be the case that other programs instead enjoy the constant-time property under the same obfuscation. In these cases, we can still use Theorem 1 to assess when the given obfuscation preserves constant-time on a specific program, in the style of translation validation [25].

3.3 Translation Validation

To make sure that a given obfuscation $\mathcal{O}$ does not break constant-time on a *specific* program i we apply the Algorithm 1. The algorithm simply checks the conditions in Definiton 5, and when they hold we confirm that the obfuscated program $[\![i]\!]_{\mathcal{O}}$ still has the constant-time property.

Algorithm 1. Translation validation.

function CT-PRESERVED($\mathcal{O}, i$)
  t are sub-instructions of i, with labels in Λ partially ordered by $\sqsubset^+$
  v are sub-instructions of $[\![i]\!]_{\mathcal{O}}$, with labels in $\Lambda_{\mathcal{O}}$ partially ordered by $\sqsubset^+_{\mathcal{O}}$
  $f\colon \Lambda \to \Lambda_{\mathcal{O}}$ be the correspondence function

  $cond_1, cond_2, cond_3 \leftarrow true$
  for all β such that $f(\beta) \in \Lambda_{\mathcal{O}}$ **do**
    $cond_1 \leftarrow cond_1 \wedge check\_ops(v^\beta) = \emptyset$
  end for
  for all β such that $f(\beta) = \alpha \in \Lambda$ **do**
    $cond_2 \leftarrow cond_2 \wedge check\_ops(v^\beta) = check\_ops(t^\alpha)$
  end for
  for all $\beta, \beta' \in \Lambda_{\mathcal{O}}, \alpha, \alpha' \in \Lambda$ such that $f(\beta) = \alpha \wedge f(\beta') = \alpha'$ **do**
    $cond_3 \leftarrow cond_3 \wedge (\beta \sqsubset^+_{\mathcal{O}} \beta' \iff \alpha \sqsubset^+ \alpha')$
  end for
  return $cond_1 \wedge cond_2 \wedge cond_3$
end function

In the next section we will present a couple of examples showing that translation validation helps.

4 Case Studies

Here, we intuitively present a few obfuscation techniques with the help of very simple examples, and we apply our condition to them to check whether they preserve cryptographic constant-time. Note that such techniques are implemented in real-world obfuscating compilers, and that when our condition does not apply, we can still use Algorithm 1 to consider programs case-by-case.

A case showing that control flow obfuscations require much care is control-flow flattening. In spite of being constant-time preserving [11], this obfuscation does not satisfy the third condition of Definition 5. Intuitively, control-flow flattening re-organizes the AST by putting the instructions in a sequence

$i_1; i_2; \ldots; i_n$ as cases of a selective structure that dispatches to the right element i_j. This is reason for control-flow flattening not to pass our test: the relation $\sqsubset^*$ is not preserved *statically*, while of course at run-time the order of the sequence is kept.

4.1 Mixed Boolean Arithmetic Transformations

The obfuscation technique called *insertion of Mixed Boolean Arithmetic expressions* (MBA for short) aims to hide the operations on data performed by a program. This obfuscation mainly consists in replacing a binary operator, e.g., $+$ or $\wedge$, and its two operands e_1 and e_2 by a complex expression involving arithmetic and bitwise operations, only applied to e_1 and e_2. There are various ways of generating MBA expressions that of course have the same meaning of the original one and that resist reverse engineering, because they create NP-hard problems for the attacker. For an algebraic presentation, we refer the reader to [31] and only present here a toy example. Note that these transformations only use variables occurring in the original expression and introduce no new ones.

Suppose we have the following program consisting of a single conditional

$$\mathit{if}\ z = x + y\ \mathit{then}\ x := x + y\ \mathit{else}\ z := z + 3$$

an obfuscated version of which follows

$$\mathit{if}\ z = (x \wedge y) + (x \vee y)\ \mathit{then}\ x := 2(x \vee y) - (x \oplus y)\ \mathit{else}\ z := 2(z + 1) + 1 - z$$

where we replace the expression $x+y$ with $(x \wedge y)+(x \vee y)$ exploiting the properties of $\wedge$ and $\vee$ with respect to $+$. Similarly, for the other expressions occurring therein. The conditions of Theorem 1 trivially hold, so the constant-time property is preserved. Even more, by looking at the way MBA transformations work, we prove that *any* MBA transformation preserves the constant-time of *any* program. Formally,

Property 1. Every transformation $mba\colon Expr \mapsto Expr$ from [31] preserves the constant-time property.

4.2 Opaque Predicate Transformations

Opaque predicate transformations are commonly used in control flow obfuscations to introduce superfluous branches and dummy code. Opaque predicates are traditionally constant expressions (they always evaluate true or always false) that use complex or hard-to-understand logic with the intention of hiding that they are constant. Different proposals have been put forward in the literature for such transformations. Here, we briefly consider two of them: *constant value* and *dynamic opaque predicates*.

Constant Value Opaque Predicates. Control code obfuscation often takes advantage of predicates, dubbed *constant opaque predicates* that always evaluate *true* (or *false*), in any program state. A typical usage of this technique consists in inserting in the code a branch instruction controlled by such a predicate. While the constant value is known a priori to the program obfuscator, it is difficult for attackers to deduce such a value. Since attackers instead ignore the constant value of the opaque predicate, they have to take into account both paths of the branch instruction and the control flow of the program gets obfuscated.

To show that the insertion of opaque predicates does not in general respect the conditions of Definition 5, so not preserving cryptographic constant-time, it suffices to consider the following trivial counterexample. Let the instruction i be

$$a[3] := 42$$

and its transformation $[\![i]\!]_{\mathcal{O}}$ be

$$\mathit{if}\ a[x] = a[x]\ \mathit{then}\ a[3] := 42\ \mathit{else}\ \mathit{if}\ a[x] = 3\ \mathit{then}\ x := 1\ \mathit{else}\ \mathit{skip}.$$

Our check fails, because instruction *if* is new and its guard $a[x] = a[x]$ has the memory access $a[x]$, so its memory operations are not empty violating the condition (1) of Definition 5. However, any run of the program will select the "*then*" branch, and will always produce the same leakage. Thus, we have a false positive when we apply this obfuscation to the program above.

Luckily, translation validation can help in showing that the same instruction i above, when obfuscated as follows, preserves constant-time, because the guards of the "*if*" instructions are now on the scalar x:

$$\mathit{if}\ x = x\ \mathit{then}\ a[3] := 42\ \mathit{else}\ \mathit{if}\ x = 3\ \mathit{then}\ x := 1\ \mathit{else}\ \mathit{skip}$$

Dynamic Opaque Predicates. A different technique is based on *dynamic* opaque predicates [24]. Roughly, one uses two (or more) predicates P and Q that are correlated, adjacent and evaluate to the same value in any given run because $P \Leftrightarrow Q$, but may assume different values in different runs. We exemplify their usage as follows. Suppose we have the following instruction i (see also Example 1):

$$a[3] := 42; x := 1; [y + 1] := a[3] + x$$

that is obfuscated as:

$$\begin{array}{l} \mathit{if}\ a[1] - 7 > 0\ \mathit{then}\ a[3] := 42\ \mathit{else}\ a[3] := 42; x := 1; \\ \mathit{if}\ 2 + a[1] > 9\ \mathit{then}\ x := 1; [y + 1] := a[3] + x\ \mathit{else}\ [y + 1] := a[3] + x \end{array}$$

This example shows a violation of the condition (1) of Definition 5 because of the guards.

Let now obfuscate i with a pair of conditionals similar to those above, but where we use expressions that only involve scalar variables just as we do for the constant value opaque predicate obfuscation above. In this case, the translation validation will certify that the constant-time property is preserved.

We have presented above two counterexamples showing that the application of opaque predicate obfuscations requires care. Of course, they suffice for stating the following property, but their effect can be mitigated to some extent. Actually, constraining both constant value and dynamic opaque predicates obfuscations to only have scalars in the conditions of the introduced branching instructions make them constant-time preserving.

Property 2. The obfuscation techniques based on either constant value or dynamic opaque predicates do not preserve the constant-time property.

4.3 Anti-Taint Analysis Transformations

The `Tigress` C compiler [29] proposes a transformation that disrupts analysis tools that make use of dynamic taint analysis. The idea of this transformation is to replace instructions performing a direct assignment with a code snippet that indirectly assign a memory location. Essentially, it replaces the assignment to a value by a loop driven by the value itself. For example, consider the instruction

$$a[3] := 0$$

and obfuscate it as

$$\textit{while } a[3] > 0 \textit{ do } a[3] := a[3] - 1$$

which is no longer constant-time because the guard of the *while* violates condition (1) of Definition 5.

On the contrary, our translation validation certifies that the following case:

$$x := 0 \qquad \text{obfuscated as} \qquad \textit{while } x > 0 \textit{ do } x := x - 1$$

passes the test because x is a scalar, and thus is constant-time.

Thus, we have the following:

Property 3. The anti-taint analysis obfuscation technique does not preserve the constant-time property.

5 Related Work

Program obfuscations are widespread transformations [13,17,19,29] designed to protect software in scenarios where the adversary has physical access to the program and can inspect or tamper with it. Many obfuscation transformations have been proposed in the literature that resist reverse engineering, making the life of attackers harder. However, we do not discuss these papers because they do not consider formal properties of the proposed transformations. We refer the interested reader to [14] for a recent survey.

Ours is one of first paper addressing the problem of security preservation for obfuscating transformations. In [11] we showed that the control-flow flattening preserves cryptographic constant-time. In that paper, we considered an imperative language without pointers and we *manually* proved our preservation theorem using a special kind of simulation relation. Differently, in this paper we consider several obfuscations. In addition, the conditions to check do not involve a simulation relation, are automatically checkable, and give rise to a translation validation procedure.

Many papers in the literature formally studied the correctness of obfuscations. We briefly describe these proposals in the following. In [26,27] a formal framework based on abstract interpretation is proposed to study the effectiveness of obfuscating techniques. This framework not only characterizes when a transformation is correct but also measures its resilience, i.e., the difficulty of undoing the obfuscation. Other work followed the research line of fully verified, obfuscating compilation chains [6–8], focusing on the correctness of the transformations, also in the setting of the CompCert C compiler. On the contrary, here we defined a sufficient condition on the syntax of obfuscations to check if a specific transformation always preserves security or otherwise if it does on a given program, through a derived translation validation procedure.

6 Conclusion

We proposed a sufficient condition to guarantee that a given obfuscation technique preserves the cryptographic constant-time property, regardless of whether the source-to-source transformations are carried out on high- or low-level programs. Obfuscations that satisfy our condition can then be freely and repeatedly applied in any order to a program, making it harder for an attacker to unveil secrets, e.g., a cryptographic key embedded in the program itself, as it happens in the white-box approach.

To assess the applicability of our condition, we have shown that cryptographic constant-time programs are still such after obfuscation transformations that hide both values (through insertion of mixed boolean arithmetic expressions) and control (through opaque predicates, under specific, mild constraints).

Other obfuscations instead do not pass our test. Yet our condition provides the basis for a translation validation algorithm to assess the preservation on a case-by-case basis. This is the case for two further techniques we considered: (unconstrained) opaque predicate transformation and `Tigress`'s anti-taint analysis transformation. Based on a simple scrutiny of both techniques, we suggest constraints on them so as they satisfy our condition and thus always preserve cryptographic constant-time.

We are currently studying more program obfuscations, and we plan to integrate our translation validation as an additional pass within one of the existing popular obfuscating compiler, like the `Tigress` C compiler [29], `O-MVLL` [23], or the LLVM obfuscator [16]. Also, rather than regarding compilers as single entities, we propose to consider their various components one by one, and study whether they preserve further, different properties, in a divide-et-impera fashion.

Acknowledgments. We are deeply indebted with the anonymous referees for their comments and suggestions, in particular with the third one who stressed the importance of our third condition. This work was partially supported by project SERICS (PE00000014) PNRR MUR - M4C2 - I 1.3 and by project PRIN PNRR AM∀DEUS (P2022EPPHM) M4C2 I 1.1 - D53D23017420001 under the MUR National Recovery and Resilience Plan funded by the European Union - NextGenerationEU and "Spatio-Temporal Enhancement of Neural nets for Deeply Hierarchical Automatised Logic - STENDHAL" (20228KXFN2).

A Proofs

It is immediate verifying that the semantics of Fig. 5 conservatively extends that of Fig. 3: for all i, s it is $\Downarrow is\ell_i s'$ if and only if $\exists\chi.\, i^\alpha s \Downarrow \ell_i(\chi, s')$.

In the following, assume that $\mathcal{O}$ is a semantic preserving obfuscation; that i is an instruction satisfying the preservation test, i.e., such that $\mathcal{O}\boxtimes i$ holds; and that f is the correspondence function between the labels β of $[\![i]\!]_\mathcal{O}$ and the labels α of i. Also, say that χ ($\chi_\mathcal{O}$, respectively) *has leakage* ℓ whenever $i^\alpha s \Downarrow \ell(\chi, s')$ ($[\![i^\beta]\!]_\mathcal{O} s \Downarrow \ell(\chi_\mathcal{O}, s')$, respectively).

The following lemma holds.

Lemma 1. (Partial Order and Traces). *If $\alpha_i \sqsubset \alpha_j$ in the AST of i (of $[\![i]\!]_\mathcal{O}$, respectively) then there exists χ such that $\chi = \chi'\alpha_i\alpha_j\chi''$.*
If $\chi = \chi'\alpha_i\alpha_j\chi''$ then $\alpha_i \sqsubset \alpha_j$ in the AST of i (of $[\![i]\!]_\mathcal{O}$, respectively).

Proof. Immediate by induction on AST of i for the first statement, recalling that instructions have no dead code. By induction on the length of χ for the second statement. □

Now, we use the correspondence function f to extract χ from a given $\chi_\mathcal{O}$ where it is embedded. Roughly, we only consider the sequence of those β in $\chi_\mathcal{O}$ that are related to α's in χ via f. For doing that we extend f as follows.

Definition 6. *Let the function $F\colon \Lambda_\mathcal{O}^* \to \Lambda$ be defined as the homomorphic extension to sequences of:*

$$g(\beta) = \begin{cases} \epsilon & \textit{if } f(\beta) = \beta \in \Lambda_\mathcal{O} \\ \alpha & \textit{if } f(\beta) = \alpha \in \Lambda \end{cases}$$

Lemma 2. (Extracting χ from $\chi_\mathcal{O}$).
For all $\chi_\mathcal{O}$ such that $[\![i^\beta]\!]_\mathcal{O} s \Downarrow \ell(\chi_\mathcal{O}, s')$ the sequence $\chi = F(\chi_\mathcal{O})$ is such that $i^\alpha s \Downarrow \ell'(\chi, s'')$ and $s' = s''$, with $f(\beta) = \alpha$.

Proof. Trivially true when there is no β in $\chi_\mathcal{O}$ such that $f(\beta) = \alpha$ or when there is a single such β. Otherwise, for all $\beta_i\chi'_\mathcal{O}\beta_j$ subtrace of $\chi_\mathcal{O}$ such that $f(\beta_i) = \alpha_i, f(\beta_j) = \alpha_j, F(\chi'_\mathcal{O}) = \epsilon$ then $\alpha_i\alpha_j$ is a substring of χ by the first implication of Lemma 1.
Since $\beta_i \sqsubset_\mathcal{O}^+ \beta_j$ then $\alpha_i \sqsubset^+ \alpha_j$ by condition (3) of Definition 5. Now, we show that $\alpha_i \sqsubset \alpha_j$ by contradiction. Suppose there exists α_k such that $\alpha_i \sqsubset^* \alpha_k \sqsubset^* \alpha_j$, but in this case condition (3) of Definition 5 implies that $F(\chi'_\mathcal{O}) \neq \epsilon$ against the hypothesis. Now the second implication of Lemma 1 suffices.
The correctness of $\mathcal{O}$ guarantees that $s' = s''$. □

Theorem 2. *Let $\mathcal{O}$ be a semantic preserving obfuscation and let i be a program enjoying the constant-time property.*
If $\mathcal{O}\boxtimes i$ then $[\![i]\!]_{\mathcal{O}}$ enjoys the constant-time property.

Proof. Take a $\chi_{\mathcal{O}} = \beta_0 \dots \beta_n$. Consider then all the β_i with $f(\beta_i) \in \Lambda_{\mathcal{O}}$ occurring in it, which are such that $check\_ops(i_i^{\beta_i}) = \emptyset$ by the condition (1) of Definition 5. All the β_i that $f(\beta_i) \in \Lambda$ are instead such that $check\_ops(i_i^{\beta_i}) = check\_ops(f(i_i^{\beta_i}))$ by the condition (2) of Definition 5. Therefore, no $\chi_{\mathcal{O}}$ introduces a memory operation that is not already present in $F(\chi_{\mathcal{O}})$, and χ and $\chi_{\mathcal{O}}$ have the same leakage.

Property 4. Every transformation $mba\colon Expr \mapsto Expr$ from [31] preserves the constant-time property.

Proof. By definition, any *mba* only transforms existing instructions, because it neither introduces new ones nor changes the control flow. The condition (1) and (3) of Definition 5 thus hold trivially. The same happens for condition (2), because any *mba* only accesses scalar variables or array variables already accessed in the original expression. Thus, all programs i are such that $\mathcal{O}\boxtimes i$ and all the *mba* of [31] preserve the constant-time property. □

$$\frac{}{(skip)^{\alpha} : s \Downarrow_{\{\}} (\alpha, s)} \qquad \frac{i_1^{\alpha_1} : s \Downarrow_{\ell_{i_1}} (\chi_1, s_1),\ i_2^{\alpha_2} : s_1 \Downarrow_{\ell_{i_2}} (\chi_2, s_2)}{(i_1; i_2)^{\alpha} : s \Downarrow_{\ell_{i_1};\ell_{i_2}} (\alpha\chi_1\chi_2, s_2)}$$

$$\frac{e \downarrow^{s}_{\ell_e} v,\ d := v \downarrow^{s}_{\ell_d} s'}{(d := e)^{\alpha} : s \Downarrow_{\ell_d := \ell_e} (\alpha, s')} \qquad \frac{e \downarrow^{s}_{\ell_e} b,\ i_b^{\alpha_b} : s \Downarrow_{\ell_i} (\chi_b, s')}{(if\ e\ then\ i_{tt}\ else\ i_{ff})^{\alpha} : s \Downarrow_{if_b(\ell_e, \ell_{i_b})} (\alpha\chi_b, s')}$$

$$\frac{e \downarrow^{s}_{\ell_e} ff}{(while\ e\ do\ i)^{\alpha} : s \Downarrow_{while_f(\ell_e)} (\alpha, s)}$$

$$\frac{e \downarrow^{s}_{\ell_e} tt,\ i_1^{\alpha_1} : s \Downarrow_{\ell_{i_1}} (\chi_1, s_1),\ (while\ e\ do\ i)^{\alpha} : s_1 \Downarrow_{\ell_w} (\chi_2, s_2)}{(while\ e\ do\ i)^{\alpha} : s \Downarrow_{while_t(\ell_e, \ell_i, \ell_w)} (\alpha\chi_1\chi_2, s_2)}$$

Fig. 5. Extended instrumented semantics. The rules for expressions are as in Fig. 3.

References

1. Albrecht, M.R., Mareková, L., Paterson, K.G., Stepanovs, I.: Four attacks and a proof for telegram. In: 2022 IEEE Symposium on Security and Privacy (SP), pp. 87–106 (2022). https://doi.org/10.1109/SP46214.2022.9833666
2. Arp, D., Yamaguchi, F., Rieck, K.: Torben: a practical side-channel attack for deanonymizing tor communication. In: Proceedings of the 10th ACM Symposium on Information, Computer and Communications Security, pp. 597–602. Association for Computing Machinery, New York (2015). https://doi.org/10.1145/2714576.2714627

3. Barthe, G., Grégoire, B., Laporte, V.: Secure compilation of side-channel countermeasures: the case of cryptographic "constant-time". In: 31st IEEE Computer Security Foundations Symposium, CSF, pp. 328–343 (2018). https://doi.org/10.1109/CSF.2018.00031
4. Barthe, G., Grégoire, B., Laporte, V., Priya, S.: Structured leakage and applications to cryptographic constant-time and cost. In: Kim, Y., Kim, J., Vigna, G., Shi, E. (eds.) CCS '21: 2021 ACM SIGSAC Conference on Computer and Communications Security, pp. 462–476. ACM (2021). https://doi.org/10.1145/3460120.3484761
5. Bernstein, D.J.: Cache-timing attacks on AES. https://cr.yp.to/antiforgery/cachetiming-20050414.pdf (2005), Access Nov 2019
6. Blazy, S., Giacobazzi, R.: Towards a formally verified obfuscating compiler. In: SSP 2012 - 2nd ACM SIGPLAN Software Security and Protection Workshop (2012)
7. Blazy, S., Hutin, R.: Formal verification of a program obfuscation based on mixed boolean-arithmetic expressions. In: Proceedings of the 8th ACM SIGPLAN International Conference on Certified Programs and Proofs, pp. 196–208 (2019). https://doi.org/10.1145/3293880.3294103
8. Blazy, S., Trieu, A.: Formal verification of control-flow graph flattening. In: Proceedings of the 5th ACM SIGPLAN Conference on Certified Programs and Proofs, pp. 176–187 (2016). https://doi.org/10.1145/2854065.2854082
9. Bulck, J.V., et al.: Foreshadow: extracting the keys to the intel SGX kingdom with transient out-of-order execution. In: USENIX Security Symposium, pp. 991–1008. USENIX Association (2018)
10. Bulck, J.V., Piessens, F., Strackx, R.: Nemesis: studying microarchitectural timing leaks in rudimentary cpu interrupt logic. In: CCS '18: 2018 ACM SIGSAC Conference on Computer & Communications Security (2018). https://doi.org/10.1145/3243734.3243822
11. Busi, M., Degano, P., Galletta, L.: Control-flow flattening preserves the constant-time policy. In: Loreti, M., Spalazzi, L. (eds.) Proceedings of the Fourth Italian Conference on Cyber Security. CEUR Workshop Proceedings, vol. 2597, pp. 82–92. CEUR-WS.org (2020). https://ceur-ws.org/Vol-2597/paper-08.pdf
12. Collberg, C., Davidson, J., Giacobazzi, R., Gu, Y.X., Herzberg, A., Wang, F.Y.: Toward digital asset protection. IEEE Intell. Syst. **26**(6), 8–13 (2011). https://doi.org/10.1109/MIS.2011.106
13. Collberg, C.S., Nagra, J.: Surreptitious Software - Obfuscation, Watermarking, and Tamperproofing for Software Protection. Addison-Wesley (2010)
14. Hosseinzadeh, S., et al.: Diversification and obfuscation techniques for software security: a systematic literature review. Inf. Softw. Technol. **104**, 72–93 (2018)
15. Jasmin Language for high-assurance and high-speed cryptography. https://github.com/jasmin-lang/jasmin (2021), Accessed Oct 2023
16. Junod, P., Rinaldini, J., Wehrli, J., Michielin, J.: Obfuscator-LLVM – software protection for the masses. In: Wyseur, B. (ed.) Proceedings of the IEEE/ACM 1st International Workshop on Software Protection, SPRO'15, pp. 3–9. IEEE (2015). https://doi.org/10.1109/SPRO.2015.10
17. Junod, P., Rinaldini, J., Wehrli, J., Michielin, J.: Obfuscator-LLVM–software protection for the masses. In: 2015 IEEE/ACM 1st International Workshop on Software Protection, pp. 3–9. IEEE (2015)
18. Kocher, P.C.: Timing attacks on implementations of Diffie-Hellman, RSA, DSS, and other systems. In: Proceedings of the 16th Annual International Cryptology Conference on Advances in Cryptology. LNCS, vol. 1109, pp. 104–113. Springer-Verlag (1996)

19. László, T., Kiss, Á.: Obfuscating c++ programs via control flow flattening. Annales Universitatis Scientarum Budapestinensis de Rolando Eötvös Nominatae, Sectio Computatorica **30**(1), 3–19 (2009)
20. Molnar, D., Piotrowski, M., Schultz, D., Wagner, D.A.: The program counter security model: automatic detection and removal of control-flow side channel attacks. In: Won, D., Kim, S. (eds.) Information Security and Cryptology - ICISC 2005, 8th International Conference. LNCS, vol. 3935, pp. 156–168 (2005)
21. Nagra, J., Collberg, C.: Surreptitious software: obfuscation, watermarking, and tamperproofing for software protection: obfuscation, watermarking, and tamperproofing for software protection. Pearson Education (2009)
22. Nielson, F., Nielson, H.R., Hankin, C.: Principles of program analysis. Springer (1999)
23. Open-Obfuscator: O-MVLL & dProtect. https://obfuscator.re/, Accessed Oct 2023
24. Palsberg, J., Krishnaswamy, S., Kwon, M., Ma, D., Shao, Q., Zhang, Y.: Experience with software watermarking. In: 16th Annual Computer Security Applications Conference (ACSAC 2000), pp. 308–316. IEEE Computer Society (2000). https://doi.org/10.1109/ACSAC.2000.898885
25. Pnueli, A., Siegel, M., Singerman, E.: Translation validation. In: Steffen, B. (ed.) Tools and Algorithms for Construction and Analysis of Systems, 4th International Conference, TACAS '98. Lecture Notes in Computer Science, vol. 1384, pp. 151–166. Springer (1998). https://doi.org/10.1007/BFB0054170
26. Preda, M.D., Giacobazzi, R.: Control code obfuscation by abstract interpretation. In: Third IEEE International Conference on Software Engineering and Formal Methods (SEFM 2005), pp. 301–310 (2005). https://doi.org/10.1109/SEFM.2005.13
27. Preda, M.D., Giacobazzi, R.: Semantics-based code obfuscation by abstract interpretation. J. Comput. Secur. **17**(6), 855–908 (2009). https://doi.org/10.3233/JCS-2009-0345
28. Shivakumar, B.A., Barthe, G., Grégoire, B., Laporte, V., Priya, S.: Enforcing fine-grained constant-time policies. In: Yin, H., Stavrou, A., Cremers, C., Shi, E. (eds.) Proceedings of the 2022 ACM SIGSAC Conference on Computer and Communications Security, CCS 2022, pp. 83–96. ACM (2022). https://doi.org/10.1145/3548606.3560689
29. The Tigress C obfuscator. https://tigress.wtf/index.html (2023), Accessed Oct 2023
30. Tramèr, F., Boneh, D., Paterson, K.: Remote side-channel attacks on anonymous transactions. In: Capkun, S., Roesner, F. (eds.) 29th USENIX Security Symposium, USENIX Security 2020, August 12-14, 2020, pp. 2739–2756. USENIX Association (2020). https://www.usenix.org/conference/usenixsecurity20/presentation/tramer
31. Zhou, Y., Main, A., Gu, Y.X., Johnson, H.: Information hiding in software with mixed boolean-arithmetic transforms. In: Proceedings of the 8th International Conference on Information Security Applications, pp. 61–75. WISA'07, Springer-Verlag, Berlin, Heidelberg (2007)

A Symbolic Computing Perspective on Software Systems

Arthur C. Norman[1] and Stephen M. Watt[2](✉)

[1] Trinity College, Cambridge CB2 1TQ, UK
acn1@cam.ed.uk

[2] Cheriton School of Computer Science, University of Waterloo, Waterloo N2L 3G1, Canada
smwatt@uwaterloo.ca
https://cs.uwaterloo.ca/~smwatt/

Abstract. Symbolic mathematical computing systems have served as a canary in the coal mine of software systems for more than sixty years. They have introduced or have been early adopters of programming language ideas such as dynamic memory management, arbitrary precision arithmetic and dependent types. These systems have the property of being highly complex while at the same time operating in a domain where results are well-defined and clearly verifiable. These software systems span multiple layers of abstraction with concerns ranging from instruction scheduling and cache pressure up to algorithmic complexity of constructions in algebraic geometry. All of the major symbolic mathematical computing systems include low-level code for arbitrary precision arithmetic, memory management and other primitives, a compiler or interpreter for a bespoke programming language, a library of high-level mathematical algorithms, and some form of user interface. Each of these parts invokes multiple deep issues.

We present some lessons learned from this environment and free flowing opinions on topics including:

- Portability of software across architectures and decades;
- Infrastructure to embrace and infrastructure to avoid;
- Choosing base abstractions upon which to build;
- How to get the most out of a small code base;
- How developments in compilers both to optimise and to validate code have always been and remain of critical importance, with plenty of remaining challenges;
- The way in which individuals including in particular Alan Mycroft who has been able to span from hand-crafting Z80 machine code up to the most abstruse high-level code analysis techniques are needed, and
- Why it is important to teach full-stack thinking to the next generation.

The key message is that the real world is often messier than presentation in papers and we need to be able to cross between very low and very high levels of abstraction to deal with this, as Alan Mycroft has done in his work.

D. Orchard et al. (Eds.): Alan Mycroft Festschrift, LNCS 15500, pp. 33–50, 2026.
https://doi.org/10.1007/978-3-032-08187-2_3

1 Introduction

This paper is to celebrate and illustrate some of the threads that have pervaded Alan Mycroft's work across the years. He has combined skill in the sort of low level detailed code constructions covered in Hakmem [2] and the Hacker's Delight [17,18] with some of his skills there honed through his support for the BCPL compiler for the Z80 and also on, perhaps particularly, the string-processing parts of the C library that accompanied the Norcroft `C` compiler [15]. But he has also put much energy into higher level code optimization using various styles of global analysis, so it is proper to look at the consequences that flow from developments in that area. He has also focused on ways that compile-time analysis can help with getting code correct—some of that will have grown out of association with Edinburgh Standard ML [13] where one starts with a language where naïve implementation may be inefficient but where the semantics are clean enough that even radical code transformations can be safe. An ideal that flows from is that users should express their needs with the very greatest clarity and generality and that the language implementation should (ideally!) arrange that performance ends up satisfactory.

We try here to look at an area that illustrates the fact that if one looks at a problem from only a single perspective, only thinking in terms of a single level of abstraction, then important aspects of a practical implementation will be lost. And a part of what we observe is that developments in optimizing compilers over the last say 30 years have made it possible to express code in a much cleaner way that had previously been possible. Our case study is the apparently simple task of long division of multi-precision integers.

In many contexts, algorithmic performance is looked at through the prism of big-O notation. It is only in special areas the improvements by less than perhaps a factor of two are viewed as worthy of discussion, and speeding things up by just a few percent is usually thought of as immaterial. But Alan has had involvement in precisely such special areas: one is compiler optimisation where over the years a succession of incremental improvements make life better for everybody. The second is in low level libraries, where even small enhancements (for instance in being able to copy strings using word not byte operations) help all users. Finally, as compilers improve, those limited areas where machine-code implementation wins have shrunk and compiler-based analysis has allowed use of higher levels of abstraction in even performance critical code. This higher abstraction has improved the prospect of static reporting of errors as well. Alan has contributed either directly or indirectly to all of these.

The particular case study we cover here is at almost the lowest level of any symbolic computation systems—exact arbitrary precision arithmetic. Software that is to manipulate algebraic expressions needs arbitrary precision integer arithmetic. Unlike the situation for those concerned with cryptography this has to cover numbers whose size can not be predicted in advance. Unlike the situation for those concerned with breaking records for high precision values of elementary constants, it almost never calls for the ultimate asymptotically best algorithms.

Because this arithmetic underpins all other activity, even small improvements to it impact the whole system.

The current market-leader for big integer arithmetic is "GMP"—the GNU multi-precision library [5]. It is notable as a widely used library that still has heavy reliance on machine code to achieve its objectives. The first version of GMP was released only in 1991, well after we became involved in implementing arithmetic, and so we started from code-bases and mind sets that predated it. Since then we have valued abstraction and readily portable code (GMP has separate bodies of assembly code for perhaps a couple of dozen architectures, all calling for maintenance) above absolute performance. But recently we have wanted to consider two questions

1. How close to GMP performance can high-level code now come?
2. Are the algorithms from Knuth Volume 2 still close enough to the the last word?

Our stance is also that low-level underpinnings for a system deserve serious review every decade or so, this view having emerged over around 50 years of experience.

2 Acceptable Absolute Performance Given Good Compilers

Going back to the times when Alan Mycroft was a student, one of us (ACN) had multiple-precision arithmetic using base 10^9 (arguing that a power of 10 base let input and output happen in linear time but left the asymptotic cost of arithmetic unchanged). Around 1989 that was replaced by a version using 2^{31} and coded in `C` rather that BCPL. Twenty five or so years later, that needed to be replaced by a version using 64-bit digits and built using `C++`. These were not capricious changes—one was triggered by the need to move from a BCPL base to a `C` base (for instance using Norcroft `C` [15] developed along with Alan!) and the other to keep up to date using `C++` in a 64-bit world. Many serious long-lasting systems will need their foundations dramatically re-worked over similar time-scales.

Meanwhile the other of us (SMW) became involved in the Scratchpad [6], Axiom [10] and Aldor [19,20] symbolic computation work at IBM after initial work on the Maple [3,4] system. Coincidentally, at its very start Scratchpad included parts of Reduce [8] which was the driver for the first work thread. Axiom was seriously concerned with generality, and this led SMW to consider both the extent to which big-number code could be written neatly parameterised by the width of digits, and how the algorithms used could be expressed so as to be directly usable in a range of other domains that were not purely numeric. His sequence of papers on "shifted inverses" [21,22] triggered the current work.

Pleasingly, by using `C++` templates to achieve specialization for small cases and with the highest level of optimization using current compilers—and a certain amount of care reading the Hacker's Delight [17]—the unsigned multiplication code written in `C++` could match or even beat GMP multiplying numbers with up to around 130 decimal digits. From there on GMP, starts to win mostly by a factor of up to two, in part due to its use of hand-written assembly code. This suggests that there remains some scope for further compiler development to help us claw back that discrepancy! At some stage beyond where Karatsuba [11] becomes the preferred scheme, GMP switches to the Toom [5] family of algorithms, before eventually moving to use of the FFT. Rather than that, the competing C++ code switches to using three threads for the three top-level sub-multiplications that Karatsuba performs, making that transition once thread management overhead is properly balanced by concurrency savings. The means that comparison between the two platforms is not quite straightforward, but of the measurement is of elapsed time on an otherwise lightly loaded system it allows the portable C++ code to be at least competitive against GMP out to well over 30000 decimals. This is typically as far as general purpose symbolic computation cares for—calculations needing more than that are not liable to terminate in a sensible amount of time anyway. This confirms what one might have hoped, that modern compiler optimisation can diminish the need for assembly code even in extreme cases. But it also confirms one's uncomfortable suspicion that it is not yet perfect so continued work in the area is called for.

With multiplication code stable and prompted by the SMW work on shifted inverses, our attention re-focused on division and this forms the main core of this paper. The observations below arise from re-working two arbitrary precision integer libraries, seen through the lens of our own experience.

3 Long Division

Way back in 1969 Knuth explained to the world how to do fast long division. His procedure is based on wanting to compute a quotient $q = u/v$ of N digit numbers. Since he is actually considering fractional values rather than integers all the numbers concerned have just N digits and his explanation will be most directly relevant to the implementation of high precision floating point.

Jebelean [9] in a paper on practical integer division stated in the introduction to his report that a scheme designed along the lines of the Knuth method would lead to long division being around 30 times as costly as a multiplication. This would render it of little practical value. We set out to see if use of a modern code-base (Jebelean's arithmetic used a base of 2^{29}), shifted inverses and a fresh round of consideration could change that judgment.

Knuth starts by computing $w = 1/v$ using an iteration $w \leftarrow w + w \times (1 - v \times w)$ performing only the last step to full precision N. The previous to $N/2$ and so on. The total cost of finding the reciprocal is then $4 \times M(N)$, where $M(N)$ is the cost of a single multiplication of two N digit fractions to obtain an N digit result. Next compute $q' = u \times w$ and it is an approximation to the final result and with care it will be correct within 1 (as the fraction is truncated) and can only be an underestimate. Finally compute $r = u - v \times q'$ and compare against v—if necessary do a minor correction. In all this has used time $6 \times M(N)$ [plus some linear cost work]. Students have been taught this scheme for generations, but in reality every single simple tiny step has greater depth.

We will look at this in detail and show the extra considerations that emerge when looking at the algorithm from a perspective where absolute rather than just asymptotic costs matter. We also have some comments on code expressiveness and compile-time validation and to make, and believe that both concern for fine-detail issues that impact performance and higher level ones relevant to correctness and maintainability are relevant here.

The Domain of Computation

A first thing to note is that Knuth's explanation is in terms of numbers with an implicit leading binary point (base 2 decimal point), in other words fractions. Even though at times this may still provide a convenient way to think, it means that the code for integer division diverts into a different domain for much of what is done. SMW properly viewed this as unsatisfactory not just on aesthetic grounds but because it complicates any attempt to have one body of code (with an associated single proof of correctness) that is applicable across multiple domains. Axiom and Aldor try hard to keep all code such that the characteristics of underlying domains (rings, fields, vector spaces, polynomials, non-commutative versions of all those...) can be used to parameterise algorithmic code. He set about re-formulating fast division so that all intermediate values were in the same domain as the inputs, but "shifted" [21,22]. The work reported here started with the idea of implementing fast division within the ACN code body (which just used classical methods for that operation), both to enhance that code and to further test and demonstrate the SMW variant of the algorithm.

We next note that given that calculation is going to be done using digits (in this case 64-bits wide) rather than just abstract numbers it is desirable to align all values to make full use of each digit. Thus the notation $1/v$ is taken as an invitation to left-shift v until its top digit is almost full. Informally this can be thought of as normalization to the range [0.5, 1). Then we compute 0.5 divided by this shifted value rather than $1/v$ and obtain a nicely normalised reciprocal also in the range [0.5, 1], save for the case where v is exactly a power of 2 which just gets treated specially. Of course the shifting has to be allowed for and in effect undone at a later stage, but that is easy so we will not mention it again, even though it represents a number of extra lines of code. Also the explanation here in terms of fractional values has to be interpreted as talking about integers with associated shift values. This is not quite like use of floating point where every intermediate value tends to be re-normalised to have its top bit set, and it is not quite like most scaled arithmetic were there will often be scaling by a fairly fixed amount—here, as we go, the amount of shifting will end up varying from step to step.

In the calculation $q = u/v$, many in the past have spoken of working with N digits. Well u and v in general have unrelated sizes, so a single parameter

N here is an over-simplification. It is more probable that the sizes of v and q are what should be thought about and performance predictions can not be uni-dimensional.

In real code, if numbers are reasonably small, it will be proper to drop back to classical methods. When an iteration is called for a starting approximation will be needed and there has to be a judgment about how accurate that should be because even if a single digit would suffice it is not obvious that such a choice will be best.

Sub-operations

We now consider the important iterative step $w \leftarrow w + w \times (1 - v \times w)$ and we assert that it has issues in every sub-operation!

At any stage we want to calculate using only values that are meaningful and we only want to generate outputs that will be necessary. So consider the inner $v \times w$. At any stage w will have (say) k digits correct, so there is no merit in looking at more digits of w than that. However the updated value we are computing will have $2k$ digits correct, and those depend on $2k$ digits from v. So in that multiplication we multiply a $2k$ digits value by a k digit one and that yields a $3k$ digit result. However, because w is already a k-digit approximation to the reciprocal of v, we know in advance that (almost) the top k of those digits will exactly cancel with the 1, and so those do not need computing. Furthermore (almost) the lower k digits of that result are not needed because they would contribute to digits beyond $2k$ in the next value of w. So what we need is an unusual form of multiplication that forms the product of a $2N$ digit number by an N digit one and just return the middle N digits on the result. But it is even messier because we actually need those middle N digits with extra guard digits surrounding them!

These cases of looking at just some of the digits of a product and the issues of looking at different numbers of digits within different values amount to just what SMW was expressing at a higher level in his papers. They are explained in grim detail here to illustrate just how much care has to be taken throughout the implementation, and how much might be lost by viewing everything at a higher and more mathematical level.

Now consider the "$w + w\times$" part. The multiplication is of a k digit w by only k digits from the term just computed because it is (almost) the case that this is not added to the existing value if w but merely concatenated on its end to (almost) double the number of correct digits. So only (almost) the top k digits of that product are required. There are two driving issues behind the repeated uses of the word "almost" here. One is that when one computes the top half (say) of the product of a pair of numbers by a scheme other than forming a full product and discarding low digits there are liable to be carries from the omitted low part of the calculation that are missed so the value formed will be slightly low. It is therefore necessary to bound that level of inaccuracy and maintain guard bits sufficient that it does not hurt the end result. The second issue is that in the Newton Raphson iteration even if at one step a value may have all bits of k digits correct and then at the next we expect to get $2k$ digits correct, there can be rounding or truncation errors relative to the full result both in the initial k digits and in the calculation that obtains the updated value. Tiny errors can escalate. This issue interacts with the fact that the eventual number of digits required may not be a power of 2, and so for instance if $2k+1$ digits are required in an end result the iteration that leads to it is liable to be starting with values stored as $k+1$ digits but where the least significant of those digits could afford to have almost half its low digits incorrect. This adds extra depth to the simple sounding statements about use of precision $N, N/2, N/4\ldots$

Another place where only high digits from a product are needed is $q' = u \times w$. The magnitude of the quotient can be estimated from the sizes of divisor and dividend. At this stage we only need to use high digits from u, and at this stage we can see that the reciprocal w needed to be computed to a number of digits to match q. Note that this level of precision may be either greater or less than the size of the divisor, and coping with that adds further detail to the iterative process—in particular the operation described above as multiplying a $2k$ digit by a k digit one will sometimes have to allow for (and take advantage of) the divisor v not having fully $2k$ digits.

The final step that Knuth presents forms $r = u - v * q'$. He has arranged that q' is either the correct quotient or just one too small, and as a result r will be in the range $0 \leq r < 2v$. That means that we can tell in advance that many high digits in the subtraction there will cancel exactly, and so this is a case where only low parts of the product are required. If we require the remainder as part of our output, this is as far as we can go, but there are occasions when division is performed and only the quotient is wanted. In such cases, computing even the full low part of $w \times q'$ is usually unnecessary.

If we did the full calculation of r and then compared it against v, that would be done by inspecting its top digit first and only working down to check lower digits if the issue had not been resolved. One might hope that, when using 64-bit digits, testing only the top digit would almost always be sufficient. That means we may be able to get away with finding just a single digit from some well-chosen place towards the middle of $v \times q'$. This can be done with controllable error in linear time rather than $M(N)$ time. However three issues intervene. The first is that the top relevant full digit of $w \times q'$ may have either almost all its bits in use or only a few. In the latter case, testing just those few bits does not provide as reliable a test as would be ideal. This can be coped with by using code that extracts a digit-sized value from a product but aligned by a bit-address rather than a digit address. This is not obviously a primitive operation widely discussed in the literature. The second issue is that a one-digit part product can have inaccuracies because carries that would have contributed to a perfect value have been missed out. Those errors need bounding and allowing for. And finally there is the issue of what the most challenging cases might be. Here that will be when $u - v \times q'$ is very close to v in value, in which case the comparison may not be resolved by inspecting just one high digit. In particular this can be the case when the division is going to prove to be exact (and q' was one too low). Exact division seems a really bad case to have badly handled in a version of division code that will not be returning a remainder! To mitigate that we round q' rather than truncate. This means that r has to be tested not just to see if it is less than v but also to see if it was negative, but it moves the case where this one-digit check for correction is insufficient from near exact divisions to one where the remainder is around $v/2$. Obviously, if the one-digit test is inconclusive, it makes sense to drop back and use the original low-half-of-product scheme. We have considered elsewhere the general case of "clipped products" in which only some of a product's digits are desired [16].

All the above makes use of a version of multiplication code that delivers some but not all the digits of the full result. Mulders [14] pioneered this. He was concerned with multiplying power series and so naturally he looked at keeping the N low terms from the product of two series each of which had N terms. He showed that he could form the product in time that was say 70% to 80% of the cost of performing a full Karatsuba style multiplication. Hanrot and Zimmerman [7] considered his scheme in some depth and in particular looked into the optimal value for his parameter β, the proportion of the product computed. There were also associated with its use in the `mpfr` multi-precision floating point library, where they will have just been concentrating on the top half of a multiplication of two equal-sized numbers, but they will have considered carry propagation carefully.

Tying it Together

For general use, it is necessary to adapt things so that the two inputs do not have to have the same number of digits, to allow for carry operations and to have versions that keep flexible numbers of high, middle or low digits from the product. That of course all depends on having underlying fast full multiplication, and so the Karatsuba procedures have to be bolstered with code that allows for inputs not balanced in terms of their digit counts. At yet lower levels performance can depend on just how carry detection and propagation is implemented, how the temporary workspace that Karatsuba and Mulders need is managed and on overheads that arise when the resulting library is built so it can work in a threaded environment.

As an implementation became close to complete, it became possible to start some performance assessment.

The first observation is that in general the cost of a classical long division u/v is only modestly greater than that of classical multiplication of v by the quotient q. This should probably not come as a big surprise! It also makes sense that when the quotient has fairly few digits any chance for the Newton-Raphson "fast" division to shine has to depend on even q being rather large and hence the two inputs u and v will be enormous.

If the divisor and quotient are about the same size, the fast method can be a winner with the cost of u/v being only about 4 times that of $v \times q$, but the various overheads mean that with the current code-base a division of a 100-digit number by a 50-digit one is still faster using classical methods. Note the ratio of the cost of clever division to Karatsuba multiplication is still not much more than 4—a long way short of the 30 that Jebelean had projected, but that of course does not invalidate the merits of the alternative scheme that he presents.

The case that we had not initially expected arises when the quotient has many more digits than the divisor and there the Newton-Raphson shows disastrously poor performance. This is of course because it is needing to compute a value of $1/v$ to the number of digits precision set by q. It becomes clear that when q is going to be significantly larger than v that the division should be conducted as if by short division by v, partitioning u into appropriate sized super-digits. That will result in all the internal divisions being of the $2N/N$ variety where the asymptotically good method actually pays off.

4 Correctness and Abstraction

It should be apparent from the above explanation of our division code that it ends up complicated enough that correctness can not be a given. In particular are all stages we want to compute with only the minimal number of digits to maintain accuracy—the closer to the wind we can sail the faster the code will be.

There are two components to the task of getting things right. The first is illustrated by a need for a bound on the error due to ignoring some potential carries when we compute just the top half of a product. In some of the work we were involved in required properly detailed coding: for instance we write `(-(from>=M+1))&(from-M)` rather than `from>=M+1?0:from-M` because, using certain compilers, the former tuned into branch-free code and ran measurably faster than the latter. But then we need to switch into mathematician mode and derive and then prove a bound on the impact carries could have on a partial product. We believe that Alan Mycroft is the sort of person with the breadth to contribute at both ends of this abstraction stack, and to all levels in between.

With regard to the low-level hackery we are very aware that compiler improvements over the years have made it possible to achieve results that previously called for lower level code. For instance some compilers now recognize fairly natural-looking idioms and generate machine code that makes proper use of carry flags and "add-with-carry" operations. But our case, where we want to generate branch-free code, shows that such a line of work has not fully run its course. But we are also strongly appreciative of compiler work that in-lines functions, maps variables onto registers and all the other clever things that allow us to write code in a cleaner and more abstract way than in the past.

We also note that way in which compilers can increasingly propagate information through code and and detect issues. We very much want that to continue to improve. The experience developing this fairly densely detailed code all intended to implement (in the end) very clear cut mathematical operations has shown that at least with the compilers currently in general use there is still plenty to be done. In a better future world all of the off-by-one and not-quite-enough-bits-for-accuracy bugs we had to detect by fairly traditional methods might ideally be spotted based on static code analysis. This of course can involve continuing the merge of proof technology with compilation.

The final issue of language design and compilation that we feel that this effort has highlighted for us is the need to be able to express actions at the highest possible level of abstraction while still maintaining fine detailed control of issues that impact performance. In some ways, this is reminiscent of other findings [1]. As an example of a conflict we faced in this style consider the fact that most of the more elaborate big-number functions need workspace sized as per their inputs. A clean way of allocating this space might be use of C++ `std::vector`, and then a reasonably plausible compiler can lead to unchecked indexed access being as efficient as use of simple C-style arrays. However in library code that is liable to allocate and release memory very frequently the potential costs of `new` and `delete` operations are a worry—leading us to provide our own scheme exploiting all our understanding of sharing and lifetime properties of our workspace. We obviously try to implement that with an interface that makes its use seem as high-level and abstract as possible (thank you templates, overloading,...) but, all in all, we find the gulf between the around 3 lines of explanation that Knuth provides and the several thousand lines of code we end up with to be rather horrifying. We are very aware that if we had coded all of this some decades ago it would have been even worse, but we very much want compiler work (including language design and code proof technology) to continue even after the retirement of one of its contributors.

5 Results

Part of the thesis behind the paper is that the real world is messier than the presentations in most research papers. For integer division we believe that most explanations of procedures have been characterised by a single parameter that gives "the number of digits involved". We observe that if an N digit number is to be divided by an M digit one that there are certainly three domains of performance—the straightforward one where N is close to $2 \times M$ but also ones where the divisor or the quotient is much smaller than the dividend. In the extreme cases the Knuth scheme—applied in a naïve manner—is unsatisfactory. If the divisor is small relative to the dividend but large enough to justify non-classical treatment, it is much better to perform an operation in the style of classical short division treating the divisor as defining a sort of digit. If the quotient is going to be small, a scheme that uses an iteration to generate a shifted inverse of the divisor is extremely good provided that all calculation is done only to a precision based on the number of quotient digits. In this case, the dominant cost of the full calculation will be multiplying quotient by divisor and subtracting to find the remainder. If the user does not actually need the remainder, almost all of that cost can be avoided most of the time, leading to dramatic savings.

As well as there being thresholds based on the relative magnitudes of divisor and quotient, there also have to be ones that reflect that until numbers become large there is no merit in abandoning the classical algorithms. Just where these will lie will depend on the relative performance of the classical division used as a baseline and on the fast multiplication used for larger products. Of course multiplication has performance that varies for inputs that are not the same size and here waters are further muddied by the use of Mulders-style multiplication that generates only some of the digits from a full product. In our case an additional complication arises. Karatsuba multiplication works by decomposing a product so that to multiply a pair of N digit values one performs three multiplications on $N/2$ ones. For large enough N that synchronization overheads are balanced by concurrency savings these three sub-products are calculated in separate threads, giving a reduction in elapsed time but not in the total number of CPU cycles executed. This certainly brings into focus the issue of whether timing reports should show elapsed or CPU time, and in the latter case how much system as distinct from user time needs to be accounted for. It also means that our multiplication cost grows in a somewhat lumpy way rather than meeting the asymptotic prediction at all early.

We need per-platform tuning within a Karatsuba multiplier, for just how Mulders-style decomposition is used for inputs that do not match in size and when it is not exactly the top of bottom half of a product needed and for the changeover from classical to notionally faster division. At this stage we have not completed all that tuning, and anyway the main focus here is to expose complicated detail rather than to claim ultimate performance. So we provide here some measurements that can at least give an idea of behaviour.

Because our division code sits firmly atop multiplication, we start with measurements for regular simple integer multiplication where the two numbers being combined each have the same number of digits. We report elapsed time on am Intel i7-8086k system running Windows 10 and using the Cygwin C++ compiler. The bit-patterns of the numbers multiplied are set up as random in such a way that successive test runs will use different random seeds (so as to avoid optimization artefects based on the exact test cases). Timings for our code are reported against those for GMP and the key inner loop is essentially

```
clk1 = std::chrono::high_resolution_clock::now();
for (std::size_t m=0; m<REPEATS; m++)
    mpn_mul((mp_ptr)c,
            (mp_srcptr)a, lena*
                (sizeof(std::uint64_t)/sizeof(mp_limb_t)),
            (mp_srcptr)b, lenb*
                (sizeof(std::uint64_t)/sizeof(mp_limb_t)),
    for (std::size_t i=0; i<lena+lenb; i++)
        gmp_check = gmp_check*MULT + c[i];
clk2 = std::chrono::high_resolution_clock::now();
```

where the value `gmp_check` both serves to give a weak confirmation that our results and those from GMP match and to reduce the changes of an over-enthusiastic compiler omitting everything because its output was unused. As well as `my_time` for the multiplication code that transitions to Karatsuba and to the GMP figure there is a reference time that is the timing for a simple version of classical long multiplication with quadratic cost (and no special casing

Table 1. Multiplication of two integers of the same length. Times are reported in seconds per multiplication.

Length	Our time	GMP time	Ref time	Ours/GMP	Ref/Ours
2	0.010	0.017	0.075	0.577	7.830
3	0.015	0.034	0.087	0.439	5.749
4	0.024	0.036	0.103	0.665	4.260
5	0.034	0.045	0.124	0.753	3.681
6	0.049	0.056	0.147	0.873	2.990
7	0.092	0.071	0.176	1.301	1.915
8	0.151	0.085	0.213	1.780	1.409
9	0.172	0.105	0.248	1.638	1.441
10	0.185	0.123	0.292	1.498	1.580
20	0.721	0.432	1.043	1.667	1.447
29	1.505	0.820	2.184	1.835	1.451
39	2.399	1.309	3.802	1.833	1.585
50	3.700	1.998	6.738	1.852	1.821
78	7.764	4.083	15.965	1.901	2.056
102	12.051	6.301	29.201	1.912	2.423
120	16.015	7.523	39.678	2.129	2.478
235	42.043	22.819	152.726	1.842	3.633
260	44.692	26.515	186.394	1.686	4.171
429	72.350	54.386	509.029	1.330	7.036
607	98.855	87.958	1024.906	1.124	10.368
740	120.235	120.761	1523.879	0.996	12.674
1043	217.381	189.216	2939.518	1.149	13.522
1546	400.686	328.835	6583.968	1.218	16.432

for short values). Number lengths are expressed in terms of 64-bit digits so for instance the line for length 1546 relates to multiplying a pair of integers each of around 30000 decimals. The lengths are not all at neat multiples of ten because this table is extracted from a larger one which uses a set of samples that grow geometrically not arithmetically. This is shown in Table 1.

We are of course very pleased with the results for length up to 6 (i.e. around 100 decimals) and for many calculations in Computer Algebra we view that range as important. We are frustrated that so far we have not been able to coax our code and compilers into matching GMP speed there. From 20 up we will be using Karatsuba and at least we manage to be within a factor of 2 of GMP. At around 200 digits (say 4000 decimals) we start to be able to use concurrency and that keeps us reasonably competitive against GMP as far as we fuss. Even though by that stage GMP will be using variants on Toom rather than just Karatsuba. We do not measure and do not really concern ourselves cases with millions of decimals.

Next we report on Mulders multiplication, and again to simplify the presentation we multiply two equal sized random numbers and keep either the full product or the top half or the bottom half. Our Mulders code is capable of

Table 2. Time to compute lower half of product of two N place values.

N	Class	Kara	Fast	Kara/Class	Fast/Class	Fast/Kara
10	0.07	0.10	0.07	132.57%	96.42%	72.73%
14	0.13	0.20	0.12	148.17%	89.80%	60.61%
18	0.21	0.29	0.18	139.22%	88.17%	63.33%
20	0.25	0.36	0.22	144.48%	88.76%	61.44%
24	0.37	0.42	0.37	114.31%	99.15%	86.74%
50	1.63	1.80	1.30	109.98%	79.73%	72.50%
55	2.04	2.17	1.59	106.62%	77.74%	72.91%
70	3.19	3.38	2.21	106.04%	69.44%	65.49%
80	4.14	3.98	2.99	96.04%	72.09%	75.06%
90	5.29	4.87	3.72	92.02%	70.37%	76.48%
95	5.78	4.69	4.02	81.13%	69.41%	85.56%
100	6.39	5.65	4.44	88.53%	69.50%	78.51%
105	7.02	6.68	4.67	95.17%	66.47%	69.84%
110	7.70	6.88	5.08	89.40%	66.02%	73.85%
135	11.51	9.71	6.65	84.30%	57.78%	68.54%
240	36.49	20.25	19.70	55.50%	53.99%	97.27%
250	39.29	21.23	20.53	54.02%	52.25%	96.72%
300	56.69	23.96	26.36	42.27%	46.50%	110.00%
700	302.47	60.42	72.48	19.97%	23.96%	119.96%
750	359.93	63.92	81.34	17.76%	22.60%	127.26%
1400	1228.45	177.73	180.51	14.47%	14.69%	101.57%
1600	1562.67	261.09	207.99	16.71%	13.31%	79.66%
1800	2033.82	337.94	314.95	16.62%	15.49%	93.20%
10000	60694.30	3520.00	3558.90	5.80%	5.86%	101.11%

delivering an arbitrary slice from the product and so any overhead associated with that generality is present. We use our Karatsuba-based multiplication as underpinning. We have code that can produce a slice of digits from a product using simple classical code, so we compare this use of Karatsuba to form a complete product (and then merely discard unwanted digits) and then Mulders. For generating a complete product our code degenerates to just use of Karatsuba with a few initial extra tests that are irrelevant by the time Karatsuba makes sense. And our comparisons show that we can compute the top half of a product in times broadly similar to those for the bottom half, so the only section of our full test results included here are for calculating the lower half of the product of two N digit values. The results are shown in Table 2.

It can be seen that for reasonably big numbers the fast methods are indeed faster than simple classical code, and for huge cases they are better by a large factor. Up to a couple of hundred (64-bit) digits, the Mulders code delivers a really useful speedup compared against just using Karatsuba and then throwing away half of the result. But at about the point where our Karatsuba implementation goes multi-threaded that benefit gets lost—perhaps because Mulders in its recursion uses a sequence of smaller full multiplications that do not use parallelism. At present we find it hard to explain why our implementation of Mulders does not do better on truly huge numbers. It perhaps means that pragmatically we should add in additional thresholds so that for numbers with a really large number of digits it does not try to be clever! Our "top half of product" code matches the bottom half performance up to around 70 (64-bit) digits but then degrades in an even worse way than the bottom-half code, so further tuning is called for – or perhaps more sophisticated optimization in the compiler.

We collected similar measurements for the "shifted inverse" code that computes a sort of scaled reciprocal. For that we could use our existing classical long division as a baseline, then code that used Newton-Raphson but performed all arithmetic to full precision and finally our version using precision that adjusted as the iteration proceeded and Mulders multiplication. As an additional assessment for this we timed multiplying the input by its computed inverse, so we can compare our best time with that of a single multiplication. Here the table of results is tidy enough that we do not need to present much of it. Using restricted precision for intermediate results and Mulders can save serious amounts of time as against using full precision everywhere (as expected). The iterative code is never slower than finding the reciprocal using classical division, but we needed to get as far as 500 digits before it was faster by a factor of 5. The shifted inverse is found in a time that in the best cases is slightly under twice as long as multiplication, is usually between 2 and 3 times and at worst still under 4 multiplies.

By this stage the multiple opportunities to adjust thresholds in the underlying code made optimization rather hard even on a single system! Note that in the above comparisons the various simpler schemes were being used not just as performance baselines but also for confirmation of output values, and with input data generated with distinct random seeds for each test run our confidence tends to grow.

Finally we come to division. Here the calculation will be to evaluate the quotient q and remainder r when a value u is divided by v. In each case we will use the corresponding lower case letter for the number of 64-bit digits in a value. We use $u = 10000$ as a case large enough that we can hope that asymptotic effects will dominate, and then consider $v = 100, 500, 5000$ and 9500 to cover the regimes of relative divisor lengths. These of course lead to quotients taking the same range of lengths.

Rather than showing absolute times we report timing ratios. We scale against the cost of (our code) multiplying v by q, and then report the cost of repeating that using classical long multiplication, using classical long division for u/v, using our shifted-inverse code to calculate quotient and remainder and finally our scheme that just finds the quotient.

Table 3 shows how behaviour changes fairly radically for divisions where the numbers have different lengths. The more traditional Table 4 only considers $2N \times N$ divisions but observes what happens as N varies.

This of course confirms that eventually fast division beats classical, but the cross over point is perhaps higher than would be nice! The final row here is the same test as the $5000, 5000$ case above and the slightly different numbers serve

Table 3. Scaled multiplication and division

v, q	100,9900	500,9500	5000,5000	9500,500	9900,100
classical mul	1.96	7.07	24.30	6.92	1.97
classical div	2.16	6.43	20.55	5.89	2.01
fast div+rem	3.99	6.86	4.16	1.32	1.04
fast quot only	4.00	6.80	3.20	0.29	0.04

Table 4. $2N \times N$ multiplication and division

size in digits	classical multiply	classical divide	fast divide	divide no rem
20	1.33	3.24	5.98	5.22
40	1.67	2.63	4.58	3.81
60	1.82	2.42	3.96	3.28
80	2.06	2.36	4.45	3.65
100	2.18	2.41	4.34	3.54
150	2.39	2.47	4.09	3.27
200	2.63	2.64	4.16	3.36
300	4.45	4.22	6.33	5.17
500	7.51	6.99	7.15	5.81
1000	11.39	9.79	6.05	4.96
5000	24.99	20.91	4.25	3.27

to remind us that measurements on modern computers are subject to all sorts of variation—an additional obstacle to refined optimization. In particular cache consequences of running a single test repeatedly so as to have a long enough time period to measure risk leading to results that may not be representative of real-world usage. These figures also make it clear that a version of division that does not compute a remainder can help with time savings when working at higher precisions.

Given that results can be sensitive to the computer used the same tests were run on a second system. A Raspberry Pi 5 was used with this choice partly motivated by Alan Mycroft's involvement in the start-up of Raspberry Pi.

For multiplication on the Raspberry Pi the `C++`-coded multiplication beats GPM up to 7 digits, but only by a small fraction and it would probably be fairer to declare a dead heat. From there on up to around 200 digits the speed ratio remains at worst 1.4 and our code is mostly no more than 15% slower than GMP. From 200-1546 digits where we use parallel Karatsuba beat GMP where the best observation was taking 65% of the GMP time to multiply a pair of 740 digit numbers.

The Mulders multiplication to find the low half of a product shows a more repeatable speed-up so that Mulders costs about 75% of Karatsuba for a wide range of number sizes, but again with ugly behaviour where a full Karatsuba

Table 5. Division with shifted inverses

v, q	100,9900	500,9500	5000,5000	9500,500	9900,100
classical mul	1.93	7.57	26.71	7.38	1.69
classical div	2.21	7.81	26.85	7.49	1.73
fast div+rem	4.09	7.86	4.28	1.73	0.94
fast quot only	4.09	7.74	3.51	0.31	0.04

goes parallel but the sub-multiplications done within Mulders are smaller and do not. In our current implementation Mulders loses from around 200-3000 digits, but beyond there it starts to be a winner again—albeit with less stability in the speed ratio. A hypothesis is that the heavy use of starting and stopping threads makes timings sensitive to internal timing in operating system thread-scheduling and given that the subsidiary tasks are fairly small this generates delays.

Shifted inverses show a pattern similar to that observed on the PC.

For division we obtain Table 5. Given the significant differences in architecture it is perhaps amazing how similar to the Intel table this is.

Looking at how well "fast" division works as input sizes grow, on the ARM we have the shifted-inverse based division matching classical somewhere between 500 and 1000 digits again just as on Intel.

The main observation is that the Raspberry Pi figures as collected on Linux look a little less scattered and incoherently variable than the Intel ones on Windows and this may in part reflect the i7-8086k having a more complicated instruction processing scheme where, while average performance is excellent detailed, timing can be very sensitive to all sorts of hard to predict interactions.

One thing which is clear from all this is that integer division following the Knuth explanation can have a cost less than 4 times that of multiplying back to recover the dividend—at least in the case where only a quotient is required not both a quotient and remainder. While this includes the special case of divisions known in advance to be exact it does not rely on that situation applying. This is very much faster than the factor of 30 that Jebelean suggested would apply but nevertheless his paper claims to achieve a factor of about 2 and so would be even better – future work should implement that and consider how it applies to quotients other than the tidy $2N \times N$ case. The other thing that emerges is that our "fast" code only really begins to shine for integers sufficiently large that we would rather avoid them arising in the first place, for instance by using modular arithmetic with a word-sized modulus. But despite these practical reservations we are very pleased with the manner in which this exercise highlights how much depth can arise when one attempts to optimise even simple-seeming schemes.

6 Conclusions and Further Thoughts About Education

All the above explains some of the additional mess that a typical implementer who is keen to achieve high performance may face. A properly pedantic implementer will be fixated both on performance and on correctness, so will need to deploy a mathematician's skills and mind-set to prove that errors never intrude as well as a low level hacker's understanding of performance issues. With caches, multiple-issue CPUs, speculative execution and various memory models that can impact how multiple cores may or may not observe that the others are up to, this has continued to become more and more challenging. Performance engineering can often involve a desire to sail as close to the wind as possible, and in this case error bounds on the "top half of an unbalanced product" will interact with the exact manner in which errors propagate through the iterative step, and careful analysis of just how accurate the initial approximations to the shifted inverse are. So the difficulty of attaining correctness has perhaps grown too.

Clearly very many programmers respond by taking the line that delivery of a product on time trumps correctness and correctness trumps performance. For many purposes their stance is completely proper, but compilers and libraries represent special cases where correctness is vital and optimization impacts enough users that it becomes truly important—perhaps especially now that machines have by and large ceases speeding up substantially and their manufacturers chase benchmarks with a combination of more cores (which will often not all be activated) and with special instructions to support important but possible niche applications.

We note that, as system developers, our own approaches start in some sense from opposite perspectives—one as specific as possible and one as generic as possible. However, we both consider the consequences of decisions on the full software stack, and end up with designs with a great deal of similarity.

Our illustration has involved integer division, which might be viewed as fairly low level and fundamental building block where there are carefully documented solutions that go back at least as far back as Knuth Volume 2 [12]. But we assert that proper implementation calls for a style of computer "renaissance" individual, able to span consideration from mathematical and abstract down to the finest detail of how to implement carry detection while combining multi-word integers. And indeed ideally one who could know how then to tune code to exploit the hardly intuitive performance consequences of modern complicated instruction execution strategies. For the future we can not count on performance improvements (and hence resource use reduction) based on raw CPU improvements. We need a new generation of programmers who—against the teaching style of several decades—value compactness and efficiency, and continue work to keep improving compilers so that they can deliver that with clearly expressed source code that can be validated effectively. If long division is messy consider almost any "real scale" challenge! We need more Mycrofts.

References

1. Agaram, K.: Bicycles for the mind have to be see-through. In: Companion Proceedings of the 4th International Conference on the Art, Science, and Engineering of Programming (Programming '20 Companion), pp. 173–186. ACM (2020)

2. Beeler, M., Gosper, R., Schroeppel, R.: Hakmem. Tech. Rep. AI memo 239, Artificial Intelligence Laboratory, MIT, Cambridge Massachusetts (1972)
3. Char, B.W., Fee, G.J., Geddes, K.O., Gonnet, G.H., Monagan, M.B., Watt, S.M.: On the design and performance of the Maple system. In: Proceedings of the 1984 Macsyma Users' Conference, pp. 199–219. General Electric Corporation (1984)
4. Char, B.W., Geddes, K.O., Gonnet, G.H., Watt, S.M.W.: Maple User's Guide. Watcom Publications (1985)
5. GMP Development Team: The GNU Multiple Precision Arithmetic Library (version 6.2.1). Free Software Foundation (2020). https://gmplib.org
6. Griesmer, J., Jenks, R.: Scratchpad/1: An interactive facility for symbolic mathematics. In: Proceedings of the second ACM Symposium on Symbolic and Algebraic Manipulation, pp. 42–58 (1971)
7. Hanrot, G., Zimmermann, P.: A long note on Mulders' short product. J. Symbolic Comput. **37**, 391–401 (2004)
8. Hearn, A.C.: REDUCE: A user-oriented interactive system for algebraic simplification. In: Klerer, M., Reinfelds, J. (eds.) Interactive Systems for Experimental Applied Mathematics, pp. 79–90. Academic Press, New York (1968)
9. Jebelean, T.: Practical division with Karatsuba complexity. In: Proc. 1997 International Symposium on Symbolic and Algebraic Computation (ISSAC 1997, pp. 339–341. ACM, New York (July 1997)
10. Jenks, R.D., Sutor, R.S.: AXIOM: The Scientific Computation System. Springer Verlag, New York (1992). https://doi.org/10.1007/978-1-4612-2940-7
11. Karatsuba, A., Yu., O.: Multiplication of many-digital numbers by automatic computers. Proc. USSR Acad. Sci. **145**, 293–294 (1962), Transl. Acad. J. Phys.-Doklady **7** (1963), pp. 595–596
12. Knuth, D.E.: The Art of Computer Programming, Volume 2: Seminumerical Algorithms. Addison-Wesley, Boston, third edn. (1997)
13. MacQueen, D., Harper, R., Reppy, J.: The history of standard ml. In: ACM on Programming Languages: Issue HOPL, vol. 4 – 86, pp. 1–100. ACM, Washington DC (2020)
14. Mulders, T.: On short multiplication and division. In: Proceedings AAECC 11, 1. pp. 69–88 (2000)
15. Mycroft, A., Norman, A., Fitch, J.: The Norcroft C compiler. Tech. rep., Codemist Ltd (1985). http://www.codemist.co.uk/ncc
16. Norman, A.C., Watt, S.M.: Computing clipped products. In: 26th International Workshop on Computer Algebra in Scientific Computing (CASC 2024), pp. 273–291. Springer Cham LNCS 14938 (2024)
17. Warren Jr., H.S.: The Hacker's Delight. Addison Wesley (2003)
18. Warren, H.S., Jr.: Hacker's Delight, 2ed. Addison Wesley-Pearson Education Inc, Boston (2013)
19. Watt, S.M., Broadbery, P.A., Dooley, S.S., Iglio, P., Steinbach, J., Sutor, R.S.: A first report on the $A^\sharp$ compiler. In: Proc. International Symposium on Symbolic and Algebraic Computation (ISSAC 1994), pp. 25–31. ACM Press, New York (1994)
20. Watt, S.M.: Aldor. In: Grabmeier, J., Kaltofen, E., Weispfenning, V. (eds.) Handbook of Computer Algebra, pp. 265–270. Springer Verlag (2003)
21. Watt, S.M.: Efficient generic quotients using exact arithmetic. In: Proceedings of the International Symposium on Symbolic and Algebraic Computation (ISSAC 2023), pp. 535–544. ACM, New York (2023)
22. Watt, S.M.: Efficient quotients of non-commutative polynomials. In: 25th International Workshop on Computer Algebra in Scientific Computing (CASC 2023), pp. 370–392. Springer Cham LNCS 14139, New York (2023)

GPU Implementations for Midsize Integer Addition and Multiplication

Cosmin E. Oancea[1] and Stephen M. Watt[2(✉)]

[1] DIKU, University of Copenhagen, 2100 Copenhagen, Denmark
cosmin.oancea@di.ku.dk

[2] Cheriton School of Computer Science, University of Waterloo, Waterloo, Canada
smwatt@uwaterloo.ca

Abstract. This paper explores practical aspects of using a high-level functional language for GPU-based arithmetic on "midsize" integers. By this we mean integers of up to about a quarter million bits, which is sufficient for most practical purposes. The goal is to understand whether it is possible to support efficient nested-parallel programs with a small, flexible code base. We report on GPU implementations for addition and multiplication of integers that fit in one CUDA block, thus leveraging temporal reuse from scratchpad memories. Our key contribution resides in the simplicity of the proposed solutions: We recognize that addition is a straightforward application of scan, which is known to allow efficient GPU implementation. For quadratic multiplication we employ a simple work-partitioning strategy that offers good temporal locality. For FFT multiplication, we efficiently map the computation in the domain of integral fields by finding "good" primes that enable almost-full utilization of machine words. In comparison, related work uses complex tiling strategies—which feel too big a hammer for the job—or uses the computational domain of reals, which may degrade the magnitude of the base in which the computation is carried. We evaluate the performance in comparison to the state-of-the-art CGBN library, authored by NvidiaLab, and report that our CUDA prototype outperforms CGBN for integer sizes higher than 32K bits, while offering comparable performance for smaller sizes. Moreover, we are, to our knowledge, the first to report that FFT multiplication outperforms the classical one on the larger sizes that still fit in a CUDA block. Finally, we examine Futhark's strengths and weaknesses for efficiently supporting such computations and find out that the significant overheads and scalability issues of the Futhark implementation are mainly caused by the absence of a compiler pass aimed at efficient sequentialization of excess parallelism.

Keywords: Big integer arithmetic · CUDA · Data-parallel programming · GPGPU · High-level parallel languages · High-performance computing

D. Orchard et al. (Eds.): Alan Mycroft Festschrift, LNCS 15500, pp. 51–79, 2026.
https://doi.org/10.1007/978-3-032-08187-2_4

1 Introduction

The work presented in this paper is ultimately aimed at extending already-parallel programs, written in high-level languages such as Futhark [18], with support for multi-precision arithmetic that runs efficiently on highly-parallel hardware such as GPGPUs. Accelerating such computations would benefit algorithms from various disciplines, such as computer algebra and cryptography.

The current work focuses on addition and multiplication of midsized integers, by which we mean integers of up to about a quarter million bits. While there is in principle no size bound on integers that may be required in symbolic computation, values of the size considered here account for almost all arithmetic in systems such as Maple, Mathematica, Reduce and so on, even taking into account algorithms such as "GCDHEU" [9] that operate by evaluate polynomials at integer points. Likewise, values of this size are adequate for most modern cryptographic computations, though some older systems, *e.g.* [27], push this limit.

A second, important, observation is that integers of this size fit in one CUDA block of threads, or in a "work group" in OpenCL terminology. This hardware level attention allows the implementation to leverage temporal reuse from fast (register+scratchpad) memory, which has significantly lower latency than global memory. In our experiments on Nvidia hardware, this range covers integers as large as about a quarter million bits.

Normally, writing GPU software attending to this sort of hardware consideration is time consuming, detailed and error-prone, with inflexible code using specific machine instructions for a particular platform. Our main interest has been to determine whether we may use a high level language to write GPU code that is elegant and flexible while being sufficiently efficient. We have found this is readily achieved. We have not at this stage been concerned with determining the best algorithms for different integer sizes (i.e. classical, versus Karatsuba, versus FFT), nor with using every trick to maximize performance (e.g. Montgomery representation for FFT).

Related Work. The most closely related work is the "Cooperative Groups Big Numbers" (CGBN) library [34], authored by NvidiaLab, that offers a high-performance implementation for integers up to 32K bits. The key technique used by CGBN to achieve top performance is to map an instance of integer computation on at most one warp of threads in order to leverage specialized Nvidia hardware that allows values to be communicated directly between registers (of the warp), i.e., without passing through scratchpad (shared) memory buffers that have significantly higher latency. Other related work aimed at integer in the target range implement

- the carry propagation of addition by mapping complex VLSI designs of hardware adders into equivalent GPU operations [13,14],
- classical (quadratic time) multiplication using tiling strategies [13], but which may require atomic updates to shared memory, or/and
- Strassen's algorithm [49] for log-linear-time multiplication by applying FFT in the domain of reals [2,13], which requires the computation to be carried in bases unfriendly to the underlying machine arithmetic (e.g., base 10).

There have been other, earlier implementations of multiple precision integer arithmetic on CUDA, but with different emphasis:

- CAMPARY [22,23] is a C library based on floating point arithmetic. The main point is to extend precision by representing real numbers as the unevaluated sum of several standard machine precision floating-point values.
- CUMP [32,33] is an older work with a primary purpose of accessing CUDA with GMP. Its stated objective was to outperform the GARPREC library [26]. Other similar works were ancestors of the CGBN package, with which we compare directly.
- Isupov [21] uses interval techniques to augment residue number arithmetic for operations that rely on magnitude for numbers with upto 4096 bits.
- Chen et al. [10] consider FFT using prime fields with generalized Fermat prime characteristics of size 504 and 992 bits to handle integers of practically unbounded size. These numbers will generally span multiple CUDA blocks, hence the work is mostly concerned with making sure that access patterns enable coalesced access to global memory. They aim to improve spatial locality, but not temporal locality (re-use from shared memory).

We have recently assisted to a proliferation of Python-embedded DSLs aimed at supporting ML practitioners—such as Tensorflow [1], PyTtoch [46] and Jax [15]. Similarly, we envision that a practically important direction refers to interfacing languages supporting multi-precision arithmetic with mainstream computer-algebra systems such as Maple [3] and Mathematica [20], thus enabling both ease of scripting and high performance. Such solutions can build on prior interoperability work aimed, for example, at supporting automatic differentiation [44,45] or parametric polymorphism [11,41,42] across language boundaries.

Contributions. This paper presents CUDA and Futhark implementations[1] for integer addition and multiplication, including both quadratic and Strassen's log-linear time algorithms. The main contribution of our solutions mainly resides in choosing the simplest tool that does the job: We recognize that addition is a straightforward application of prefix sum [4]—a.k.a., scan: a basic-block of parallel programming—for which efficient GPU implementations are folklore [28]. For classical multiplication we use a simple partitioning technique that assigns to each thread a load-balanced computation of entire elements of the result, so that updates do not need to be atomic and are performed directly in low-latency registers. For Strassen (FFT) multiplication, we conduct the computation in the integral domain by using computer-algebra reasoning to find good prime fields that maximize the utilization of machine-supported arithmetic. This allows for example to represent integers using 15 bits of each half word or 31 bits of each word.

In comparison to CGBN, our implementation does not rely on specialized hardware instructions and, we surmise, is likely to translate the performance to other hardware from different vendors, such as AMD. Instead of mapping integer operations to execute at warp level, our implementation allows them to

[1] Implementations are available at https://github.com/coancea/midint-arithmetic/.

occupy as much as an entire CUDA block of threads, and relies on the classical technique of efficiently sequentializing parallelism in excess[2] to amortize each access to shared memory across several register accesses.

We evaluate the performance of our implementations in comparison with CGBN—on programs performing one addition, one multiplication and fusion of such operations—and report that CGBN is faster on integer ranges up to 2^{13} bits, but our CUDA implementation gains the upper hand on ranges of $2^{15} - 2^{16}$ bits, and outperforms CGBN on integers consisting of 2^{17} and 2^{18} bits. In fairness, CGBN offers near-perfect scalability on fused operations.

Our Futhark implementation exhibits significant overheads in comparison to our CUDA prototype. The performance bottlenecks are caused by the absence of a compiler pass that automatically performs efficient sequentialization. Implementing it by hand is possible in Futhark, but still sub-optimal in several ways: *First*, intermediate results are always mapped by the compiler to shared-memory buffers and there does not exist a way for the programmer to change the mapping to register memory. *Second*, the suboptimal shared-memory mapping may restrict the maximal size of the integer that fits in a CUDA block. *Finally*, the user code implementing efficient sequentialization is likely to degrade the performance of other semantically-equivalent code versions that, for example, support execution even when the integer is too big to fit in one CUDA block.

In summary, the contributions of this paper are:

- a demonstration that high level languages (C++ and Futhark) can be used to implement big integer arithmetic concisely and efficiently for GPU computation,
- simple and efficient GPU implementations for multi-precision addition and multiplication,
- an experimental evaluation that demonstrates significant performance gains in comparison to CGBN library on integer sizes in the range of 2^{15} to 2^{18} bits,
- to our knowledge, the first demonstration that FFT-based multiplication outperforms an efficient implementation of the quadratic algorithm on sizes that fit in a CUDA block (by factors as high as $5\times$ on the largest size),
- a presentation that (we hope) allows to reproduce the implementations directly from the information in the paper.

Outline. This paper is structured in a straightforward fashion: Sects. 2, 3 and 4 present our implementations of addition, quadratic and log-linear time multiplication, respectively. Section 5 discusses the strengths and weaknesses of the current Futhark compiler infrastructure for supporting multi-precision arithmetic. Section 6 reports experimental results, and Sect. 7 concludes.

[2] In simple words, this refers to having one thread compute in a sequential-efficient fashion several elements of the result instead of just one.

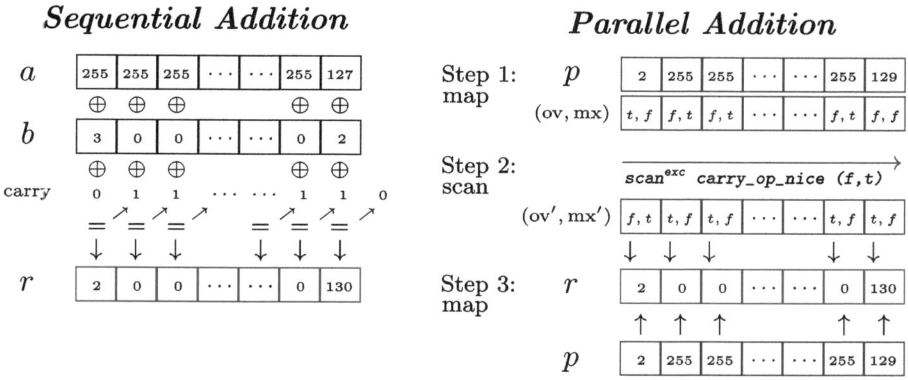

Fig. 1. Sequential and parallel procedures for addition `a+b` base 2^8: linear vs log time.

2 Integer Addition

We represent a big unsigned integer—referred from now on as an integer—as an array a containing M elements of type *uint*, which allows to store $M{\cdot}8{\cdot}\texttt{sizeof(uint)}$ bits. The elements can be seen as the coefficients of a polynomial in (base) $x = 2^{8\cdot\texttt{sizeof(uint)}}$, i.e., $a = a_0{+}a_1{\cdot}x{+}\ldots a_{M-1}{\cdot}x^{M-1}$. In our implementation of addition and multiplication, the result has the same length and element type as the input integers, e.g., $add\ :\ [M]uint\ \rightarrow\ [M]uint\ \rightarrow\ [M]uint$.

Adding two such integers can be accomplished by a (well known) iterative procedure, illustrated on the left side of Fig. 1, that adds (in a bigger type of double size) the corresponding elements of a and b together with the carry from the previous operation, and then it computes the result element and the carry for the next iteration as the remainder and quotient of the division of the sum to the integer's base. This is commonly implemented by performing the additions within the domain of *uint* and by checking for overflow.

The procedure described above is inherently sequential, since the carry computation gives rise to a cycle of cross-iteration true dependencies. Furthermore, Fig. 1 shows a pathological case in which the carry of the first addition is propagated all the way to the last element of the result, which, at first sight, would seem that it does not allow any chunks of computations to be performed in parallel, i.e., independently of each other.

However, Blelloch leaves it as an exercise [4]—that was solved by Topalovic, Restelli-Nielsen and Olesen among others [50]—that a data-parallel implementation can be straightforwardly obtained by reasoning in terms of the basic blocks of parallel programming—particularly scan [6], a.k.a., prefix sum. The procedure, illustrated on the right side of Fig. 1 requires three parallel steps:

(1) a `map` operation that independently sums up corresponding elements within the *uint* domain, and computes a partial result *uint* $p_i = a_i + b_i$, together with two booleans ov_i and mx_i that record whether (i) the addition has

overflow, i.e., there is a carry, and (ii) the result of the addition is the highest element of *uint*, i.e., $ov_i = (p_i < a_i)$ and $mx_i = (p_i == uint.highest)$.
(2) an exclusive `scan` that combines the overflow-highest pairs across elements, and
(3) another `map` that adds the partial result obtained in step (1) with the carry (overflow) result obtained from the scan in step (2).

Before zooming on step (2), we recall the type and semantics of *exclusive* scan:

$$\text{scan}^{exc} \;:\; (\tau \to \tau \to \tau) \;\to\; \tau \;\to [n]\tau \;\to\; [n]\tau$$

$$\text{scan}^{exc} \;\odot\; e_\odot\; [a_0, \ldots, a_{n-1}] \;\equiv\; [e_\odot,\; a_0,\; a_0 \odot a_1,\; \ldots,\; a_0 \odot \ldots \odot a_{n-2}]$$

where $\odot$ is an arbitrary *associative* binary operator with neutral element $e_\odot$. Scan has parallel work $O(n)$ and depth $O(\log n)$. Carries can be propagated by means of a scan with an operator that is expressed in a friendly way as below:

```
-- neutral element is (false, true)
def carry_op_nice (ov1: bool, mx1: bool)
                  (ov2: bool, mx2: bool) : (bool, bool) =
    ( (ov1 && mx2) || ov2,  mx1 && mx2 )
```

The operator can be derived by human reasoning in the divide-and-conquer, list-homomorphic style [17]: Assuming that `(ov1,mx1)` and `(ov2,mx2)` are the partial results of two half problems, figuring out the operator comes down to reasoning how to combine the half results into a full result. One can reason that:

- The whole addition overflows *if and only if* either (i) the second addition overflows, i.e., `ov2` holds, or (ii) the first addition overflows and the second addition has resulted in the maximal element, i.e., `(ov1 && mx2)` holds.
- The whole addition results in the maximal element *if and only if* both half additions have resulted in the maximal element (of half size), i.e., `(mx1 && mx2)` .

Topalovic, Restelli-Nielsen and Olesen prove that the operator is associative [50] and accepts `(false,true)` as its neutral element, which is easy to see.

Figure 2 shows a more involved Futhark implementation, denoted `badd`, which is intended to be mapped at the CUDA-block level of parallelism, such that all intermediate arrays are maintained and accessed from fast (scratchpad or register) memory. The pseudocode specializes for simplicity `uint` to 32-bit unsigned integer (`u32`) and computes `IPB` instances of additions in a CUDA block—e.g., to optimize the case when `M` is too small for a good block size. Details are:

- `carry_op_eff` is very similar to `carry_op_nice`, excepts that it packs the tuple of boolean values in the last two bits of an `u32` value. The rationale is that this (i) requires only one scratchpad buffer (instead of two), and (ii) GPU hardware is optimized for `u32` accesses; otherwise one can also use `u8`.
- However, since we aim to compute `IPB` (independent) instances within a CUDA block, step (2) needs to perform a segmented scan instead of a scan. This is typically achieved by lifting the scan's operator to operate over tuples formed by the original datatype and a boolean which, when set, indicates the start of a segment. `carry_op_sgm` encodes the lifted operator of the segmented scan by encoding the start of the segment in the third-last bit.

```
1   -- neutral element is 2 for both carry_op_eff and carry_op_sgm
2   def carry_op_eff (c1: u32) (c2: u32) =
3       (c1 & c2 & 2) | ( ((c1 & (c2 >> 1)) | c2) & 1 )
4
5   def carry_op_sgm (c1: u32) (c2: u32) =
6       if (c2 & 4) != 0 then c2
7       else ( (carry_op_eff c1 c2) | ( (c1 | c2) & 4 ) )
8
9   -- computes IPB instances but without efficient sequentialization
10  def badd [IPB][M] (as : [IPB*M]u32) (bs : [IPB*M]u32) : [IPB*M]u32 =
11      let f a b i =
12          let p = a + b
13          let b = ((u32.bool (i % M == 0)) << 2)
14                | ((u32.bool (p == u32.highest)) << 1)
15                | (u32.bool (p < a))
16          in (p, b)
17      let (part_res, carry_elms) = map3 f as bs (0..<IPB*M) ▷ unzip
18
19      let carries = scan^exc carry_op_sgm 2 carry_elms -- carry propagation
20
21      let g r c = r + u32.bool ( c & 1 == 1 )
22      in  map2 g part_res carries
23
24  def bbadd [N][IPB][M]
25          (ass : [n][IPB*M]u32) (bss : [n][IPB*M]u32) : [n][IPB*M]u32 =
26      map2 badd ass bss
```

Fig. 2. Futhark pseudocode for performing a batch of `IPB` additions of big numbers, each represented as an array of `M` 32-bit unsigned integers. Function `badd` is supposed to be mapped at CUDA-block level (where arrays are mapped to scratchpad memory). Efficient sequentialization is not shown, albeit it is critical for good performance.

- the implementation of `badd` follows the three parallel steps mentioned before: the first corresponds to `map3 f` at line 17, which computes the partial result and the input to the (segmented) scan, the second step corresponds to `scan carry_op_sgm 2` at line 19, which propagates the carries, and the third step—`map2 g` at line 22—adds the resulting carries to each partial result.
- the `bbadd` function performs an arbitrary batch (N) of `badd` computations, hence the `map2` at line 26 is intended to be mapped on CUDA's grid of blocks.

A final optimization that we apply (not shown) is the classical *efficient sequentialization of excess parallelism*. In our case, this corresponds to having each thread process independently a parametric (statically-known, smallish) number of elements, rather than just one, as a way of reducing the inter-thread communication overhead for operators such as scan and reduce.[3]

The practical manner of implementing efficient sequentialization in CUDA is by mapping logical arrays to register (thread-private) memory whenever possible, and by using shared memory preferably only as staging buffers—e.g., for copying in a coalesced way to/from global to register memory or for storing intermediate results (of reduced size) produced in the internal implementation of `reduce` and `scan`. (Of course, some operations force manifestation of logical arrays in shared

[3] Our CUDA implementation of block-level scan and reduce follows the standard strategy [28] that (de)composes the implementation hierarchically, at each level of the hardware: CUDA thread, warp and block level.

memory, e.g., when the same element is read by multiple threads, or in the presence of gather/scatter operations that access statically unknown indices.) This strategy has several well known advantages:

- it allows to maximize the utilization of both register and shared memory,
- it promotes accesses from registers, which has lower latency, do not suffer bank conflicts, and are more numerous (in terms of bytes per thread) than shared memory,
- it minimizes the live range of shared-memory buffers, thus promoting their reuse, while register usage is automatically optimized by register allocation.

In summary, efficient sequentialization is a performance critical optimization that reduces inter-thread communication and the latency of memory accesses, generating significant speedups, higher than 2× in cases. More importantly, it enables the implementation to *efficiently support larger integers*, since in our context, their size is tied with that of the CUDA block: On the one hand, the quantity of resources utilized by a CUDA block is typically proportional with its size, hence a suboptimal mapping will lower the size of the CUDA block that can be launched and thus the magnitude of the integer. One the other hand, the size of a CUDA block is hard constrained to a maximal number of 1024 threads, hence a one-to-one mapping would limit the integers to $[1024]uint$, while an efficient sequentialization factor $Q = 8$ would support $[8196]uint$. In principle, for addition, the integer size is constrained by registers, not by shared memory, because all logical arrays can be mapped to register memory.

3 Classical, Quadratic Multiplication

Discussion is organized as follows: Sect. 3.1 provides the high-level rationale of our implementation strategy in comparison with the popular approach of applying tiling to optimize convolution-based code. Section 3.2 gives the birds-eye-view of our CUDA implementation, and Sect. 3.3 zooms in on the main computational step (the convolution).

3.1 Key Insights

The classical algorithm for multiplication corresponds to the formula:

$$C_k = \sum_{\substack{i+j=k \\ 0 \leq i,j,k<M}} A_i \cdot B_j \tag{1}$$

which assumes that the element type $uint'$ of the result C is large enough to prevent overflow. Denoting with $uint$ the element type of A and B, practical implementations commonly perform the product $A_i \cdot B_j$ inside a type $ubig$ which has double the size of $uint$, thus guaranteeing no overflow, and represent the element type of C as a tuple $(ubig, uint32)$ in which the second term denotes the carry

```
template<uint, ubig, uint32_t M, uint32_t T> __global__
void bmulTiled ( uint* Aglb, uint* Bglb, ubig* Cglb ) {
    __shared__ uint Ash[T], uint Bsh[T]; __shared__ ubig Csh[2*T];
    int ii = blockIdx.y*T, i = threadIdx.y; // 0 <= i < T
    int jj = blockIdx.x*T, j = threadIdx.x; // 0 <= j < T
    // copy A and B from global to shared memory & initialize Csh
    if(threadIdx.y == 0) {
        Ash[j] = Aglb[ii+j]; Csh[j    ] = 0;
        Bsh[j] = Bglb[jj+j]; Csh[j + T] = 0;
    }
    __syncthreads();
    if(ii+jj + i+j < M) {
        ubig prod = ((ubig)Ash[i]) * ((ubig)Bsh[j]);
        atomicAdd(&Csh[i+j], prod);  // atomic in shared memory
    }
    __syncthreads();
    int tid = i*T + j;
    if(tid < 2*T && ii+jj + tid < M) // atomic in global memory
        atomicAdd( &Cglb[ii+jj + tid], Csh[tid] );
}
```

Fig. 3. Sketch of a simple CUDA kernel for the tiled version of quadratic multiplication.

that accounts for the potential overflow of summation. Alternatively, one may use a triple $(uint, uint, uint32)$ in which the first two terms correspond to the low and high part of *ubig*. This section is aimed to highlight the key differences between implementation choices and thus will work directly with formula (1) and ignore the overflow details.

Tiling Approach. Related approaches [2,13,14] predominantly use block tiling to implement formula (1); this results in C-like code similar to the one below, which uses for simplicity the same tile size `T` that is assumed to evenly divide `M`:

```
for(int k = 0; k < M; k++) C[k] = 0;

for (int ii = 0; ii < M; ii+=T)    // mapped on CUDA Grid.y
  for (int jj = 0; jj < M; jj+=T) // mapped on CUDA Grid.x
    for (int i = 0; i < T; i++)    // mapped on CUDA Block.y
      for (int j = 0; j < T; j++) // mapped on CUDA Block.x
        if (ii+jj + i+j < M)
          C[ii+jj + i+j] += A[ii+i] * B[jj+j];
```

The tiled code minimizes the temporal reuse distance of the accesses to A, B and C. For example, the read indices of A are invariant to loop `j` (and `jj`). It follows that the slice of `A[ii : ii+T]` can be remapped to a scratchpad memory buffer of length `T` just inside the `jj` loop and reused from there within the body of the loop, i.e., one access to global memory is amortized across T accesses to scratchpad memory. Similar thoughts apply to arrays B and C. However, the loop nest above is a generalized reduction [25,38], whose parallelization requires inter-thread communication, because the same element of `C` may be updated by different threads, hence the additive updates need to be atomic.

$$
\begin{array}{lll}
C_0 & = A_0 \cdot B_0 & \texttt{1 term} \\
C_1 & = A_0 \cdot B_1 + A_1 \cdot B_0 & \texttt{2 terms} \\
C_2 & = A_0 \cdot B_2 + A_1 \cdot B_1 + A_2 \cdot B_1 & \texttt{3 terms} \\
\ldots & \quad \ldots & \\
C_{M-3} & = A_0 \cdot B_{M-3} + \ldots + A_{M-3} \cdot B_0 & \texttt{M-3 terms} \\
C_{M-2} & = A_0 \cdot B_{M-2} + \ldots + A_{M-3} \cdot B_1 + A_{M-2} \cdot B_0 & \texttt{M-2 terms} \\
C_{M-1} & = A_0 \cdot B_{M-1} + A_1 \cdot B_{M-2} + \ldots + A_{M-2} * B_1 + A_{M-1} \cdot B_0 & \texttt{M-1 terms}
\end{array}
$$

Fig. 4. A load-balanced embarrassingly parallel partitioning is to assign thread 0 to compute C_0 and C_{M-1}, thread 1 to compute C_1 and C_{M-2}, thread 2 to compute C_2 and C_{M-3}, and so on. All threads perform a total M multiply-fused add operations.

Figure 3 sketches a toy CUDA kernel implementing the tiled version, which assumes a two-dimensional block of size `T`×`T`. This approach optimizes temporal locality and enables maximal parallelism but has two shortcomings:

- `C` is not only maintained in shared memory, which has higher latency than registers, but its updates use *expensive* atomic operations: `T`·`T` times from shared memory (line 14 in Fig. 3) and 2·`T` times from global memory (line 19).
- it prevents producer-consumer fusion—e.g., with following additions and multiplications—because the atomic add in global memory requires a global barrier across all blocks, which is not possible in CUDA other than by ending the execution of the current kernel.

Load Balanced Partitioning of the Result Across Threads. We choose instead a strategy that partitions the elements of the result in a manner that is load balanced, and assigns the computation of an entire partition to the same thread. Figure 4 illustrates the partitioning that computes two elements of the result with each thread, i.e., the identically coloured elements are computed by the same thread and they require the same number (M) of terms. One could increase the sequentialization degree, denoted Q, by computing $Q = 4$ or $Q = 8$ elements of the result per thread, which would result in $2 \cdot M$ and $4 \cdot M$ terms computed by each thread, respectively. This strategy has the advantages that it:

- allows the result C to be mapped to register memory, and to be computed in an embarrassingly parallel fashion, while enabling efficient sequentialization,
- allows multiple addition/multiplication operations to be fused within a CUDA block, such that intermediate results are reused from fast memory.

The downside is that it sequentializes completely an entire parallel dimension of size `M`. We found however that this is a small price to pay, given the advantages, especially when considering that

- we aim at integrating such arithmetic inside programs that are already parallel, which makes it unlikely that the parallel hardware will be starved,
- classical multiplication has suboptimal $O(M^2)$ work, in comparison with the $O(M \ \log M)$ FFT algorithm, hence it makes sense to use it as a niche specialization aimed at squeezing maximal performance from the hardware.

```
template<class Base,uint32_t IPB,uint32_t M,uint32_t Q> __device__ void
bmulRegs( typename Base::uint*Ash,        typename Base::uint*Bsh,
          typename Base::uint Areg[2*Q], typename Base::uint Breg[2*Q],
          typename Base::uint Rreg[2*Q]
) {
    using uint = typename Base::uint;
    using ubig = typename Base::ubig;

    // 1. copy from register to shared memory
    cpReg2Shm<uint, 2*Q>( Areg, Ash );
    cpReg2Shm<uint, 2*Q>( Breg, Bsh );
    __syncthreads();

    // 2. perform the convolution
    uint lhcs[2][Q+2];
    wrapperConv<uint, ubig, M, Q>( Ash, Bsh, lhcs );
    __syncthreads();

    // 3. publish low parts & high and carry (hcs[:][Q:]) in Lsh & Hsh
    typename Base::uint *Lsh = Ash, *Hsh = Bsh;
    publishReg2Shmem<uint, M, Q>( lhcs, Lsh, Hsh );
    __syncthreads();

    // 4. load back to register and perform the addition of the carries.
    uint Lrg[2*Q], Hrg[2*Q];
    cpShm2Reg<uint, 2*Q>( Lsh, Lrg );
    cpShm2Reg<uint, 2*Q>( Hsh, Hrg );
    __syncthreads();
    baddRegs<uint, M, 2*Q, Base::HIGHEST>( Lsh, Lrg, Hrg, Rreg );
}
```

Fig. 5. Main CUDA wrapper function that computes quadratic integer multiplication.

3.2 Birds-Eye View of Implementation

Figure 5 shows the core function `bmulRegs` that implements the quadratic multiplication algorithm. The implementation denotes by `Q` half the sequentialization factor, i.e., each thread computes 2·`Q` elements of the result, and assumes that 2·`Q` evenly divides `M`, which has been (previously) ensured by padding the numbers to the closest multiple of `Q`. As before, `IPB` denotes the number of instances solved within a CUDA block, and the integer consists of `M` elements of type `uint`. Thus the size of the CUDA block of threads is: `IPB*M / (2*Q)`.

The function input `Areg` and `Breg` and result `Rreg` are allocated in register memory. `Ash` and `Bsh` are shared-memory staging buffers of length `[IPB*M]`*uint*. It follows that one CUDA block requires `2*IPB*M*sizeof(uint)` bytes of shared memory, and the maximal problem size `M*sizeof(uint)` that is computable for `IPB=1` is half the total size (in bytes) of the shared memory available on a SM.

Prior to calling `bmulRegs`, the kernel has copied (not shown) the input from global to register memory in two stages: First, the input is copied from global to shared memory in `2*Q` sequential steps, such that consecutive threads read consecutive elements of global memory, thus ensuring coalesced accesses. Second, each thread packs `2*Q` consecutive elements from shared to its register memory.

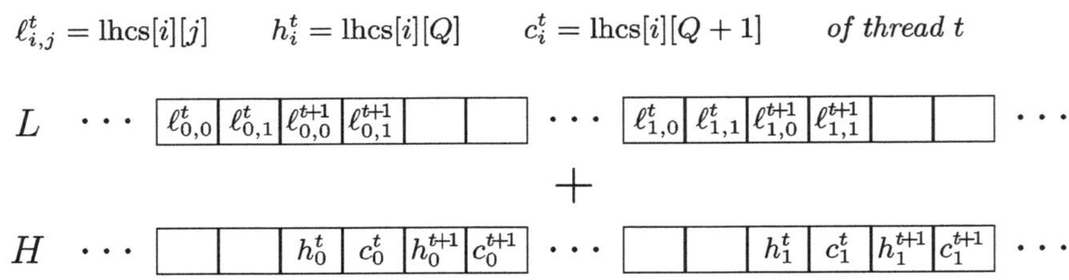

Fig. 6. Illustrating the placement of thread-private array `lhcs`: $[2][Q+2]uint$ in shared-memory arrays L and H for $Q = 2$. L and H are then added to complete the algorithm.

The implementation manifests numbers A and B in shared memory (at lines 10–11), because computing the convolution (line 16) corresponding to formula (1) requires multiple threads to access overlapping elements of A and B.

The per-thread result of the convolution (line 16) is the array named `lhcs` which has type $[2][Q+2]uint$. The rationale is that each thread processes two contiguous sub-partitions of Q elements: one from the first half of the integer and its symmetric opposite across the midpoint. The result of each sub-partition is represented as an array of size $Q+2$ of *uint*s that addresses overflow concerns:

- the first Q elements are the low parts of the sequentially aggregated result,
- the next element corresponds to the high part of the aggregated result, and the last one to an additional carry (in case the high part overflows).

Next, the function `publishReg2Shmem` manifests the per-thread aggregated `lhcs` result into two shared-memory buffers denoted `Lsh` and `Hsh` in the manner depicted in Fig. 6. (Note that these are in fact reusing the shared-memory buffers of `Ash` and `Bsh`, which are dead after convolution). Finally, the low, high and carry parts are aggregated across threads by simply adding together, with the procedure from Sect. 2, the integers represented by the arrays L and H: This is accomplished by the call to `baddReg` at line 29, which requires its arguments to be remapped as registers (at lines 26 and 27).

3.3 Implementing the Convolution

Figure 7 details the implementation of the convolution step:

- Function `wrapperConv` calls twice function `convolution` at lines 54 and 55, each call processing one of the contiguous sub-partitions corresponding to Q elements of the result,
- Function convolution computes each of the Q results independently in the two loops at lines 35–44. The two loops are necessary since each element of the result requires incrementally more terms.

```
1  template<class uint,class ubig, uint32_t M,uint32_t Q> __device__
2  void combine( ubig accums[Q], uint32_t carrys[Q], S lhcs[Q+2] ) {
3      const uint32_t SHFT = 8 * sizeof(uint);
4      lhcs[0] = (uint) accums[0];
5      uint h_res = (uint) (accums[0] >> SHFT);
6      uint c_res = carrys[0];
7
8      for(int q=1; q<Q; q++) {
9          uint l = (uint) accums[q];
10         uint h = (uint) (accums[q] >> SHFT);
11         lhcs[q] = l + h_res;
12         h_res = h + (c_res + (lhcs[q] < l));
13         c_res = carrys[q] + (h_res < h);
14     }
15     lhcs[Q]   = h_res;
16     lhcs[Q+1] = c_res;
17 }
18
19 template<class uint, class ubig> __device__  void
20 convIter( uint32_t i, uint32_t j, uint* Ash, uint* Bsh,
21           ubig& accum, uint32_t& carry
22 ) {
23     const uint32_t SHFT = 8*sizeof(S);
24     uint accum_prev = (uint) (accum >> SHFT);
25     accum += ((ubig)Ash[i]) * ((ubig)Bsh[j]);
26     carry += (  ((uint)(accum >> SHFT)) < accum_prev );
27 }
28
29 template<class uint,class ubig, uint32_t M,uint32_t Q> __device__
30 void convolution(uint32_t k1, uint* Ash, uint* Bsh, uint lhcs[Q+2]) {
31     ubig accums[Q];  uint32_t carries[Q];
32     for(int q=0; q<Q; q++) {
33         accums[q] = 0; carries[q] = 0;
34     }
35     for(int kk = 0; kk <= k1; kk++) {
36         uint32_t i = kk;
37         uint32_t j = k1 - i;
38         for(int q=0; q<Q; q++)
39           convIter<uint,ubig>(i,j+q, Ash,Bsh, accums[q],carries[q]);
40     }
41     for(int q=1; q<Q; q++) {
42         for(int i=0; i<Q-q; i++)
43           convIter<uint,ubig>(k1+q,i,Ash, sh,accums[i+q], carries[i+q]);
44     }
45     combine<uint,ubig,M,Q>(accums, carries, lhcs);
46 }
47
48 template<class uint, class ubig, uint32_t M, uint32_t Q> __device__
49 void wrapperConv( uint* Ash0, uint* Bsh0, uint lhcs[2][Q+2] ) {
50     const uint32_t offset = ( threadIdx.x / (M/(2*Q)) ) * M;
51     uint *Ash = Ash0 + offset, *Bsh = Bsh0 + offset;
52     uint32_t ltid = threadIdx.x % (M/(2*Q));
53
54     convolution<uint,ubig,M,Q>( Q * ltid,     Ash, Bsh, lhcs[0]); //first half
55     convolution<uint,ubig,M,Q>( M-Q*(ltid+1), Ash, Bsh, lhcs[1]); //second half
56 }
```

Fig. 7. CUDA code for computing the per-thread convolution.

- Function `convIter`, called at lines 39 and 43 adds one more term to the result. We represent the result at this stage as a tuple between `accum` of type *ubig* (which has double the size of *uint*) and a `carry` of type `uint32_t`. The new term $A_i \cdot B_j$ is computed in the *ubig* type (line 25), which prevents overflow. However the additive update of `accum` may result in overflow, which is accounted for at line 26.

- After all results have been computed, they are aggregated together by the call to `combine` at line 45 which computes half of the `lhcs` array—the other half is computed by the second call to `convolution`.

The reported code allows for all but one loops to be unrolled—the exception is the loop at line 35—thus enabling scalarization of the arrays `lhcs`, `carries`, `accum`. We have found that the best performance is obtained when maximizing the size of *uint*, i.e., when *uint* and *ubig* are instantiated to `uint64_t` and `unsigned __int128`, respectively. This is as expected, since their implementation is sequentially handcrafted for that specific size, and hence offers better performance than our generic algorithm. Finally, our implementation:

- utilizes two shared-memory buffers of size `IPB*M*sizeof(uint)` bytes, which are necessary in order to make the elements of arrays A and B available to all threads during the convolution step.
- promotes fusion by holding the logical arrays to registers and using shared-memory buffers transiently for each operation. It follows that fusion can only be hampered by excessive register use.

4 FFT-Based Integer Multiplication

This section presents our implementation for the log-linear time integer multiplication. Several related approaches use the domain of reals to perform the DFFT transformation, which has the potential to affect the accuracy of the computation. Ensuring that errors do not manifest is often handled by restricting the base in which the computation is carried [2,13] to values that are unfriendly to the hardware (e.g., base 10 or 11). Section 4.1 presents the algebraic construction of suitable prime fields that promote efficient DFFT implementation directly in the integral domain by exposing bases that allow near-optimal utilization of the underlying machine arithmetic. While this construction is not necessarily a novelty in the computer-algebra domain, we believe that its application to integer multiplication has merits and it is in the least instructive to the non expert.

Finally, Sect. 4.2 sketches a relatively straightforward implementation of the log-linear time integer multiplication based on the Cooley-Tukey Algorithm [12], which, as before, performs an instance of multiplication with an entire (CUDA) block of threads, such as to allow reuse from fast memory.

4.1 Construction of Integer Prime Fields for DFFT

Strassen's algorithm [49] builds on the intuition that integer multiplication:

$$C_k = \sum_{\substack{i+j=k \\ 0 \leq i,j,k < M}} A_i \cdot B_j$$

can be translated in the DFFT domain by applying the convolution theorem:

$$DFFT(C) \;=\; DFFT(A) \cdot DFFT(B)$$

```
template<typename P> class zmod_t {
    using rep_t   = typename P::uint;
    using ubig_t = typename P::ubig;
    static const rep_t modulus = P::p;
public:
    __host__ __device__ static rep_t norm(const rep_t v)  {
        return (0 <= v && v < modulus) ? v : v % modulus;
    }
    __host__ __device__ static rep_t add (const rep_t x, const rep_t y) {
        ubig_t r = ((ubig_t) x) + ((ubig_t) y);
        if (r >= modulus) r -= modulus;
        return (rep_t)r;
    }
    __host__ __device__ static rep_t sub (const rep_t x, const rep_t y) {
        rep_t r = x;
        if (x < y) r += modulus;
        return (r - y);
    }
    __host__ __device__ static rep_t mul(const rep_t x, const rep_t y) {
        ubig_t r = ((ubig_t) x) * ((ubig_t) y);
        return (r % (ubig_t)modulus);
    } ...
};
```

Fig. 8. A sketch of the prime-field implementation that omits the negation, inversion and power operators.

hence the result C can be computed in $M \cdot log(M)$ time as:

$$C \;=\; IDFT(\; DFT(A) \;\cdot\; DFT(B)\;)$$

Finding a good prime field that enables efficient DFFT computation in the integral domain comes down to finding good prime numbers of shape:

$$p = k \cdot 2^n + 1$$

that accept 2^n distinct roots of unity for a large enough n. Applying the Little Theorem of Fermat, it follows that:

$$\forall a, \;\; a^{k \cdot 2^n} \;\equiv\; 1 \pmod{p} \tag{2}$$

By denoting $g = a^k$ for some a, it follows from Eq. 2 that $g^{2^n} \equiv 1 \pmod{p}$. To compute a g that is a 2^n-th root of unity, one can iterate through the elements a of $\mathbf{Z}_p$ and chose the first one (if any) that also verifies $g^q \neq 1, \; \forall q < 2^n$.

Once such a g was successfully found, one can easily construct a M-th root of unity, named ω, for any M that is a power of 2 and $M < 2^n$:

$$\omega \;=\; g^{2^n/M} \;=\; g^{2^{n-\log_2(M)}}$$

for example, one can easily check that $\omega^M \;\equiv\; g^{2^n} \; (mod\; p) \;\equiv\; 1 \; (mod\; p)$.

A simple Maple program has revealed in less than 15 minutes of computation the following "good" primes that conform with the desired shape:

$PrimeField32$**:** $(p = 3221225473, k = 3, n = 30, g = 13)$
$PrimeField64$**:** $(p = 4179340454199820289, k = 29, n = 57, g = 21)$

*PrimeField*32 allows (i) to represent an integer (input) as an array of type $[M]uhlf$ with $uhlf$ = `unsigned short`, in which only the first 15 out of 16 bits are utilized, (ii) the FFT computation to be carried on in extended representation $[M]uint$, in which $uint$ = `uint32_t`, and (iii) some of the prime-field computation—such as addition, multiplication, division—need to be performed in a double-sized type $ubig$ = `uint64_t`. Similarly, *PrimeField*64 uses the following instantiations: $uhlf$ = `uint32_t` such that only the first 31 out of 32 bits are utilized, $uint$ = `uint64_t` and $ubig$ = `unsigned __int128`. The implementation of several of the prime-field operations is shown in Fig. 8.

4.2 Straightforward Acceleration of Cooley-Tukey Algorithm

Figure 9 gives a relatively-straightforward CUDA implementation of the Cooley-Tukey algorithm, adapted from [24] to use roots of unity in a finite field rather than on the unit circle in the complex plane. The entry function, denoted `bmulFFT`, assumes that M is a power of two and that the total sequentialization factor Q is greater or equal to 2 and it evenly divides M—this is ensured by suitable padding. It follows that the CUDA block size is $\frac{M}{Q}$. The arguments are: `invM` is the (pre-computed) inverse of M in prime field P, `lgM` is the base-2 logarithm of M, `omegas` and `omegas_inv` are (pre-computed) arrays holding the M-roots of unity, i.e.,

```
omegas     = scan^exc (P::mul) 1 (replicate M ω)
omegas_inv = scan^exc (P::mul) 1 (replicate M ω^-1)
```

Finally, `shmem` is a shared-memory staging buffer of type $[M]uint$, and `Ahlf` and `Bhlf` represent the input arrays of element type $uhlf$, which were already copied in coalesced way from global to register memory. `Bhlf` is the place-holder for the result and it is mapped to register memory as well.

The implementation applies FFT to the input arrays (lines 52–56), then multiplies together the FFT results within the given prime field (line 58), and applies the inverse FFT transform (line 59), whose result is stored in `Rreg`.

Function `splitFftReg`, whose implementation is not shown, is called at line 62 to change the base in which the computation is carried from $2^{8\cdot\texttt{sizeof(uint)}}$ back to $2^{8\cdot\texttt{sizeof(uhlf)}-1}$:

- it first aggregates the Q per-thread results of element type $uint$ into Q low parts, one high part and a carry, all of element type $uhlf$; the procedure is similar to the one described in Sect. 3.2 for classical multiplication,
- then it places the result in a shared-memory buffer in a manner similar to the one depicted in Fig. 6—except that there is no "symmetrical" part,
- finally, it loads the results back again to register memory, denoted `Rlw` and `Rhc`—such that each thread holds the elements at the same indices from the logical arrays `Rlw` and `Rhc`.

```
template<typename P, uint32_t M, uint32_t Q> __device__ void
fft ( typename P::uint_t* shmem, uint32_t lgM, typename P::uint_t* omegas,
      typename P::uint_t Areg[2*Q], typename P::uint_t Rreg[2*Q]
) {
    using uint_t = typename P::uint_t; using PF = zmod_t<P>;
    cpReg2Shm<uint_t,2*Q>( Arg, shmem );
    __syncthreads();

    for( int32_t q = 0; q < 2*Q; q++ ) {
        int32_t vtid = threadIdx.x + q*blockDim.x;
        permute<uint_t>( vtid, lgM, shmem );
    }
    __syncthreads();

    for(int32_t t = 1; t <= lgM; t++) {
        uint32_t L = 1 << t,   Ld2 = L >> 1,   r = M >> t;
        for(int32_t q = 0; q < Q; q++) {
            int32_t vtid = threadIdx.x + q*blockDim.x;
            int32_t k = vtid >> (t-1);
            int32_t j = vtid &  (Ld2 - 1);
            int32_t kLj = k*L + j;
            uint_t omega_pow = omegas[r*j];
            uint_t tau       = PF::mul( omega_pow , shmem[kLj + Ld2] );
            uint_t x_kLj     = shmem[kLj];
            shmem[kLj]       = PF::add(x_kLj, tau);
            shmem[kLj + Ld2] = PF::sub(x_kLj, tau);
        }
        __syncthreads();
    }
    cpShm2Reg<uint_t,2*Q>( shmem, Rrg );
    __syncthreads();
}

template<typename P, uint32_t M, uint32_t Q> __device__ void
ifft( typename P::uint_t  invM,     uint32_t lgM,
      typename P::uint_t* shmem,    typename P::uint_t* omegas_inv,
      typename P::uint_t Areg[2*Q], typename P::uint_t Rreg[2*Q]
) {
    fft<P,M,Q>( shmem, lgM, omegas_inv, Areg, Rreg );
    for(int i=0; i<2*Q; i++) Rreg[i] = zmod_t<P>::mul(invM, Rreg[i]);
}

template<typename P, uint32_t M, uint32_t Q> __device__ void
bmulFFT ( typename P::uint  invM,   uint32_t lgM,
          typename P::uint* omegas, typename P::uint_t* omegas_inv,
          typename P::uint* shmem,  typename P::uhlf Ahlf[Q],
          typename P::uhlf Bhlf[Q], typename P::uhlf Rhlf[Q]
) {
    using uint = typename P::uint; using uhlf = typename P::uhlf;
    uint_t Areg[Q], Afft[Q], Breg[Q], Bfft[Q], Treg[Q], Rreg[Q];

    for(int q=0; q<Q; q++) Areg[q] = Ahlf[q];
    fft<P,M,Q/2>(shmem, lgM, omegas, Areg, Afft);

    for(int q=0; q<Q; q++) Breg[q] = Bhlf[q];
    fft<P,M,Q/2>(shmem, lgM, omegas, Breg, Bfft);

    for(int q=0; q<Q; q++) Treg[q] = zmod_t<P>::mul(Afft[q], Bfft[q]);
    ifft<P,M,Q/2>(shmem, invM, lgM, omegas_inv, Treg, Rreg);

    uhlf_t Rlw[Q], Rhc[Q];
    splitFftReg<P,Q>(Rreg, (uhlf*)shmem, Rlw, Rhc);
    baddRegMul2Fft<P, M, 2*Q, 0>( (uhlf*)shmem, Rlw, Rhc, Rhlf );
}
```

Fig. 9. Main CUDA wrapper function that computes FFT multiplication, where the input (`Ahlf`, `Bhlf`) and result (`Rhlf`) are stored in register memory.

The numbers represented by logical arrays `Rlw` and `Rhc` are finally summed up (carry propagation included) by the call to function `baddRegMul2Fft` at line 63. Since the addition needs to be performed in base $2^{8\cdot\texttt{sizeof(uhlf)}-1}$, we multiply all elements of `Rlw` and `Rhc` by two, perform the addition in the machine base $2^{8\cdot\texttt{sizeof(uhlf)}}$, then divide back by 2 while reapplying the carries. (An element resulted from addition was subject to a carry if its value is odd).

The implementation of `fft` and `ifft` are standard. FFT-based multiplication can operate with integers having (close to) the same size as the classical multiplication ($\mathcal{CM}$): on the one hand its input uses half the element type of $\mathcal{CM}$ (i.e., *uhlf vs. uint*), but on the other hand it uses only one memory buffer of size $M \cdot \texttt{sizeof(uint)}$ instead of two buffers with $\mathcal{CM}$. To be exact, the maximal supported size is a bit smaller than the one of $\mathcal{CM}$, because only 15 out of 16 bits can be used with $PrimeField32$ and 31 out of 32 bits with $PrimeField64$.

Short Discussion on Overflow. Exact multiplication of an integer of size M by an integer of size N gives a result of size at most $M + N$. For FFT-based methods, one pads both arguments to this size with leading zeros. Unlike classical multiplication, if the area for the result is insufficient to hold the exact product value, then the result will not give an approximation to a leading or trailing part of the product.

The implementation we have presented is correct as long as the result is exact in multi-precision, *i.e.*, as long as the multiplication does not "overflow". The performance evaluation of Sect. 6.3 uses the overflow-unsafe implementation. We consider that this version provides a more fair comparison to the $\mathcal{CM}$ implementation because modifying the latter to compute the full result would similarly double its shared-memory requirements and *quadruple* its work.

5 Futhark's Strengths and Weaknesses

5.1 Futhark Optimizations Relevant for Big Integer Arithmetic

Incremental Flattening. Futhark supports expression of parallel programs that operate on regular multi-dimensional arrays. The arbitrarily-nested application parallelism is flattened [5,7], by a technique dubbed "incremental flattening" [19] that utilizes map fission and map-loop interchange to create semantically-equivalent code versions that systematically map more and more levels of application parallelism to the hardware. Essentially, when a new `map f` operation is discovered in the top-down traversal of the program, the analysis adds the new `map` to the parallel context—that represents an enclosing perfect nest of `map` operations—and then it:

(1) maps the parallel context to the hardware by creating a first code version corresponding to a CUDA kernel in which each thread executes (independently) an application of f.
(2) creates a second code version in which the parallel context (i.e., the enclosing `map` operations discovered so far) is mapped on the CUDA grid, and the parallelism inside function f is recursively flattened and mapped to CUDA

block level, such that intermediate arrays are stored in shared memory. This is dubbed an *intra-group kernel.*

(3) incremental flattening continues recursively, by applying map-fission and map-loop interchange on the body of f, such as to qualify more levels of application parallelism to the hardware.

The resulting code versions are independently optimized and combined into one program by guarding each of them with a predicate that compares a dynamic program measure[4] with a threshold. Threshold values are autotuned—so as to select the best combination of code versions—based on a deterministic procedure that is guaranteed to produce a near-optimal result in a minimal number of runs, as long as the dynamic measure conforms with a monotonic property [30].

This compilation strategy has proved valuable in enabling high-performance implementation of real-world applications from domains such as computer vision [43], remote-sensing [16,48] and computational finance [35], and, as well, in optimizing code synthesized by program-level transformations such as automatic differentiation [8,47]. As well, incremental flattening is essential to supporting multi-precision computations in a high-level architecture-neutral language such as Futhark: On the one hand, choice (2) produces the intra-group kernel that we are aiming for, i.e., that leverages the use of fast (shared) memory and supports efficient fusion of such operations. One the other hand, it provides a fail-safe platform: the computation will still be carried on, albeit less efficiently so, on large integers that do not fit the intra-group kernel, by means of the versions generated by choices (1) and (3).

Memory Optimizations. A set of analyses that come handy in our context refer to reducing the memory footprint [29] and at eliminating unnecessary copy operations, dubbed short-circuiting analysis [31]. The former corresponds to applying register-like allocation to operate on memory buffers instead of registers, thus allowing buffers' reuse once their liveness ended. This reduces the shared-memory requirements of the kernel and enables larger integers and fusion.

Short-circuiting analysis [31] addresses an inefficiency common to functional languages whose type systems enforce correct-by-construction parallelism: some parallel loops—e.g., appearing in LUD or Needleman-Wunsch algorithms—cannot be expressed directly because they both read and write (non-overlapping slices of) elements of the same matrix. The typical type system does not perform dependence-analysis on arrays [39,40] and will demand to separate the parallel loop into two parallel operations, typically: a `map` that reads from the original matrix and results into a temporary buffer, and another parallel-write operation that updates the corresponding slice of the matrix with the buffer elements.

The analysis introduces a notion of memory and attempts to map the memory space of the buffer directly to the corresponding memory space of the matrix—whenever it can guarantee safety—such that the parallel write becomes a `noop`

4 In practice, the dynamic measure is the degree of parallelism utilized by a kernel.

```
1  let badd [ipb][n] (as: [ipb*(4*n)]u32) (bs: [ipb*(4*n)]u32) : [ipb*(4*n)]u32 =
2    let g = ipb * n
3    let cpGlb2Sh (i : i64) = #[unsafe]
4          ( ( as[i], as[g + i], as[2*g + i], as[3*g + i] )
5          , ( bs[i], bs[g + i], bs[2*g + i], bs[3*g + i] ) )
6
7    let ( ass, bss ) = map cpGlb2Sh (0...<g) ▷ unzip
8    let (a1s, a2s, a3s, a4s) = unzip4 ass
9    let (b1s, b2s, b3s, b4s) = unzip4 bss
10   let ash = a1s ++ a2s ++ a3s ++ a4s
11   let bsh = b1s ++ b2s ++ b3s ++ b4s
12   ...
```

Fig. 10. Futhark code illustrating coalesced copying from global to shared memory for an efficient sequentialization factor $Q = 4$.

and the buffer does not actually allocates any extra space. A trivial example is:

$$\texttt{let}\ x = \texttt{concat}\ a\ b$$

If a or b are lastly used in the above statement, then their memory is allocated directly in the corresponding memory space of x and the `concat` becomes a `noop`.

We have used this compiler feature to support efficient sequentialization in our Futhark implementations. Figure 10 shows the prelude of the function that performs integer addition, which is intended to be mapped at CUDA block level. The `map cpGlb2Sh` operation on line 7 reads four elements of `as` and `bs` with each of the `g` threads (of the block) in a coalesced way from global to shared memory—i.e., consecutive threads access consecutive words in global memory. The following `concat` operations at lines 10 and 11 put the results together in the correct order in arrays `ash` and `bsh`, which will be mapped to shared memory. Short-circuiting analysis ensures that only two shared-memory buffers are allocated (for the final `ash` and `bsh`), and that the `concat` operation cost nothing—since `a1s`...`a4s` are allocated directly in the memory space of `ash`.

5.2 Shortcomings of Futhark's Compiler Infrastructure

The experimental evaluation, reported in the next section, shows that our Futhark implementation has sub-optimal performance and scalability in comparison to our CUDA prototype and the CGBN library. The central reason is the absence of a compiler pass aimed at supporting efficient sequentialization. Rationale is:

First, performing efficient sequentialization by hand is not only "un-natural" and results in less elegant code, but, more importantly it has the potential of degrading the performance of the other semantically-equivalent code versions. For example, if the integer size is too large to fit in the intra-group kernel, then the code in Fig. 10—which was intended to copy in coalesced way from global to shared memory—performs in a convoluted way two expensive and completely unnecessary copies (global-to-global memory).

Second, logical array created inside the intra-group kernel are currently mapped by the compiler to shared-memory only, since this guarantees that their elements are accessible to any threads. This mapping has serious performance implications since shared memory has higher latency than registers, and there is no manner in which this mapping can be altered by the programmer. It also follows that Futhark kernels will require more shared memory than necessary, which limits the magnitude of the supported integer. For example, in the case of addition, our CUDA prototype utilizes one memory buffer (and this can be further reduced), while Futhark requires twice as much.

Third, the Futhark FFT implementation currently uses a `scatter` (parallel write) operation as the result of a loop (body), which requires two shared-memory buffers that are aliased across the loop (double buffering). This circular aliasing prevents the current compiler to reuse the space of these buffers for subsequent operations, even when their liveness interval has ended. We observe that if the corresponding array was mapped to register memory instead, then only one shared-memory buffer would be necessary, and furthermore the double buffering of that array would be efficiently supported by the register allocation of the underlying compiler (e.g., `nvcc`).

Finally, Futhark does not yet supports an 128-bit integer, which would offer a significant boost to the performance of the classical multiplication.

6 Experiments

This section evaluates the performance of our implementations for addition, multiplication and fusion of such operations. We compare our results with those of the "Cooperative Groups Big Numbers" library,[5] (CGBN) authored by NVlabs. that offers a framework for performing unsigned multiple precision integer arithmetic in CUDA. The current release (XMP 2.0 Beta) offers state-of-the-art performance on small to medium sized integers: 2^5 bits through 2^{15} bits, but also seems to support larger integers, albeit without top-performance guarantees.

The key design decision in CGBN is that one operation is performed within (at most) one warp of threads, such that the implementation can leverage specialized hardware (instructions) that enable very efficient (low-latency) communication of register values within a warp. This also promotes the scalability of fused operations. In comparison, our implementation does not rely on specialized hardware instructions, and maps an integer instance to be solved by at most one CUDA block of threads. We thus expect to achieve higher performance on larger integers, where CGBN is likely to be affected by high-register pressure.

6.1 Hardware, Benchmark, Performance Measures, Methodology

Our evaluation uses an Nvidia A100 GPU that offers 6912 cores, peak global-memory bandwidth of 1.555 TB/sec and FP32 peak performance of 19.49 Tflops.

We evaluate our implementations in comparison with CGBN by running programs that perform batches of (i) one addition **1-Add**, (ii) six additions **6-Add**,

[5] https://github.com/NVlabs/CGBN.

(iii) one multiplication **1-Mul**, and (iv) a polynomial computation **Poly** involving four multiplications and two additions. All four programs correspond to the execution of one kernel such that related sequences of additions and multiplications are performed inside the same CUDA block—i.e., **6-ADD** and **Poly** are intended to evaluate the scalability of block-level fusion, in which intermediate results are maintained in fast memory. Ideally, the evaluation would include bigger benchmarks that heavily use addition and multiplication, such as **Poly**. However, constructing such practically-relevant programs requires to support at least division (which we do not), e.g., which would enable GCD computations.

The target programs are evaluated on eight combinations of values for the size in bits *NumBits* of the integer and the total number of (integer) instances *NumInsts*, such that $NumBits \cdot NumInsts = 2^{32}$. We report the performance of

addition: in GB/sec—because addition is memory bound—and we compute the number of bytes accessed by **1-Add** and **6-Add** with the *same* formula:[6]

$$\texttt{number} - \texttt{of} - \texttt{bytes} - \texttt{accessed} = 3 NumInsts \cdot \frac{NumBits}{8}$$

multiplication: in terms of Giga 32-bit unit operations per second (Gu32ops/sec), since multiplication is compute bound. **1-Mul** uses as number of operations:

$$\texttt{1} - \texttt{Mul} - \texttt{num} - \texttt{u32} - \texttt{ops}{=}300 \cdot NumInsts \cdot m \cdot \log m, \text{ where } m = \frac{M \cdot \texttt{sizeof(uint)}}{4}$$

For **Poly** we consider the number of unit operations to be four times that of **1-Mul**, i.e., we only consider the four multiplications and ignore the two additions. The rationale for the constant 300 is that the algorithm performs three FFT transformations, each of them using about $100 \cdot m \cdot \log m$ unit operations.[7] However, the constant does not matter much: the key is that the measure implements a normalized runtime that allows meaningful comparison across different implementations and also across different datasets.

Since all CUDA programs consist of one kernel call, we measure the runtime as the average of 500 kernel runs for **1-Add**, **6-Add** and **1-Mul** and of 125 runs for **Poly**. For Futhark, we use the option `bench -backend=cuda` that (i) measures all overheads except for device initialization, kernel compilation and data transfers between host and device, and (ii) performs enough runs until the 95%-confidence percentile average stabilizes.

---

[6] Ideally, both programs read two integers from global memory and write one as result.

[7] We have used test programs to measure the latency of 32 and 64 bit operations such as addition, multiplication, modulo, in comparison with 32-bit integer addition (as the unit), and we have counted that FFT multiplication instantiated to `FftPrime32` requires about 100 units inside its $M \cdot \log M$ loop nest. In fact one modulo operation on `uint64_t` alone accounts for the time of ~ 78 additions.

Table 1. Performance of Addition in **GB/sec**. A100's peak bandwidth is **1555** GB/s.

Num Bits	Num Insts	1-Add CGBN	1-Add Our-Cuda	1-Add Futhark	6-Add CGBN	6-Add Our-Cuda	6-Add Futhark
2^{18}	2^{14}	369	**1320**	737	362	**570**	294
2^{17}	2^{15}	368	**1331**	1172	353	**803**	350
2^{16}	2^{16}	376	**1358**	**1343**	353	**853**	313
2^{15}	2^{17}	329	**1363**	**1363**	321	**856**	431
2^{14}	2^{18}	581	**1334**	**1370**	546	**836**	434
2^{13}	2^{19}	1238	**1350**	**1364**	**1207**	816	435
2^{12}	2^{20}	**1329**	**1359**	**1364**	**1189**	856	435
2^{11}	2^{21}	1275	**1366**	**1364**	**1167**	855	435

6.2 Performance of Addition

Table 1 shows the performance of integer addition expressed as memory bandwidth, i.e., in GB/sec. The peak global-memory bandwidth of the Nvidia A100 hardware is 1.555TB/sec. The first two columns correspond to the number of bits of the integer (*NumBits*) and the total number of instances performed *NumInsts*. The columns denoted CGBN correspond to the performance of the CGBN library, while the columns denoted by **Our-CUDA** and **Futhark** correspond to the performance of our CUDA and Futhark implementations.

For CGBN we set the thread-per-instance parameter for *NumBits* equal to 2^{11} and 2^{12} to 16 and 8, respectively, and to 32 for the rest of *NumBits* values; we have observed that best performance is achieved for these instantiations (for both addition and multiplication). For our CUDA and Futhark implementations, we instantiate *uint* to `uint64_t` and the sequentialization factor Q to 4, i.e., each thread computes $4 \cdot 64 = 256$ bits sequentially.

Key observations derived from Table 1 are:

1-Add: both our CUDA and Futhark implementations outperform CGBN on integers whose number of bits are in the interval $2^{14} \ldots 2^{18}$. For example, CGBN commonly achieves less than 25% of the peak bandwidth, while our implementations commonly achieve higher than 85% of the peak bandwidth. CGBN offers competitive performance on $NumBits = 2^{11} \ldots 2^{13}$.

6-Add: CGBN offers near-perfect scalability, i.e., it takes about the same amount of time to perform six addition as it takes to perform one. We attribute this to the low-latency of specialized-register instructions for transferring values within a warp of threads. However, while CGBN offers excellent performance on integers of size $2^{11} \ldots 2^{13}$ bits (up to 1.5× faster than ours), **Our-CUDA** still holds the upper hand on sizes $2^{14} \ldots 2^{18}$ (up to 2.7× faster than CGBN).

6-Add: our CUDA implementation offers decent scaling: except for 2^{18} bits, computing six additions takes less than 1.65× the time of one addition.

6-Add: the scalability of the Futhark implementation is severely handicapped by the layout that maps intermediate arrays in shared-memory buffers rather than registers: six additions require (more than) 3× the time of one addition.

Table 2. Performance of multiplication in Gu32ops/sec (the higher the better); the number of 32-bit operations for **1-Mul** is computed as $300 \cdot \mathit{NumInsts} \cdot m \cdot \log m$, where $m = \frac{M \cdot \mathtt{sizeof(uint)}}{4}$. **Poly** computes $(a \cdot a + b) \cdot (b \cdot b + b) + a \cdot b$ using four multiplications and two additions; its number of operations is considered to be four times that of **1-Mul**.

Num Bits	Num Insts	1-Mul CGBN	1-Mul Cu-Q	1-Mul Fu-Q	1-Mul Cu-F	1-Mul Fu-F	Poly CGBN	Poly Cu-Q	Poly Fu-Q	Poly Cu-F	Poly Fu-F
2^{18}	2^{14}	72	----	**1813**	**11590**	----	49	----	**1795**	**11351**	----
2^{17}	2^{15}	997	**4471**	3296	**11789**	----	192	**4027**	3259	**12130**	----
2^{16}	2^{16}	6482	**7843**	5901	**11466**	----	5837	**7148**	5820	**11679**	----
2^{15}	2^{17}	11640	**13460**	10091	**12779**	10187	**12246**	**12247**	9889	**12621**	8395
2^{14}	2^{18}	**21461**	**21608**	15856	14297	11259	**21454**	**19455**	15093	13899	10742
2^{13}	2^{19}	**34004**	**31658**	24267	15791	11651	**34165**	**27876**	20677	15173	11620
2^{12}	2^{20}	**54465**	**49328**	39861	15264	11051	**53846**	**42673**	30569	11189	9641
2^{11}	2^{21}	**86252**	**70661**	61333	13554	10099	**86182**	**60819**	44094	10884	8801

6.3 Performance of Multiplication

Table 2 shows the performance of multiplication expressed in Gu32ops/sec (see Sect. 6.1), where the best two numbers are displayed in bold text—the higher the number the better the performance. Cells filled with ---- denote that kernel launch failed due to running out of resources.[8] As before, the first two columns report the integer size in bits and the number of instances performed, and the columns denoted CGBN correspond to the performance of the CGBN library. The columns denoted **Cu-Q** and **Cu-F** correspond to our CUDA implementation for the classical (quadratic time) and FFT (log-linear time), respectively, and similarly, the columns denoted **Fu-Q** and **Fu-F** correspond to Futhark.

Our implementation of classical multiplication specializes *uint* to `uint64_t` and use a total sequentialization factor of 4, i.e., each thread computes two elements from the first half and their two symmetric opposites across the middle, as in Fig. 6. For FFT multiplication we use (i) the smallest sequentialization factor (greater or equal than two) that allows the computation to fit in a CUDA block, which is constrained to 1024 threads, and (ii) the `FftPrime32` field, in which *uint* is `uint32_t` and *ubig* is `uint64_t`. Using `FftPrime64` is a bit slower mainly because it requires a modulo operation on 128-bit integers, which is very expensive. Key observations derived from Table 2 are:

(1) On both **1-Mul** and **Poly**, our CUDA implementation of classical (quadratic) multiplication is faster than CGBN for integer sizes in the range $2^{15} \dots 2^{18}$. Size 2^{15} is also very close to the split point from which on, our CUDA FFT implementation starts outperforming the quadratic implementation.
(2) CGBN is faster on the smaller integer sizes $2^{11} \dots 2^{13}$ by factors as high as $1.2\times$ and $1.4\times$ on **1-Mul** and **Poly**, respectively, but our **Cu-Q** is faster on sizes $2^{15} \dots 2^{17}$ by factors as high as $4.5\times$ and $21\times$.

[8] We prevented Futhark from switching to the slower versions described in Sect. 5.1.

(3) Our CUDA FFT implementation is faster than the best quadratic running implementation (i) by factors of 6.3× on integer size 2^{18}, and (ii) by 2.6× and 3.0× factors on integer size 2^{17} on **1-Mul** and **Poly**, respectively.
(4) CGBN demonstrates excellent (super-linear) scalability on integer sizes between $2^{11} \ldots 2^{15}$, since its performance on **Poly** is very-close to or better than the one on **1-Mul**, even when the two additions are not counted.
(5) Our CUDA FFT implementation also demonstrates excellent scalability on sizes higher than or equal to 2^{15}, which is all that matters because 2^{15} seems to be the split point from which point on FFT gains the upper hand.
(6) We attribute the performance gap between our CUDA and Futhark quadratic implementations on **1-Mul** to the fact that Futhark lacks support for 128-bit integers, and hence it uses less-efficient 64-bit arithmetic that computes the high and low parts. Similar to addition, Futhark's scalability (for **Poly**) is worse due to logical arrays being always mapped to shared memory.
(7) Finally, the Futhark FFT implementation runs out of resource for sizes of 2^{16} to 2^{18} bits, due to the last issue reported in Sect. 5.2.

6.4 Brief Performance Discussion on GPUs Other Than A100

A systematic investigation of the performance of our implementations on GPU hardware other than A100 is outside the scope of this paper. We can however report that running the benchmark on an RTX A4500 Nvidia GPU results in very similar performance metrics as the ones for A100, once we adjust to the peak bandwidth, the peak-compute performance, and to the amount of shared memory per SM of the RTX A4500 GPU. Notably, the scalability trends are the same, and the maximal problem size is downgraded one level because the A100 provides more shared memory per SM.

We have not yet translated our CUDA implementation to OpenCL or HIP, and as such, we do not have results to report in this sense. However, we have run the Futhark implementations using the `opencl` and `hip` compiler back ends on an AMD MI100 GPU. The scalability trends are similar to the one of the A100. We have observed that the performance is about half of the A100 performance and the maximal problem size is downgraded by one or two levels. The latter "makes sense" since MI100 offers only 48 `KB` of scratchpad memory per SM, while the A100 offers up to 128 `KB`.

7 Conclusions

We have shown that high-level languages (`C++` and Futhark) can be used to implement big integer addition and multiplication concisely and efficiently for GPU computation. These implementations are simple and efficient for big integers of practical size, comparing favourably to the CGBN library for integers of size from 2^{15} to 2^{18} bits (i.e., up to about 79,000 digits). We have seen that an FFT-based multiplication can, by factors as high as 5×, outperform an efficient implementation of the classical multiplication on sizes that fit in a CUDA block.

This is achieved using a naive implementation of finite field arithmetic—further improvement would be expected using Montgomery representation. The paper has presented the implementation in sufficient detail to be reproduced as desired by others. For C++ template CUDA code has been provided.

We have measured the performance of these implementations against the high quality CGBN library, testing up to sizes of 2^{18} bits. For addition, our CUDA code outperforms the CGBN library by a factor of about 2× to 4× for integers of more than about 2^{14} bits. For most tests, our functional Futhark code also outperforms the CGBN library. For classical quadratic multiplication, our simple CUDA code is comparable to the CGBN library for numbers with up to 2^{14} bits and superior to CGBN for larger sizes. The Futhark implementation is comparable over most of the range of sizes. The CUDA FFT implementation of multiplication is superior for sizes greater than 2^{15} bits, becoming about 160 times faster at 2^{18} bits. For tests involving a combination of operations (the "Poly" tests), our CUDA implementation using classical arithmetic performs significantly better than CGBN for sizes above 2^{15} bits and within a factor of 2 below that size. While the Futhark implementation meets the criterion of being concise and flexible, further compiler support is required to approach the efficiency of our CUDA code. The present investigation has identified specific areas of Futhark compiler enhancement that together may lead to performance comparable to our CUDA code.

Acknowledgments. The authors were originally inspired to consider non-uniform memory architectures in a collaboration with Alan Mycroft [36,37], without whom we never would have ended up here!

Disclosure of Interests. The authors have no conflicts of interest to declare.

References

1. Abadi, M., et al.: TensorFlow: a system for large-scale machine learning. In: 12th USENIX Symposium on Operating Systems Design and Implementation (OSDI 16), pp. 265–283 (2016)
2. Bantikyan, H.: Big integer multiplication with CUDA FFT(CUFFT) library. Int. J. Innovative Res. Comput. Commun. Eng. **2**, 6317–6325 (2014). https://api.semanticscholar.org/CorpusID:14759606
3. Bernardin, L., et al.: Maple Programming Guide, Maplesoft, a division of Waterloo Maple Inc. (1996–2023)
4. Blelloch, G.E.: Scans as primitive parallel operations. IEEE Trans. Comput. **38**(11), 1526–1538 (1989)
5. Blelloch, G.E.: Vector Models for Data-Parallel Computing, vol. 75. MIT Press Cambridge (1990)
6. Blelloch, G.E.: Programming parallel algorithms. Commun. ACM (CACM) **39**(3), 85–97 (1996)
7. Blelloch, G.E., Hardwick, J.C., Sipelstein, J., Zagha, M., Chatterjee, S.: Implementation of a portable nested data-parallel language. J. Parallel Distrib. Comput. **21**(1), 4–14 (1994)

8. Bruun, L.M., Larsen, U.S., Hinnerskov, N.H., Oancea, C.E.: Reverse-mode ad of multi-reduce and scan in futhark. In: Proceedings of the 35th Symposium on Implementation and Application of Functional Languages, IFL 2023. Association for Computing Machinery, New York, NY, USA (2024). https://doi.org/10.1145/3652561.3652575
9. Char, B.W., Geddes, K.O., Gonnet, G.H.: GCDHEU: heuristic polynomial GCD algorithm based on integer GCD computation. J. Symb. Comput. **7**, 31–48 (1989)
10. Chen, L., Covanov, S., Mohajerani, D., Moreno Maza, M.: Big prime field FFT on the GPU. In: Proceedings 2017 International Symposium on Symbolic and Algebraic Computation (ISSAC 2017), pp. 85–92. ACM Press (2017)
11. Chicha, Y., Lloyd, M., Oancea, C., Watt, S.M.: Parametric polymorphism for computer algebra software components. In: Proceedings 6th International Symposium on Symbolic and Numeric Algorithms for Scientific Computing, pp. 119–130. Mirton Publishing House (2004)
12. Cooley, J.W., Tukey, J.W.: An algorithm for the machine calculation of complex Fourier series. Math. Comput. **19**(90), 297–301 (1965). http://www.jstor.org/stable/2003354
13. Dieguez, A.P., Amor, M., Doallo, R., Nukada, A., Matsuoka, S.: Efficient high-precision integer multiplication on the GPU. Int. J. High Performance Comput. Appl. **36**(3), 356–369 (2022). https://doi.org/10.1177/10943420221077964
14. Emmart, N., Weems, C.: High precision integer addition, subtraction and multiplication with a graphics processing unit. Parallel Process. Lett. **20**, 293–306 (2010). https://doi.org/10.1142/S0129626410000259
15. Frostig, R., Johnson, M.J., Leary, C.: Compiling machine learning programs via high-level tracing. Syst. Mach. Learn., 23–24 (2018)
16. Gieseke, F., Rosca, S., Henriksen, T., Verbesselt, J., Oancea, C.E.: Massively-parallel change detection for satellite time series data with missing values. In: 2020 IEEE 36th International Conference on Data Engineering (ICDE), pp. 385–396 (2020). https://doi.org/10.1109/ICDE48307.2020.00040
17. Gorlatch, S.: Systematic extraction and implementation of divide-and-conquer parallelism. In: Kuchen, H., Doaitse Swierstra, S. (eds.) Programming Languages: Implementations, Logics, and Programs, pp. 274–288. Springer, Heidelberg (1996)
18. Henriksen, T., Serup, N.G.W., Elsman, M., Henglein, F., Oancea, C.E.: Futhark: purely functional GPU-programming with nested parallelism and in-place array updates. In: Proceedings of the 38th ACM SIGPLAN Conference on Programming Language Design and Implementation, PLDI 2017, pp. 556–571. ACM, New York, NY, USA (2017). https://doi.org/10.1145/3062341.3062354
19. Henriksen, T., Thorøe, F., Elsman, M., Oancea, C.: Incremental flattening for nested data parallelism. In: Proceedings of the 24th Symposium on Principles and Practice of Parallel Programming, PPoPP 2019, pp. 53–67. ACM, New York, NY, USA (2019). https://doi.org/10.1145/3293883.3295707
20. Wolfram Research, Inc.: Mathematica, Version 14.0, Champaign, IL (2024). https://www.wolfram.com/mathematica
21. Isupov, K.: Using floating-point intervals for non-modular computations in residue number system. IEEE Access **8**, 58603–58619 (2020)
22. Joldes, M., Muller, J., Popescu, V., Tucker, W.: CAMPARY: CUDA multiple precision arithmetic library and applications. In: Greuel, G., Koch, T., Paule, P., Sommese, A. (eds.) Mathematical Software – ICMS 2016. LNCS 9725, pp. 232–240. Springer Cham (2016)
23. Joldes, M., Muller, J., Popescu, V., Tucker, W.: CAMPARY library (2017). https://homepages.laas.fr/mmjoldes/campary/

24. van Loan, C.: Computational Frameworks for the Fast Fourier Transform. SIAM (1992)
25. Lu, B., Mellor-Crummey, J.: Compiler optimization of implicit reductions for distributed memory multiprocessors. In: Proceedings of the First Merged International Parallel Processing Symposium and Symposium on Parallel and Distributed Processing, pp. 42–51 (1998). https://doi.org/10.1109/IPPS.1998.669887
26. Lu, M., He, B., Luo, Q.: Supporting extended precision on Grahics processors. In: Proceedings Sixth International Workshop on Data Management on New Hardware (DaMoN 2010), pp. 19–26. ACM (2010)
27. McEliece, R.J.: A public-key cryptosystem based on algebraic coding theory. DSN Progress Rep. **44**, 114–116 (1978)
28. Merrill, D., Garland, M.: Single-pass parallel prefix scan with decoupled lookback. Technical report NVR-2016-002, NVIDIA Corporation, March 2016. https://research.nvidia.com/sites/default/files/pubs/2016-03_Single-pass-Parallel-Prefix/nvr-2016-002.pdf
29. Munksgaard, P.: Static and dynamic analyses for efficient GPU execution. Ph.D. thesis, Department of Computer Science, Faculty of Science, University of Copenhagen (2023). https://di.ku.dk/english/research/phd/phd-theses/2023/Philip_Munksgaard_Thesis.pdf
30. Munksgaard, P., Breddam, S.L., Henriksen, T., Gieseke, F.C., Oancea, C.: Dataset sensitive autotuning of multi-versioned code based on monotonic properties. In: Zsók, V., Hughes, J. (eds.) Trends in Functional Programming, pp. 3–23. Springer International Publishing, Cham (2021)
31. Munksgaard, P., Henriksen, T., Sadayappan, P., Oancea, C.: Memory optimizations in an array language. In: Proceedings of the International Conference on High Performance Computing, Networking, Storage and Analysis, SC 2022. IEEE Press (2022). https://doi.org/10.1109/SC41404.2022.00036
32. Nakayama, T., Takahashi, D.: Implementation of multiple-precision floating-point arithmetic for GPU computing. In: Proceedings 23rd IASTED International Conference on Parallel and Distributed Computing and Systems (PDCS 2011), pp. 343–349. IASTED (2011)
33. Nakayama, T.: CUMP library (2017). https://github.com/skystar0227/CUMP
34. NVlabs: Cooperative Groups Big Numbers (CGBN) Library (2018). https://github.com/NVlabs/CGBN
35. Oancea, C.E., Andreetta, C., Berthold, J., Frisch, A., Henglein, F.: Financial software on GPUs: between Haskell and Fortran. In: Proceedings of the 1st ACM SIGPLAN Workshop on Functional High-performance Computing, FHPC 2012, pp. 61–72. ACM, New York, NY, USA (2012). https://doi.org/10.1145/2364474.2364484
36. Oancea, C.E., Mycroft, A.: Set-congruence dynamic analysis for thread-level speculation (TLS). In: Amaral, J.N. (ed.) Languages and Compilers for Parallel Computing, pp. 156–171. Springer, Heidelberg (2008)
37. Oancea, C.E., Mycroft, A., Watt, S.M.: A new approach to parallelising tracing algorithms. In: Proceedings 2009 International Symposium on Memory Management (ISMM 2009), pp. 10–19. ACM Press (2009)
38. Oancea, C.E., Rauchwerger, L.: Logical inference techniques for loop parallelization. In: Proceedings of the 33rd ACM SIGPLAN Conference on Programming Language Design and Implementation, PLDI 2012, pp. 509–520. ACM, New York, NY, USA (2012). https://doi.org/10.1145/2254064.2254124

39. Oancea, C.E., Rauchwerger, L.: A hybrid approach to proving memory reference monotonicity. In: Rajopadhye, S., Mills Strout, M. (eds.) Languages and Compilers for Parallel Computing, pp. 61–75. Springer, Heidelberg (2013)
40. Oancea, C.E., Rauchwerger, L.: Scalable conditional induction variables (CIV) analysis. In: Proceedings of the 13th Annual IEEE/ACM International Symposium on Code Generation and Optimization, CGO 2015, pp. 213–224. IEEE Computer Society, Washington, DC, USA (2015). http://dl.acm.org/citation.cfm?id=2738600.2738627
41. Oancea, C.E., Watt, S.M.: Domains and expressions: an interface between two approaches to computer algebra. In: Proceedings of the 2005 International Symposium on Symbolic and Algebraic Computation, ISSAC 2005, pp. 261–268. Association for Computing Machinery, New York, NY, USA (2005).https://doi.org/10.1145/1073884.1073921
42. Oancea, C.E., Watt, S.M.: Parametric polymorphism for software component architectures. In: Proceedings of the 20th Annual ACM SIGPLAN Conference on Object-Oriented Programming, Systems, Languages, and Applications, OOPSLA 2005, pp. 147–166. Association for Computing Machinery, New York, NY, USA (2005). https://doi.org/10.1145/1094811.1094823
43. Oancea, C.E., Robroek, T., Gieseke, F.: Approximate nearest-neighbour fields via massively-parallel propagation-assisted K-D trees. In: 2020 IEEE International Conference on Big Data (Big Data), pp. 5172–5181 (2020). https://doi.org/10.1109/BigData50022.2020.9378426
44. O'Malley, D., E. Santos, J., Lubbers, N.: Interlingual automatic differentiation: software 2.0 between PyTorch and Julia. In: Association for the Advancement of Artificial Intelligence (2022)
45. Pascual, V., Hascoët, L.: Mixed-language automatic differentiation. Optim. Methods Softw. **33**(4-6), 1192–1206 (2018). https://doi.org/10.1080/10556788.2018.1435650
46. Paszke, A., et al.: PyTorch: an imperative style, high-performance deep learning library. In: Advances in Neural Information Processing Systems, vol. 32, pp. 8026–8037 (2019)
47. Schenck, R., Rønning, O., Henriksen, T., Oancea, C.E.: AD for an array language with nested parallelism. In: Proceedings of the International Conference on High Performance Computing, Networking, Storage and Analysis, SC 2022. IEEE Press (2022). https://doi.org/10.1109/SC41404.2022.00063
48. Serykh, D., et al.: Seasonal-trend time series decomposition on graphics processing units. In: 2023 IEEE International Conference on Big Data (BigData), pp. 5914–5923 (2023). https://doi.org/10.1109/BigData59044.2023.10386208
49. Strassen, V., Schönhage, A.: Schnelle multiplikation großer zahlen. Computing **7**(3–4), 281–292 (1971)
50. Topalovic, A., Restelli-Nielsen, W., Olesen, K.: Multiple-precision integer arithmetic. Final project of the "Data Parallel Programming" MSc-level course, Department of Computer Science, University of Copenhagen (2022). https://futhark-lang.org/student-projects/dpp21-mpint.pdf

Static Analysis

The Contributions of Alan Mycroft to Abstract Interpretation

Patrick Cousot(✉)

CIMS, CS, New York University, New York, NY, USA
pmc309@nyu.edu

Abstract. We summarize and contextualize the most influential contributions of Alan Mycroft in the field of static analysis. Some of Alan's seminal contributions are well-known such as his work on strictness analysis and completeness, but others have been largely overlooked, namely his thesis work on linked data structures and his precursory work on predicate abstraction.

1 Introduction

Abstract interpretation started in the late 70's in Grenoble, France. At that time Rod Burstall was visiting the computer science department (IMAG), and Radhia and I have had numerous conversations (and steak-frites-salade lunches at the GUC (Grenoble University Club) restaurant) with Rod. I suspect that Alan Mycroft got news about abstract interpretation far north in Edinburgh, Scotland, thanks to Rod Burstall supervising his thesis together with Robin Milner. This led to his first publication [16] in 1980 and his thesis "Abstract Interpretation and Optimising Transformations for Applicative Programs" [17] in 1982 (his second most cited paper on Google Scholar, not so common for a thesis). His work originated a lot of research on strictness analysis and more generally the static analysis of functional programs, a crucial contribution to the theory, diffusion, and application of abstract interpretation.

Alan Mycroft has had a very productive career with numerous applied and theoretical achievements in various domains of computer science and so my overview of his contributions will be restricted to those explicitly connected to abstract interpretation.

2 Strictness Analysis

The first problem Alan Mycroft solved was to determine statically when a lazy call by need (or call by name) in a side-effect free, higher-order, functional language (where the formal parameter is reevaluated in the context of the call whenever (or the first time) it is used in the function body) can be replaced by a more efficient call by value (where the formal parameter is evaluated at call time and stored in the context/environment of evaluation of the function body).

D. Orchard et al. (Eds.): Alan Mycroft Festschrift, LNCS 15500, pp. 83–100, 2026.
https://doi.org/10.1007/978-3-032-08187-2_5

Because of the absence of side effects, the only difference is when the evaluation of the parameter does not terminate and it is never used in the function body/definition so that call be need/name will terminate while call by value will not, as in `let f x = f x and g y = if true then 0 else y in g (f 0)`. The two call methods are therefore equivalent when the function call evaluated with call by need/name does not terminates when the evaluation of the parameter does not terminate (assuming the "observations" of a functional program execution is its final value or nontermination). Explained in terms of denotational semantics, this is $f(\bot) = \bot$, where $\bot$ denotes nontermination, which is the infimum in Scott domains, meaning that f is strict, hence the term "strictness analysis".

2.1 Alan Mycroft's Starting Point

Alan Mycroft relied on the theory of abstract interpretation. At the time [2], it was essentially for reachability/invariant verification/analysis of transition systems $\langle \Sigma, \tau \rangle$[1]. Σ is a set of states (with memory and control components) and the transition relation $\tau \subseteq \Sigma \times \Sigma$ specifies the possible effects of a computation step from one state to a next one.

We let $\tau^* \subseteq \Sigma \times \Sigma$ be the reflexive transitive closure of τ. τ^* relates a state to any of its possible successors that can be reached after 0 or more computation steps. Formally, τ^0 is the identity relation on the set of states Σ and $\tau^{n+1} \triangleq \tau^n \circ \tau$ is the relation power defined by recurrence on the natural $n \in \mathbb{N}$.

The reflexive transitive closure of $\tau \in \wp(\Sigma \times \Sigma)$ is $\tau^* \triangleq \bigcup_{n \in \mathbb{N}} \tau^n$ in that it relates any state to its successors after n computation steps for all naturals $n \in \mathbb{N}$. $\tau^* = \mathsf{lfp}^{\subseteq} T$ can be characterized as the least fixpoint of the function $T(X) \triangleq \tau^0 \cup \tau \circ X$ because $\tau^* = \tau^0 \cup \tau \circ \tau^*$ and if $X = \tau^0 \cup \tau \circ X$ then $\tau^* \subseteq X$.

The objective of static analysis is to automatically infer an invariant $I \in \wp(\Sigma)$ which always holds during any execution starting from given initial states $P \in \wp(\Sigma)$. This means that any state reachable from P should belong to the invariant I, but I may also contain other states, since it may be an over approximation of the reachable states from P. Formally, the invariant over approximates the reachable states means that $\{\sigma' \mid \exists \sigma \in P \,.\, \langle \sigma, \sigma' \rangle \in \tau^*\} \subseteq I$.

Define $\mathsf{post}(r)P \triangleq \{\sigma' \mid \exists \sigma \in P \,.\, \langle \sigma, \sigma' \rangle \in r\}$ to be the right-image of the states in P by the relation r on states. We look for an invariant I such that $\mathsf{post}(\tau^*)P = \mathsf{post}(\mathsf{lfp}^{\subseteq} T)P \subseteq I$. The function $\boldsymbol{\lambda} X \bullet \mathsf{post}(X)P$ is an abstraction function. $\boldsymbol{\lambda} X \bullet \mathsf{post}(X)P$ provides some information on X while also loosing some information on X. Take for example $X = \tau^*$. The abstraction $\mathsf{post}(\tau^*)P$ says nothing on the states reachable from initial states not in P while τ^* does. Even for initial states in P, some information is lost. Assume a state $\sigma_0 \in P$ is in P and that from σ_0 a number of transitions reach σ_1 and then σ_2, that is $\langle \sigma_0, \sigma_1 \rangle \in \tau^*$ and $\langle \sigma_1, \sigma_2 \rangle \in \tau^*$. This shows that there is a computation in which σ_0, σ_1, and σ_2 do appear in this order. Therefore, they all belong to

[1] Alan and his followers refer to "flowchart abstract interpretation" whereas in my thesis and POPL79, I had moved from flowcharts to transition systems for conciseness.

$\mathsf{post}(\tau^*)P$. However the information $\sigma, \sigma' \in \mathsf{post}(\tau^*)P$ provides no information whether there exists a computation in which σ appears before σ' since the order of computation is lost.

Proposition 1 below, shows that, like many abstractions, $\boldsymbol{\lambda} X \cdot \mathsf{post}(X)P$ is the lower adjoint α of a Galois connection $\langle C, \preceq\rangle \xleftarrow[\alpha]{\gamma} \langle A, \preccurlyeq\rangle$ with upper adjoint (or concretization) γ. $\langle C, \preceq\rangle$ and $\langle A, \preccurlyeq\rangle$ are posets where the partial orders $\preceq$ and $\preccurlyeq$ can be interpreted as concrete and abstract logical implications. Moreover, $\forall x \in C \,.\, \forall y \in A \,.\, \alpha(x) \preccurlyeq y$ if and only if $x \preceq \gamma(y)$. Such Galois connections have numerous properties. For example α and γ are increasing, which means that they preserve logical implications. Moreoever, α preserves existing least upper bound (lubs/joins). This means that if $S \subseteq C$ has a lub $\bigvee S$ in C, then the image $\{\alpha(x) \mid x \in S\}$ of S by α has a least upper bound $\alpha(\bigvee S)$ in A. This property is essential in the proof of forthcoming Proposition 2 essentially stating that the abstraction if a fixpoint is a fixpoint. Proofs are relegated to the appendix.

Proposition 1. *Given $P \in \wp(\Sigma)$, we have the Galois connection* $\langle \wp(\Sigma \times \Sigma), \subseteq\rangle \xleftarrow[\boldsymbol{\lambda} r \cdot \mathsf{post}(r)P]{\gamma_P} \langle \wp(\Sigma), \subseteq\rangle$.

As the lower adjoint of a Galois connection, $\boldsymbol{\lambda} r \cdot \mathsf{post}(r)P$ preserves exists joins and so $\mathsf{post}(\tau^*)P = \mathsf{post}(\bigcup_{n\in\mathbb{N}} \tau^n)P = \bigcup_{n\in\mathbb{N}} \mathsf{post}(\tau^n)P$.

Proposition 2. *For all $P \in \wp(\Sigma)$, we have the following commutation property $\boldsymbol{\lambda} r \cdot \mathsf{post}(r)P \circ T = F_P \circ \boldsymbol{\lambda} r \cdot \mathsf{post}(r)P$ with $T(X) \triangleq \tau^0 \cup \tau \circ X$ and $F_P(X) \triangleq P \cup \mathsf{post}(\tau)X$.*

If follows that $\mathsf{post}(\mathsf{lfp}^{\subseteq} T) = \mathsf{lfp}^{\subseteq} F_P$, as shown by the following Proposition 3 on the exactness of fixpoint abstraction under this commutation condition. For simplicity, we assume that functions f and $\bar{f}$ are continuous, meaning that they preserve least upper bound of increasing chains.

Proposition 3. *if $\langle C, \preceq\rangle$ and $\langle A, \preccurlyeq\rangle$ are CPO's (every increasing chain has a lub, including the empty chain, so has an infimum), $f \in C \xrightarrow{c} C$ and $\bar{f} \in A \xrightarrow{c} A$ are continuous, $\langle C, \preceq\rangle \xleftarrow[\alpha]{\gamma} \langle A, \preccurlyeq\rangle$ is a Galois connection, then the commutation condition $\alpha \circ f = \bar{f} \circ \alpha$ (respectively semi-commutation $\alpha \circ f \mathrel{\dot{\preccurlyeq}} \bar{f} \circ \alpha$, pointwise) implies that $\alpha(\mathsf{lfp}^{\preceq} f) = \mathsf{lfp}^{\preceq} \bar{f}$ (resp. $\alpha(\mathsf{lfp}^{\preceq} f) \preccurlyeq \mathsf{lfp}^{\preccurlyeq} \bar{f}$).*

The problem is thus to find an invariant I such that $\mathsf{lfp}^{\subseteq} F_P \subseteq I$. It is essential to remark that the computation ordering used for the fixpoint $\mathsf{lfp}^{\subseteq} F_P$ and the logical ordering in $\mathsf{lfp}^{\subseteq} F_P \subseteq I$ to over approximate the reachable states are the same so that the above fixpoint approximate abstraction under the semi-commutation condition is directly applicable

Therefore, by Proposition 3, using a Galois connection $\langle \wp(\Sigma), \subseteq\rangle \xleftarrow[\alpha]{\gamma} \langle A, \leqslant\rangle$, the problem can be reduced to the computation of an abstract invariant $\mathsf{lfp}^{\leqslant} \alpha \circ F_P \circ \gamma$ such that $\mathsf{lfp}^{\subseteq} F_P \subseteq \gamma(\mathsf{lfp}^{\leqslant} \alpha \circ F_P \circ \gamma)$, as desired.

Using a semi-commuting over approximation $\bar{F}_P$ such that $\alpha \circ \bar{F}_P \mathrel{\dot{\leqslant}} F_P \circ \alpha$ is also feasible since then $\mathsf{lfp}^{\subseteq} F_P \subseteq \gamma(\mathsf{lfp}^{\leqslant} \bar{F}_P)$, by Proposition 3.

2.2 Alan Mycroft's Pioneer Strictness Analysis

Alan Mycroft formulates strictness analysis by first defining the denotational semantics of the (recursive) function as a fixpoint $\mathsf{lfp}^{\sqsubseteq} F \in \mathcal{D}_\perp \xrightarrow{c} \mathcal{D}_\perp$ where the domain $\mathcal{D}_\perp$ is a CPO $\langle \mathcal{D}_\perp, \sqsubseteq, \perp, \sqcup \rangle$ with ordering $\sqsubseteq$, infimum $\perp$, lub $\sqcup$ of increasing chains, and the functional $F \in (\mathcal{D}_\perp \xrightarrow{c} \mathcal{D}_\perp) \xrightarrow{c} (\mathcal{D}_\perp \xrightarrow{c} \mathcal{D}_\perp)$ is continuous. (F is defined on pages 38/39 of his thesis by structural induction on the functional programs he considers. As stated in [17, page 54], $\sqsubseteq$ is taken to be Scott ordering $\perp \sqsubseteq \perp \sqsubset x \sqsubseteq x, x \in D$ on the flat domain $\mathcal{D}_\perp = D \cup \{\perp\}$ where $\perp \notin D$ denotes nontermination).

Example. Consider the lazy function $f(x, y) = \mathsf{if}\ (x = 0)\ (1, 1)\ \mathsf{else}\ f(x - 1, y)$ so that $D_\perp = \mathbb{Z}_\perp \times \mathbb{Z}_\perp$ is ordered component wise by Scott ordering $\sqsubseteq$ where the component wise infimum is $(\perp, \perp)$[2]. A parameter equal to $\perp$ means that its evaluation does not terminate. $f(x, y) = (\perp, \perp)$ means that the call of f for parameters x and y does not terminate.

Then $F = \boldsymbol{\lambda} f \bullet \boldsymbol{\lambda}(x, y) \bullet\ \mathsf{if}\ (x = \perp)\ (\perp, \perp)\ \mathsf{elsif}\ (x = 0)\ (1, 1)\ \mathsf{else}\ f(x - 1, y)$. The iterates from $F^0 = \boldsymbol{\lambda}(x, y) \bullet (\perp, \perp)$ are $F^1 = F(F^0) = \boldsymbol{\lambda}(x, y) \bullet\ \mathsf{if}\ (x = 0)\ (1, 1)\ \mathsf{else}\ (\perp, \perp)$, $F^2 = F(F^1) = \boldsymbol{\lambda}(x, y) \bullet\ \mathsf{if}\ (0 \leqslant x \leqslant 1)\ (1, 1)\ \mathsf{else}\ (\perp, \perp)$, so that, by recurrence, $F^n = \mathsf{if}\ (0 \leqslant x \leqslant n - 1)\ (1, 1)\ \mathsf{else}\ (\perp, \perp)$ and passing to the limit $\mathsf{lfp}^{\sqsubseteq} F = \boldsymbol{\lambda}(x, y) \bullet\ \mathsf{if}\ (0 \leqslant x)\ (1, 1)\ \mathsf{else}\ (\perp, \perp)$ meaning that the function f returns the pair $(1, 1)$ for $x \geqslant 0$ and does not terminate for $x < 0$ or $x = \perp$ whichever is the y parameter, including when $y = \perp$.

The collecting semantics of a function with denotational semantics $f \in \mathcal{D}_\perp \xrightarrow{c} \mathcal{D}_\perp$ is $\mathsf{post}(f)P \triangleq \{f(x) \mid x \in P\}$ where $P \in \wp(\mathcal{D}_\perp)$ is a set of possible values of the parameter (including $\perp$ in case of non termination) and $\mathsf{post}(f)P$ provides the possible results of the function for these parameters.

Example. Continuing the above example let $P = \{(x, \perp) \mid x \in \mathbb{N}\}$ so that x is a positive integer and the evaluation of the parameter y does not terminate. Then $\mathsf{post}(f)P = \{(1, 1)\}$. If $P' = \{(x, y) \mid x < 0\ \mathsf{and}\ y \in \mathbb{Z}\}$ then $\mathsf{post}(f)P' = \{(\perp, \perp)\}$, which is the infimum of $\mathbb{Z}_\perp \times \mathbb{Z}_\perp$. More generally, $\mathsf{post}(f)P = \{(1, 1) \mid P \cap (\mathbb{N} \times \mathbb{Z}_\perp) \neq \emptyset\} \cup \{(\perp, \perp) \mid P \cap (\{\perp\} \times \mathbb{Z}_\perp) \neq \emptyset\} \cup \{(\perp, \perp) \mid P \cap (\{x \in \mathbb{Z} \mid x < 0\} \times \mathbb{Z}_\perp) \neq \emptyset\}$.

Since the considered functions are total and deterministic, the image of a singleton is a singleton. Moreover, post preserves arbitrary joins so that the collecting semantics $\mathsf{post}(f)$ belongs to $\wp(\mathcal{D}_\perp) \xrightarrow{1\cup} \wp(\mathcal{D}_\perp)$ defined as

$$\wp(\mathcal{D}_\perp) \xrightarrow{1\cup} \wp(\mathcal{D}_\perp) \triangleq \{\phi \in \wp(\mathcal{D}_\perp) \longrightarrow \wp(\mathcal{D}_\perp) \mid \forall x \in \mathcal{D}_\perp \,.\, |\phi(\{x\})| = 1 \wedge \forall X \in \wp(\wp(\mathcal{D}_\perp)) \,.\, \phi(\bigcup_{P \in X} P) = \bigcup_{P \in X} \phi(P)\}$$

as well a $\mathsf{post}(f) \in \wp(\mathcal{D}_\perp) \setminus \{\emptyset\} \xrightarrow{1\cup} \wp(\mathcal{D}_\perp) \setminus \{\emptyset\}$ since $\mathsf{post}(f)X = \emptyset$ if and only if $X = \emptyset$.

[2] Note that $(\perp, \perp) \in \mathbb{Z}_\perp \times \mathbb{Z}_\perp$ in the example is the infimum $\perp$ of $\mathcal{D}_\perp$ in the general discussion.

Proposition 4. *We have the Galois connection* $\langle \mathcal{D}_\perp \longrightarrow \mathcal{D}_\perp,\ \dot{\sqsubseteq}\rangle \underset{\mathsf{post}}{\overset{\hat{\gamma}}{\longleftrightarrow}} \langle \wp(\mathcal{D}_\perp) \setminus \{\emptyset\} \xrightarrow{1\cup} \wp(\mathcal{D}_\perp) \setminus \{\emptyset\},\ \dot{\hat{\sqsubseteq}}\rangle$ *where* $\hat{\gamma}(\phi) \triangleq \boldsymbol{\lambda} x \bullet \mathsf{let}\ \{y\} = \phi(\{x\})\ \mathsf{in}\ y$, $\hat{\sqsubseteq}$ *is Egli-Milner preordering* $X \mathrel{\hat{\sqsubseteq}} Y \triangleq (\forall x \in X \,.\, \exists y \in Y \,.\, x \sqsubseteq y \wedge \forall y \in Y \,.\, \exists x \in X \,.\, x \sqsubseteq y)$, *and* $\dot{\preceq}$ *is the pointwise extension of* $\preceq$ *(that is* $f \mathrel{\dot{\preceq}} g$ *if and only if* $\forall x \,.\, f(x) \preceq g(x)$*).*

In order to characterize $\mathsf{post}(\mathsf{lfp}^{\sqsubseteq} F)$ as a fixpoint, we consider the commutation condition

Proposition 5. $\mathsf{post} \circ F = \hat{F} \circ \mathsf{post}$ *with* $\hat{F}(\phi)P \triangleq \mathsf{post}(F(\hat{\gamma}(\phi)))P$.

By Propositions 4, 5, and 3, we have

$$\mathsf{post}(\mathsf{lfp}^{\dot{\sqsubseteq}} F) = \mathsf{lfp}^{\dot{\hat{\sqsubseteq}}} \hat{F} \tag{1}$$

(where $\hat{F}$ is defined by the equations on top of page 42 of Alan's thesis). Beyond Alan's use of $\mathsf{lfp}^{\dot{\hat{\sqsubseteq}}} \hat{F}$ for strictness analysis, this collecting semantics is of interest for any static analysis of lazy functional programs.

Example. For our running example,

$$\begin{aligned}
& \hat{F}(\phi)P \\
\triangleq\ & \mathsf{post}(F(\hat{\gamma}(\phi)))P && \text{(def. } \hat{F}\text{)} \\
=\ & \{(F(\hat{\gamma}(\phi)))(x,y) \mid (x,y) \in P\} && \text{(def. post)} \\
=\ & \{(F(\mathsf{let}\ \{p'\} = \phi(\{p\})\ \mathsf{in}\ p'))(x,y) \mid (x,y) \in P\} && \text{(def. } \hat{\gamma}\text{)} \\
=\ & \{\mathsf{if}\ (x = \perp)\ (\perp,\perp)\ \mathsf{elsif}\ (x = 0)\ (1,1)\ \mathsf{else}\ \mathsf{let}\ \{p'\} = \phi(\{(x-1,y)\})\ \mathsf{in}\ p' \mid \\
& (x,y) \in P\} && \text{(def. } F\text{)}
\end{aligned}$$

The iterates of $\hat{F}$ from $\hat{F}^0 = \boldsymbol{\lambda} P \bullet \{(\perp,\perp)\}$ are

$$\begin{aligned}
\hat{F}^1 =\ & \hat{F}(\hat{F}^0) && \text{(def. iterates)} \\
=\ & \boldsymbol{\lambda} P \bullet \{\mathsf{if}\ (x = \perp)\ (\perp,\perp)\ \mathsf{elsif}\ (x = 0)\ (1,1)\ \mathsf{else}\ \mathsf{let}\ \{p'\} = \hat{F}^0(\{(x - \\
& 1,y)\})\ \mathsf{in}\ p' \mid (x,y) \in P\} && \text{(def. } \hat{F}\text{)} \\
=\ & \boldsymbol{\lambda} P \bullet \{\mathsf{if}\ (x = 0)\ (1,1)\ \mathsf{else}\ (\perp,\perp) \mid (x,y) \in P\} && \text{(def. } \hat{F}^0\text{)}
\end{aligned}$$

$$\begin{aligned}
\hat{F}^2 =\ & \hat{F}(\hat{F}^1) && \text{(def. iterates)} \\
=\ & \boldsymbol{\lambda} P \bullet \{\mathsf{if}\ (x = \perp)\ (\perp,\perp)\ \mathsf{elsif}\ (x = 0)\ (1,1)\ \mathsf{else}\ \mathsf{let}\ \{p'\} = \hat{F}^1(\{(x - \\
& 1,y)\})\ \mathsf{in}\ p' \mid (x,y) \in P\} && \text{(def. } \hat{F}\text{)} \\
=\ & \boldsymbol{\lambda} P \bullet \{\mathsf{if}\ (x = \perp)\ (\perp,\perp)\ \mathsf{elsif}\ (x = 0)\ (1,1)\ \mathsf{else}\ \mathsf{let}\ \{p'\} = \{\mathsf{if}\ (x' = \\
& 0)\ (1,1)\ \mathsf{else}\ (\perp,\perp) \mid (x',y') \in \{(x-1,y)\}\ \mathsf{in}\ p' \mid (x,y) \in P\} && \text{(def. } \hat{F}^1\text{)} \\
=\ & \boldsymbol{\lambda} P \bullet \{\mathsf{if}\ (x = \perp)\ (\perp,\perp)\ \mathsf{elsif}\ (x = 0)\ (1,1)\ \mathsf{elsif}\ (x - 1 = 0)\ (1,1)\ \mathsf{else}\ (\perp,\perp) \mid \\
& (x,y) \in P\} && \text{(def. } \in\text{)} \\
=\ & \boldsymbol{\lambda} P \bullet \{\mathsf{if}\ (0 \leqslant x \leqslant 1)\ (1,1)\ \mathsf{else}\ (\perp,\perp) \mid (x,y) \in P\} && \text{(grouping cases)}
\end{aligned}$$

By recurrence $\hat{F}^n = \hat{F}(\hat{F}^{n-1}) = \boldsymbol{\lambda} P \bullet \{\mathsf{if}\ (0 \leqslant x \leqslant n-1)\ (1,1)\ \mathsf{else}\ (\perp,\perp) \mid (x,y) \in P\}$.

Passing to the limit $\mathsf{lfp}^{\dot{\hat{\sqsubseteq}}} \hat{F} = \boldsymbol{\lambda} P \bullet \{\mathsf{if}\ (x \in \mathbb{N})\ (1,1)\ \mathsf{else}\ (\perp,\perp) \mid (x,y) \in P\}$.

If P is a set of possible values for the parameters x and y of f, then $(1,1) \in \mathsf{post}(f)P$ if some (x,y) of P has $x \geqslant 0$ and $(\bot,\bot) \in \mathsf{post}(f)P$ if some (x,y) of P has $x < 0$ or $x = \bot$. The result of $f(x,y)$ does not depend on y.

To introduce strictness analysis, Mycroft defines the abstractions $\alpha^\sharp(S) \triangleq (\!|\, S = \{\bot\} \mathrel{?} 0 \mathrel{:} 1 \,|\!)$ and $\alpha^\flat(S) \triangleq (\!|\, \bot \in S \mathrel{?} 0 \mathrel{:} 1 \,|\!)$ on page 53 (where the conditional is $(\!|\, \mathsf{true} \mathrel{?} a \mathrel{:} b \,|\!) = a$ and $(\!|\, \mathsf{false} \mathrel{?} a \mathrel{:} b \,|\!) = b$). It follows that

Proposition 6. *Let* $\mathbb{B} \triangleq \{0,1\}$ *and* $\leq$ *be logical implication. Then* $\langle \wp(D_\bot)\setminus\{\emptyset\}, \subseteq\rangle \underset{\alpha^\sharp}{\overset{\gamma^\sharp}{\longleftrightarrow}} \langle \mathbb{B}, \leq\rangle$ *and* $\langle \wp(D_\bot), \subseteq\rangle \underset{\alpha^\flat}{\overset{\gamma^\flat}{\longleftrightarrow}} \langle \mathbb{B}, \leq\rangle$ *with* $\gamma^\sharp(b) = (\!|\, b = 0 \mathrel{?} \{\bot\} \mathrel{:} D_\bot \,|\!)$, $\gamma^\flat(b) = (\!|\, b = 1 \mathrel{?} D \mathrel{:} D_\bot \,|\!)$, *and* $0 < 1$.

Observe that $\langle \wp(D_\bot) \setminus \{\emptyset\}, \hat{\sqsubseteq}\rangle \underset{\alpha^\sharp}{\overset{\gamma^\sharp}{\longleftrightarrow}} \langle \mathbb{B}, \leq\rangle$ does <u>not</u> hold since e.g. for Scott ordering, we have $\alpha^\sharp(S) \leq 1$ but not $S \mathrel{\hat{\sqsubseteq}} \gamma^\sharp(1) = D_\bot$ since for $S \subset D$ and $y \in D \setminus S \subseteq D_\bot$ we don't have $\exists x \in S \,.\, x \sqsubseteq y$ since for Scott flat ordering the only possibility is $x = y \notin S$. So Proposition 3 is not applicable to express $\alpha^\sharp(\mathsf{post}(\mathsf{lfp}^{\dot{\sqsubseteq}} F) = \alpha^\sharp(\mathsf{lfp}^{\dot{\hat{\sqsubseteq}}} \hat{F}))$ as a fixpoint. This is the main difficulty that Alan Mycroft had to solve with the theory of abstract interpretation, as available at the time [2]. The required generalization of Proposition 3 is the following

Proposition 7. *Let* $\langle C, \bot, \sqsubseteq, \sqcup\rangle$ *be a concrete CPO for the computational ordering* $\sqsubseteq$ *and* $f \in C \xrightarrow{c} C$ *be continuous. Let* $\langle C, \leq\rangle$ *be a poset for the approximation ordering* $\leq$.

Let $\langle A, \bot^\sharp, \sqsubseteq^\sharp, \sqcup^\sharp\rangle$ *be an abstract CPO and* $f^\sharp \in A \xrightarrow{c} A$ *be continuous.*

Let $\langle C, \leq\rangle \underset{\alpha}{\overset{\gamma}{\longleftrightarrow}} \langle A, \sqsubseteq^\sharp\rangle$ *be an abstraction such that*

$$\bot \leq \gamma(\bot^\sharp) \tag{2}$$

$$\forall x \in C, y \in A \,.\, (x \leq \gamma(y)) \Rightarrow (f(x) \leq \gamma(f^\sharp(y)) \tag{3}$$

for all increasing chains $\langle x_i,\, i \in \mathbb{N}\rangle$ *for* $\sqsubseteq$ *and* $\langle y_i,\, i \in \mathbb{N}\rangle$ *for* $\sqsubseteq^\sharp$.

$$(\forall i \in \mathbb{N} \,.\, x_i \leq \gamma(y_i)) \Rightarrow \bigsqcup_{i\in\mathbb{N}} x_i \leq \gamma(\bigsqcup_{j\in\mathbb{N}}^{\sharp} y_j) \tag{4}$$

Then $\mathsf{lfp}^{\sqsubseteq} f \leq \gamma(\mathsf{lfp}^{\sqsubseteq^\sharp} f^\sharp)$.

Notice that in Proposition 7, the computational ordering $\sqsubseteq$ and the approximation ordering $\leq$ may differ, whereas in Proposition 3 they must be the same. This solves Alan problem for strictness analysis.

Define $\overrightarrow{\alpha}^\sharp(f) \triangleq \alpha^\sharp \circ f \circ \gamma^\sharp$ and $\overrightarrow{\gamma}^\sharp(f) \triangleq \gamma^\sharp \circ f \circ \alpha^\sharp$ so that

$$\langle \wp(\mathcal{D}_\bot) \xrightarrow{1\cup} \wp(\mathcal{D}_\bot),\, \dot{\subseteq}\rangle \underset{\overrightarrow{\alpha}^\sharp}{\overset{\overrightarrow{\gamma}^\sharp}{\longleftrightarrow}} \langle \mathbb{B} \xrightarrow{i} \mathbb{B},\, \dot{\leq}\rangle \tag{5}$$

where $\mathbb{B} \xrightarrow{i} \mathbb{B}$ is the set of $\leq$-increasing Boolean functions.

Define $\hat{F}^\sharp \triangleq \overrightarrow{\alpha}^\sharp \circ \hat{F} \circ \overrightarrow{\gamma}^\sharp$ so that the hypotheses (2), (3), and (4) of Proposition 7 are satisfied with $C = \wp(\mathcal{D}_\bot) \xrightarrow{1\cup} \wp(\mathcal{D}_\bot)$, $\sqsubseteq = \dot{\hat{\sqsubseteq}}$, $A = \mathbb{B} \xrightarrow{i} \mathbb{B}$, $\sqsubseteq^\sharp = \dot{\leq}$, $\leq = \dot{\subseteq}$, $\alpha = \overrightarrow{\alpha}^\sharp$, and $\gamma = \overrightarrow{\gamma}^\sharp$.

Example.

$$\begin{aligned}
\hat{F}^\sharp &\triangleq \overrightarrow{\alpha}^\sharp \circ \hat{F} \circ \overrightarrow{\gamma}^\sharp && \text{(def. } \hat{F}^\sharp\text{)}\\
&= \boldsymbol{\lambda}\phi \bullet \overrightarrow{\alpha}^\sharp(\hat{F}(\overrightarrow{\gamma}^\sharp(\phi))) && \text{(def. function composition } \circ\text{)}\\
&= \boldsymbol{\lambda}\phi \bullet \overrightarrow{\alpha}^\sharp(\hat{F}(\gamma^\sharp \circ \phi \circ \alpha^\sharp)) && \text{(def. } \overrightarrow{\gamma}^\sharp\text{)}\\
&= \boldsymbol{\lambda}\phi \bullet \overrightarrow{\alpha}^\sharp(\hat{F}(\boldsymbol{\lambda}P \bullet \gamma^\sharp(\phi(\alpha^\sharp(P))))) && \text{(def. function composition } \circ\text{)}\\
&= \boldsymbol{\lambda}\phi \bullet \alpha^\sharp \circ (\hat{F}(\boldsymbol{\lambda}P \bullet \gamma^\sharp(\phi(\alpha^\sharp(P))))) \circ \gamma^\sharp && \text{(def. } \overrightarrow{\alpha}^\sharp\text{)}\\
&= \boldsymbol{\lambda}\phi \bullet \boldsymbol{\lambda}(b_x, b_y) \bullet \alpha^\sharp(\hat{F}(\boldsymbol{\lambda}P \bullet \gamma^\sharp(\phi(\alpha^\sharp(P))))(\gamma^\sharp(b_x, b_y)))\\
& && \text{(def. function composition } \circ\text{)}
\end{aligned}$$

$= \boldsymbol{\lambda}\phi \bullet \boldsymbol{\lambda}(b_x, b_y) \bullet \alpha^\sharp(\{\text{if } (x = \bot)\ (\bot,\bot) \text{ elsif } (x = 0)\ (1,1) \text{ else let } \{p'\} = (\boldsymbol{\lambda}P \bullet \gamma^\sharp(\phi(\alpha^\sharp(P))))(\{(x-1, y)\}) \text{ in } p' \mid (x,y) \in \gamma^\sharp(b_x, b_y)\})$

(since $\hat{F}(\phi)P = \{\text{if } (x = \bot)\ (\bot,\bot) \text{ elsif } (x = 0)\ (1,1) \text{ else let } \{p'\} = \phi(\{(x-1,y)\}) \text{ in } p' \mid (x,y) \in P\}$ so that $\hat{F}(\boldsymbol{\lambda}P \bullet \gamma^\sharp(\phi(\alpha^\sharp(P))))(\gamma^\sharp(b_x, b_y)) = \{\text{if } (x = \bot)\ (\bot,\bot) \text{ elsif } (x = 0)\ (1,1) \text{ else let } \{p'\} = (\boldsymbol{\lambda}P \bullet \gamma^\sharp(\phi(\alpha^\sharp(P))))(\{(x-1,y)\}) \text{ in } p' \mid (x,y) \in \gamma^\sharp(b_x, b_y)\}$)

$= \boldsymbol{\lambda}\phi \bullet \boldsymbol{\lambda}(b_x, b_y) \bullet \alpha^\sharp(\{\text{if } (x = \bot)\ (\bot,\bot) \text{ elsif } (x = 0)\ (1,1) \text{ else let } \{p'\} = (\boldsymbol{\lambda}P \bullet \gamma^\sharp(\phi(\alpha^\sharp(P))))(\{(x-1,y)\}) \text{ in } p' \mid (x,y) \in (\llparenthesis\, b_x = 0 \mathrel{?} \{\bot\} \mathrel{⁏} D_\bot \rrparenthesis, \llparenthesis\, b_y = 0 \mathrel{?} \{\bot\} \mathrel{⁏} D_\bot \rrparenthesis)\})$ (def. $\gamma^\sharp$)

$= \boldsymbol{\lambda}\phi \bullet \boldsymbol{\lambda}(b_x, b_y) \bullet \alpha^\sharp(\{\text{if } (x = \bot)\ (\bot,\bot) \text{ elsif } (x = 0)\ (1,1) \text{ else let } \{p'\} = \gamma^\sharp(\phi(\alpha^\sharp(\{(x-1,y)\}))) \text{ in } p' \mid (x,y) \in (\llparenthesis\, b_x = 0 \mathrel{?} \{\bot\} \mathrel{⁏} D_\bot \rrparenthesis, \llparenthesis\, b_y = 0 \mathrel{?} \{\bot\} \mathrel{⁏} D_\bot \rrparenthesis)\})$ (function application)

$= \boldsymbol{\lambda}\phi \bullet \boldsymbol{\lambda}(b_x, b_y) \bullet \alpha^\sharp(\text{if } (b_x = 0)\ \{(\bot,\bot)\} \text{ else } \{\text{if } (x = \bot)\ (\bot,\bot) \text{ elsif } (x = 0)\ (1,1) \text{ else let } \{p'\} = \gamma^\sharp(\phi(\alpha^\sharp(\{(x-1,y)\}))) \text{ in } p' \mid (x,y) \in D_\bot, \llparenthesis\, b_y = 0 \mathrel{?} \{\bot\} \mathrel{⁏} D_\bot \rrparenthesis\})$ (case analysis, if $b_x = 0$ then $x = \bot$ else $b_x = 1$ and $x \in D_\bot$)

$= \boldsymbol{\lambda}\phi \bullet \boldsymbol{\lambda}(b_x, b_y) \bullet \alpha^\sharp(\text{if } (b_x = 0)\ \{(\bot,\bot)\} \text{ else } \{(\bot,\bot),(1,1) \cup \{p' \mid (x,y) \in D_\bot, \llparenthesis\, b_y = 0 \mathrel{?} \{\bot\} \mathrel{⁏} D_\bot \rrparenthesis) \wedge \{p'\} = \gamma^\sharp(\phi(\alpha^\sharp(\{(x-1,y)\})))\}\})$

(if $x \in D_\bot$ then both $x = \bot$ and $x = 0$ are possible)

$= \boldsymbol{\lambda}\phi \bullet \boldsymbol{\lambda}(b_x, b_y) \bullet \text{if } (b_x = 0)\ (0,0) \text{ else } (1,1)$

(since $\alpha^\sharp(\{(\bot,\bot)\}) = (0,0)$ while $\alpha^\sharp(\{(\bot,\bot),(1,1)\} \cup S) = (1,1)$) □

Proposition 7 applies to $\hat{F}^\sharp$.

Proposition 8. $\mathit{lfp}^{\dot{\sqsubseteq}}\, \hat{F} \mathrel{\dot{\subseteq}} \overrightarrow{\gamma}^\sharp(\mathit{lfp}^{\dot{\leq}}\, \hat{F}^\sharp)$

Therefore by (1) and Proposition 8, we have soundness $\mathsf{post}(\mathsf{lfp}^{\dot{\sqsubseteq}}\, F) = \mathsf{lfp}^{\dot{\sqsubseteq}}\, \hat{F} \mathrel{\dot{\subseteq}} \overrightarrow{\gamma}^\sharp(\mathsf{lfp}^{\dot{\leq}}\, \hat{F}^\sharp)$ Since $\hat{F}^\sharp$ operates on a finite domain, $f^\sharp = \mathsf{lfp}^{\dot{\leq}}\, \hat{F}^\sharp$ is computable for any functional program. Assume that $f^\sharp(0) = 0$. Then $\mathsf{post}(\mathsf{lfp}^{\dot{\sqsubseteq}}\, F)\{\bot\} \subseteq \gamma^\sharp(0) = \{\bot\}$, proving strictness $F(\bot) = \bot$.

Example. For our example, $\hat{F}^\sharp = \boldsymbol{\lambda}\phi \bullet \boldsymbol{\lambda}(b_x, b_y) \bullet \text{if } (b_x = 0)\ (0,0) \text{ else } (1,1)$ does not depends on the parameter ϕ so $\mathsf{lfp}^{\dot{\leq}}\, \hat{F}^\sharp = \boldsymbol{\lambda}(b_x, b_y) \bullet \text{if } (b_x = 0)\ (0,0) \text{ else } (1,1)$ meaning that if the parameter x does not terminate (since $b_x = 0$) then the function f does not terminate for sure else nothing is known on the result. This information is sufficient to conclude that f is strict in x while it is unknown if f is strict in y.

Mycroft's strictness analysis method is sound (and also incomplete by Rice's theorem, like any abstract interpretation computing a non trivial property of programs).

Alan applies the same approach to the lower abstraction $\alpha^\flat$ but this is of limited applicability since function nontermination can be proved with this abstraction only when it does not depend upon the values of the parameters. However, it is anticipating the present-day interest in under approximation verification and static analysis for incorrectness proofs!

For functions with multiple parameters, Mycroft uses a Cartesian abstraction in the collecting semantics [17, top of page 42] which is more efficient but less precise that a relational analysis.

The thesis goes on in Chap. 4 to show that call-by-need can be replaced by call-by-value for strict functions, see also [16].

2.3 The Large Body of Research on Strictness Analysis in the 1980/90 s

Alan Mycroft strictness analysis originated an enormous amount of work on the subject in the 80's and early 90's, see e.g. [1]. Strictness analysis has routinely found its way in modern compilers for lazy purely functional languages such as Haskell [3].

Although purely Boolean, strictness analysis suffers combinatorial explosions at higher-orders, although widenings, which have not been much investigated in this context, might certainly have helped [12].

2.4 Connection Between Call-by-Value and Call-by-Name

In his thesis, Alan proved that call-by-need strict functions without side effects can be replaced by call-by-value functions. Nearly 40 years later, he came back to the subject, establishing a Galois connection between call-by-name and call-by-value for functions with limited side effects [13–15]. The Galois connection is between pre-ordered programs, where programs can be understood as encoding their set-based semantics, which establishes the link with abstract interpretation.

3 Sharing Analysis

In Chap. 5 of his thesis [17], Alan Mycroft considers Lisp-like lists and two versions of LISP, a pure applicative LISP-A (declarative without side effect)

[3] e.g. in the open source compiler and interactive environment GHC wiki. haskell.org/Performance/Strictness or the strictness analysis of The Helium Compiler for a subset of Haskell.

and destructive LISP-D (with data structure alteration rplaca, rplacd, nconc, expressed using an explicit deallocation by free). The objective is to analyse declarative programs and optimize them into destructive ones.

To go into more details of LISP-A (we don't consider LISP-D and the transformation of LISP-A into LISP-D described in [17, section 5.8] and proved correct in [17, section 5.9]). Let $\mathbb{A}$ be a set of atoms, $\mathbb{L}$ be a disjoint set of locations and $\mathbb{V} = \mathbb{A} \cup \mathbb{L}$, with $\mathbb{A} \cap \mathbb{L} = \emptyset$ be the set of values. Assume that the memory heap/store is represented by binary directed acyclic graphs (DAGs) $H \in \mathbb{H}$ which are sets of nodes/cells $\langle v,\ v_h,\ v_t,\ f\rangle \in H$ such that $v \in \mathbb{L}$ is the location of the node on the heap, $v_h, v_t \in \mathbb{V}$ are the respective left/car/head and right/cdr/tail values of the node, and $f \in \mathbb{B}$ is a Boolean recording whether the node has been explicitly freed. The locations uniquely identify nodes in that if $H \ni \langle v,\ v_h,\ v_t,\ f\rangle \neq \langle v',\ v'_h,\ v'_t,\ f'\rangle \in H$ then $v \neq v'$. If $v \in \mathbb{L}$, we define the head $\mathsf{h}(v) = v_h$ and the tail $\mathsf{t}(v) = v_t$, this is an error if $v_h, v_t \in \mathbb{A}$ (because nodes $\langle v,\ v_h,\ v_t,\ f\rangle$ can only be accessed through their location v on the heap and atoms are not locations) or $f = \mathtt{true}$ (because the node has been freed). The locations allocated in the heap H are $\mathsf{L}(H) \triangleq \{v \mid \langle v,\ v_h,\ v_t,\ f\rangle \in H\}$. The roots $\mathsf{R}(H)$ of the graph H have no predecessors $\mathsf{R}(H) \triangleq \{v \in \mathsf{L}(H) \mid \forall v', v'', f \,.\, \langle v',\ v,\ v'',\ f\rangle \notin H \wedge \langle v',\ v'',\ v,\ f\rangle \notin H\}$. The heap/graph has no cycles, meaning that if $v_1 \ldots v_n \in \mathsf{L}(H)^n$, $n \geqslant 0$ is any sequence of heap locations such that $v_{i+1} \in \{\mathsf{h}(v_i), \mathsf{t}(v_i)\}$, $i \in [1, n]$, then $\forall\, 0 \leqslant i < j \leqslant n \,.\, v_i \neq v_j$. The construction operation c (cons) is $\mathsf{c}(v_h, v_t)H \triangleq \mathsf{let}\ v \notin \mathsf{L}(H)\ \mathsf{in}\ H \cup \{\langle v,\ v_h,\ v_t,\ \mathsf{false}\rangle\}$ where $v_h, v_t \in \mathbb{A} \cup \mathsf{L}(H)$ are atoms or locations of nodes allocated in H. It follows that $\mathsf{h}(\mathsf{c}(v_h, v_t)) = v_h$ and $\mathsf{t}(\mathsf{c}(v_h, v_t)) = v_t$.

The considered language [17, page 154] is a functional language with a denotation for atoms, primitives including c, h, t, free, atom (checking for atomicity). The fixpoint denotational semantics of a function denotation [17, Section 5.12] for LISP-D is a function F taking the value $v \in \mathsf{A} \cup \mathsf{L}(H)$ of the actual parameter and a memory heap H as a parameter and returning the possibly modified heap H' and a returned value $v' \in \mathsf{A} \cup \mathsf{L}(H')$ or $\bot$ in case of non termination (so $F \in \mathbb{L} \times \mathbb{H} \to \mathbb{L} \cup \{\bot\} \times \mathbb{H}$) [17, Section 5.12.3] is an isomorphic tuple-based semantics for LISP-A (S-expressions in LISP), where $t(v)H = v$ when $v \in \mathbb{A}$, $t(\langle v,\ v_h,\ v_t,\ \mathsf{false}\rangle\})H = \langle t(v_h)H,\ t(v_t)H\rangle$, when $v \in \mathbb{L}$ (since no node is ever freed in LISP-A and is well-defined for DGAs).

Alan looks for "an approximation to the set of paths which will actually exist at run time, but as usual in abstract interpretation (see Chap. 2) the paths we infer will be a superset of those which can occur at run time". He claims [17, Section 5.7, page 134] that his abstraction was inspired and generalizes the isolation classes of Jacob T. Schwarz[4], to provide information on "how shared an object might be".

---

[4] citing Schwarz, J. *Verifying the safe use of destructive operations in applicative programs.* Program Transformations - Proc. of the 3rd Int'l Symp. on Programming, Dunod Informatique, 1978, pp. 395–411, also DAI research report 55, Dept. of Artificial Intelligence, Edinburgh University, published while Jacob was visiting Edinburgh.

Given a heap $H \in \mathbb{H}$, $v, v' \in \mathsf{L}(H)$, the paths $\Pi(H)\langle v,\ v'\rangle$ from v to v' are

$$\Pi(H)\langle v,\ v'\rangle \triangleq \{x_0 \ldots x_n \in \mathsf{L}(H)^n \mid x_0 = v \wedge \forall i \in [0, n[.\ x_{i+1} \in \{\mathsf{h}(x_i), \mathsf{t}(x_i)\} \wedge x_n = v'\}$$

$\Pi(H)\langle v,\ v'\rangle$ is empty when v or v' is an atom (including erroneous h and t). Let $O(H)$ be the set of locations on the heap H reachable from the roots of H through heads and tails by one path only.

$$O(H) \triangleq \{v \in \mathbb{A} \cup \mathsf{L}(H) \cup \{\bot\} \mid (v \in \mathsf{L}(H)) \Rightarrow (\forall v' \in \mathsf{R}(H)\ .\ |\Pi(H)\langle v',\ v\rangle| = 1)\}$$

(where $|S|$ is the cardinality of a set S). $\Delta_{\mathsf{h}}(H)v$ (respectively $\Delta_{\mathsf{t}}(H)v$, $\Delta(H)v$) is the set of descendants of location $v \in \mathsf{L}(H)$ in the heap H going exclusively through heads (resp. through tails only, through heads or tails).

$$\begin{aligned}
\Delta_{\mathsf{h}}(H)v &\triangleq \{v' \mid \exists x_0 \ldots x_n \in \mathsf{L}(H)^n\ .\ x_0 = v \wedge \forall i \in [0, n[.\ x_{i+1} = \mathsf{h}(x_i) \wedge x_n = v'\}\\
\Delta_{\mathsf{t}}(H)v &\triangleq \{v' \mid \exists x_0 \ldots x_n \in \mathsf{L}(H)^n\ .\ x_0 = v \wedge \forall i \in [0, n[.\ x_{i+1} = \mathsf{t}(x_i) \wedge x_n = v'\}\\
\Delta(H)v &\triangleq \{v' \mid \Pi(H)\langle v,\ v'\rangle \neq \emptyset\}
\end{aligned}$$

The abstract domain is the (complete) lattice

A = 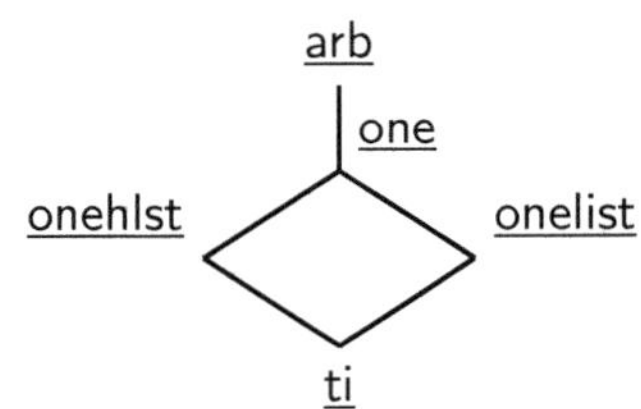

The meaning of the abstract values (called "isolation classes") is as follows.

- The supremum $\underline{\mathsf{arb}}$ can denote any atom (including error), element on the heap, or non termination. $\gamma(\underline{\mathsf{arb}}) \triangleq \{\langle v,\ H\rangle \mid H \in \mathbb{H} \wedge v \in \mathbb{A} \cup \mathsf{L}(H) \cup \{\bot\}\}$.
- The abstract value $\underline{\mathsf{one}}$ can denote any atom, non termination, or element on the heap accessible from the roots of the heap by one path only, so, "the object described [by $\underline{\mathsf{one}}$] cannot be a shared CONS node" [17, page 138]. $\gamma(\underline{\mathsf{one}}) \triangleq \{\langle v,\ H\rangle \mid H \in \mathbb{H} \wedge v \in O(H)\}$.
- The abstract value $\underline{\mathsf{onehlst}}$ can denote any atom, non termination, or element on the heap accessible from the roots of the heap by one path only, and such that all its descendants by the head h are not accessible from the roots in any other way. $\gamma(\underline{\mathsf{onehlst}}) \triangleq \{\langle v,\ H\rangle \mid \forall v' \in \Delta_{\mathsf{h}}(H)v\ .\ v' \in O(H)\}$ (this includes $v' = v$).
- The abstract value $\underline{\mathsf{onelist}}$ is similar, but for tails only. So these nodes are uniquely accessible from the roots of H and so are all their descendants through tails only. $\gamma(\underline{\mathsf{onelist}}) \triangleq \{\langle v,\ H\rangle \mid \forall v' \in \Delta_{\mathsf{t}}(H)v\ .\ v' \in O(H)\}$
- The infimum $\underline{\mathsf{ti}}$ denotes any atom, nontermination, or location on the heap such that all its descendants are accessible form the roots by one path only ("objects totally unshared from other objects" [17, page 135]). $\gamma(\underline{\mathsf{ti}}) \triangleq \{\langle v,\ H\rangle \mid \forall v' \in \Delta(H)v\ .\ v' \in O(H)\}$

Observe that $\gamma(\underline{\mathsf{onehlst}}) \sqcap \gamma(\underline{\mathsf{onelist}}) = \gamma(\underline{\mathsf{ti}})$ so we have a Galois connection with the abstraction of $P \in \wp(\mathbb{V} \times \mathbb{H})$ such that $\alpha(P) \triangleq \bigsqcap\{\underline{a}) \in A \mid P \subseteq \gamma(\underline{a})\}$. The abstraction is extended to increasing functions of the collecting semantics $\bar{F} \in \wp(\mathbb{V} \times \mathbb{H}) \xrightarrow{i} \wp(\mathbb{V} \times \mathbb{H})$ by $\dot{\alpha}\ (\bar{F}) \triangleq \alpha \circ \bar{F} \circ \gamma$. This provides a fixpoint definition of the isolation class of a function in terms of the isolation classes of its parameters and its textual definition" [17, page 140], provided variables are handled correctly, as in [17, section 5.7.5], as roots of the DAG. Since the abstract domain is finite, the abstraction is computable for each subexpression appearing in a program.

3.1 Static Analysis of Shared Data Structures

Alan is one of the early users of abstract interpretation[5] for analyzing programs manipulating shared recursive data structures, a complex problem which, with parallelism, is still a hot research subject nowadays.

4 Main Contributions of Alan Mycroft to Static Program Analysis

We have already underlined the pioneering work of Alan Mycroft on strictness analysis in Sect. 2.3 and linked data structure analysis in Sect. 3.1. In this section, we outline other important contributions to static program analysis (excluding dynamic analysis).

4.1 Denotational Semantics Based Abstract Interpretation

The work of Alan Mycroft [16,17] originated the used of denotational semantics as a standard semantics, as opposed to operational semantics, for abstract interpretation [21]. "The motivation is that abstract interpretation of denotational language definitions allows approximation of a wide class of programming language properties" [10, section 1.5]. The interest in denotational semantics, which is an abstract interpretation of operational semantics, later declined since it is not expressive enough (e.g. for trace or hyper properties) although basic principles like structural induction on the program syntax have persisted.

4.2 Static Analysis

Alan's interest in static program analysis has persisted all along his scientific carrier, including for strictness analysis [4], analysis of procedures and functions [9,20], microcode [18], hardware [27,28], although his concerns in correctness

[5] following Cousot and Cousot, IFIP FDPC, 1978.

proofs somewhat faded while concentrating on data flow analysis (in which programs are represented by graphs[6] and analysis algorithms are traditionally postulated rather than proved sound with respect to a semantics[7]) [5,7,8]. This informal approach is nevertheless with some exceptions, mainly without reference to a formal semantics [6,11,25].

4.3 Completeness in Abstract Interpretation

Alan Mycroft was one of the first [19] to develop completeness[8] in abstract interpretation, a subject that has since proliferated. His example of multiplication complete for sign analysis but not addition, is provided as introductory example in (almost) all papers on the subject! Moreover, [19] introduces predicate abstraction, somewhat before the standard reference[9]. Unfortunately fixpoints are postponed to later research. The fixpoint abstraction completeness problem is not yet solved satisfactorily.

4.4 Types and Effects

Alan Mycroft most cited work is on types and type inference [22] and he has also maintained interest and important contributions on the subject [3,24], including effect systems [23,26]. Alan certainly understood the close link between types and abstract interpretation. An example is his thesis "There is an analogy between the system described here and the "most general type" inference system used in a language such as ML [17]"[10] [17, page 67]. Another is "Control-flow operators also provide a link to abstract interpretation" citing [2] in [23]. Primitive effectful operations in the concrete semantics are abstracted to effects in an effect algebra." [23, page 18]. Finally in [19], he writes "Mycroft and Jones [10] manage to exhibit the Hindley-Milner type system as an abstract interpretation of the untyped λ-calculus but the result is much more unwieldly to use than the inference rule formulation." (where [10] in this citation is our [20]).

He has certainly been too overwhelmed by new ideas to take time to explore this connection in more depth.

---

[6] ironically close to decried "flowchart abstract interpretation".

[7] for example the classical liveness analysis in [7] is wrong since use is a syntactic over approximation of the semantic notion of use of a variable value, whereas, being negated, it should be an underapproximation, see Patrick Cousot: *Syntactic and Semantic Soundness of Structural Dataflow Analysis*. SAS 2019: 96-117.

[8] Cousot and Cousot, POPL, 1979.

[9] Susanne Graf, Hassen Saïdi: *Construction of Abstract State Graphs with PVS.* CAV 1997: 72-83.

[10] where [17] refers to Michael J. C. Gordon, Robin Milner, F. Lockwood Morris, Malcolm C. Newey, Christopher P. Wadsworth: *A Metalanguage for Interactive Proof in LCF.* POPL 1978: 119-130.

5 Conclusion

Starting from his PhD thesis [17], we have taken a rapid tour of Alan Mycroft's publications related to abstract interpretation, where he played an outstanding pioneer role and went on to regularly introduce new inspiring ideas in the field. Personally, I would have hoped that he spend more time on the subject since he is one of the few who, beyond theory, have a strong interest in applicability and practical applications as his other works in other domains do show.

A Proofs for Section 2 (Strictness Analysis)

Proof (proposition 1).

$$\begin{array}{ll}
& \mathsf{post}(r)P \subseteq Q \\
\Leftrightarrow & \{\sigma' \mid \exists \sigma \,.\, \sigma \in P \wedge \langle\sigma,\, \sigma'\rangle \in r\} \subseteq Q \hfill \wr\text{def. } \mathsf{post}\int \\
\Leftrightarrow & \forall \sigma' \,.\, (\exists \sigma \,.\, \sigma \in P \wedge \langle\sigma,\, \sigma'\rangle \in r) \Rightarrow \sigma' \in Q \hfill \wr\text{def. } \subseteq\int \\
\Leftrightarrow & \forall \sigma' \,.\, \forall \sigma \,.\, (\sigma \in P \wedge \langle\sigma,\, \sigma'\rangle \in r) \Rightarrow \sigma' \in Q) \hfill \wr\text{def. } \Rightarrow\int \\
\Leftrightarrow & \forall \sigma \,.\, \forall \sigma' \,.\, (\langle\sigma,\, \sigma'\rangle \in r) \Rightarrow (\sigma \in P \Rightarrow \sigma' \in Q) \hfill \wr\text{def. } \forall \text{ and } \Rightarrow\int \\
\Leftrightarrow & r \subseteq \{\langle\sigma,\, \sigma'\rangle \mid \sigma \in P \Rightarrow \sigma' \in Q\} \hfill \wr\text{def. } \subseteq\int \\
\Leftrightarrow & r \subseteq \gamma_P(Q) \qquad \wr\text{by defining } \gamma_P(Q) = (P \times Q) \cup (\Sigma \setminus P) \times \Sigma\int \qquad \square
\end{array}$$

Proof (proposition 2).

$$\begin{array}{ll}
& \boldsymbol{\lambda} r \bullet \mathsf{post}(r)P \circ T(X) \\
= & \mathsf{post}(T(X))P \hfill \wr\text{def. function composition } \circ\int \\
= & \mathsf{post}(\tau^0 \cup \tau \circ X)P \hfill \wr\text{def. } T\int \\
= & \mathsf{post}(\tau^0)P \cup \mathsf{post}(\tau \circ X)P \hfill \wr\mathsf{post}\text{ preserves arbitrary unions}\int \\
= & P \cup \mathsf{post}(\tau)(\mathsf{post}(X)P) \hfill \wr\text{def. } \mathsf{post}\int \\
= & P \cup \mathsf{post}(\tau)(\boldsymbol{\lambda} r \bullet \mathsf{post}(r)(X)) \hfill \wr\text{def. function application}\int \\
= & F_P(\boldsymbol{\lambda} r \bullet \mathsf{post}(r)(X)) \hfill \wr\text{ with } F_P(X) \triangleq P \cup \mathsf{post}(\tau)X \int \\
= & F_P \circ \boldsymbol{\lambda} r \bullet \mathsf{post}(r)(X) \hfill \wr\text{def. function composition } \circ\int \qquad \square
\end{array}$$

Proof (proposition 3). Let f^n and $\bar{f}^n$, $\in \mathbb{N}$ be the iterates of f and $\bar{f}$ from the infima $\bot$ and $\bar{\bot}$. In a Galois connection, α preserves existing arbitrary joins in particular the infimum so $\alpha(f^0) = \alpha(\bot) = \bar{\bot} = \bar{f}^0$. Assume $\alpha(f^n) = \bar{f}^n$ by induction hypothesis. By the commutation condition, $\alpha(f^{n+1}) = \alpha(f(f^n)) = \bar{f}(\alpha(f^n)) = \bar{f}(\bar{f}^n) = \bar{f}^{n+1}$. By recurrence, $\forall n \in \mathbb{N} \,.\, \alpha(f^n) = \bar{f}^n$. Since f and $\bar{f}$ are continuous, they are increasing (isotone/monotone), so their iterates are increasing, and their limits do exist in the CPO. By continuity $\alpha(\mathsf{lfp}^{\preceq} f) = \alpha(\bigcup_{n\in\mathbb{N}} f^n) = \bigvee_{n\in\mathbb{N}} \alpha(f^n) = \bigvee_{n\in\mathbb{N}} \bar{f}^n = \mathsf{lfp}^{\preccurlyeq} \bar{f}$. The proof is similar in the inequality case. $\square$

Proof (proposition 4).

$\mathsf{post}(f) \mathrel{\dot{\hat{\sqsubseteq}}} \phi$

$\Leftrightarrow \forall P \in \wp(D_\perp) \mathrel{.} \mathsf{post}(f)P \mathrel{\hat{\sqsubseteq}} \phi(P)$ ⦃pointwise def. of $\dot{\hat{\sqsubseteq}}$⦄

$\Leftrightarrow \forall P \in \wp(D_\perp) \mathrel{.} \{f(x) \mid x \in P\} \mathrel{\hat{\sqsubseteq}} \phi(P)$ ⦃def. post⦄

$\Leftrightarrow \forall P \in \wp(D_\perp) \mathrel{.} (\forall x \in \{f(x) \mid x \in P\} \mathrel{.} \exists y \in \phi(P) \mathrel{.} x \sqsubseteq y \wedge \forall y \in \phi(P) \mathrel{.} \exists x \in \{f(x) \mid x \in P\} \mathrel{.} x \sqsubseteq y)$ ⦃def. $\hat{\sqsubseteq}$⦄

$\Leftrightarrow \forall P \in \wp(D_\perp) \mathrel{.} (\forall x \in P \mathrel{.} \exists y \in \phi(P) \mathrel{.} f(x) \sqsubseteq y \wedge \forall y \in \phi(P) \mathrel{.} \exists x \in P \mathrel{.} f(x) \sqsubseteq y)$ ⦃def. $\in$⦄

$\Leftrightarrow \forall x \in D_\perp \mathrel{.} f(x) \sqsubseteq \mathsf{let}\ \{y\} = \phi(\{x\})\ \mathsf{in}\ y$

⦃($\Rightarrow$) Take $P = \{x\}$, $x \in D_\perp$, then $\exists y \in \phi(\{x\}) \mathrel{.} f(x) \sqsubseteq y$. By $\phi \in \wp(\mathcal{D}_\perp) \xrightarrow{1\cup} \wp(\mathcal{D}_\perp)$, we have $\{y\} = \phi(\{x\})$ so $f(x) \sqsubseteq \mathsf{let}\ \{y\} = \phi(\{x\})\ \mathsf{in}\ y$.

($\Leftarrow$) Assume that $P \in \wp(D_\perp)$ and $x \in P$. Then $\{y\} = \phi(\{x\}) \subseteq \bigcup_{z\in P} \phi(\{z\}) = \phi(\bigcup_{z\in P}\{z\}) = \phi(P)$ proving $\exists y \in \phi(P) \mathrel{.} f(x) \sqsubseteq y$.

Moreover, take any $y \in \phi(P) = \phi(\bigcup_{x\in P}\{x\}) = \bigcup_{x\in P} \phi(\{x\})$, there exists $x \in P$ such that $y \in \phi(\{x\})$, that is $\{y\} = \phi(\{x\})$ since $\phi(\{x\})$ is a singleton, proving $f(x) \sqsubseteq y$ by hypothesis.⦄

$\Leftrightarrow f \mathrel{\dot{\sqsubseteq}} \boldsymbol{\lambda} x \bullet \mathsf{let}\ \{y\} = \phi(\{x\})\ \mathsf{in}\ y$ ⦃pointwise def. $\dot{\sqsubseteq}$⦄

$\Leftrightarrow f \mathrel{\dot{\sqsubseteq}} \hat{\gamma}(\phi)$ ⦃def. $\hat{\gamma}$⦄

It follows that $\langle \mathcal{D}_\perp \longrightarrow \mathcal{D}_\perp,\ \dot{\sqsubseteq}\rangle \underset{\mathsf{post}}{\overset{\hat{\gamma}}{\longleftrightarrow}} \langle \wp(\mathcal{D}_\perp) \xrightarrow{1\cup} \wp(\mathcal{D}_\perp),\ \dot{\hat{\sqsubseteq}}\rangle$ so that by restriction to the continuous functions, we also have $\langle \mathcal{D}_\perp \xrightarrow{c} \mathcal{D}_\perp,\ \dot{\sqsubseteq}\rangle \underset{\mathsf{post}}{\overset{\hat{\gamma}}{\longleftrightarrow}} \langle \wp(\mathcal{D}_\perp) \xrightarrow{1\cup} \wp(\mathcal{D}_\perp),\ \dot{\hat{\sqsubseteq}}\rangle$. Moreover $\mathsf{post}(f)X = \emptyset$ if and only if $X = \emptyset$ so that $\langle \mathcal{D}_\perp \xrightarrow{c} \mathcal{D}_\perp,\ \dot{\sqsubseteq}\rangle \underset{\mathsf{post}}{\overset{\hat{\gamma}}{\longleftrightarrow}} \langle \wp(\mathcal{D}_\perp \setminus \{\emptyset\}) \xrightarrow{1\cup} \wp(\mathcal{D}_\perp \setminus \{\emptyset\}),\ \dot{\hat{\sqsubseteq}}\rangle$. □

Proof (proposition 5). Given $F \in (\mathcal{D}_\perp \longrightarrow \mathcal{D}_\perp) \longrightarrow (\mathcal{D}_\perp \longrightarrow \mathcal{D}_\perp)$ and $f \in \mathcal{D}_\perp \longrightarrow \mathcal{D}_\perp$, we have

$\mathsf{post}(F(f))P$

$= \mathsf{post}(F(\boldsymbol{\lambda} x \bullet f(x)))P$ ⦃def. $\boldsymbol{\lambda}$ notation⦄

$= \mathsf{post}(F(\boldsymbol{\lambda} x \bullet \mathsf{let}\ \{y\} = \{f(x)\}\ \mathsf{in}\ y))P$ ⦃def. singleton equality⦄

$= \mathsf{post}(F(\boldsymbol{\lambda} x \bullet \mathsf{let}\ \{y\} = \{f(z) \mid z \in \{x\}\}\ \mathsf{in}\ y))P$ ⦃def. $\in$⦄

$= \mathsf{post}(F(\boldsymbol{\lambda} x \bullet \mathsf{let}\ \{y\} = \boldsymbol{\lambda} X \bullet \{f(x) \mid x \in X\}(\{x\})\ \mathsf{in}\ y))P$ ⦃def. application⦄

$= \mathsf{post}(F(\hat{\gamma}(\boldsymbol{\lambda} X \bullet \{f(x) \mid x \in X\})))P$ ⦃def. $\hat{\gamma}$⦄

$= \mathsf{post}(F(\hat{\gamma}(\mathsf{post}(f))))P$ ⦃def. post⦄

$= \hat{F}(\mathsf{post}(f))P$ ⦃def. $\hat{F}(\phi)P \triangleq \mathsf{post}(F(\hat{\gamma}(\phi)))P$⦄ □

Proof (proposition 6). Let $S \in \wp(D_\perp) \setminus \{\emptyset\}$ and $b \in \mathbb{B}$.

– $\alpha^\sharp(S) \leq b$

$\Leftrightarrow (\!| S = \{\perp\} \mathrel{?} 0 \mathrel{\mathring{\imath}} 1 |\!) \leq b$ ⦃def. $\alpha^\sharp$⦄

$\Leftrightarrow (\!| S \subseteq \{\bot\} \mathrel{?} 0 \mathrel{:} 1 |\!) \leq b$ $\quad$ (since $S \in \wp(D_\bot) \setminus \{\emptyset\}$)

$\Leftrightarrow (b = 0) \Rightarrow (S \subseteq \{\bot\})$ $\quad$ (by cases 0 or 1 for b with $0 \leq 0$ and $1 \not\leq 0$)

$\Leftrightarrow S \subseteq (\!| b = 0 \mathrel{?} \{\bot\} \mathrel{:} D_\bot |\!)$ $\quad$ ($S \subseteq D_\bot$)

$\Leftrightarrow S \subseteq \gamma^\sharp(b)$ $\quad$ (def. $\gamma^\sharp$)

- $\alpha^\flat(S) \leq b$

$\Leftrightarrow (\!| \bot \in S \mathrel{?} 0 \mathrel{:} 1 |\!) \leq b$ $\quad$ (def. $\alpha^\flat$)

$\Leftrightarrow (b = 0) \Rightarrow (\bot \in S)$ $\quad$ (by cases 0 or 1 for b with $0 \leq 0$ and $1 \not\leq 0$)

$\Leftrightarrow (b = 1) \Rightarrow (\bot \notin S)$ $\quad$ (by cases $b = 0$ or $b = 1$)

$\Leftrightarrow S \subseteq (\!| b = 1 \mathrel{?} D \mathrel{:} D_\bot |\!)$ $\quad$ (since $S \subseteq D_\bot$)

$\Leftrightarrow S \subseteq \gamma^\flat(b)$ $\quad$ (def. $\gamma^\flat$) $\square$

Proof (proposition 7). Let $\langle f^n,\ n \in \mathbb{N}\rangle$ be the increasing iterates of f from $\bot$ such that $\mathsf{lfp}^{\sqsubseteq} f = \bigsqcup_{n\in\mathbb{N}} f^n$. Let $\langle f^{\sharp n},\ n \in \mathbb{N}\rangle$ be the increasing iterates of $f^\sharp$ from $\bot^\sharp$ such that $\mathsf{lfp}^{\sqsubseteq^\sharp} f^\sharp = \bigsqcup^\sharp_{l\in\mathbb{N}} f^{\sharp n}$. By (2), we have $f^0 = \bot \leq \gamma(\bot^\sharp) = \gamma(f^{\sharp 0})$. Assume by induction hypothesis that $f^n \leq \gamma(f^{\sharp n})$. Then by (3), we have $f^{n+1} = f(f^n) \leq \gamma(f^\sharp(f^{\sharp n})) = \gamma(f^{\sharp n+1})$, proving that $\forall n \in \mathbb{N}\ .\ f^n \leq \gamma(f^{\sharp n})$. By (4), we have $\mathsf{lfp}^{\sqsubseteq} f = \bigsqcup_{n\in\mathbb{N}} f^n \leq \gamma(\bigsqcup^\sharp_{n\in\mathbb{N}} f^{\sharp n}) = \gamma(\mathsf{lfp}^{\sqsubseteq^\sharp} f^\sharp)$.[11] $\square$

Proof (of (5)).

$\vec{\alpha}^\sharp(f) \mathrel{\dot{\leq}} f^\sharp$

$\Leftrightarrow \forall b \in \mathbb{B}\ .\ \alpha^\sharp \circ f \circ \gamma^\sharp(b) \leq f^\sharp(b)$ $\quad$ (pointwise def. $\dot{\subseteq}$ and def. $\vec{\alpha}^\sharp$)

$\Leftrightarrow \forall b \in \mathbb{B}\ .\ f \circ \gamma^\sharp(b) \subseteq \gamma^\sharp \circ f^\sharp(b)$ $\quad$ (Galois connection in prop. (6))

$\Leftrightarrow \forall X \in \wp(\mathcal{D}_\bot)\ .\ f(X) \subseteq \gamma^\sharp \circ f^\sharp \circ \alpha^\sharp(X)$

(($\Leftarrow$) Take $X = \gamma^\sharp(b)$ and $\gamma^\sharp \circ f^\sharp(b) \subseteq \gamma^\sharp \circ f^\sharp \circ \alpha^\sharp \circ \gamma^\sharp(b)$ since $\alpha^\sharp \circ \gamma^\sharp$ is reductive in $\langle \wp(D_\bot) \setminus \{\emptyset\},\ \subseteq\rangle \xrightleftharpoons[\alpha^\sharp]{\gamma^\sharp} \langle \mathbb{B},\ \leq\rangle$ of prop. 6, and $\gamma^\sharp$ and $f^\sharp(b)$ hence their composition is reductive.

($\Rightarrow$) $\gamma^\sharp \circ \alpha^\sharp$ is expansive in $\langle \wp(D_\bot) \setminus \{\emptyset\},\ \subseteq\rangle \xrightleftharpoons[\alpha^\sharp]{\gamma^\sharp} \langle \mathbb{B},\ \leq\rangle$ of prop. 6, f preserves joins so is increasing, so that taking $b = \alpha^\sharp(X)$ we have $f(X) \subseteq f \circ \gamma^\sharp \circ \alpha^\sharp(X) \subseteq \gamma^\sharp \circ f^\sharp(\alpha^\sharp(X)b)$)

$\Leftrightarrow \forall X \in \wp(\mathcal{D}_\bot)\ .\ f(X) \subseteq \vec{\gamma}^\sharp(f^\sharp)X$ $\quad$ (def. $\vec{\gamma}^\sharp$)

$\Leftrightarrow f \mathrel{\dot{\subseteq}} \vec{\gamma}^\sharp(f^\sharp)$ $\quad$ (pointwise def. $\dot{\subseteq}$) $\square$

[11] We have not used the Galois connection hypothesis which is useful to rephrase the hypotheses using α. It is also possible to require equality, see Patrick Cousot, Radhia Cousot: *Galois Connection Based Abstract Interpretations for Strictness Analysis (Invited Paper)*. Formal Methods in Programming and Their Applications 1993: 98-127.

Proof (of 8).

- $\bot \leq \vec{\gamma}^\sharp(\bot^\sharp)$

$\Leftrightarrow \boldsymbol{\lambda} X \cdot \{\bot\} \mathrel{\dot{\subseteq}} \vec{\gamma}^\sharp(\boldsymbol{\lambda} x \cdot 0)$ ⟅def. $\bot$ and $\bot^\sharp$⟆

$\Leftrightarrow \forall X \in \wp(\mathcal{D}_\bot) \,.\, \{\bot\} \subseteq \gamma^\sharp \circ \boldsymbol{\lambda} x \cdot 0 \circ \alpha^\sharp(X)$ ⟅pointwise def. of $\dot{\subseteq}$ and def. $\vec{\gamma}^\sharp$⟆

$\Leftrightarrow \{\bot\} \subseteq \gamma^\sharp(0)$ ⟅def. function composition $\circ$⟆

$\Leftrightarrow \{\bot\} \subseteq \{\bot\}$ ⟅def. $\gamma^\sharp$, which is true, proving (2)⟆

- Let $f \in \wp(\mathcal{D}_\bot) \xrightarrow{1\cup} \wp(\mathcal{D}_\bot)$, $f^\sharp \in \mathbb{B} \xrightarrow{i} \mathbb{B}$ be such that $f \leq \vec{\gamma}^\sharp(f^\sharp)$. Then

$\hat{F}(f)$

$\dot{\subseteq}\ \hat{F}(\vec{\gamma}^\sharp(f^\sharp))$

⟅$f \leq \vec{\gamma}^\sharp(f^\sharp)$ and the composition $\hat{F}^\sharp$ of increasing functions is increasing⟆

$\dot{\subseteq}\ \vec{\gamma}^\sharp(\vec{\alpha}^\sharp \circ \hat{F} \circ \vec{\gamma}^\sharp(f^\sharp))$

⟅by the Galois connection $\langle \vec{\alpha}^\sharp,\, \vec{\gamma}^\sharp \rangle$, $\vec{\gamma}^\sharp \circ \vec{\alpha}^\sharp$ is extensive⟆

$=\ \vec{\gamma}^\sharp(\hat{F}^\sharp(f^\sharp))$ ⟅def. $\hat{F}^\sharp \triangleq \vec{\alpha}^\sharp \circ \hat{F} \circ \vec{\gamma}^\sharp$, proving hypothesis (3) of Proposition 7⟆

- Let $\langle f_i,\, i \in \mathbb{N} \rangle$ be an increasing chain for $\dot{\hat{\sqsubseteq}}$ and $\langle f_i^\sharp,\, i \in \mathbb{N} \rangle$ be an increasing chain for $\dot{\leq}$ such that $\forall i \in \mathbb{N} \,.\, f_i \mathrel{\dot{\subseteq}} \vec{\gamma}^\sharp(f_i^\sharp)$. We have

$$\dot{\hat{\bigsqcup_{i \in \mathbb{N}}}} f_i \mathrel{\dot{\subseteq}} \vec{\gamma}^\sharp(\dot{\bigvee_{j \in \mathbb{N}}} f_j^\sharp)$$

$\Leftrightarrow \forall X \in \wp(\mathcal{D}_\bot) \,.\, \hat{\bigsqcup_{i \in \mathbb{N}}} f_i(X) \subseteq \vec{\gamma}^\sharp(\dot{\bigvee_{j \in \mathbb{N}}} f_j^\sharp)(X)$ ⟅pointwise def. $\dot{\hat{\sqsubseteq}}$ and $\dot{\leq}$⟆

⟅proving (4)⟆

$\Leftrightarrow \forall X \in \wp(\mathcal{D}_\bot) \,.\, \hat{\bigsqcup_{i \in \mathbb{N}}} f_i(X) \subseteq \gamma^\sharp \circ (\dot{\bigvee_{j \in \mathbb{N}}} f_j^\sharp) \circ \alpha^\sharp(X)$ ⟅def. $\vec{\gamma}^\sharp(f) \triangleq \gamma^\sharp \circ f \circ \alpha^\sharp$⟆

$\Leftrightarrow \forall X \in \wp(\mathcal{D}_\bot) \,.\, \hat{\bigsqcup_{i \in \mathbb{N}}} f_i(X) \subseteq \gamma^\sharp(\bigvee_{j \in \mathbb{N}} f_j^\sharp(\alpha^\sharp(X)))$ ⟅def. composition $\circ$⟆ (6)

Since $\langle f_j^\sharp,\, j \in \mathbb{N} \rangle$ is $\dot{\leq}$-increasing, $\langle f_j^\sharp(\alpha^\sharp(X)),\, j \in \mathbb{N} \rangle$ is $\leq$-increasing so is either a sequence of 0s or a sequence of 0s followed by 1s. There are two cases.

- If $\langle f_j^\sharp(\alpha^\sharp(X)),\, j \in \mathbb{N} \rangle$ is a sequence of 0s then $\bigvee_{j \in \mathbb{N}} f_j^\sharp(\alpha^\sharp(X)) = 0$. Moreover the hypothesis $\forall i \in \mathbb{N} \,.\, f_i \mathrel{\dot{\subseteq}} \vec{\gamma}^\sharp(f_i^\sharp) = \gamma^\sharp \circ f_i^\sharp \circ \alpha^\sharp$ implies that $\forall i \in \mathbb{N} \,.\, f_i(X) = \gamma^\sharp(f_i^\sharp(\alpha^\sharp(X))) = \gamma^\sharp(0) = \{\bot\}$. Therefore

⟅(6)⟆

$\Leftrightarrow \hat{\bigsqcup_{i \in \mathbb{N}}} f_i(X) \subseteq \gamma^\sharp(0)$ ⟅case $\langle f_j^\sharp(\alpha^\sharp(X)),\, j \in \mathbb{N} \rangle = \langle 0,\, j \in \mathbb{N} \rangle$⟆

$\Leftrightarrow \hat{\bigsqcup_{i \in \mathbb{N}}} \{\bot\} \subseteq \{\bot\}$ ⟅def. $\gamma^\sharp(b) = (\!| b = 0 \mathrel{?} \{\bot\} \mathrel{\text{;}} D_\bot |\!)$⟆

$\Leftrightarrow \{\bot\} \subseteq \{\bot\}$

$\wr$by def. of the least upper bound $\hat{\bigsqcup}$ for $\hat{\sqsubseteq}$, proving (4) in this first case$\int$

- Otherwise $\langle f_j^\sharp(\alpha^\sharp(X)),\ j \in \mathbb{N}\rangle$ is a sequence of 0s followed by 1s so $\bigvee_{j\in\mathbb{N}} f_j^\sharp(\alpha^\sharp(X)) = 1$ in (6) and therefore $\hat{\bigsqcup}_{i\in\mathbb{N}} f_i(X) \subseteq \gamma^\sharp(1) = D_\bot$ since $\hat{\bigsqcup}_{i\in\mathbb{N}} f_i(X) \in \wp(D_\bot)$ by def. of the lub in the poset $\langle \wp(D_\bot),\ \hat{\sqsubseteq}\rangle$. Again (4) holds in this second case. □

References

1. Abramsky, S., Hankin, C. (eds.): Abstract Interpretation of Declarative Languages. Ellis Horwood (1987)
2. Cousot, P., Cousot, R.: Abstract interpretation: a unified lattice model for static analysis of programs by construction or approximation of fixpoints. In: Graham, R.M., Harrison, M.A., Sethi, R. (eds.) Conference Record of the Fourth ACM Symposium on Principles of Programming Languages, Los Angeles, California, USA, January 1977, pp. 238–252. ACM (1977)
3. Dolan, S., Mycroft, A.: Polymorphism, subtyping, and type inference in MLSUB. In: POPL, pp. 60–72. ACM (2017)
4. Ernoult, C., Mycroft, A.: Untyped strictness analysis. J. Funct. Program. **5**(1), 37–49 (1995)
5. Feigin, B., Mycroft, A.: Formally efficient program instrumentation. In: Barringer, H., Falcone, Y., Finkbeiner, B., Havelund, K., Lee, I., Pace, G., Roşu, G., Sokolsky, O., Tillmann, N. (eds.) RV 2010. LNCS, vol. 6418, pp. 245–252. Springer, Heidelberg (2010). https://doi.org/10.1007/978-3-642-16612-9_19
6. Gharat, P.M., Khedker, U.P., Mycroft, A.: Generalized points-to graphs: A precise and scalable abstraction for points-to analysis. ACM Trans. Program. Lang. Syst. **42**(2), 8:1–8:78 (2020)
7. Ivaskovic, A., Mycroft, A., Orchard, D.: Data-flow analyses as effects and graded monads. In: FSCD. LIPIcs, vol. 167, pp. 15:1–15:23. Schloss Dagstuhl - Leibniz-Zentrum für Informatik (2020)
8. Jaiswal, S., Khedker, U.P., Mycroft, A.: A unified model for context-sensitive program analyses: the blind men and the elephant. ACM Comput. Surv. **54**(6), 114:1–114:37 (2022)
9. Jones, N.D., Mycroft, A.: Data flow analysis of applicative programs using minimal function graphs. In: POPL, pp. 296–306. ACM Press (1986)
10. Jones, N.D., Nielson, F.: Abstract interpretation: a semantics-based tool for program analysis. In: Abramsky, S., Gabbay, D.M., Maibaum, T.S.E. (eds.) Handbook of Logic in Computer Science. Volume 4. Semantic modelling, pp. 527–636. Clarendon Press (1995)
11. Khedker, U.P., Dhamdhere, D.M., Mycroft, A.: Bidirectional data flow analysis for type inferencing. Comput. Lang. Syst. Struct. **29**(1–2), 15–44 (2003)
12. Mauborgne, L.: Abstract interpretation using typed decision graphs. Sci. Comput. Program. **31**(1), 91–112 (1998)
13. McDermott, D., Mycroft, A.: Call-by-need effects via coeffects. Open Comput. Sci. **8**(1), 93–108 (2018)

14. McDermott, D., Mycroft, A.: Extended call-by-push-value: reasoning about effectful programs and evaluation order. In: Caires, L. (ed.) ESOP 2019. LNCS, vol. 11423, pp. 235–262. Springer, Cham (2019). https://doi.org/10.1007/978-3-030-17184-1_9
15. McDermott, D., Mycroft, A.: Galois connecting call-by-value and call-by-name. In: FSCD. LIPIcs, vol. 228, pp. 32:1–32:19. Schloss Dagstuhl - Leibniz-Zentrum für Informatik (2022)
16. Mycroft, A.: The theory and practice of transforming call-by-need into call-by-value. In: Robinet, B. (ed.) Programming 1980. LNCS, vol. 83, pp. 269–281. Springer, Heidelberg (1980). https://doi.org/10.1007/3-540-09981-6_19
17. Mycroft, A.: Abstract interpretation and optimising transformations for applicative programs. Ph.D. thesis, University of Edinburgh, UK (1982)
18. Mycroft, A.: A study on abstract interpretation and 'validating microcode algebraically'. In: Abramsky and Hankin [1], pp. 199–218
19. Mycroft, A.: Completeness and predicate-based abstract interpretation. In: PEPM, pp. 179–185. ACM (1993)
20. Mycroft, A., Jones, N.D.: A relational framework for abstract interpretation. In: Ganzinger, H., Jones, N.D. (eds.) Programs as Data Objects. LNCS, vol. 217, pp. 156–171. Springer, Heidelberg (1986). https://doi.org/10.1007/3-540-16446-4_9
21. Mycroft, A., Nielson, F.: Strong abstract interpretation using power domains. In: Diaz, J. (ed.) ICALP 1983. LNCS, vol. 154, pp. 536–547. Springer, Heidelberg (1983). https://doi.org/10.1007/BFb0036935
22. Mycroft, A., O'Keefe, R.A.: A polymorphic type system for prolog. In: Logic Programming Workshop, pp. 107–122. Núcleo de Intelligência Artificial, Universidade Nova De Lisboa, Portugal (1983)
23. Probst, C.W., Hankin, C., Hansen, R.R. (eds.): Semantics, Logics, and Calculi. LNCS, vol. 9560. Springer, Cham (2016). https://doi.org/10.1007/978-3-319-27810-0
24. Orchard, D.A., Mycroft, A.: Efficient and correct stencil computation via pattern matching and static typing. In: DSL. EPTCS, vol. 66, pp. 68–92 (2011)
25. Rodriguez-Prieto, O., Mycroft, A., Ortin, F.: An efficient and scalable platform for java source code analysis using overlaid graph representations. IEEE Access **8**, 72239–72260 (2020)
26. Schrijvers, T., Mycroft, A.: Strictness meets data flow. In: Cousot, R., Martel, M. (eds.) SAS 2010. LNCS, vol. 6337, pp. 439–454. Springer, Heidelberg (2010). https://doi.org/10.1007/978-3-642-15769-1_27
27. Thompson, S., Mycroft, A.: Abstract interpretation of combinational asynchronous circuits. In: Giacobazzi, R. (ed.) SAS 2004. LNCS, vol. 3148, pp. 181–196. Springer, Heidelberg (2004). https://doi.org/10.1007/978-3-540-27864-1_15
28. Thompson, S., Mycroft, A.: Abstract interpretation of combinational asynchronous circuits. Sci. Comput. Program. **64**(1), 166–183 (2007)

A Fixed Point Iteration Technique for Proving Correctness of Slicing for Probabilistic Programs

Torben Amtoft[1(✉)] and Anindya Banerjee[2]

[1] Kansas State University, Manhattan, KS 66506, USA
tamtoft@ksu.edu
[2] IMDEA Software Institute, Pozuelo de Alarcon, Madrid, Spain
anindya.banerjee@imdea.org

Abstract. When proving the correctness of a method for slicing probabilistic programs, it was previously discovered by the authors that for a fixed point iteration to work one needs a non-standard starting point for the iteration. This paper presents and explores this technique in a general setting; it states the lemmas that must be established to use the technique to prove the correctness of a program transformation, and sketches how to apply the technique to slicing of probabilistic programs.

Keywords: Fixed Point Iteration · Program Slicing · Probabilistic Programming

1 Setting

We wish to reason about the correctness of a program transformation of a "source semantics" ϕ into a "target semantics" γ, each semantics defined on a universe $\mathcal{U}$ of "subprograms". Typically, such correctness is established by demonstrating some "correctness relation" R such that $R\ \phi\ \gamma$ can be proved. But we shall show that for a certain application, the standard technique for such a proof cannot be adapted directly but requires modification.

We assume that for each $x \in \mathcal{U}$, $\phi(x)$ and $\gamma(x)$ are *continuous* functions from D to D where D is a *complete partial order* (cpo). Recall[1] that

– a cpo D is a set equipped with a partial order $\sqsubseteq$ that satisfies:
  if $\{d_i \mid i \geq 0\}$ is a chain (that is $d_i \sqsubseteq d_{i+1}$ for all $i \geq 0$) then it has a least upper bound, written $\sqcup\{d_i \mid i \geq 0\}$, thus:
  - $d_i \sqsubseteq \sqcup\{d_i \mid i \geq 0\}$ for all $i \geq 0$, and
  - if $d_i \sqsubseteq d'$ for all $i \geq 0$ then $\sqcup\{d_i \mid i \geq 0\} \sqsubseteq d'$.

  If in addition there is a least element $\bot$ (thus $\bot \sqsubseteq d$ for all $d \in \mathsf{D}$) we say that D is a *pointed* cpo.

[1] Throughout we employ elementary concepts of domain theory; see, e.g., Winskel's textbook [5].

D. Orchard et al. (Eds.): Alan Mycroft Festschrift, LNCS 15500, pp. 101–113, 2026.
https://doi.org/10.1007/978-3-032-08187-2_6

- a function f, from a cpo D_1 into a cpo D_2, is continuous if for all chains $\{d_i \mid i \geq 0\}$ in D_1 it holds that
  - $\{f(d_i) \mid i \geq 0\}$ is a chain in D_2 (this implies that f is monotone)
  - $f(\sqcup\{d_i \mid i \geq 0\}) = \sqcup\{f(d_i) \mid i \geq 0\}$.

  We write $\mathsf{D}_1 \rightarrow_c \mathsf{D}_2$ for the space of continuous functions from D_1 to D_2.
- if D_1 and D_2 are cpos then also $\mathsf{D}_1 \rightarrow_c \mathsf{D}_2$ is a cpo, with the partial order defined pointwise, as is the least upper bound:

$$\sqcup \{f_k \mid k \geq 0\} = \lambda d \in \mathsf{D}_1. \sqcup \{f_k(d) \mid k \geq 0\}$$

  and if $\perp$ is least in D_2 then $\lambda d.\perp$ is least in $\mathsf{D}_1 \rightarrow_c \mathsf{D}_2$.

2 Goal

We want ϕ and γ to be related as prescribed by a given correctness relation R over $(\mathsf{D} \rightarrow_c \mathsf{D})$; that is we shall require $R\ \phi\ \gamma$ which is an abbreviation of

$$\forall x \in \mathcal{U} : R\ (\phi\ x)\ (\gamma\ x). \tag{1}$$

We shall aim at finding a widely applicable recipe for establishing (1), but shall see that the most straightforward approach does not always work.

We shall assume that R is *admissible* in that if $\{f_i \mid i \geq 0\}$ and $\{g_i \mid i \geq 0\}$ are chains in $\mathsf{D} \rightarrow_c \mathsf{D}$ then

$$\text{if } R\ f_i\ g_i \text{ for all } i \geq 0 \text{ then } R\ (\sqcup\{f_i \mid i \geq 0\})\ (\sqcup\{g_i \mid i \geq 0\}). \tag{2}$$

3 Example Setting

We shall consider *probabilistic programming* (with [4] a seminal contribution and [3] giving a recent overview) where the effect of a program is to transform probability distributions, and shall express a program as a *probabilistic control-flow graph* [1]. In that setting,

- the subprograms in $\mathcal{U}$ are of the form (u, u') where u, u' are nodes such that u' postdominates u (that is, u' occurs on every path from u to an end node).
- the members of D are probability distributions where a probability distribution D maps a store, which is a (partial) map from program variables to integers or booleans, into a real number in [0..1] which is the "probability" of that store.

  With $D_1 \sqsubseteq D_2$ defined to hold iff $D_1(s) \leq D_2(s)$ for all stores s, D will be a pointed cpo where
  - the least element is $\lambda s.0$
  - the least upper bound of a chain $\{D_i \mid i \geq 0\}$ is $\lambda s.S(s)$ where $S(s)$ is the supremum of the chain $\{D_i(s) \mid i \geq 0\}$.

We can think of $\phi(u, u')$ as denoting the distribution transformation done along the path(s) from u to u': if D describes how stores are distributed at point u, then $\phi(u, u')(D)$ describes how stores are distributed at point u'.

4 Example

We shall consider the probabilistic structured program in Fig. 1 which

1. assigns 0 to the variables p and q
2. assigns random boolean values to the variables b and h, with the choices independent and unbiased so that each outcome (say $b = \text{true}$ and $h = \text{false}$) has probability $\frac{1}{2} \cdot \frac{1}{2} = \frac{1}{4}$
3. if h is true, enters an infinite loop
4. if b is true (false), increments p (q) until a random boolean choice becomes true (which in each iteration will happen with probability $\frac{1}{2}$)

The corresponding control-flow graph is depicted in Fig. 2.

```
p := 0; q := 0
b := random boolean value
h := random boolean value
if h
    while true
        skip
else
    skip
if b
    repeat
        p := p + 1
    until random boolean choice becomes true
else
    repeat
        q := q + 1
    until random boolean choice becomes true
```

Fig. 1. The source code of our running example.

Table 1. The distribution produced by the source semantics.

s	$\phi(\mathsf{start}, \mathsf{end})\,(D)$	
$\{b \mapsto T,\ h \mapsto F,\ p \mapsto k,\ q \mapsto 0\}$	$\frac{1}{2^{k+2}}$	for $k \geq 1$
$\{b \mapsto F,\ h \mapsto F,\ p \mapsto 0,\ q \mapsto k\}$	$\frac{1}{2^{k+2}}$	for $k \geq 1$

We will expect that for arbitrary initial D, the distribution $\phi(\mathsf{start}, \mathsf{end})\,(D)$ is given by Table 1. To understand why say $\{b \mapsto F,\ h \mapsto F,\ p \mapsto 0,\ q \mapsto 2\}$ has probability $\frac{1}{2^{2+2}} = \frac{1}{2^4}$, observe that to obtain this store we need four fortunate binary outcomes:

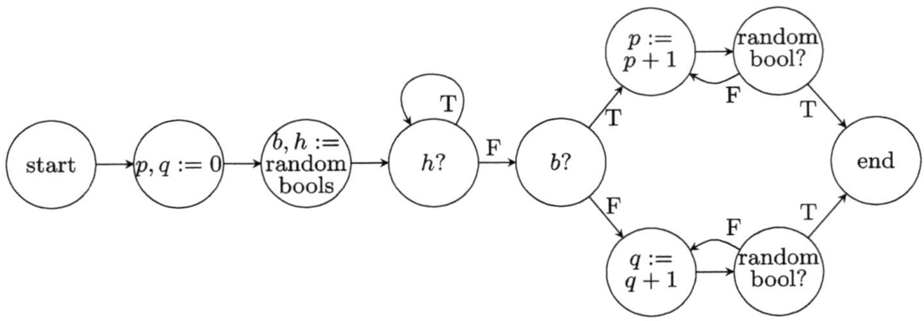

Fig. 2. The source control-flow graph of our running example.

1. b becomes F (so that q, rather than p, is incremented)
2. h becomes F (so the infinite loop is not taken)
3. the first random choice is F (so q will become 2)
4. the second random choice is T (so q remains 2)

Observe that the probabilities add up to $\frac{1}{2}$, since if $h = T$ we never get to end.

5 Slicing the Example

In general, if we care about only certain variables, we would like to *slice* away all parts of the program that do not affect those variables; see Danicic et al. [2] for a unifying framework for program slicing.

For our example, assume that the part of the store we care about is the value of q, whereas we do not care about the value of p. Observe that we still need to care about the value of b because it is *relevant* in that it determines whether q is incremented, but p is irrelevant, as is h as it does not impact the *relative* distribution of q (since h and b are independent). Accordingly, we can abstract the distribution from Table 1 into Table 2.

We then slice the given program so as to eliminate irrelevant operations, such as the assignments to p and h, and even the loop on h (as we consider *termination-insensitive* slicing). Figure 3 shows the resulting control-flow graph, which can be further simplified and corresponds to the structured program in Fig. 4.

That control-flow graph induces the target semantics γ. It is easy to see that for arbitrary initial D, the distribution $\gamma(\mathsf{start}, \mathsf{end})\,(D)$ is given by Table 3.

By comparing Tables 2 and 3 we see:

$$\phi(\mathsf{start}, \mathsf{end})\,(D) = \frac{1}{2} \cdot \gamma(\mathsf{start}, \mathsf{end})\,(D)$$

and indeed, for this application, our correctness relation R requires:

$$R\ (\phi(u, u'))\ (\gamma(u, u')) \text{ iff } \forall D \in \mathsf{D}\ \exists c : \phi(u, u')(D) = c \cdot \gamma(u, u')(D).$$

Table 2. The relevant part of the distribution produced by the source semantics.

s	$\phi(\mathsf{start}, \mathsf{end})\ (D)\ s$	
$\{b \mapsto T,\ q \mapsto 0\}$	$\frac{1}{4}$	
$\{b \mapsto F,\ q \mapsto k\}$	$\frac{1}{2^{k+2}}$	for $k \geq 1$

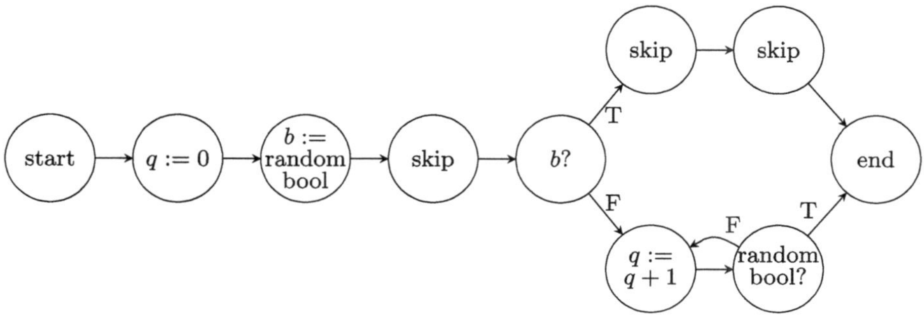

Fig. 3. The target control-flow graph of our example program.

That is, the transformation must not affect the *relative* probabilities of the various stores.

We shall now study how to *prove* that this correctness relation holds.

6 Basic Approach

Recall the fixed-point theorem for cpos:

> if D is a pointed cpo, and F belongs to $\mathsf{D} \to_c \mathsf{D}$, then $\{F^i(\bot) \mid i \geq 0\}$ is a chain with
> $$F(\sqcup\{F^i(\bot) \mid i \geq 0\}) = \sqcup\{F^i(\bot) \mid i \geq 0\}.$$
> The chain property follows by induction, with the base case being $F^0(\bot) = \bot \sqsubseteq F^1(\bot)$, and the inductive step using that F is monotone:
> $$F^{i+1}(\bot) = F(F^i(\bot)) \sqsubseteq F(F^{i+1}(\bot)) = F^{i+2}(\bot).$$

$q := 0$; $b :=$ random boolean value
if b
    skip
else
    repeat
        $q := q + 1$
    until random boolean choice becomes true

Fig. 4. The target code of our example program.

Table 3. The distribution produced by the target semantics.

s	$\gamma(\mathsf{start}, \mathsf{end})\ (D)\ (s)$	
$\{b \mapsto T,\ q \mapsto 0\}$	$\frac{1}{2}$	
$\{b \mapsto F,\ q \mapsto k\}$	$\frac{1}{2^{k+1}}$	for $k \geq 1$

That the least upper bound is a fixed point follows from the continuity of F:

$$F(\sqcup\{F^i(\bot) \mid i \geq 0\}) = \sqcup\{F(F^i(\bot)) \mid i \geq 0\} = \sqcup\{F^i(\bot) \mid i \geq 0\}$$

and it is actually the least fixed point since if also f is a fixed point then for all $i \geq 0$ we have $F^i(\bot) \sqsubseteq f$, as can be proved by induction with the inductive step being $F^{i+1}(\bot) = F(F^i(\bot)) \sqsubseteq F(f) = f$.

It will typically be the case that ϕ and γ have been defined as

$$\begin{aligned} \phi &= \sqcup\{F^i(\bot) \mid i \geq 0\} \\ \gamma &= \sqcup\{G^i(\bot) \mid i \geq 0\} \end{aligned}$$

for functionals F and G with functionality

$$F, G : (\mathcal{U} \to \mathsf{D} \to_c \mathsf{D}) \to_c (\mathcal{U} \to \mathsf{D} \to_c \mathsf{D}).$$

where $\mathcal{U} \to \mathsf{D} \to_c \mathsf{D}$ is a pointed cpo since

- $\mathsf{D} \to_c \mathsf{D}$ is a pointed cpo, since D is
- equipped with the discrete partial order, $\mathcal{U}$ is a cpo and all functions from $\mathcal{U}$ are continuous.

Thus the fixed point theorem can be applied; we shall often write ϕ_k for $F^k(\bot)$ and γ_k for $G^k(\bot)$.

To accomplish our goal (1), that is to prove that $R\ \phi\ \gamma$, due to R being admissible (2) it thus suffices to show that

$$R\ \phi_k\ \gamma_k \text{ for all } k \geq 0 \tag{3}$$

which indeed often can be proved by induction in k. But we shall now see that (3) may *not* always hold.

7 Problem

In the setting of control flow graphs, we will expect ϕ_k and γ_k to be the meaning of the program assuming we are allowed at most $k-1$ "backwards moves", that is control flowing away from the end node (as will necessarily happen each time a loop is iterated). In particular, ϕ_1 will allow only forward moves, and thus we would expect (ignoring the values of h and p) that $\phi_1(\mathsf{start},\mathsf{end})\,(D)$ is given by

s	$\phi_1(\mathsf{start},\mathsf{end})\,(D)$
$\{b \mapsto T,\ q \mapsto 0\}$	$\frac{1}{8}$
$\{b \mapsto F,\ q \mapsto 1\}$	$\frac{1}{8}$

whereas ϕ_2 allows for at most one backwards move and thus we would expect that $\phi_2(\mathsf{start},\mathsf{end})\,(D)$ is given by

s	$\phi_2(\mathsf{start},\mathsf{end})\,(D)$
$\{b \mapsto T,\ q \mapsto 0\}$	$\frac{1}{8}+\frac{1}{16}$
$\{b \mapsto F,\ q \mapsto 1\}$	$\frac{1}{8}$
$\{b \mapsto F,\ q \mapsto 2\}$	$\frac{1}{16}$

Thus the probability that execution ends with $q = 0$ is $\frac{3}{16}$, which makes sense since for this to happen we need two independent events:

- b becomes T and h becomes F; this has probability $\frac{1}{4}$
- the random choice at the upper branch becomes T either first time or second time; this has probability $\frac{3}{4}$.

In general, for $k \geq 1$, we would expect that the distribution $\phi_k(\mathsf{start},\mathsf{end})\,(D)$ is given by Table 4, in particular we have

$$\begin{aligned}
&\phi_k(\mathsf{start},\mathsf{end})\,(D)\ \{b \mapsto T,\ q \mapsto 0\}\\
=&\sum_{i=1}^{k}\phi_k(\mathsf{start},\mathsf{end})\,(D)\ \{b \mapsto T,\ p \mapsto i,\ q \mapsto 0\}\\
=&\sum_{i=1}^{k}\frac{1}{2^{i+2}} = \frac{1}{8}+\frac{1}{16}+\ldots\frac{1}{2^{k+2}} = \frac{1}{4}-\frac{1}{2^{k+2}}
\end{aligned}$$

Table 4. The relevant part of the source distribution after $k \geq 1$ iterations.

s	$\phi_k(\mathsf{start},\mathsf{end})\,(D)$	
$\{b \mapsto T,\ q \mapsto 0\}$	$\frac{1}{4}-\frac{1}{2^{k+2}}$	
$\{b \mapsto F,\ q \mapsto i\}$	$\frac{1}{2^{i+2}}$	when $1 \leq i \leq k$

Table 5. The relevant part of the target distribution after $k \geq 1$ iterations.

s	$\gamma_k(\mathsf{start},\mathsf{end})\,(D)$	
$\{b \mapsto T,\ q \mapsto 0\}$	$\frac{1}{2}$	
$\{b \mapsto F,\ q \mapsto i\}$	$\frac{1}{2^{i+1}}$	when $1 \leq i \leq k$

On the other hand, looking at the target control-flow graph (Fig. 3), we see that no backwards moves are needed for q to end up being 0, and hence we would expect that the distribution $\gamma_k(\mathsf{start},\mathsf{end})\,(D)$ is given by Table 5.

By comparing Tables 4 and 5 we see that (3) does **not** hold, in particular

$$\phi_k(\mathsf{start},\mathsf{end})\,(D) \neq \frac{1}{2} \cdot \gamma_k(\mathsf{start},\mathsf{end})\,(D).$$

We shall now show how to repair this, by replacing $\{\phi_k \mid k \geq 0\}$ by a more appropriate chain.

8 Refined Approach

To prepare for the correctness proof, the idea is to first transform the source control-flow graph. This involves replacing loops that are irrelevant, and eventually terminate, by skip.

In our setting, with p considered irrelevant, this will result in the control-flow graph depicted in Fig. 5.

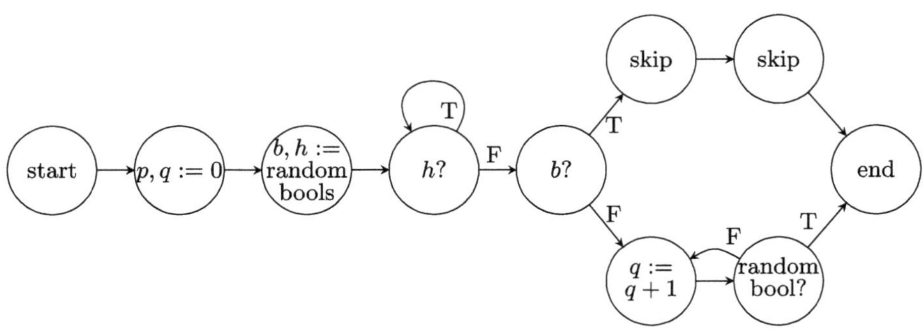

Fig. 5. The modified source control-flow graph of our example program.

With that control-flow graph as our starting point, we may define a chain $\{\phi'_k \mid k \geq 0\}$ where for $k \geq 1$, we would expect that the distribution $\phi'_k(\mathsf{start},\mathsf{end})\,(D)$ is given by Table 6.

Table 6. The relevant part of the revised source distribution after $k \geq 1$ iterations.

s	$\phi'_k(\mathsf{start}, \mathsf{end})\,(D)$	
$\{b \mapsto T,\ q \mapsto 0\}$	$\frac{1}{4}$	
$\{b \mapsto F,\ q \mapsto i\}$	$\frac{1}{2^{i+2}}$	when $1 \leq i \leq k$

By comparing Tables 6 and 5 we see that for $k \geq 1$,

$$\phi'_k(\mathsf{start}, \mathsf{end})\,(D) = \frac{1}{2} \cdot \gamma_k(\mathsf{start}, \mathsf{end})\,(D)$$

which suggests that we do indeed have $R\ \phi'_k\ \gamma_k$ when $k \geq 1$.

This is a special case, of the general idea that we shall now present.

9 General Result

Recall the setting: with D a pointed cpo, $\mathcal{U}$ a set of subprograms, F and G functionals of type $(\mathcal{U} \to \mathsf{D} \to_c \mathsf{D}) \to_c (\mathcal{U} \to \mathsf{D} \to_c \mathsf{D})$, and with R an admissible correctness relation, we want to prove $R\ \phi\ \gamma$ where

$$\begin{aligned} \phi &= \sqcup\{F^i(\bot) \mid i \geq 0\} \\ \gamma &= \sqcup\{G^i(\bot) \mid i \geq 0\}. \end{aligned}$$

For that purpose, we might be able to use the following result:

Theorem 1. *With $X \subseteq \mathcal{U}$ given, for $k \geq 0$ define $\phi'_k = F^k(\phi'_0)$ with ϕ'_0 given by*

$$\begin{aligned} \phi'_0(x) &= \phi(x) && \textit{if } x \in X \\ \phi'_0(x) &= \bot && \textit{otherwise} \end{aligned}$$

(thus the starting point for the iteration may be above *the standard starting point $\bot$), and similarly for $k \geq 0$ define $\gamma'_k = G^k(\gamma'_0)$ where γ'_0 is given by:*

$$\begin{aligned} \gamma'_0(x) &= \gamma(x) && \textit{if } x \in X \\ \gamma'_0(x) &= \bot && \textit{otherwise.} \end{aligned}$$

Now assume that the below 3 properties all hold:

$$\forall k \geq 0 : R\ \phi'_k\ \gamma'_k \tag{4}$$

$$\forall x \in X : \phi(x) \sqsubseteq \phi'_1(x) \tag{5}$$

$$\forall x \in X : \gamma(x) \sqsubseteq \gamma'_1(x). \tag{6}$$

Then we do have $R\ \phi\ \gamma$.

Proof. Observe that due to (4) and (2), our goal $R\ \phi\ \gamma$ will follow if we can prove that

$\{\phi'_k \mid k \geq 0\}$ is a chain with $\sqcup\{\phi'_k \mid k \geq 0\} = \phi$
$\{\gamma'_k \mid k \geq 0\}$ is a chain with $\sqcup\{\gamma'_k \mid k \geq 0\} = \gamma$

and by symmetry it suffices to prove the first property. To do so, first observe that

$$\forall x \in \mathcal{U} : \phi'_0(x) \sqsubseteq \phi'_1(x)$$

which is trivial if $x \notin X$ and otherwise follows from (5). By monotonicity of F, this implies that $\{\phi'_k \mid k \geq 0\}$ is a chain. Writing ϕ_i for $F^i(\bot)$ (with $i \geq 0$), we obviously have

$$\phi_0 \sqsubseteq \phi'_0 \sqsubseteq \phi$$

which implies (since F is monotone and has ϕ as a fixed point)

$$\phi_1 \sqsubseteq \phi'_1 \sqsubseteq F(\phi) = \phi$$

and in general (by induction in k)

$$\phi_k \sqsubseteq \phi'_k \sqsubseteq \phi \text{ for all } k \geq 0$$

Because $\sqcup\{\phi_k \mid k \geq 0\} = \phi$, we obtain the desired $\sqcup\{\phi'_k \mid k \geq 0\} = \phi$.

To summarize, we see that the successful application of our approach requires choosing a suitable set X, to be called an *exclusion set* as it is excluded from the iteration process, and then establishing (4) (5) (6).

In the next section, we shall see that our example setting does allow a suitable X to be found; we shall not address whether there are heuristics for that in a general setting.

10 An Application

We have presented a recipe for proving the correctness of an algorithm for slicing probabilistic programs. An elaborate, albeit unmotivated, proof of correctness was furnished in the authors' earlier work [1]. In contrast, the technique proposed in Sect. 9 abstracts the essence of the proof structure, and clarifies the key lemmas that are needed.

In [1], slicing involves finding suitable node sets Q and Q_0, where Q are those nodes that impact the variable(s) of interest, whereas Q_0 are those of the remaining nodes that may cause non-termination. The exclusion set X (cf. Sect. 9) is then defined to contain the pairs $(v, v') \in \mathcal{U}$ where (using the terminology of [1]) "v stays outside $Q \cup Q_0$ until v'", a property which (as proved in [1][Lemma 5.8]) ensures that from v, control will eventually (without risk of non-termination) reach v', without affecting relevant variables.

For the control-flow graph in Fig. 2, two nodes are not in $Q \cup Q_0$: the node that increments p, and its successor (the node that tests h may cause non-termination, and all other nodes impact q). With u_p the node that increments p we thus have

$$(u_p, \mathsf{end}) \in X \tag{7}$$

In Sect. 9 we listed the properties sufficient for correctness: (4), (5), (6) and admissibility (2). They are all stated in [1] (though with quite different naming conventions[2]):

- property (4) is stated as [1][Lemma 6.9] (proved by induction in k, and with a case analysis on $(v, v') \in \mathcal{U}$)
- property (5) is a special case of [1][Lemma 6.2] which (renamed) states that $\phi'_k(x) = \phi(x)$ for all $x \in X$ and all $k \geq 0$
- property (6) is a special case of [1][Lemma 4.31] which (renamed) entails that $G(g_1)(x) = G(g_2)(x)$ for all $x \in X$ and all functions g_1, g_2, from which we for $x \in X$ infer $\gamma(x) = G(\gamma)(x) = G(\gamma'_0)(x) = \gamma'_1(x)$
- property (2) follows from the calculation in [1][Proof of Theorem 6.6], except that we need to *rectify* [1][Lemma 6.13]. That lemma claims that a certain sequence of reals is a chain; this is not necessarily the case, but (as shown in Appendix A) still the sequence will have a limit, and that is sufficient to establish property (2).

11 The Intuition Behind the Exclusion Set

In our application, where the source control-flow graph of Fig. 2 is transformed into the target control-flow graph of Fig. 3. rather than paths from start to end along which b becomes true, thus causing the value of q at end to be 0.

- For the target program (Fig. 3), the only such path is the one that takes the upper branch. That path has no loops and hence the fixed point (which assigns $q = 0$ the probability $\frac{1}{2}$) is reached already in the first iteration, as can be seen by comparing the first row of Table 5 with the first row of Table 3.
- On the other hand, for the source program (Fig. 2), there are denumerably many such paths; all will follow the upper branch but one path will not loop, another path will loop once, another path will loop twice, etc. Hence the fixed point (which assigns $q = 0$ the probability $\frac{1}{4}$) is reached only in the limit of the iterations, as can be seen by comparing the first row of Table 4 with the first row of Table 2.

We conclude that source iteration and target iteration get out of lockstep, which is why we cannot establish the correctness relation between the iterands.

Our approach is to let the iteration on the source program start with the parts in the exclusion set X already at their fixed point. This is accomplished by ensuring that if (u, u') in X then no path from u to u' has loops. Recall (7) that with u_p the node that increments p we have $(u_p, \text{end}) \in X$. And indeed, no path from u_p to end has loops in the control-flow graph in Fig. 5, as we put skip at node u_p and at its successor.

As a consequence, the revised iterands of the source program (Table 6) are in lockstep with the iterands of the target program (Table 5), with each iterand of the source being $\frac{1}{2}$ of the corresponding iterand of the target.

---

[2] [1] uses "ω" for what the current paper calls "ϕ", uses "γ" for "ϕ'", uses "ϕ" for "γ", uses "Φ" for "γ'", uses "H_V" for "F", and uses "H_Q" for "G".

12 Perspectives

We have distilled a proof technique that in at least one (recently published) situation [1] comes to the rescue when the standard technique falls short. We conjecture that other applications exist, and encourage the discovery of such.

More generally, while we were surprised that we had to begin the fixed point iteration above the bottom element, we believe it likely that other researchers have encountered and reported similar situations, though so far we have not come across it in our literature search.

We offer this paper as a tribute to Alan Mycroft who has inspired the authors since early in their careers, by his kindness and enthusiasm, and his work on program analysis where the computation of fixed points is ubiquitous.

Acknowledgments. We thank the anonymous reviewers for their comments which in various ways helped improve the presentation of the paper, and also thank Patrick Cousot for looking into our findings. Banerjee's research is based on work supported by the National Science Foundation (NSF), while working at the Foundation. Any opinions, findings, and conclusions or recommendations expressed in this paper are those of the authors and do not necessarily reflect the views of the NSF.

A Rectifying Lemma 6.13 in [1]

We shall refer to the setting of [1], where $\mathcal{U}$ is the set of pairs (v, v') such that v' postdominates v, and D is the set of probability distributions. With $c_{k,D}^{v,v'}$ a real number as defined in Definition 6.10, we shall replace Lemma 6.13 by the following result:

> **Lemma 6.13, restated.** Assume $\{D_k \mid k \geq 0\}$ is a chain in D, and that $\{f_k \mid k \geq 0\}$ is a chain of functions in $\mathsf{D} \rightarrow_c \mathsf{D}$.
> Then for all $(v, v') \in \mathcal{U}$, the limit $lim_{k\rightarrow\infty}\, c_{k,f_k(D_k)}^{v,v'}$ does exist.

Observe that as a special case, with each f_k the identity and each D_k equal D, we have

For all $(v, v') \in \mathcal{U}$ and $D \in \mathsf{D}$, there does exist a real number c such that

$$lim_{k\rightarrow\infty}\, c_{k,D}^{v,v'} = c$$

which suffices to prove Theorem 6.6, stating the correctness of slicing in [1].

We shall prove the restated Lemma 6.13 by induction in the maximum length of an acyclic path from v to v', where two cases are non-trivial; in each we let v'' denote the first proper postdominator of v:

- Assume $v' \neq v$ and $v' \neq v''$. We can inductively assume that there exists c'', c' such that

$$\begin{aligned} lim_{k\to\infty}\, c^{v,v''}_{k,f_k(D_k)} &= c'' \\ lim_{k\to\infty}\, c^{v'',v'}_{k,\gamma_k^{(v,v'')}(f_k(D_k))} &= c' \end{aligned}$$

but then

$$lim_{k\to\infty}\, c^{v,v'}_{k,f_k(D_k)} = lim_{k\to\infty}\, (c^{v,v''}_{k,f_k(D_k)} \cdot c^{v'',v'}_{k,\gamma_k^{(v,v'')}(f_k(D_k))}) = c'' \cdot c'.$$

- Assume $v' = v''$ but v does not stay outside Q_0 until v'.
Since $\{f_k(D_k) \mid k \geq 0\}$ and $\{\gamma_k^{(v,v')}(f_k(D_k)) \mid k \geq 0\}$ are chains in the cpo D, there exists D_1 and D_2 such that

$$\begin{aligned} lim_{k\to\infty}\, f_k(D_k) &= D_1 \\ lim_{k\to\infty}\, \gamma_k^{(v,v')}(f_k(D_k)) &= D_2. \end{aligned}$$

By Lemma 4.1 we see that

$$\begin{aligned} lim_{k\to\infty}\, (\sum f_k(D_k)) &= \sum D_1 \\ lim_{k\to\infty}\, (\sum \gamma_k^{(v,v')}(f_k(D_k))) &= \sum D_2. \end{aligned}$$

If $D_1 = 0$ we for all k have $f_k(D_k) = 0$ and thus $c^{v,v'}_{k,f_k(D_k)} = 1$ making the claim trivial. We can thus assume that $D_1 \neq 0$, in which case we see that

$$lim_{k\to\infty}\, c^{v,v'}_{k,f_k(D_k)} = lim_{k\to\infty} \frac{\sum \gamma_k^{(v,v')}(f_k(D_k))}{\sum f_k(D_k)} = \frac{\sum D_2}{\sum D_1}$$

which yields the claim.
But observe that while $\{c^{v,v'}_{k,f_k(D_k)} \mid k \geq 0\}$ has a limit, we apparently have no assurance it is a chain (it is rather a *ratio* between two chains) and thus the original Lemma 6.13 makes an unwarranted claim.

References

1. Amtoft, T., Banerjee, A.: A theory of slicing for imperative probabilistic programs. ACM Trans. Program. Lang. Syst. **42**(2) (2020). https://doi.org/10.1145/3372895
2. Danicic, S., Barraclough, R.W., Harman, M., Howroyd, J.D., Kiss, Á., Laurence, M.R.: A unifying theory of control dependence and its application to arbitrary program structures. Theoret. Comput. Sci. **412**(49), 6809–6842 (2011). https://doi.org/10.1016/j.tcs.2011.08.033
3. Gordon, A.D., Henzinger, T.A., Nori, A.V., Rajamani, S.K.: Probabilistic programming. In: Future of Software Engineering Proceedings, pp. 167—-181. FOSE 2014, Association for Computing Machinery, New York, NY, USA (2014). https://doi.org/10.1145/2593882.2593900
4. Kozen, D.: Semantics of probabilistic programs. J. Comput. Syst. Sci. **22**(3), 328–350 (1981). https://doi.org/10.1016/0022-0000(81)90036-2
5. Winskel, G.: The Formal Semantics of Programming Languages. MIT Press, Cambridge, MA, USA (1993). https://doi.org/10.7551/mitpress/3054.001.0001

On Graded Coeffect Types for Information-Flow Control

Vilem-Benjamin Liepelt[1(✉)], Danielle Marshall[1,3], Dominic Orchard[1,2], Vineet Rajani[1], and Michael Vollmer[1]

[1] University of Kent, Canterbury, UK
mail@vilem.net
[2] University of Cambridge, Cambridge, UK
[3] University of Glasgow, Glasgow, UK

Abstract. Graded types are an overarching paradigm that provides fine-grained reasoning by reflecting the structure of typing rules into a system of type annotations. A significant subset of graded type systems is that of *coeffect systems*, originally introduced by Petricek, Orchard, and Mycroft as a dual to effect systems, capturing the dataflow of values in a calculus by annotating variables and function types with elements of a semiring. A particularly useful instance of these graded coeffect systems is to capture security properties of data to enforce information-flow control. We examine this particular use case and give a new characterisation of a subclass of semirings which enable the key non-interference theorem of information-flow control: that less privileged observers are unable to distinguish the dependence of computations on more privileged inputs. The result relies on a logical relations proof and is mechanised in Agda. We consider its relationship to other characterisations of non-interference in the recent literature on graded types and in the historical context of coeffect and graded systems. We leverage these results for programming with security in the Granule programming language, a research language for graded types. We conclude with extensions to Granule that go beyond non-interference to *declassification*, leveraging graded types to control deliberate information leakage.

1 Introduction

An important consideration in the design of a software system is how security is handled. A typical program has access to various data sources that must be kept secret. Therefore, it is vital that such a program carefully manage data that comes from secret inputs, ensuring that the data only flows to corresponding secret outputs. A program that fails to manage this correctly can leak secret data and is said to violate *confidentiality*. To guarantee this does not happen, a system designer may choose to enforce some security policy, but how?

A well-studied method for ensuring that programs obey a specified security policy is *Information Flow Control* (IFC) [28]. IFC is a form of dependence analysis, which ensures that secret inputs do not flow to public outputs, whether

D. Orchard et al. (Eds.): Alan Mycroft Festschrift, LNCS 15500, pp. 114–148, 2026.
https://doi.org/10.1007/978-3-032-08187-2_7

this be through bug or malice. In a language-based setting, aspects of IFC can be achieved statically [1] or dynamically [28]. IFC analyses typically associate *labels* (secrecy annotations) to data, tracking these labels through a program's data and control flow.

For example, consider a function with two integer inputs that computes a pair, the first component of which is an arithmetic expression over both inputs and the second component is just the first input:

$$\texttt{process} = \lambda x.\lambda y.(x + y, x)$$

A static IFC type system might then permit the following type specification for this function, where the first input has been annotated as low security (public) and the second as high security (secret) and thus the first component of the pair is high security, and the second component is low security:

$$\texttt{process} : \texttt{Integer}^{\mathsf{Lo}} \rightarrow \texttt{Integer}^{\mathsf{Hi}} \rightarrow (\texttt{Integer}^{\mathsf{Hi}} * \texttt{Integer}^{\mathsf{Lo}})$$

Such a system would disallow a typing of the output pair that has both components marked as low security as this would constitute a potential leak of the first input. In this work we focus on using types for IFC analysis, in particular using the framework of *coeffect-and-type systems* whose notation differs to the above example, but which captures the same fundamental ideas.

Coeffect-and-type systems (hereafter *coeffect systems* for brevity) were proposed by Petricek, Orchard, and Mycroft as a dual to effect systems [52,53], providing a general type-based analysis of context dependence in programs. Later work brought effect and coeffect systems under the umbrella of *graded type systems* [21]. In general, graded type systems provide a principled approach for analysing programs by augmenting a base type system with annotations (called *grades*) consisting of some algebraic structure which reflects aspects of the underlying system (such as semantic structure or proof structure). They can be used to reason about a variety of program properties [46], including IFC as first suggested by Petricek, Orchard, and Mycroft [52].

Most of the prior work on graded type theories for IFC is in the *effect* style (e.g., Abdadi et al.'s DCC [1]). The idea is to prevent information leaks by constraining the *outputs* that can be produced by a given program. This is often implemented using a graded monad to track the flow of information with security labels as the grades. However, there is also a less explored dual approach, which achieves IFC in the *coeffect* style via a graded comonad. The idea here is to protect information leaks by constraining the *inputs* that can be fed to a given program. In this style, grades are typically drawn from a semiring (or semiring-like structure), capturing dataflow. Prior works [2,18,21,43] have proposed instantiating a semiring-graded system with a lattice of security labels to capture information-flow for the purpose of data security properties. We examine this use case in detail and propose that there is a more general class of semirings which can be used for IFC and which enforce the crucial non-interference property: that less privileged observers cannot distinguish the dependence of a computation on more privileged inputs.

We begin with a tour through the history and development of coeffect systems, starting with the work of Alan Mycroft and his students, joining together various threads from the literature culminating in the general graded types paradigm (Sect. 2). From this historical narrative, we define a core graded coeffect calculus, called GrBase, based on the structural coeffect systems of Petricek, Orchard, and Mycroft [53], but reformulated within the context of the last decade of developments in graded types (Sect. 3). This captures the essential core of many systems in the literature discussed in Sect. 2. We then define a logical-relation-based semantic model for GrBase and use this to prove non-interference for a general class of pre-ordered semirings with some additional axioms which we call *non-interfering semirings* (Sect. 4). This serves to clarify a minimal set of constraints that need to hold of a coeffect analysis to enforce the key IFC property of non-interference. Our result is formalised in Agda.[1] The mechanisation covers the entire relational model for the graded type system and its non-interference result, but admits as postulates some basic results about substitution and strong normalisation that have been proved elsewhere in the literature for such systems.

Section 5 demonstrates an in-depth practical example of coeffect-based IFC using the functional programming language Granule,[2] where we have implemented these ideas. Section 6 concludes with a discussion of the related work of other approaches to information-flow typing and graded types. We also consider extensions to *declassification* (controlled leakage), outside of our non-interference result, and how graded types can be used to control information leakage.

2 The Road to Graded Coeffects

We define in Sect. 3 a core calculus with a graded type system for tracking coeffects given by a pre-ordered semiring structure. This system has arisen independently in a few forms and from a few different starting points, but, most notably for this festschrift, first due to Alan Mycroft and his students. We begin by giving a recap of the history and an overview of this space.

2.1 Coeffects as Dual to Effect Systems

In a 2013 ICALP paper *Coeffects: Unified static analysis of context-dependence*, Petricek, Orchard, and Mycroft initiated a programme of work studying a general type-based framework for analysis of *context dependence* in programs [52].

The central idea is that there is a sensible dualisation of the type-and-effect systems (hereafter *effect systems*) of Gifford and Lucassen [24,36]. This dualisation yields a useful and flexible system for tracking program properties relating to how a program uses its context. The work builds on the close connections between effect systems and monads, fleshed out by Wadler and Thiemann [67]:

[1] https://github.com/granule-project/security-coeffects-mechanization.
[2] https://github.com/granule-project/granule.

for an effect judgment $\Gamma \vdash t : A, F$ describing that program t produces (at most) side effects F (where F is a member of a semilattice) then there is a translation to an equivalent judgment in a monadic meta-language $[\![\Gamma]\!] \vdash_M [\![t]\!] : M_F[\![A]\!]$ where the monadic type constructor M is annotated by the effect information F. The following two rules capture the composition of side effectful computations whilst concordantly composing the effect information in types:

$$\frac{\Gamma \vdash_M t : A}{\Gamma \vdash_M \mathsf{return}\ t : M_\bot A}\text{RET} \qquad \frac{\Gamma \vdash_M t_1 : M_F A \qquad \Gamma, x : A \vdash_M t_2 : M_G B}{\Gamma \vdash_M \mathsf{do}\ x \leftarrow t_1; t_2 : M_{F \vee G} B}\text{BIND}$$

Later work formalises this "annotated" monad structure M_F as the more general notion of *graded monads* [33,50]. (Mycroft et al. later generalised this further, considering in depth the paradigm of capturing effects via grading [44]).

From this starting point of the relationship between effects and monads, the ICALP 2013 paper sought to find the corresponding annotated type system for *comonads*, which were gaining in popularity for structuring notions of context dependence in semantics [14,62], computational logic [7,11,12] (by former PhD students of Alan), and programming [48,49,60,61], amongst others.

The result of that paper is a general type-and-coeffect system (hereafter *coeffect system*) with judgments of the form [52]:

$$C^S \Gamma \vdash t : A$$

capturing that for a program t of type A, alongside the usual free variables Γ, the program also requires (at least) the 'context' S (with C merely representing a syntactical anchor for the comonadic denotational model) where S is drawn from a lattice $\mathcal{S}$ with additional monoid structure $(\otimes, 1)$.[3] Key typing rules:

$$\frac{x : A \in \Gamma}{C^1 \Gamma \vdash x : A}\text{VAR} \qquad \frac{C^{R \wedge S}(\Gamma, x : A) \vdash t : B}{C^R \Gamma \vdash \lambda x.t : C^S A \to B}\text{ABS}$$
$$\frac{C^R \Gamma \vdash t_1 : C^S A \to B \quad C^T \Gamma \vdash t_2 : A}{C^{R \vee (S \otimes T)} \Gamma \vdash t_1\ t_2 : B}\text{APP}$$

The (VAR) rule describes that using a variable amounts to some usage of the context denoted by the $1 \in \mathcal{S}$ element. Reading top-down, the (ABS) rule says that the context-dependence of a function's body can be split between the 'call site' by capturing the dependence S on the function arrow (written $C^S A \to B$) leaving the remaining requirements R to be made at the 'definition site'. Reading bottom-up, the (ABS) says that the context *available* to a function is a combination of the current context R and the context provided by the function argument S. The (APP) rule then shows how these requirements/capabilities come together when applying a function, using the monoidal $\otimes$ to combine the context T of the argument t_2 with the requirements S of the function t_1.

The paper gives various examples, including one using sets of labels to capture resources required from the context, e.g., hardware devices or global variables,

[3] The ICALP 2013 paper actually uses $\oplus$ and e as its syntax for the monoidal part of the coeffect algebra structure, but thinking of this monoid in multiplicative terms fits better with the literature that came after.

with $\mathcal{S} = \mathcal{P}(resources)$. The usual lattice of sets and monoid $\otimes = \cup$ and $1 = \emptyset$ is used with a primitive for accessing resources $C^{\{?\mathsf{a}\}}\Gamma \vdash ?\mathsf{a} : \rho$. For example:

$$C^{\{?\mathsf{gps},?\mathsf{compass}\}} \ldots \vdash (\lambda c.\ \mathit{locate}?\mathsf{gps}\ c)?\mathsf{compass} : \ldots$$

An interactive web-based essay by Tomas Petricek (Alan's student at the time) provides a playground exploring this example and others,[4] and Petricek's PhD thesis discusses 'systems capabilities as coeffects' in more detail [51].

This line of work has been picked up by several practical programming languages. One example of this is Hack, via its *contexts and capabilities* [59].

The paper then develops a categorical semantics which introduces the notion of *indexed comonads* which, in modern terminology, are known as *graded comonads* [21], dualising graded monads but with additional structure for managing the more complex structure of contexts.

A key aspect of the paper is that the system is general, parameterised by a coeffect algebra $\mathcal{S}$ which can then be instantiated to various interesting and useful analyses. The paper includes an example based on whether the entire free variable context Γ is used (live) or is unused (dead). The paper concludes by pointing out that it would be more useful in that case to track liveness of variables (whether they are 'relevant') on a *per variable* basis rather than *per context* and suggests the notion of a 'structural' coeffect system where coeffect annotations are formed out of finite products matching the structure of the context, e.g., with abstraction rule:

$$\frac{C^{R \times S}(\Gamma, x : A) \vdash t : B}{C^{R}\Gamma \vdash \lambda x.t : C^{S}A \to B}\text{ABS}'$$

These structural coeffects (which the present paper builds on in Sect. 3) then lend themselves to analysing how variables are used, separately to wider notions of context dependence which were the main focus of the ICALP 2013 paper. In this teasing of the more fine-grained structural coeffect system, the authors suggested that such a system could be used for tracking secure information flow along the lines of DCC [1], the topic of the present paper.

A follow-up paper at ICFP 2014, titled *Coeffects: A calculus of context-dependent computation* also by Petricek, Orchard, and Mycroft, builds a unified system in which both the ICALP 2013 'flat' (whole context) coeffects and structural (per variable) coeffects can be expressed as instances of a single system via a coeffect structure akin to a (shape-indexed) module over a semiring. We do not replay the full generality of the system here but briefly overview a subset specialised to the subclass of coeffect structures which encode structural coeffects. In this approach judgments have the form:

$$\Gamma @ R \vdash t : A$$

[4] https://tomasp.net/coeffects/.

where R is a vector $\langle r_1, \ldots, r_n \rangle$ of coeffect annotations $r_i \in \mathcal{R}$ drawn from a pre-ordered semiring[5] where $n = |\Gamma|$, i.e., the structure and shape of R matches the context. Selected key typing rules are then:

$$\frac{}{x : A @ \langle 1 \rangle \vdash x : A} \text{VAR}$$

$$\frac{\Gamma, x : A @ R \times \langle r \rangle \vdash t : B}{\Gamma @ R \vdash \lambda x.t : A \xrightarrow{r} B} \text{ABS} \qquad \frac{\Gamma_1 @ R \vdash t_1 : A \xrightarrow{r} B \quad \Gamma_2 @ S \vdash t_2 : A}{\Gamma_1, \Gamma_2 @ R \times (r * S) \vdash t_1\, t_2 : B} \text{APP}$$

$$\frac{\Gamma_1, y : B, z : B, \Gamma_2 @ R \times \langle s, t \rangle \times Q \vdash t : A}{\Gamma_1, x : B, \Gamma_2 @ R \times \langle s + t \rangle \times Q \vdash [x/z][x/y]t : A} \text{CONTR} \qquad \frac{\Gamma @ R \vdash t : A}{\Gamma, x : B @ R \times \langle 0 \rangle \vdash t : A} \text{WEAK}$$

The (VAR) rule now annotates a singleton context with a singleton vector using the multiplicative unit $1 \in \mathcal{R}$ of the semiring to denote usage. The (ABS) splits off the coeffect for the variable being bound, where the syntax is now $A \xrightarrow{r} B$ for a function which uses its input according to r (rather than $C^r A \to B$ as in the ICALP 2013 paper). The (APP) rule composes two disjoint contexts but scales the requirements of S for the argument by the coeffect of the function r, where the semiring's multiplication is lifted to a scalar multiplication of a coeffect vector by a coeffect. Lastly, the (CONTR) and (WEAK) rules provide contraction and weakening using the additive part of the semiring. A somewhat similar approach will be used and explained in more detail in the present paper.

2.2 Coeffects as a Generalisation of Bounded Linear Logic

Independently to Petricek, Orchard, and Mycroft's ICALP 2013 paper, two very similar systems arose independently of each other in ESOP 2014 (by Ghica and Smith [23] and Brunel et al. [15]), coming from a different angle: generalising *bounded linear logic* (BLL), which is itself is a generalisation of linear logic.

Linear logic is a logic of *resources* in which propositions must be used exactly once, i.e., they cannot be discarded and cannot be copied [25]. A corresponding system of linear types can then be used to control data as a resource [66]; for example, to enforce stateful protocols, e.g., that a file handle is opened, read from and written to, then closed once and never accessed again after [68]. Non-linearity is provided by the !-modality (pronounced 'of course' or 'bang') which gives a binary view, delineating linear and non-linear propositions or values. Bounded Linear Logic (BLL) refines the binary view, replacing ! with a *family* of indexed modal operators $!_r$ where the index r provides an upper bound on usage [26], e.g., $!_4 A$ represents a value A which may be used up to 4 times.

[5] In fact, the ICFP 2014 paper refers to this as the *coeffect scalar* structure $\mathcal{R}$ which comprises a pair of monoids with distributive laws between them but does not mention the need for 0 (called ign in ICFP 2014) to be absorbing or that + is commutative, however the paper points to the proofs in the thesis of Orchard which explains additional axioms which are required of the coeffect scalar in order for subject reduction/type preservation to hold [47] albeit on a slightly different presentation of the structure. The modern rendering in terms of semiring is more clear.

Dal Lago and Gaboardi applied linear typing to PCF with BLL-style modalities indexed by usage bounds which could depend on type-level natural number indices [20, 34]. Observing that the natural number terms form a semiring and the system can be usefully generalised to arbitrary semirings, this approach was generalised by Brunel, Gaboardi, Mazza, and Zdancewic in an ESOP 2014 paper *A Core Quantitative Coeffect Calculus* [15]. The work was developed independently of the work on coeffects, but the authors discovered the terminology of coeffects towards the end of their project[6] and so helpfully worked that terminology into their description of the system.

The core system has typing contexts which can contain both linear variables and non-linear variables, which are marked with an element of a semiring. A dual-calculus style presentation is possible, splitting the contexts, though the ESOP 2014 work combined these into a single context syntax. A family of modal operators $\Box_r A$ where r is drawn from the semiring is then used to internalise the coeffect information, with the following subset of its typing rules:

$$\frac{}{x : A \vdash x : A}\text{var} \quad \frac{\Gamma, x : A \vdash t : B}{\Gamma \vdash \lambda x.t : A \multimap B}\text{abs} \quad \frac{\Gamma \vdash t_1 : A \multimap B \quad \Delta \vdash t_2 : A}{\Gamma + \Delta \vdash t_1\ t_2 : B}\text{app}$$

$$\frac{\Gamma, x : A \vdash x : A}{\Gamma, x : [A]_1 \vdash x : A}\text{der} \quad \frac{\Gamma \vdash t : A}{r * \Gamma \vdash [t] : \Box_r A}\text{pr}$$

The variable and abstraction rules are standard for linear type systems. The application rule is also standard but includes a context addition operation that is undefined if the contexts are not disjoint in their linear assumptions and which adds together (using the semiring addition) the coeffects of any non-linear variable assumptions that appear in both contexts. The 'dereliction' rule (der) links linearity with coeffects, marking a linear assumption with 1 of the semiring. The 'promotion' rule (pr) then introduces a coeffect-graded modality at grade r, requiring that the inputs are also scaled by r (and implicitly that the context contains no linear variables).

Independently to the work of Brunel et al., another paper appeared at the very same ESOP (2014) proposing essentially the same idea: Ghica and Smith provided a generalisation of BLL in their paper *Bounded Linear Types in a Resource Semiring* [23]. Whilst they explicitly generalise BLL, the calculus presented does not provide a base notion of linearity. Instead, similarly to structural coeffects, every assumption is associated with an element of a semiring and the function type always has a semiring element associated with its input (in their case written as $(J.A) \multimap B$ for semiring element J, calling back to the linear logic roots at least via the appearance of $\multimap$). The resulting system has very similar expressivity and power to that of Brunel et al., with 1 of the semiring denoting usage, 0 denoting discarding, multiplication for composition and addition for contraction. Ghica and Smith give a particularly interesting use case for coeffects for capturing 'hardware schedules' in circuit synthesis.

[6] Personal communication.

2.3 The Graded Types Paradigm and Further Systems

In summary, the notion of coeffects as a semiring (or semiring-like) type-based analysis of how a program depends on its variables arose independently as both a generalisation of effects (ICALP 2013, 2014) and a generalisation of bounded linear logic (ESOP 2014, two independent papers).

At ICFP 2016, Gaboardi et al. went on to generalise the ESOP 2014 paper of Brunel et al., using now the terminology of *grading*, providing a linear logic with a *graded comonadic* modality (essentially like the system of Brunel et al.) but also adding graded monads for tracking effects and (graded) distributive laws for capturing effect-coeffect interaction [21]. One of the examples given in their work is a graded comonad with a two-point lattice of 'high' and 'low' security markers for tracking security as a coeffect. This is the first such instance actually showing the details of using coeffects for security, following the cursory mention by Petricek, Orchard, and Mycroft in ICALP 2013. However, the example was not developed to the point of proving non-interference, though the categorical semantics captures the idea implicitly.

Following this calculus with graded monads and comonads, Orchard et al. presented an implementation of the Gaboardi et al.'s work as a functional programming language, called Granule, extended with polymorphism and GADTs [46]. The language has served as a research vehicle for exploring the applications of graded type systems, including for example program synthesis [30–32] and capturing uniqueness and borrowing for mutable structures [38,40]. The paper proposes the general paradigm of *graded modal types*, encompassing both graded comonadic types for coeffects, graded monadic types for effects, and suggesting there may be other flavours of graded modality. The general paradigm is that

> "graded modal types carry information about the semantic structure of programs, and along with a suitably expressive type system, provide a mechanism for specifying and verifying properties not captured by existing type systems" [46].

Various other works have since proposed related general systems or have deployed such systems. For example, Abel and Bernardy give a general characterisation of semiring-graded type systems (similar to structural coffects but also with an added graded modality) and study in detail its semantic models [2]. They consider information-flow control as a key application and prove a non-interference result, which we discuss in this paper in more detail in Sect. 4.

As a notable application of graded types, GHC Haskell now provides linear types as an extension, the implementation of which uses a structural coeffect system, providing a way to describe linear typing via a $\{0, 1, \omega\}$ ("none, one, tons") semiring [8].

Lastly, coeffect-like grading has also been a subject of much study in the context of dependent types. Notably, McBride proposed a dependent type theory with coeffects for tracking whether values are used or not as a way of reconciling linear and dependent types [41]. The system was refined by Atkey under the name Quantitative Type Theory (QTT) [6], which has then become the basis for the Idris 2 implementation [13]. Several other dependent type systems have then included graded types for capturing coeffects, including GRAD [18], Graded Modal Dependent Type Theory (GrTT) [43], and a similar fully formalised version by Abel et al. with universes and erasure properties [3].

Our focus here is on simple and polymorphic type systems, rather than dependent type theories; applying the ideas here to a more powerful dependent type theory is further work.

2.4 Linear Base Versus Graded Base

As seen, there has been a proliferation in graded type systems, particularly focusing on coeffects, in the last decade. A common theme is the use of a (preordered) semiring to structure the coeffect analysis. There are two dominant styles of system that have emerged in this vein: those which take linear logic as a basis and those which do not. In the former case ("linear base"), contexts comprise a mixture of linear assumptions and graded assumptions, function types are linear functions $\multimap$, and a graded modality $\Box_r$ internalises the grading from the context. Such systems include the ESOP 2014 system of Brunel et al. [15], the ICFP 2016 system of Gaboardi et al. [21], and Granule [46]. In the latter case ("graded base"), coeffect information is pervasive: every typing assumption has a grade, function types are annotated with a grade describing the input use, and the inclusion of a graded modality is optional (though useful for flexibility). Such systems include the original coeffect systems of Petricek, Orchard, and Mycroft [47,52], the ESOP 2014 system of Ghica and Smith [23], the general system of Abel and Bernardy [2], and the dependent type systems mentioned above. Recent theoretical work by Vollmer et al. has illustrated the relationship between these two styles more closely, by showing that there is a mutual embedding between the two approaches in their system [63].

The main differences between the types and contexts of linear vs. graded base systems can be summarised as follows:

(linear base)	(graded base)
$A ::= \Box_r A \mid A \multimap B$ $\Gamma ::= \emptyset \mid \Gamma, x : A \mid \Gamma, x : [A]_r$	$A ::= \Box_r A \mid A^r \rightarrow B$ $\Gamma ::= \emptyset \mid \Gamma, x :_r A$

Linear base has two kinds of assumptions (linear and graded) and a linear arrow; graded base has one kind of assumption (graded) with a graded function arrow.

It has recently been shown that both styles are equally expressive, i.e. any linear base term can be emulated in graded base and vice versa [35]. In this work, we continue in the graded base style, used in the early coeffect systems, using this as our basis for a core calculus in which we can then study IFC via coeffects.

3 A Core Graded Coeffect Calculus

Following the approaches described in the previous section, we focus on GrBase, a minimal core calculus in the style of Petricek, Orchard, and Mycroft's structural coeffect system [53], but using the language and terminology of grades. We thus describe our system as having *graded coeffects* structured by a *pre-ordered semiring*: grades are associated to every free variable in the context and track how it is used, with a graded function type to describe how the input is used. Thus there is no base notion of linearity as found in systems building directly from the linear logic tradition (i.e., [15,21]), but we do include explicit graded modalities for internalising grades into types separately to functions as this allows more flexibility. As discussed in the previous section this style of core calculus is becoming routine and appears in various works now in slightly different forms [2,8,18,23,41,53,69].

We supplement the presentation of GrBase with real examples written in the Granule programming language. (Real, in the sense that they are embedded in the source of this paper such that they can be type checked by the Granule system.) As mentioned in Sect. 2.4, Granule, by default, represents a linear base system. However, it can be run in graded base mode via the `language GradedBase` pragma, which we are doing for this paper, as this makes Granule a strict superset of GrBase. Granule features a rich pattern language and equational-style function definitions with syntax similar to Haskell's.

3.1 Syntax and Typing

The syntax of GrBase is essentially that of the λ-calculus extended with a graded necessity modality and products (along with their unit), and booleans (for control flow). The syntax of types is:

$$A ::= \quad A \otimes B \mid \mathsf{Unit} \mid \mathbb{B} \mid A^r \rightarrow B \mid \Box_r A \qquad (\textit{types})$$

Types comprise products, units, booleans, graded functions $A^r \rightarrow B$, and a graded modality $\Box_r A$. The calculus is parameterised by a pre-ordered semiring $(\mathcal{R}, \cdot, 1, +, 0, \leq)$ where $\cdot$ and $+$ are monotonic with respect to the pre-order $\leq$. For function types, a grade $r \in \mathcal{R}$ is associated with the input type, describing the usage of the input within the inhabiting function. The graded modality $\Box_r A$ captures a *capability* to use a value typed A according to grade $r \in \mathcal{R}$.

The syntax of GrBase is as follows (explained later with reference to typing):

$$\begin{aligned} t ::= \;& \underbrace{x \mid t_1\, t_2 \mid \lambda x.t}_{\lambda\text{-calculus}} \mid \underbrace{[t] \mid \mathsf{let}\,[x] = t_1\, \mathsf{in}\, t_2}_{\text{graded modality}} \qquad (\textit{terms}) \\ & \mid \underbrace{(t_1, t_2) \mid \mathsf{let}\ (x, y) = t_1\ \mathsf{in}\ t_2}_{\text{products}} \mid \underbrace{() \mid \mathsf{let}\ () = t_1\ \mathsf{in}\ t_2}_{\text{unit}} \\ & \mid \underbrace{\mathtt{ff} \mid \mathtt{tt} \mid \mathsf{if}\ t_1\ \mathsf{then}\ t_2\ \mathsf{else}\ t_3}_{\text{booleans}} \end{aligned}$$

Typing is via judgments $\Gamma \vdash t : A$, assigning a type A to term t under the context Γ. Every free variable type assumption in Γ has an associated semiring element called its *grade*:

$$\Gamma ::= \emptyset \mid \Gamma, x :_r A$$

The order of assumptions in contexts is not relevant, i.e., contexts can be arbitrarily reordered.

$$\frac{}{0 \cdot \Gamma, x :_1 A \vdash x : A}\ \textsc{Var} \qquad \frac{\Gamma, x :_r A \vdash t : B}{\Gamma \vdash \lambda x.t : A^r \to B}\ \textsc{Abs}$$

$$\frac{\Gamma_1 \vdash t_1 : A^r \to B \qquad \Gamma_2 \vdash t_2 : A}{\Gamma_1 + r \cdot \Gamma_2 \vdash t_1\, t_2 : B}\ \textsc{App} \qquad \frac{\Gamma, x :_r A, \Gamma' \vdash t : B \qquad s \leq r}{\Gamma, x :_s A, \Gamma' \vdash t : B}\ \textsc{Approx}$$

$$\frac{\Gamma \vdash t : A}{r \cdot \Gamma \vdash [t] : \Box_r A}\ \textsc{Pr} \qquad \frac{\Gamma_1 \vdash t_1 : \Box_r A \qquad \Gamma_2, x :_r A \vdash t_2 : B}{\Gamma_1 + \Gamma_2 \vdash \mathsf{let}\, [x] = t_1\, \mathsf{in}\, t_2 : B}\ \textsc{BoxElim}$$

$$\frac{\Gamma_1 \vdash t_1 : A \qquad \Gamma_2 \vdash t_2 : B}{\Gamma_1 + \Gamma_2 \vdash (t_1, t_2) : A \otimes B}\ \textsc{PairIntro}$$

$$\frac{\Gamma_1 \vdash t_1 : A_1 \otimes A_2 \qquad \Gamma_2, x : A_1, y : A_2 \vdash t_2 : B}{\Gamma_1 + \Gamma_2 \vdash \mathsf{let}\ (x, y) = t_1\ \mathsf{in}\ t_2 : B}\ \textsc{PairElim}$$

$$\frac{}{0 \cdot \Gamma \vdash () : \mathsf{Unit}}\ \textsc{UnitIntro} \qquad \frac{\Gamma_1 \vdash t_1 : \mathsf{Unit} \qquad \Gamma_2 \vdash t_2 : B}{\Gamma_1 + \Gamma_2 \vdash \mathsf{let}\ () = t_1\ \mathsf{in}\ t_2 : B}\ \textsc{UnitElim}$$

$$\frac{}{0 \cdot \Gamma \vdash \mathtt{tt} : \mathbb{B}}\ \textsc{True} \qquad \frac{}{0 \cdot \Gamma \vdash \mathtt{ff} : \mathbb{B}}\ \textsc{False}$$

$$\frac{\Gamma_1 \vdash t_1 : \mathbb{B} \qquad \Gamma_2 \vdash t_2 : A \qquad \Gamma_2 \vdash t_3 : A \qquad r \leq 1}{(r \cdot \Gamma_1) + \Gamma_2 \vdash \mathsf{if}\ t_1\ \mathsf{then}\ t_2\ \mathsf{else}\ t_3 : A}\ \textsc{If}$$

Fig. 1. Typing rules for GRBASE. Regarding the direction of the ordering in APPROX, note Remark 1.

Figure 1 provides the typing rules. The VAR rule accounts for the use of a particular variable, annotated via the grade $1 \in \mathcal{R}$ meaning it has been used. The remaining variables in the context are all graded 0, provided by scaling Γ by 0 and the semiring property that 0 is absorbing. *Scalar multiplication* is defined:

Definition 1 (Scalar context multiplication). *For all r, Γ then $r \cdot \Gamma$ is defined by induction on Γ:*

$$r \cdot \emptyset = \emptyset$$
$$r \cdot (\Gamma, x :_s A) = (r \cdot \Gamma), x :_{r \cdot s} A$$

In the conclusion of the application rule we also see the use of scalar context multiplication where $r \cdot \Gamma_2$ scales the grades of Γ_2 by r to account for the usage of the argument t_2 by the function t_1.

The ABS rule is standard modulo capturing of the assumption's grade r onto the function arrow (the *latent coeffect* [53]). The APP rule shows a key principle of combining the typing contexts for subterms using the *context addition* operation $\Gamma + \Gamma'$ which is used in the typing rules any time the contexts of two subterms need to be combined, applying semiring addition on the grades of variables occurring in each context:

Definition 2 (Pointwise context addition). *For all Γ_1, Γ_2 of the same shape (where the shape of a context is the list of variable-type assumptions),* context addition *is defined recursively as:*

$$\emptyset + \emptyset = \emptyset$$
$$(\Gamma, x :_r A) + (\Gamma', x :_s A) = (\Gamma + \Gamma'), x :_{r+s} A$$

Example 1. A classic example is the semiring of natural numbers $\mathbb{N}$ with the multiplicative and additive parts provided by multiplication and addition on naturals. Taking the ordering to be equality (i.e. $\leq$ is defined as $\equiv$), we obtain an analysis of exact usage, meaning that, the graded modalities 'count' how many times, exactly, a variable is referenced.

For example, the following typing derivation fragment shows the role of multiplicative scaling to account for how many times a variable is used:

$$\dfrac{\dfrac{\emptyset \vdash (\lambda y.(y, y)) : (A \otimes A)^2 \to (A \otimes A) \otimes (A \otimes A) \qquad x :_2 A \vdash (x, x) : A \otimes A}{x :_4 A \vdash (\lambda y.(y, y))\,(x, x) : (A \otimes A) \otimes (A \otimes A)}\ \textsc{App}}{\emptyset \vdash \lambda x.(\lambda y.(y, y))\,(x, x) : A^4 \to (A \otimes A) \otimes (A \otimes A)}\ \textsc{Abs}$$

Thus the type of the innermost function $\lambda y.(y, y)$ captures that its input its used twice; the type of (x, x) captures that x is used twice; the application $(\lambda y.(y, y))\,(x, x)$ therefore is typed with x graded at 4 due to multiplication.

In Granule, graded function types $A^r \to B$ are written as `A % r → B`, where `r` is of kind coeffect. This syntax is reminiscent of Linear Haskell and becomes available in Granule through the `language GradedBase` pragma.

We capture an example in Granule similar to the above (but β-reduced) as the following polymorphic function:

```
quad : ∀ {a : Type}. a \% 4 → ((a, a), (a, a))
quad x = ((x, x), (x, x))            -- o.k.
```

The next (non)example has an incorrect type, showing that for discrete naturals, we cannot over-approximate the usage:

```
quad_bad : ∀ {a : Type}. a \% 5 → ((a, a), (a, a))
quad_bad x = ((x, x), (x, x))        -- type error!
```

Graded modalities are introduced by 'promotion' (TyPr), scaling graded assumptions in Γ via scalar multiplication. Graded modalities are eliminated by $\mathsf{let}\,[x] = t_1\ \mathsf{in}\ t_2$ connecting the graded modal box at r in the type of t_1 with an assumption of grade r in the free variable context of t_2.

Example 2. The grade on function types is rather coarse grained: it summarises how the *entire* input is used. In the case of a compound type, e.g. products, we may want more fine-grained information about how each subpart is used, for which we can use the graded modality. For example, to define first projection on pairs we use the graded modality at grade 0 for the unused second component:

$$\dfrac{\dfrac{}{z :_1 A \otimes \Box_0 B \vdash z : A \otimes \Box_0 B}\ \textsc{Var} \qquad \dfrac{\dfrac{}{y :_1 \Box_0 B \vdash y : \Box_0 B}\ \textsc{Var} \qquad \dfrac{}{x :_1 A, y' :_0 B \vdash x : A}\ \textsc{Var}}{x :_1 A, y :_1 \Box_0 B \vdash \mathsf{let}\,[y'] = y\ \mathsf{in}\ x : A}\ \textsc{BoxE}}{\dfrac{z :_1 A \otimes \Box_0 B \vdash \mathsf{let}\ (x, y) = z\ \mathsf{in}\ \mathsf{let}\,[y'] = y\ \mathsf{in}\ x : A}{\emptyset \vdash \lambda z.\mathsf{let}\ (x, y) = z\ \mathsf{in}\ \mathsf{let}\,[y'] = y\ \mathsf{in}\ x : (A \otimes \Box_0 B)^1 \to A}\ \textsc{Abs}}\ \textsc{PairE}$$

Thus, we first eliminate the incoming product value z into its components x and y which both get used once. The component y however is graded modal, of type $\Box_0 B$, and is eliminated to a graded assumption $y' :_0 B$ which can thus be discarded due to the 0 grade.

In Granule, sticking to the constructs supported by GrBase, we would write the following equivalent function:

```
fst' : ∀ {a b : Type} . (a, b [0]) \% 1 → a
fst' = \z → let (x, y) = z in let [y'] = y in x
```

Granule provides additional syntactic sugar whereby elimination of graded modalities can be folded into pattern matching. Furthermore, we can elide the grade on an arrow if it is 1. A more idiomatic Granule equivalent to the above is thus:

```
fst : ∀ {a b : Type}. (a, b [0]) → a
fst (a, [b]) = a
```

In the case of **if-then-else**, we introduce an additional grade r to scale the incoming context of t_1 with the requirement that the grade r must approximate 1 (written $r \leq 1$) as computing a conditional incurs a usage to inspect the boolean. Once control flow is in the picture, *approximation* becomes important.

Example 3. A useful semiring is that of *intervals* over another semiring, e.g., the semiring of natural numbers intervals, formed by pairs $\mathbb{N} \times \mathbb{N}$, written here as $r..s$ in which s is always greater than or equal r under the normal ordering for $\mathbb{N}$. The semiring operations are then those of interval arithmetic, with ordering:

$$r_1..r_2 \leq s_1..s_2 = r_1 \leq_{\mathbb{N}} s_1 \wedge s_2 \leq_{\mathbb{N}} r_2$$

Thus the interval $r_1..r_2$ approximates $s_1..s_2$ if it is larger in conventional natural number terms (Remark 1 discusses the direction of the ordering and why it looks opposite to how we expect it for numbers). The following shows an example of the typing for conditionals using this semiring and approximation (eliding the typing of the 'else' branch):

$$\dfrac{\dfrac{}{x :_{1..1} \mathbb{B} \vdash x : \mathbb{B}}\ \textsc{Var} \qquad \dfrac{\dfrac{}{y :_{1..1} A, z :_{0..0} A \vdash y : A}\ \textsc{Var}}{y :_{0..1} A, z :_{0..1} A \vdash y : A}\ \textsc{Approx} \qquad r..r \leq 1..1}{x :_{r..r} \mathbb{B}, y :_{0..1} A, z :_{0..1} A \vdash \mathsf{if}\ x\ \mathsf{then}\ y\ \mathsf{else}\ z : A}\ \textsc{If}$$

Approximation means that we can approximate the grades for both x and y to be 0..1, capturing that they are used either 0 or 1 times in this computation.

The typing of the conditional requires that $r..r \leq 1..1$ (since $1 = 1..1$ in this semiring) and thus we ensure that the usage of x, to decide the conditional, is recorded faithfully.

Granule provides a range of builtin semirings, including:

`Nat` Discrete naturals, denoting exact usage.

`Sec` Security levels `Lo` and `Hi`, similar to the lattice used in this paper (defined soon in Definition 3).

`Q` Rationals for sensitivity analyses (somewhat emulating Gaboardi et al.'s system for differential privacy [20]).

Semirings can also be built from other data or combined using the following higher-order operations:

`Set` –	Sets of user-defined labels, where $* = \cup$ and $+ = \cap$.
`SetOp` –	Sets of user-defined labels, where $* = \cap$ and $+ = \cup$.
`Interval` –	Lower and upper bounds on usage.
– × –	Product of two semirings, e.g. one to three usages at level `Hi` is provided by a product `(1..3, Hi) : Interval Nat` × `Sec`.

`Set` and `SetOp` present a set-based lattice coeffect over user-defined labels. Intervals can be used to give lower and upper bounds; and products of coeffects allow the combination of coeffects via pointwise products.

Granule supports grade polymorphism, but also polymorphism on the semiring itself, allowing general definitions that can be instantiated at arbitrary semirings. Granule introduced semiring-polymorphism, which is appearing now in other, similar systems; Bianchini et al. adapt graded coeffects to an Object-Oriented setting, supporting different semirings within a single system and user-defined semirings via inheritance [9,10]. In Granule, new semirings can currently only be defined by extending the implementation. Exposing an interface for user-defined semirings, akin to Bianchini et al., is further work.

Granule generalises GrBase to include sum types and arbitrary, user-defined algebraic data types. We present GrBase as a simple core here, with just booleans for control flow to focus on the essential details for the model and non-interference result of Sect. 4.

Since lattices are semirings, we can consider instantiating GrBase with lattices, where the elements of the lattice provide some kind of labeling on data.

Such a semiring has been proposed as a way to capture IFC, with the grades as security levels [2,18,21,43]. We focus on a 2-point lattice for now:

Definition 3 (2-point semiring of security levels [21]**).** *Let $\mathcal{L} := \{H, L\}$ be a set of abstract labels, denoting 'high' and 'low' security permissions respectively, with a lattice formed by the total order with $L \leq H$. This lattice is a semiring with multiplicative structure $\cdot := \vee$ and $1 := L$ and additive $+ := \wedge$ and $0 := H$.*

The additive part means contraction serves to gives us the most permissive label (the greatest-lower bound) to avoid passing secrets to the public domain, e.g.:

$$\frac{\Gamma, x : [A]_{\mathsf{H}} \vdash t : B \qquad \Gamma', x : [A]_{\mathsf{L}} \vdash t' : B'}{(\Gamma + \Gamma'), x : [A]_{\mathsf{L}} \vdash (t, t') : B \otimes B'} \tag{1}$$

since $\mathsf{H} + \mathsf{L} = \mathsf{H} \wedge \mathsf{L} = \mathsf{L}$, i.e., x must be labelled as L in the concluding term since the subterm t' uses x in a low-security way.

We argue in Sect. 4 that a lattice is more general than what is needed to establish non-interference; instead, there is an intermediate point between semirings and lattices which provides enough structure to guarantee non-interference.

Remark 1 (On the direction of the ordering). Note that since we have $1 = \mathsf{L}$, $0 = \mathsf{H}$ and $\mathsf{L} \leq \mathsf{H}$, we have $1 \leq 0$. While this is unusual vis à vis the coeffect literature [46], the ordering turns out to be an arbitrary choice. In this work we chose the option that is common in the security literature (see e.g. [1]), as it avoids having 'high less than low' ($\mathsf{H} \leq \mathsf{L}$).

By the ordering and the semiring structure, high-security inputs H cannot flow to low security outputs L and thus there are no typing derivations for:

$$\nvdash \lambda x.[x] : A^{\mathsf{H}} \rightarrow \Box_{\mathsf{L}} A \qquad \nvdash \lambda x.x : A^{\mathsf{H}} \rightarrow A$$

In the latter, the base notion of usage at grade 1 (L) prevents us returning x.

A classic attack on data processing systems, that should also be guarded against, is via an *implicit flow*, in which some form of equality checking and control flow is used to leak information. This is known as a *control flow attack*. These are avoided in GrBase since the typing of **if-then-else** requires $r \leq 1$. Therefore the following is not valid:

$$\frac{x :_{\mathsf{L}} \mathbb{B} \vdash x : \mathbb{B} \quad \mathsf{H} \leq 1}{x :_{\mathsf{H}} \mathbb{B} \vdash \mathsf{if}\ x\ \mathsf{then}\ \mathtt{tt}\ \mathsf{else}\ \mathtt{ff} : \mathbb{B}} \ \textsc{If}\ (\textit{not valid})$$

Recall that $1 = \mathsf{L}$. Now, since $\mathsf{H} \nleq \mathsf{L}$, this derivation is *not valid* as the second premise does not hold, and thus the program is rejected. This is the same solution as employed by Abel and Bernardy ([2]) and Choudhury et al. [18].

In Granule, the 2-point security semiring is given as the `Sec` type with constructor `Hi` for H and `Lo` for L. The equivalent of the above (non)example in Granule is thus also ill-typed, written as:

```
leak : Bool \% Hi → Bool
leak x = if x then True else False    -- type error!
```

The **leak** function does not use the data-flow of variables to convey the input to the output, but rather uses the information gained via the conditional to reconstruct the input value. Since `Lo` is the 1 (top) element of the two-point security level lattice, we can however type the following:

```
public_not : Bool \% Lo → Bool
public_not b = if b then False else True
```

We can also allow secret inputs to flow to secret outputs, e.g., as:

```
secret_not : Bool \% Hi → Bool [Hi]
secret_not b = [if b then False else True]
```

Crucially here, the promotion on the outside of the conditional means that all the variable usage inside is scaled by `Hi`, which is the absorbing 0 element of the semiring, and thus the input here can be typed with `Hi` grade.

The original work on Granule introduced a different lattice for security levels, which did not prevent control flow attacks [46, Def 4.2]. This has since been removed from the language, replaced by the approach described in this paper (see, e.g., work by Hughes and Orchard on program synthesis from graded types which uses the above `Sec` semiring in Granule [31]).

3.2 Operational Semantics

Figure 2 gives the operational semantics for GrBase, which is standard and call-by-name, with the most interesting case being graded modal elimination.

A key property of the calculus is that of substitution admissibility, which is then used to establish syntactic type safety.

Lemma 1 (Admissibility of substitution). *If* $\Gamma_1 \vdash t_1 : A$ *and* $\Gamma_2, x : r\, A \vdash t_2 : B$ *then* $\Gamma_1 + r \cdot \Gamma_2 \vdash [t_1/x]t_2 : B$.

Proposition 1 (Syntactic type safety). *If* $\Gamma_1 \vdash t_1 : A$ *then either* t_1 *is a value or* $t_1 \rightsquigarrow t_1'$ *with* $\Gamma_1 \vdash t_1' : A$.

Other models have been proposed for capturing soundness of grading with regards an operational model, e.g., the heap semantics of Grad [18], also used by Marshall et al. [38], and the abstract machine of Abel and Bernardy [2]. Our focus here (and next) is however on a relational model to establish non-interference.

4 Semantic Model and Non-interfering Coeffects

We define the semantics of types by building a logical relation model following Rajani et al. [55]. The key difference from the work of Rajani et al. is that our calculus is call-by-name rather than call-by-value, and performs a coeffect-based rather than an effect-based security analysis. Following their approach,

$$\frac{}{(\lambda x.t_1)\ t_2 \rightsquigarrow [t_2/x]t_1}\ \beta \qquad \frac{}{\mathsf{let}\ [x] = [t_1]\ \mathsf{in}\ t_2 \rightsquigarrow [t_1/x]t_2}\ \Box_\beta$$

$$\frac{}{\mathsf{let}\ (x, y) = (t_1, t_2)\ \mathsf{in}\ t_3 \rightsquigarrow [t_1/x][t_2/y]t_3}\ \otimes_\beta \qquad \frac{}{\mathsf{let}\ () = ()\ \mathsf{in}\ t \rightsquigarrow t}\ \mathsf{Unit}_\beta$$

$$\frac{}{\mathsf{if}\ \mathtt{tt}\ \mathsf{then}\ t_1\ \mathsf{else}\ t_2 \rightsquigarrow t_1}\ \mathsf{if}_{\mathtt{tt}\beta} \qquad \frac{}{\mathsf{if}\ \mathtt{ff}\ \mathsf{then}\ t_1\ \mathsf{else}\ t_2 \rightsquigarrow t_2}\ \mathsf{if}_{\mathtt{ff}\beta}$$

(a) β-rules

$$\frac{t_1 \rightsquigarrow t_1'}{t_1\ t_2 \rightsquigarrow t_1'\ t_2}\ \rightarrow_{\text{CONG}} \qquad \frac{t_1 \rightsquigarrow t_1'}{\mathsf{let}\ [x] = t_1\ \mathsf{in}\ t_2 \rightsquigarrow \mathsf{let}\ [x] = t_1'\ \mathsf{in}\ t_2}\ \Box_{\text{CONG}}$$

$$\frac{t_1 \rightsquigarrow t_1'}{\mathsf{let}\ (x, y) = t_1\ \mathsf{in}\ t_2 \rightsquigarrow \mathsf{let}\ (x, y) = t_1'\ \mathsf{in}\ t_2}\ \otimes_{\text{CONG}} \qquad \frac{t_1 \rightsquigarrow t_1'}{\mathsf{let}\ () = t_1\ \mathsf{in}\ t_2 \rightsquigarrow \mathsf{let}\ () = t_1'\ \mathsf{in}\ t_2}\ \mathsf{Unit}_{\text{CONG}}$$

$$\frac{t \rightsquigarrow t'}{\mathsf{if}\ t\ \mathsf{then}\ t_1\ \mathsf{else}\ t_2 \rightsquigarrow \mathsf{if}\ t'\ \mathsf{then}\ t_1\ \mathsf{else}\ t_2}\ \mathsf{if}_{\text{CONG}}$$

(b) Congruence rules

Fig. 2. Operational semantics for GrBase

the semantic model is split into two relations: a unary relation and a binary relation, the latter of which is key to relating terms based on grades and with relation to an observer (who has some security level).

$$\begin{aligned}
&(expression) & [A]_\mathcal{E} &= \{t \mid t \rightsquigarrow^* v \implies v \in [A]_\mathcal{V}\}\\
&(value) & [\mathbb{B}]_\mathcal{V} &= \{\mathtt{tt}, \mathtt{ff}\}\\
& & [\mathsf{Unit}]_\mathcal{V} &= \{1\}\\
& & [A \otimes B]_\mathcal{V} &= \{(t_1, t_2) \mid t_1 \in [A]_\mathcal{V} \wedge t_2 \in [B]_\mathcal{V}\}\\
& & [A^s \rightarrow B]_\mathcal{V} &= \{\lambda x.t \mid (\forall t'.\ [t'] \in [\Box_s A]_\mathcal{E} \implies [t'/x]t \in [B]_\mathcal{E})\\
& & [\Box_r A]_\mathcal{V} &= \{[t] \mid t \in [A]_\mathcal{E}\}\\
&(context) & [\Gamma] &= \{\gamma \mid x :_r A \in \Gamma \wedge [\gamma(x)] \in [\Box_r A]_\mathcal{E}\}
\end{aligned}$$

Fig. 3. Unary value, expression and context relations.

The unary relation is fairly straightforward; it is only required to interpret secret (and thus potentially unrelated terms) in the two executions. The type-indexed family $[A]_\mathcal{V}$ defines the unary value interpretation as the set of values (irreducible terms) that inhabit the type A. Similarly, $[A]_\mathcal{E}$ defines the unary expression interpretation as the set of expressions (reducible terms) that inhabit the type A. Formally, $[A]_\mathcal{V}$ and $[A]_\mathcal{E}$ are defined in Fig. 3 as mutually inductive definitions. For the value interpretation, we only explain the function and the graded types here, as the other cases are self explanatory. For the function type, $A^s \rightarrow B$, the values inhabiting its interpretation are lambda terms $\lambda x.t$ where the substitution of any term t' into the body is in the interpretation of the expression relation at the result type (due to the call-by-name semantics of our language). The interpretation of the graded modal type $\Box_r A$ is the set of terms which are the promotions of terms in the interpretation A. Note that, since the purpose of the grade r is to relate two values of type A, the unary relation completely ignores the grade. The importance of grades only shows up in the binary relation (as explained below). Finally, the $[\Gamma]$ relation defines an interpretation of the context Γ as a set of maps from variables to expressions (written as γ) that can be substituted for each variable.

$$
\begin{aligned}
\textit{(expression)}\quad [\![A]\!]_{\mathcal{E}}^{adv} &= \{(t_1, t_2) \mid t_1 \rightsquigarrow^* v_1 \;\wedge\; t_2 \rightsquigarrow^* v_2 \implies (v_1, v_2) \in [\![A]\!]_{\mathcal{V}}^{adv}\}\\
\textit{(value)}\quad [\![\mathbb{B}]\!]_{\mathcal{V}}^{adv} &= \{(\mathtt{tt}, \mathtt{tt}), (\mathtt{ff}, \mathtt{ff})\}\\
[\![\mathsf{Unit}]\!]_{\mathcal{V}}^{adv} &= \{(1, 1)\}\\
[\![A \otimes B]\!]_{\mathcal{V}}^{adv} &= \{((t_1, t_2), (t_1', t_2')) \mid (t_1, t_1') \in [\![A]\!]_{\mathcal{V}}^{adv} \;\wedge\; (t_2, t_2') \in [\![B]\!]_{\mathcal{V}}^{adv}\}\\
[\![A^s \to B]\!]_{\mathcal{V}}^{adv} &= \{(\lambda x.t_1, \lambda y.t_2) \mid (\forall t, t'.([t], [t']) \in [\![\Box_s A]\!]_{\mathcal{E}}^{adv} \implies\\
&\qquad\qquad ([t/x]t_1, [t'/y]t_2) \in [\![B]\!]_{\mathcal{E}}^{adv})\\
&\qquad \wedge (\forall t.[t] \in [\Box_s A]_{\mathcal{E}} \implies [t/x]t_1 \in [B]_{\mathcal{E}})\\
&\qquad \wedge (\forall t.[t] \in [\Box_s A]_{\mathcal{E}} \implies [t/y]t_2 \in [B]_{\mathcal{E}})\ \}\\
[\![\Box_r A]\!]_{\mathcal{V}}^{adv} &= \begin{cases} \{([t_1], [t_2]) \mid (t_1, t_2) \in [\![A]\!]_{\mathcal{E}}^{adv}\} & \textit{when } r \leq adv\\ \{([t_1], [t_2]) \mid t_1 \in [A]_{\mathcal{E}} \wedge t_2 \in [A]_{\mathcal{E}}\} & \textit{when } \neg(r \leq adv)\end{cases}\\
\textit{(context)}\quad [\![\Gamma]\!]^{adv} &= \{(\gamma_1, \gamma_2) \mid x :_r A \in \Gamma \;\wedge\; [\gamma_1(x), \gamma_2(x)] \in [\![\Box_r A]\!]_{\mathcal{E}}^{adv}\}
\end{aligned}
$$

Fig. 4. Binary expression, value and context relations

The binary relation (Fig. 4) formalises the key security requirements with respect to grades. Like the unary, the binary relation is defined for values and expressions. However, the key difference is that the binary interpretation of a type is a set of *pairs of terms*, as opposed to just a set of terms as in the unary case. The binary interpretation is also parameterised by a grade representing the adversary level *adv* against whom we desire *indistinguishability* of secrets.

We explain the binary expression relation first: $[\![A]\!]_{\mathcal{E}}^{adv}$ relates two expressions of type A when the values obtained by reducing them can be related under the binary value interpretation at the same type. Since we only relate the resulting values when both the expressions terminate, our logical relation internalises what is known as 'termination-insensitive non-interference' [64]. We believe that our current development can be generalised to a termination sensitive version of non-interference by additionally proving co-termination of the two executions. We leave that part as an interesting direction for future work.

For the binary value interpretation ($[\![A]\!]_{\mathcal{V}}^{adv}$), like in the unary case, we focus only on the function and the graded types here. The interpretation of the function type $A^s \to B$ relates two λ-expressions, when given related expressions at an input type ($\Box_s A$) the bodies of the λ-expression with the substitutions should be related at the output type B. The additional unary clauses are required for technical purposes (as we desire an invariant that any two terms that are related by the binary relation must also be separately in the unary relation at the same type). The value interpretation for the graded type $\Box_r A$ is now the most critical point in the model for security. It relates two promoted terms $[t_1]$ and $[t_2]$ as follows: if the grade r is less than or equal to the adversary level *adv* (i.e., $r \leq adv$) then t_1 and t_2 must be related by the binary expression relation at A, otherwise t_1 and separately t_2 are just in the unary expression interpretation of A and thus cannot be distinguished; an adversary who is at the low security level (L) cannot distinguish values which are designated as secret (at the high security level) by being in inside a H-graded box, since $\neg(\mathsf{H} \leq \mathsf{L})$.

Finally, $[\![\Gamma]\!]^{adv}$ defines the binary relation for relating substitutions in the two runs, reusing the interpretation of the graded modality to capture grading.

4.1 Fundamental Theorems and Non-interference

A key property of our model is the so-called 'fundamental theorem' which connects the syntactic type system with its semantic interpretation: any expression subject to a syntactic typing is member of the semantic typing. We define a unary (Theorem 1) and a binary (Theorem 2) version of the fundamental theorem, corresponding to the two logical relations.

Theorem 1 (Unary fundamental theorem). *For all well-typed terms $\Gamma \vdash t : A$, if $\gamma \in [\Gamma]$ then $\gamma\ t \in [A]_{\mathcal{E}}$ (where the $\gamma\ t$ applies a substitution of the mapping from variables to terms given by γ).*

Proof. (**`utheorem`**, **`UnaryFundamentalTheorem.agda`**) By induction on typing.

The unary fundamental theorem says that if t is a term of type A in a context Γ, and γ is a unary substitution in the interpretation of Γ then $\gamma\ t$ is in the unary expression relation at the type A.

The binary fundamental theorem instead leverages the binary relation, which is where we get the interaction between an external observer (the 'adversary') and the grading. It is at this stage that we need additional structure to enable the binary fundamental lemma as the crucial step to non-interference. This additional structure delineates a subclass of semirings which we call *non-interfering*:

Definition 4 (Non-interfering semiring). *A non-interfering semiring $\mathcal{R}$ is a pre-ordered semiring with four additional axioms:*

- *lax idempotence*[7] *of multiplication:* $r \cdot r \leq r$
- *antisymmetry:* $(r \leq s) \wedge (s \leq r) \implies r = s$
- *multiplicative unit is minimal (bottom):* $1 \leq r$

[7] There seems to be no universally accepted name for this property. *Weak* idempotence is used in [4] to denote the property $r^4 = r^2$, hence we opted for the modifier *lax*.

– *additive unit is maximal (top):* $r \leq 0$

Proposition 2 (Derived properties). *For a non-interfering semiring, then we have the following derived properties:*

– *(decreasing +) If* $r_1 \leq r_2$ *then* $(r_1 + s) \leq r_2$
(which follows from 0 *being the top and the usual semiring properties of* + *monotonicity and* 0 *being the additive unit).*
– *(increasing* $\cdot$*) If* $r_1 \leq r_2$ *then* $r_1 \leq (s \cdot r_2)$ *and* $r_1 \leq (r_2 \cdot s)$
(which follows from 1 *being the bottom and the usual semiring properties of* $\cdot$ *monotonicity and* 1 *being the multiplicative unit).*

From these two properties we can conversely derive the minimality of 1 *and the maximality of* 0 *respectively.*

Proposition 3 (2-point security lattice is non-interfering). *The semiring induced by the lattice on* $\mathcal{L} = \{\mathsf{H}, \mathsf{L}\}$ *with* $\mathsf{L} \leq \mathsf{H}$*, where* $0 = \mathsf{H}$ *and* $1 = \mathsf{L}$*, is non-interfering, with lax idempotence of multiplication trivial since* $\cdot = \vee$*, with the ordering providing antisymmetry, minimality of* 1*, and maximality of* 0.

We can now give the binary fundamental theorem on this subclass of semirings:

Theorem 2 (Binary fundamental theorem). *For all well-typed terms* $\Gamma \vdash t : A$ *with a semiring* $\mathcal{R}$ *parameterising the calculus that is* non interfering, *if* $(\gamma_1, \gamma_2) \in [\![\Gamma]\!]^{adv}$ *then* $(\gamma_1\ t, \gamma_2\ t) \in [\![A]\!]^{adv}_{\mathcal{E}}$ *(where the* $\gamma_1\ t$ *and* $\gamma_2\ t$ *applies a multi-substitution of the mapping from variables to terms given by* γ_1 *and* γ_2*).*

The binary fundamental theorem is similar to the unary, but relates the syntactic typing to the semantic typing according to the binary expression relation. Both of these theorems are proved by induction on the typing derivation.

Proof. Formalised (`biFundamentalTheorem`, `BinaryFundamentalTheorem.agda`).

The theorem follows by induction over typing derivations. We sketch some of the pertinent cases here which show where the axioms of the *non-interfering semiring* are used. (Note uses of axioms are typeset in green.) The interesting cases typically occur when incoming context has a grade that is not observable by the adversary (i.e., some r such that $\neg(r \leq adv)$) but some premise requires a context with a grade s that is observable by the adversary (i.e., some s such that $s \leq adv$).

– (var) with typing $0 \cdot \Gamma, x : 1\, A \vdash x : A$, and goal $[\![A]\!]^{adv}_{\mathcal{E}}$.
Thus the interpretation of the context in the assumption of the theorem provides $([t_1], [t_2]) \in [\![\Box_1 A]\!]^{adv}_{\mathcal{E}}$ with two possible cases for its meaning:
  - $1 \leq adv$ and $(t_1, t_2) \in [\![A]\!]^{adv}_{\mathcal{E}}$ satisfying the goal of the theorem.
  - $\neg(1 \leq adv)$ and thus $t_1 \in [A]_{\mathcal{E}} \wedge t_2 \in [A]_{\mathcal{E}}$ which cannot satisfy the goal of $[\![A]\!]^{adv}_{\mathcal{E}}$. However there is a contradiction here since 1 is the bottom element ($\forall r.1 \leq r$) in a non-interfering semiring, and thus this case holds by *ex falso quod libet.*

– (app) with typing $\Gamma_1 + r \cdot \Gamma_2 \vdash t_1\, t_2 : B$ and premises $\Gamma_1 \vdash t_1 : A^r \rightarrow B$ and $\Gamma_2 \vdash t_2 : A$.
Thus we have a context interpretation $(\gamma_1, \gamma_2) \in [\![r \cdot \Gamma_1 + \Gamma_2]\!]^{adv}$ from which we need to derive a context $(\gamma_1', \gamma_2') \in [\![\Gamma_1]\!]^{adv}$ to compute the left-hand side t_1. For every x such that $x :_{r_1} A \in \Gamma_1$ and $x :_{r_2} A \in \Gamma_2$ then this requires us to map from $([t_3], [t_4]) \in [\![\Box_{r_1 + r \cdot r_2} A]\!]^{adv}_{\mathcal{E}}$ to $([t_3], [t_4]) \in [\![\Box_{r_1} A]\!]^{adv}_{\mathcal{E}}$ in the interpretation of the context in order to apply induction over the first typing premise. In the case where $\neg(r_1 + r \cdot r_2 \leq adv)$ but $r_1 \leq adv$ then we have a contradiction since $r_1 \leq adv$ implies $r_1 + r \cdot r_2 \leq adv$ by the decreasing property of $+$ (i.e., that 0 is the top element, see Proposition 2). A similar use of this property occurs in every other case where the context need splitting, i.e., expressions comprising more than two subterms.
– (pr) with typing $r \cdot \Gamma \vdash [t] : \Box_r A$ and premise $\Gamma \vdash t : A$.
For all $x :_s B \in \Gamma$ then context interpretation contains some $([t_1], [t_2]) \in [\![\Box_{(r \cdot s)} B]\!]^{adv}_{\mathcal{E}}$ from which we need that $([t_1], [t_2]) \in [\![\Box_s B]\!]^{adv}_{\mathcal{E}}$ in order to induct on the premise.
In the case where $r \leq adv$ but $\neg(r \cdot s \leq adv)$ and thus $[\![\Box_{(r \cdot s)} B]\!]^{adv}_{\mathcal{E}} = [B]_{\mathcal{E}} \wedge t_2 \in [B]_{\mathcal{E}}$ then we have $\neg(s \leq adv)$ by lax idempotence of $*$ (and a proof by contradiction) and thus $[\![\Box_s B]\!]^{adv}_{\mathcal{E}} = [B]_{\mathcal{E}} \wedge t_2 \in [B]_{\mathcal{E}}$ which is satisfied by the context here.
– (if) with typing $(r \cdot \Gamma_1) + \Gamma_2 \vdash \mathsf{if}\ t_1\ \mathsf{then}\ t_2\ \mathsf{else}\ t_3 : A$ and $r \leq 1$.
For all $x :_{r_1} B \in \Gamma_1$ and $x :_{r_2} B \in \Gamma_2$ then context interpretation contains some $([t_1], [t_2]) \in [\![\Box_{(r \cdot r_1 + r_2)} B]\!]^{adv}_{\mathcal{E}}$.
In the case where $\neg((r \cdot r_1) + r_2) \leq adv$ then due to the typing requiring $r \leq 1$ it follows that $\neg r_1 \leq adv$ by, i.e.,

$$
\begin{array}{lll}
(0) & \neg((r \cdot r_1) + r_2) \leq adv & (\mathit{assumption}) \\
(1) & r_1 \leq adv & (\mathit{assumption}) \\
(2) & r \leq 1 & (\mathit{typing}) \\
(3) & r \cdot r_1 \leq adv \cdot 1 & (\mathit{monotone}\ \cdot\ (1), (2)) \\
(4) & r \cdot r_1 \leq adv & (\mathit{multiplicative\ unit}\ (3)) \\
(5) & ((r \cdot r_1) + r_2) \leq adv & (\mathit{decreasing}\ +\ (4)) \\
(6) & \bot & (\neg\text{-}\mathit{elim}\ (0),(5)) \\
(7) & \neg(r_1 \leq adv) & (\neg\text{-}\mathit{intro}\ (1),(6))
\end{array}
$$

Thus the incoming context interpretation suffices for the context interpretation of t_1.

Note that the proof does not make use of the antisymmetry property yet, which instead arises in the final central theorem:

Theorem 3 (Non-Interference). *For all judgments $x :_s A \vdash t : \Box_{adv} \mathbb{B}$ where $adv \leq s$ and $adv \neq s$ then given $\emptyset \vdash v_1 : A$ and $\emptyset \vdash v_2 : A$ then $[v_1/x]t \equiv [v_2/x]t$.*

(where $\equiv$ is full β-equality of terms, derived from the operational semantics).

Proof. (`nonInterference`, `NonInterFerence.agda`) We sketch some interesting details here, but the binary fundamental theorem does most of the heavy lifting.

First, promote the typing of v_1 and v_2, i.e., to $\emptyset \vdash [v_1] : \Box_s A$ and $\emptyset \vdash [v_2] : \Box_s A$ and to both apply the binary fundamental theorem, yielding:

$$(\emptyset, \emptyset) \in [\![\emptyset]\!]^{adv} \implies ([v_1], [v_1]) \in [\![\Box_s A]\!]^{adv}_{\mathcal{E}} \tag{2}$$

$$(\emptyset, \emptyset) \in [\![\emptyset]\!]^{adv} \implies ([v_2], [v_2]) \in [\![\Box_s A]\!]^{adv}_{\mathcal{E}} \tag{3}$$

The antecedents are trivially satisfied and both (2), (3) are each equivalent to:

$$([v_1], [v_1]) \in ([\Box_s A]_{\mathcal{E}} \times [\Box_s A]_{\mathcal{E}})$$
$$([v_2], [v_2]) \in ([\Box_s A]_{\mathcal{E}} \times [\Box_s A]_{\mathcal{E}})$$

by the meaning of $[\![\Box_s A]\!]^{adv}_{\mathcal{E}}$ and since $adv \leq s$ from the premise and the fact that if we had also $s \leq adv$ then by antisymmetry it would follow $adv = s$ which is contradicted by the premise that $adv \neq s$. We then apply the binary fundamental theorem with $(\{x \mapsto v_1\}, \{x \mapsto v_2\}) \in [\![x :_s A]\!]^{adv} \in [x :_s A] \times [x :_s A]$ to obtain $([v_1/x]t, [v_2/x]t) \in [\![\Box_{adv} \mathbb{B}]\!]^{adv}_{\mathcal{E}}$. By reflexivity of $\leq$, such that $adv \leq adv$, this interpretation is necessarily equal to $[\![\mathbb{B}]\!]^{adv}_{\mathcal{E}}$ and thus by the definition of the binary fundamental lemma $[v_1/x]t$ and $[v_2/x]t$ reduce to terms v and v' such that $(v, v') \in [\![\mathbb{B}]\!]^{adv}_{\mathcal{V}}$ which necessarily means $v \equiv v'$. □

Remark 2. The definition of non-interfering semirings (Definition 4) permits the trivial, singleton semiring where $0 = 1$. This semiring would appear to permit interference since it conflates 0 and 1. However, the non-interference theorem assumes $adv \neq s$, thus the theorem holds trivially for the singleton semiring.

Another useful non-interfering semiring is the lattice of sets over labels:

Example 4 (Set semiring). Let $\mathcal{T}$ be a set of arbitrary abstract labels from which we form a semiring **Set** of sets generated by $\mathcal{P}(\mathcal{T})$ (the powerset of $\mathcal{T}$) under subset inclusion with multiplicative structure $\cdot := \cup$ with $1 := \emptyset$ and additive structure $+ := \cap$ with $0 := \top$.

This gives one of the staples of secure information flow tracking [19], which serves as the (hard-coded) basis of other information flow control systems such as Flow Caml [58]. This semiring is also supported in Granule, where labels are defined via a sum type with unit constructors. As a concrete example, we define a datatype `Privilege` to model privileged data sources on a mobile device:

```
data Privilege = Camera | Contacts | Location | Microphone

myLocation : String [{Location}]
myLocation = ["051.28N 001.08E"]

myFavouriteContact : String [{Contacts}]
myFavouriteContact = ["Alice"]
```

We have a value `myLocation` that is marked as needing location access via its graded modal type and a value `myFavouriteContact` that is marked as needing access to contacts. Use of these values in other parts of the program propagates their requirements, as shown by these two examples:

```
honest : String [{Contacts, Location}]
honest =
  let [x] = myLocation;
      [y] = myFavouriteContact
  in [stringAppend x y]

dishonest : String [{Contacts}]
dishonest =
  let [x] = myLocation;
      [y] = myFavouriteContact
  in [stringAppend x y]     -- type error!
```

Here, `honest` requires the caller to provide a privilege context including at least contacts and location access, i.e. the union of the privileges of `myLocation` and `myFavouriteContact`. A type error is raised for `dishonest`, as it fails to require location access.

Dually to the **Set** semiring defined above, we have another valid (non-interfering) semiring given by: $\mathbf{Set}^{\mathsf{op}} := (\mathcal{R} := \mathcal{P}(\mathcal{T}), \cdot := \cap, 1 := \top, + := \cup, 0 := \emptyset, \leq := \supseteq)$. We leave its interpretation open.

4.2 Comparison with Related Results in the Literature

Abel and Bernardy (2021). From Abel and Bernardy's 'unified view' [2], §4.3 considers 'informational applications' of graded types in which "it does not matter how many times variables are used, but rather *in which context* they are used." In this setting they restrict themselves to semirings in which the + is the meet derived from an ordering and multiplication is the join, explicitly mentioning that this means that multiplication is idempotent (which exceeds the lax idempotence required by our definition). Their system is defined over a ringoid– a semiring with a meet-semilattice– with a partial order defined by the meet, hence providing the antisymmetry property. In §4.3.2. they assume that everything "above 1 in the lattice is secret", and give the 2-point H/L example, noting "the construction generalises however to any lattice of information modalities as specified". Any semiring in their class of 'informational semirings' is non-interfering[8] since defining the + as the $\wedge$ and $\cdot$ as $\vee$ implies the + is decreasing and $\cdot$ is increasing, and thus by Proposition 2 we have that 0 is maximal and 1 is minimal.

Based on a relational model, they prove a non-interference theorem (Theorem 7.10) for terms of the type (in our syntax) $f : A^1 \to B^0 \to \mathbb{B}$ showing that $[\![f]\!]\ u\ b_1 = [\![f]\!]\ u\ b_2$ for $u \in [\![A]\!]$ and $b_1, b_2 \in [\![B]\!]$. This theorem resembles ours but is more specialised, focusing just on the 0 and 1 grades (where their result type $\mathbb{B}$ can be read equivalently as $\Box_1 \mathbb{B}$).

It should be noted that their work provides a more general relational model which can be used to consider properties beyond just non-interference. On the other hand, the work presented here has a more general non-interference result and defines a larger class of semirings with this property.

[8] (`informationalImpliesNonInterfering, Semiring.agda`).

Abel et al. (2023). Formalising a graded modal dependent type theory, Abel et al. (2023) provide a graded system with many features, generalising the core calculus described here [3]. They define a semiring-based grading algebra over a partial ordering, and requiring the existence also of a meet operation. They consider an in-depth case study looking at *erasure*, in which grading is used to track which parts of a program are not used and can be erased—a similar property to non-interference: erasable arguments are non-interfering. They define a subclass of grading structures, said to have a *well-behaved zero* (similar to what Moon et al. [43] call a 'quantitative semiring') if:

- Additive is positive: if $p + q = 0$ then $p = 0$ and $q = 0$;
- Meet is positive: if $p \wedge q = 0$ then $p = 0$ and $q = 0$;
- The zero-product property holds: if $p \cdot q = 0$ then $p = 0$ or $q = 0$;
- Non-triviality $0 \neq 1$.

They point out that the second property implies that 0 is maximal. They establish a logical relations model with a fundamental theorem for erasure for those well-behaved zero algebras (Theorem 6.10), with a thorough formalisation to go with it. From this they establish non-interference for the 2-point semiring and point out that more fine-grained lattices with 1 as minimal can also give the same result. Again, this result overlaps with that here, but requiring more structure compared to our 'leaner', more general approach.

5 Practical Example of Mandatory Access Control

In this section we explore a practical case study of our security coeffects in Granule. These examples take inspiration from Haskell's Mandatory Access Control (MAC) library [57], though the code in that paper is written in a monadic effect-based style. We instead represent these local side-effects using Granule's linearly-typed session channels [39] (which are based on the GV calculus [22]). This provides an interface for channels `LChan : Protocol → Type` where:

```
data Protocol = Send Type Protocol | Recv Type Protocol | End
```

with the following (non-monadic) linear functions:

```
send : ∀ {a : Type, p : Protocol} . LChan (Send a p) → a → LChan p
recv : ∀ {a : Type, p : Protocol} . LChan (Recv a p) → (a, LChan p)
forkLinear  : ∀ {p : Protocol} . (LChan p → ()) → LChan (Dual p)
close : LChan End → ()
```

The `Dual` type family is defined internally as follows:

```
Dual (Send a p) = Recv a (Dual p)
Dual (Recv a p) = Send a (Dual p)
Dual End        = End
```

The first example below defines a function `attemptLogin` which will authenticate a (public) user ID and (secret) password, logging each attempt by sending only the ID over a public channel to be printed. Note that the boolean result is given in a **Hi** context, meaning that the result can only be used at this level of confidentiality.

```
attemptLogin : Int
             → String \% Hi
             → LChan (Send Int End) -- logging channel
             → Bool [Hi]
attemptLogin uid pass c =
  let c = send c uid;
      () = close c
  in validateLogin uid pass
```

Here, the auxiliary `validateLogin` function has the type:

```
validateLogin : Int → String \% Hi → Bool [Hi]
```

Thus, we take in the ID and password and return the result stating whether the login has been validated or not. As one might expect, this result must be secret, since the password was itself secret data.

In the `attemptLogin` function, if we tried to leak secret data by logging `pass` over the channel rather than `uid`, this would be disallowed by the type system.

We can now extend this example and write a function `doQuery`, which authenticates a user and then performs a query on secret data, returning, in a secret context, a string representing the query result if the user's password is correct and otherwise returning an error.

```
doQuery : Int                                -- uid
        → String \% Hi                        -- password
        → (LChan (Recv (String [Hi]) End))   -- secret data!
        → (Either Error String) [Hi]
doQuery uid pass secret =
  let c = forkLinear logLoginAttempt in
  let [login] : Bool [Hi] = attemptLogin uid pass c in
  [ if login
    then
      Left AuthErr
    else
      let [secr] : String [Hi] = getSecret secret
      in Right secr
  ]
```

The auxiliary `logLoginAttempt` function here is of type

```
logLoginAttempt : LChan (Recv (Int [Lo]) End) → ()
```

Since this function is public-facing, it would not be possible to log secret data such as the password or even the boolean result stating whether the login was successful; all we can log is that an attempt to login has occurred.

Note also that once we discriminate on the result of `attemptLogin`, we enter a secret context, and so even though `uid` is still public data it would no longer be possible to log this or anything else after we have reached this point. Thus, an implicit leak is prevented. The case expression has the same typing as conditional shown in Sect. 3.

The next example is based on the main case study demonstrated in Haskell in the MAC paper. Here, we define a function `isCommonPW` which checks whether a given password is in a standard list of common passwords. The list is public information, but the password given to the function is of course secret data, and so the result from the function must also be secret.

```
isCommonPW : String \% Hi → List String → Bool [Hi]
isCommonPW password commonPasswords =
    [ case commonPasswords of
        Nil → False;
        Cons x xs →
          case strEq x password of
            [True] →
              let () = drop @(List String) xs in True;
            [False] →
              let [isCommon] = isCommonPW password xs in isCommon
    ]
```

where `strEq : String % Hi → String % Hi → Bool [Hi]` is omitted for brevity. The list of common passwords (second parameter) is public, against which we compare our secret password recursively, returning a secret result about whether the password is in the common list or not. This makes use of a few additional Granule features, like the `drop @(List String)` feature which, based on the type after `@`, derives a discarding function for the list of strings [32]. The main takeaway here is that security reasoning with coeffects scales to practical examples involving algebraic data types and recursion.

6 Discussion and Conclusion

Section 2 considered the background related work on coeffects and graded type systems in depth. Section 4 also considered closely the most pertinent related work here with regards the coeffect-style to IFC. To round out the related work discussion, we consider relationship with the effect-style approach to IFC.

6.1 Alternate Presentations of Information-Flow Control

Fine-grained information-flow type systems like SLAM [29], Flow Caml [54] also use an (annotated) modal type constructor to associate labels with every type. For example, a pair of type A and B has labels associated to each component and the pair as a whole, e.g., $(A^{L1} \times B^{L2})^{L3}$. GrBase on the other hand has a coeffectful approach to labeling, explicit labels on inputs are mandatory, but explicit labels on outputs are not: instead the output is essentially equivalent to being graded at 1.

In contrast, coarse-grained type systems like DCC [1] associate and track dependencies for a language without side-effects, with annotations on *monadic constructors* (essentially extending Moggi's monadic meta language [42]). Type systems like HLIO [16] and CG [55,56] extend the coarse-grained approach for languages with higher-order mutable state. However, both HLIO and CG use a different modal type constructor to associate labels with a type, and a monad for tracking the flows. Unlike all these systems, GRBASE uses (comonadic) coeffect grades for explicit labeling. As a result, our logical relation model for GRBASE draws inspiration from the model of the fine-grained system FG due to Rajani et al. [55].

A modern perspective on DCC is that it leverages a *graded monad* to package the monad along with its structured annotations (to see this, one might follow the thread from Wadler and Thiemann's 'marriage of effects and monads' forming a lattice of monads [67], to the more general notion of graded monads; Mycroft et al. trace the history of these developments and the overall paradigm [44]). Algehed examines the monadic structure of DCC in more detail [5], showing that DCC embeds a graded monad T_ℓ with grades ℓ drawn from the two-point lattice $\mathsf{L} \leq \mathsf{H}$ (also used here) but with additional structure. This additional structure amounts to a kind of distributive law that provides $T_\ell T_{\ell'} A \rightarrow T_{\ell'} T_\ell A$. Choudhury conducts a similar but more thorough study of the structure of DCC from both a graded monadic vs. graded comonadic perspective, noting that "the monadic aspect of dependency analysis might be just half of the story [...] experience shows us that security constraints can be enforced not only by restricting outflow but also by restricting inflow" [17]. Choudhury shows, similarly to Algehed, that DCC is not just graded monadic but encodes a distributive law in its calculus. He goes on to show that this distributive law can be captured by a structure which is *both* a graded monad and graded comonad, whose operations are mutually inverse, with a derivation $T_\ell T_{\ell'} A \xrightarrow{\mu} T_{\ell \vee \ell'} A \equiv T_{\ell' \vee \ell} A \xrightarrow{\delta} T_{\ell'} T_\ell A$. In essence, DCC has both graded monadic and graded comonadic aspects. Here we focused on just the graded comonadic side of this equation via coeffects and the coeffect-graded modality. Granule however allows the missing graded monadic part to be recovered by its 'double unboxing' pattern matching [46], with:

```
joinSec : ∀ {a : Type, l l' : Sec} . (a [l]) [l'] → a [l * l']
joinSec [[x]] = [x]
```

Following Choudhury's analysis, adding this as a primitive to our GRBASE calculus here would yield a system which is equivalent in power to DCC [17]. Choudhury's calculus has a slightly different form to our own (with no linearity nor graded assumptions or functions, but explicit graded comonad operations instead), so a little more work is needed to formalise this result, which we leave as further work. Our system is yet more general though by the use of the general class of non-interfering semirings.

6.2 Declassification

The approach to IFC here features non-interference, but is extremely restrictive: there cannot be any flow from a high security level to a lower. In reality, we often want software systems to leak a small amount of information in a controlled way. This is known as *declassification* [45,65].

Our existing notion of a non-interfering semiring permits a generalisation of the 2-point lattice considered here which, along with some built-in primitives, can be used to capture the number of bits declassified in a computation as a further instance of non-interfering semirings:

Example 5 (Declassification semiring) The $\mathsf{L} \leq \mathsf{H}$ semiring can be generalised to a semiring over $\mathcal{R} = \mathbb{N} \cup \{\omega\}$ to capture the *number of declassified bits*, where L (which was the multiplicative unit 1) is replaced by ω to represent an arbitrarily large number of bits being declassified and H (which is 0) being replaced by $0 \in \mathbb{N}$ to represent 0-bits being declassified. In between are all possible representations of a finite number of bits being declassified with the pre-ordering defined by $\omega \leq \ldots \leq 1 \leq 0$. Addition is then the maximum on $\mathbb{N} \cup \{\omega\}$, i.e., the number of bits declassified by two subterms is the largest number (which according to this ordering is the 'meet' $\wedge$, since the ordering is going down towards infinity) and multiplication is then the minimum ('join' $\vee$ on this ordering), i.e., the number of bits declassified by a composed term is the smaller number.

A declassification primitive then acts as the operation of this graded modality, declassifying a precise number of bits for various data types, for example, for integers, there is a primitive function of indexed type:

```
declassifyInt : ∀ {n : Nat} . Nat n → Int [n] → Int
```

Then, a program declassifying 3-bits and then 5-bits of information from its argument overall has to be typed as declassifying 5-bits: the maximum number of declassified bits (via $+$). A program declassifying 3-bits of its argument and then composing this with a function which declassifies 5-bits of its argument declassifies only 3-bits of information overall, i.e., the minimum (via $\cdot$).

This declassification semiring is a non-interfering semiring.

Future work is to consider a quantitative non-interference theorem that allows reasoning about such declassification operations and their effect on non-interference; we need some model that can account for the above declassification operation and then a generalisation to our non-inference theorem here. Specifically we would like to explore how to integrate work on declassification from the literature, such as Relative Secrecy [65]. This is further work.

An alternate approach to declassification by Hainry and Péchoux requires that declassification operations can only happen outside of loops [27], preventing control-flow attacks from iteratively transferring information from secret to public data. We can emulate this idea in Granule, not by restricting the language or using some additional static analysis, but by leveraging grading to enforce a linearity constraint.

We sketch out a more tentative implementation of this idea by introducing an abstract data type `DeclassCap` capturing a declassification capability. This could then be consumed by the following primitive function, which compares two secret strings, producing a result which is public, but requiring a declassification capability to be consumed once:

```
equality : DeclassCap \% (1 : Nat)
         → String \% Hi → String \% Hi → Bool [Lo]
```

Remark 3. Any definition that allows for some declassification needs to be provided as an axiom, i.e. a primitive in the compiler, as it is not internally derivable. And so much the better, since this technically introduces a violation of non-interference!

There would be no constructor for `DeclassCap`, instead a special compilation mode would expect the entry-point of a program to be a function receiving a graded declassification capability that can be used a finite number of times:

```
mainDeclass : ∀ {n : Nat} . DeclassCap \% n → Int [Hi]
```

In this way we use grading to restrict declassification to a specified number of comparisons only.

6.3 Critical Analysis and Flat Coeffects for Security?

One criticism of the approach described here, for example considering the two-point lattice, is that conflating high security (H) with non-usage (0 of the semiring) leads to unintuitive proofs and typing. For instance, the derivation below (Eq. 4) is valid in GRBASE because if we can prove B from 0 copies of A then we can also prove $\Box_{\mathsf{L}} B$ from 0 copies of A:

$$\frac{x : [A]_{\mathsf{H}} \vdash t : B}{x : [A]_{\mathsf{H}} \vdash t : \Box_{\mathsf{L}} B} \tag{4}$$

since the context here has the grade calculated by $\mathsf{L} \cdot \mathsf{H} = \mathsf{L} \vee \mathsf{H} = \mathsf{H}$.

This concluding type on its own looks very worrying for non-interference: we have a computation that takes a high-security (secret) input and produces an output which can be used in a low-security (public) context. However, the fact that $0 = \mathsf{H}$, coupled with the rest of the structure of the type system, means that non-interference holds (as proved in Sect. 4). Instead, we could imagine a system in which we avoid conflating 0 and H but require that a term producing a low-security result requires all its dependencies to be low security.

Thus, whilst the type system is sound (it gives us non-interference), the grades require some additional thought. Furthermore, the system severely restricts expressivity in order to gain non-interference and avoid control-flow attacks: as seen, we can only guard control-flow on a secret value if the entire control-flow expression is promoted, e.g.

```
pnot : Bool \% Hi → Bool [Hi]
pnot x = [if x then True else False]
```

Instead, we ask, what would it take it allow the following alternate implementation, which is not well-typed under the system of this paper?

```
pnot' : Bool \% Hi → Bool [Hi]
pnot' x = if x then [True] else [False]
```

One approach could be to return to the *flat coeffects* of the original ICALP 2013 paper by Petricek, Orchard, and Mycroft [52] adding an ambient coeffect affected by control-flow. Thus guarding a conditional with a secret value would introduce an ambient security requirement into the context which must be respected by each branch. Exploring this is future work.

6.4 Concluding Remarks

The coeffect types paradigm set out by Alan Mycroft and his students sought to capture various context-dependent analyses via a unified type system. This sprung from trying to dualise effect types, but later work by Alan and his students circled back to effects to reconsider them in the light of the lessons learned from the coeffect system and its semantics [44]. This lead to the umbrella approach of *graded modal types* or more generally just *graded types*. As we've seen in the GrBase style: we do not necessarily need the explicit graded modality, but can instead have a type system with pervasive grading. Our focus here was on security, an application picked up in a number of other graded types works [2,3,21], but many questions remain about how to generalise these ideas to declassification for more practical programming. It would also be interesting to explore how to capture the notion of *integrity* (dual in a sense to security/confidentiality) in a more general manner than has been previously discussed [37].

An opportunity presents itself for the further impact of these ideas through the GHC Haskell compiler, which already implements a simple graded coeffect type system internally to enable its **LinearTypes** extension [8]. Perhaps some day in the future there may even be a **SecurityTypes** or **CoeffectTypes** extension that generalises that implementation, building on the more general systems laid down by Mycroft et al. and as seen in the Granule language.

Acknowledgments. This work was partly supported by EPSRC grant EP/T013516/1 (*Verifying Resource-like Data Use in* Programs via Types). Orchard also received support through Schmidt Sciences, LLC. Rajani was supported in part by the EPSRC grant EP/Y003535/1 (*Type-based information declassification and its secure compilation*). Rajani and Orchard also received support through ARIA's Safeguarded AI programme. Vollmer was supported in part by EPSRC grant EP/X021173/1.

The authors warmly thank Professor Alan Mycroft for all his inspiration, wisdom, patience, enthusiasm, and ideas that have gone into this work and the many other works described here. Enjoy your retirement Alan, you've earned it!

References

1. Abadi, M., Banerjee, A., Heintze, N., Riecke, J.G.: A core calculus of dependency. In: Appel, A.W., Aiken, A. (eds.) POPL 1999, Proceedings of the 26th ACM SIGPLAN-SIGACT Symposium on Principles of Programming Languages, San Antonio, TX, USA, 20–22 January 1999, pp. 147–160. ACM (1999). https://doi.org/10.1145/292540.292555
2. Abel, A., Bernardy, J.: A unified view of modalities in type systems. Proc. ACM Program. Lang. **4**(ICFP), 90:1–90:28 (2020). https://doi.org/10.1145/3408972
3. Abel, A., Danielsson, N.A., Eriksson, O.: A graded modal dependent type theory with a universe and erasure, formalized. Proc. ACM Program. Lang. **7**(ICFP), 920–954 (2023). https://doi.org/10.1145/3607862
4. Abera, T., Yitayew, Y., Wasihun, D., Kolluru, V.: Ordered weak idempotent rings. Palest. J. Math. **13**(3) (2024)
5. Algehed, M.: A perspective on the dependency core calculus. In: Alvim, M.S., Delaune, S. (eds.) Proceedings of the 13th Workshop on Programming Languages and Analysis for Security, PLAS@CCS 2018, Toronto, ON, Canada, 15–19 October 2018, pp. 24–28. ACM (2018). https://doi.org/10.1145/3264820.3264823
6. Atkey, R.: Syntax and semantics of quantitative type theory. In: Dawar, A., Grädel, E. (eds.) Proceedings of the 33rd Annual ACM/IEEE Symposium on Logic in Computer Science, LICS 2018, Oxford, UK, 09–12 2018, pp. 56–65. ACM (2018). https://doi.org/10.1145/3209108.3209189
7. Benton, N., Bierman, G., de Paiva, V., Hyland, M.: Linear λ-calculus and categorical models revisited. In: Börger, E., Jäger, G., Kleine Büning, H., Martini, S., Richter, M.M. (eds.) CSL 1992. LNCS, vol. 702, pp. 61–84. Springer, Heidelberg (1993). https://doi.org/10.1007/3-540-56992-8_6
8. Bernardy, J., Boespflug, M., Newton, R.R., Jones, S.P., Spiwack, A.: Linear Haskell: practical linearity in a higher-order polymorphic language. Proc. ACM Program. Lang. **2**(POPL), 5:1–5:29 (2018). https://doi.org/10.1145/3158093
9. Bianchini, R., Dagnino, F., Giannini, P., Zucca, E.: A Java-like calculus with heterogeneous coeffects. Theor. Comput. Sci. **971**, 114063 (2023). https://doi.org/10.1016/J.TCS.2023.114063
10. Bianchini, R., Dagnino, F., Giannini, P., Zucca, E.: Multi-graded featherweight Java. In: Ali, K., Salvaneschi, G. (eds.) 37th European Conference on Object-Oriented Programming, ECOOP 2023, Seattle, Washington, United States, 17–21 July 2023. LIPIcs, vol. 263, pp. 3:1–3:27. Schloss Dagstuhl - Leibniz-Zentrum für Informatik (2023). https://doi.org/10.4230/LIPICS.ECOOP.2023.3
11. Bierman, G.M., De Paiva, V.C.: Intuitionistic necessity revisited. School of Computer Science research reports-University of Birmingham CSR (1996)
12. Bierman, G.M., de Paiva, V.: On an intuitionistic modal logic. Stud. Logica. **65**(3), 383–416 (2000). https://doi.org/10.1023/A:1005291931660
13. Brady, E.C.: Idris 2: quantitative type theory in practice. In: Møller, A., Sridharan, M. (eds.) 35th European Conference on Object-Oriented Programming, ECOOP 2021, Aarhus, Denmark,, 11–17 July 2021 (Virtual Conference). LIPIcs, vol. 194, pp. 9:1–9:26. Schloss Dagstuhl - Leibniz-Zentrum für Informatik (2021). https://doi.org/10.4230/LIPICS.ECOOP.2021.9
14. Brookes, S., Geva, S.: Computational comonads and intensional semantics. Carnegie-Mellon University, Department of Computer Science (1991)
15. Brunel, A., Gaboardi, M., Mazza, D., Zdancewic, S.: A core quantitative coeffect calculus. In: Shao, Z. (ed.) ESOP 2014. LNCS, vol. 8410, pp. 351–370. Springer, Heidelberg (2014). https://doi.org/10.1007/978-3-642-54833-8_19

16. Buiras, P., Vytiniotis, D., Russo, A.: HLIO: mixing static and dynamic typing for information-flow control in Haskell. In: Fisher, K., Reppy, J.H. (eds.) Proceedings of the 20th ACM SIGPLAN International Conference on Functional Programming, ICFP 2015, Vancouver, BC, Canada, 1–3 September 2015, pp. 289–301. ACM (2015). https://doi.org/10.1145/2784731.2784758
17. Choudhury, P.: Monadic and comonadic aspects of dependency analysis. Proc. ACM Program. Lang. **6**(OOPSLA2), 1320–1348 (2022). https://doi.org/10.1145/3563335
18. Choudhury, P., III, H.E., Eisenberg, R.A., Weirich, S.: A graded dependent type system with a usage-aware semantics. Proc. ACM Program. Lang. **5**(POPL), 1–32 (2021). https://doi.org/10.1145/3434331
19. Denning, D.E.: A lattice model of secure information flow. Commun. ACM **19**(5), 236–243 (1976). https://doi.org/10.1145/360051.360056
20. Gaboardi, M., Haeberlen, A., Hsu, J., Narayan, A., Pierce, B.C.: Linear dependent types for differential privacy. In: Giacobazzi, R., Cousot, R. (eds.) The 40th Annual ACM SIGPLAN-SIGACT Symposium on Principles of Programming Languages, POPL 2013, Rome, Italy, 23–25 January 2013, pp. 357–370. ACM (2013). https://doi.org/10.1145/2429069.2429113
21. Gaboardi, M., Katsumata, S., Orchard, D.A., Breuvart, F., Uustalu, T.: Combining effects and coeffects via grading. In: Garrigue, J., Keller, G., Sumii, E. (eds.) Proceedings of the 21st ACM SIGPLAN International Conference on Functional Programming, ICFP 2016, Nara, Japan, 18–22 September 2016, pp. 476–489. ACM (2016). https://doi.org/10.1145/2951913.2951939
22. Gay, S.J., Vasconcelos, V.T.: Linear type theory for asynchronous session types. J. Funct. Program. **20**(1), 19–50 (2010). https://doi.org/10.1017/S0956796809990268
23. Ghica, D.R., Smith, A.I.: Bounded linear types in a resource semiring. In: Shao, Z. (ed.) ESOP 2014. LNCS, vol. 8410, pp. 331–350. Springer, Heidelberg (2014). https://doi.org/10.1007/978-3-642-54833-8_18
24. Gifford, D.K., Lucassen, J.M.: Integrating functional and imperative programming. In: Scherlis, W.L., Williams, J.H., Gabriel, R.P. (eds.) Proceedings of the 1986 ACM Conference on LISP and Functional Programming, LFP 1986, Cambridge, Massachusetts, USA, 4–6 August 1986, pp. 28–38. ACM (1986). https://doi.org/10.1145/319838.319848
25. Girard, J.Y.: Linear logic. Theoret. Comput. Sci. **50**(1), 1–101 (1987). https://doi.org/10.1016/0304-3975(87)90045-4
26. Girard, J., Scedrov, A., Scott, P.J.: Bounded linear logic: a modular approach to polynomial-time computability. Theor. Comput. Sci. **97**(1), 1–66 (1992). https://doi.org/10.1016/0304-3975(92)90386-T
27. Hainry, E., Péchoux, R.: A type-based complexity analysis of object oriented programs. Inf. Comput. **261**, 78–115 (2018). https://doi.org/10.1016/J.IC.2018.05.006
28. Hedin, D., Sabelfeld, A.: A perspective on information-flow control. In: Nipkow, T., Grumberg, O., Hauptmann, B. (eds.) Software Safety and Security - Tools for Analysis and Verification, NATO Science for Peace and Security Series - D: Information and Communication Security, vol. 33, pp. 319–347. IOS Press (2012). https://doi.org/10.3233/978-1-61499-028-4-319
29. Heintze, N., Riecke, J.G.: The slam calculus: programming with secrecy and integrity. In: MacQueen, D.B., Cardelli, L. (eds.) POPL 1998, Proceedings of the 25th ACM SIGPLAN-SIGACT Symposium on Principles of Programming Languages, San Diego, CA, USA, 19–21 January 1998, pp. 365–377. ACM (1998). https://doi.org/10.1145/268946.268976

30. Hughes, J., Orchard, D.: Resourceful program synthesis from graded linear types. In: Fernández, M. (ed.) Logic-Based Program Synthesis and Transformation - 30th International Symposium, LOPSTR 2020, Bologna, Italy, 7–9 September 2020, Proceedings. LNCS, vol. 12561, pp. 151–170. Springer (2020). https://doi.org/10.1007/978-3-030-68446-4_8
31. Hughes, J., Orchard, D.: Program synthesis from graded types. In: Weirich, S. (ed.) Programming Languages and Systems - 33rd European Symposium on Programming, ESOP 2024, Held as Part of the European Joint Conferences on Theory and Practice of Software, ETAPS 2024, Luxembourg City, Luxembourg, 6–11 April 2024, Proceedings, Part I. LNCS, vol. 14576, pp. 83–112. Springer (2024). https://doi.org/10.1007/978-3-031-57262-3_4
32. Hughes, J., Vollmer, M., Orchard, D.: Deriving distributive laws for graded linear types. In: Lago, U.D., de Paiva, V. (eds.) Proceedings Second Joint International Workshop on Linearity & Trends in Linear Logic and Applications, Linearity&TLLA@IJCAR-FSCD 2020, Online, 29–30 June 2020. EPTCS, vol. 353, pp. 109–131 (2020). https://doi.org/10.4204/EPTCS.353.6
33. Katsumata, S.: Parametric effect monads and semantics of effect systems. In: Jagannathan, S., Sewell, P. (eds.) The 41st Annual ACM SIGPLAN-SIGACT Symposium on Principles of Programming Languages, POPL 2014, San Diego, CA, USA, 20–21 January 2014, pp. 633–646. ACM (2014). https://doi.org/10.1145/2535838.2535846
34. Lago, U.D., Gaboardi, M.: Linear dependent types and relative completeness. Log. Methods Comput. Sci. **8**(4) (2011). https://doi.org/10.2168/LMCS-8(4:11)2012
35. Liepelt, V.B., Orchard, D., Marshall, D.: Same coeffect, different base: graded types with and without linearity (2024, under review)
36. Lucassen, J.M., Gifford, D.K.: Polymorphic effect systems. In: Ferrante, J., Mager, P. (eds.) Conference Record of the Fifteenth Annual ACM Symposium on Principles of Programming Languages, San Diego, California, USA, 10–13 January 1988, pp. 47–57. ACM Press (1988). https://doi.org/10.1145/73560.73564
37. Marshall, D., Orchard, D.: Graded modal types for integrity and confidentiality. In: 17th Workshop on Programming Languages and Analysis for Security (PLAS 2022) (2022). https://arxiv.org/abs/2309.04324
38. Marshall, D., Orchard, D.: Functional ownership through fractional uniqueness. Proc. ACM Program. Lang. **8**(OOPSLA1), 1040–1070 (2024). https://doi.org/10.1145/3649848
39. Marshall, D., Orchard, D.: Non-linear communication via graded modal session types. Inf. Comput. **301**, 105234 (2024). https://doi.org/10.1016/J.IC.2024.105234
40. Marshall, D., Vollmer, M., Orchard, D.: Linearity and uniqueness: an entente cordiale. In: Sergey, I. (ed.) Programming Languages and Systems - 31st European Symposium on Programming, ESOP 2022, Held as Part of the European Joint Conferences on Theory and Practice of Software, ETAPS 2022, Munich, Germany, 2–7 April 2022, Proceedings. LNCS, vol. 13240, pp. 346–375. Springer (2022). https://doi.org/10.1007/978-3-030-99336-8_13
41. McBride, C.: I got plenty o' Nuttin'. In: Lindley, S., McBride, C., Trinder, P., Sannella, D. (eds.) A List of Successes That Can Change the World. LNCS, vol. 9600, pp. 207–233. Springer, Cham (2016). https://doi.org/10.1007/978-3-319-30936-1_12
42. Moggi, E.: Notions of computation and monads. Inf. Comput. **93**(1), 55–92 (1991). https://doi.org/10.1016/0890-5401(91)90052-4

43. Moon, B., Eades III, H., Orchard, D.: Graded modal dependent type theory. In: ESOP 2021. LNCS, vol. 12648, pp. 462–490. Springer, Cham (2021). https://doi.org/10.1007/978-3-030-72019-3_17
44. Mycroft, A., Orchard, D., Petricek, T.: Effect systems revisited—control-flow algebra and semantics. In: Probst, C.W., Hankin, C., Hansen, R.R. (eds.) Semantics, Logics, and Calculi. LNCS, vol. 9560, pp. 1–32. Springer, Cham (2016). https://doi.org/10.1007/978-3-319-27810-0_1
45. Myers, A.C.: JFlow: practical mostly-static information flow control. In: Appel, A.W., Aiken, A. (eds.) POPL 1999, Proceedings of the 26th ACM SIGPLAN-SIGACT Symposium on Principles of Programming Languages, San Antonio, TX, USA, 20–22 January 1999, pp. 228–241. ACM (1999). https://doi.org/10.1145/292540.292561
46. Orchard, D., Liepelt, V., III, H.E.: Quantitative program reasoning with graded modal types. PACMPL **3**(ICFP), 110:1–110:30 (2019). https://doi.org/10.1145/3341714
47. Orchard, D.A.: Programming contextual computations. Technical report, University of Cambridge (2014). https://ethos.bl.uk/OrderDetails.do?uin=uk.bl.ethos.708000
48. Orchard, D.A., Bolingbroke, M., Mycroft, A.: Ypnos: declarative, parallel structured grid programming. In: Petersen, L., Pontelli, E. (eds.) Proceedings of the POPL 2010 Workshop on Declarative Aspects of Multicore Programming, DAMP 2010, Madrid, Spain, 19 January 2010, pp. 15–24. ACM (2010). https://doi.org/10.1145/1708046.1708053
49. Orchard, D., Mycroft, A.: A notation for comonads. In: Hinze, R. (ed.) IFL 2012. LNCS, vol. 8241, pp. 1–17. Springer, Heidelberg (2013). https://doi.org/10.1007/978-3-642-41582-1_1
50. Orchard, D.A., Petricek, T., Mycroft, A.: The semantic marriage of monads and effects. CoRR **abs/1401.5391** (2014). http://arxiv.org/abs/1401.5391
51. Petricek, T.: Context-aware programming languages. Ph.D. thesis, University of Cambridge (2017)
52. Petricek, T., Orchard, D., Mycroft, A.: Coeffects: unified static analysis of context-dependence. In: Fomin, F.V., Freivalds, R., Kwiatkowska, M., Peleg, D. (eds.) ICALP 2013, Part II. LNCS, vol. 7966, pp. 385–397. Springer, Heidelberg (2013). https://doi.org/10.1007/978-3-642-39212-2_35
53. Petricek, T., Orchard, D.A., Mycroft, A.: Coeffects: a calculus of context-dependent computation. In: Jeuring, J., Chakravarty, M.M.T. (eds.) Proceedings of the 19th ACM SIGPLAN international conference on Functional programming, Gothenburg, Sweden, 1–3 September 2014, pp. 123–135. ACM (2014). https://doi.org/10.1145/2628136.2628160
54. Pottier, F., Simonet, V.: Information flow inference for ML. ACM Trans. Program. Lang. Syst. **25**(1), 117–158 (2003). https://doi.org/10.1145/596980.596983
55. Rajani, V., Garg, D.: Types for information flow control: labeling granularity and semantic models. In: 31st IEEE Computer Security Foundations Symposium, CSF 2018, Oxford, United Kingdom, 9–12 July 2018, pp. 233–246. IEEE Computer Society (2018). https://doi.org/10.1109/CSF.2018.00024
56. Rajani, V., Garg, D.: On the expressiveness and semantics of information flow types. J. Comput. Secur. **28**(1), 129–156 (2020). https://doi.org/10.3233/JCS-191382
57. Russo, A.: Functional pearl: two can keep a secret, if one of them uses Haskell. In: Fisher, K., Reppy, J.H. (eds.) Proceedings of the 20th ACM SIGPLAN International Conference on Functional Programming, ICFP 2015, Vancouver, BC,

Canada, 1–3 September 2015, pp. 280–288. ACM (2015). https://doi.org/10.1145/2784731.2784756
58. Simonet, V., Rocquencourt, I.: Flow Caml in a nutshell. In: Proceedings of the First APPSEM-II Workshop, pp. 152–165 (2003)
59. Snider, D., et al.: HHVM and Hack User Documentation. https://web.archive.org/web/20240824005941/https://docs.hhvm.com/hack/contexts-and-capabilities/introduction
60. Uustalu, T., Vene, V.: The essence of dataflow programming. In: Yi, K. (ed.) APLAS 2005. LNCS, vol. 3780, pp. 2–18. Springer, Heidelberg (2005). https://doi.org/10.1007/11575467_2
61. Uustalu, T., Vene, V.: Signals and comonads. J. Univers. Comput. Sci. **11**(7), 1310–1326 (2005). https://doi.org/10.3217/JUCS-011-07-1311
62. Uustalu, T., Vene, V.: Comonadic notions of computation. In: Adámek, J., Kupke, C. (eds.) Proceedings of the Ninth Workshop on Coalgebraic Methods in Computer Science, CMCS 2008, Budapest, Hungary, 4–6 April 2008. Electronic Notes in Theoretical Computer Science, vol. 203, pp. 263–284. Elsevier (2008). https://doi.org/10.1016/J.ENTCS.2008.05.029
63. Vollmer, V., Marshall, D., Eades III, H., Orchard, D.: A mixed linear and graded logic: proofs, terms and models. In: 33rd EACSL Annual Conference on Computer Science Logic (CSL 2025) (2025). https://doi.org/10.4230/LIPIcs.CSL.2025.32
64. Volpano, D.M., Irvine, C.E., Smith, G.: A sound type system for secure flow analysis. J. Comput. Secur. **4**(2/3), 167–188 (1996). https://doi.org/10.3233/JCS-1996-42-304
65. Volpano, D.M., Smith, G.: Verifying secrets and relative secrecy. In: POPL 2000, Proceedings of the 27th ACM SIGPLAN-SIGACT Symposium on Principles of Programming Languages, Boston, Massachusetts, USA, 19–21 January 2000, pp. 268–276 (2000). https://doi.org/10.1145/325694.325729
66. Wadler, P.: Linear types can change the world! In: Broy, M., Jones, C.B. (eds.) Programming Concepts and Methods: Proceedings of the IFIP Working Group 2.2, 2.3 Working Conference on Programming Concepts and Methods, Sea of Galilee, Israel, 2–5 April 1990, p. 561. North-Holland (1990)
67. Wadler, P., Thiemann, P.: The marriage of effects and monads. ACM Trans. Comput. Log. **4**(1), 1–32 (2003). https://doi.org/10.1145/601775.601776
68. Walker, D.: Substructural type systems. Adv. Top. Types Program. Lang., 3–44 (2005)
69. Wood, J., Atkey, R.: A linear algebra approach to linear metatheory **353**, 195–212 (2020). https://doi.org/10.4204/EPTCS.353.10

Hardware

Static Analysis for Hardware Design

Mads Rosendahl(✉) and Maja H. Kirkeby

Computer Science, Roskilde University, Roskilde, Denmark
madsr@ruc.dk, kirkebym@acm.org

Abstract. Implementing algorithms in hardware can be a substantial engineering challenge. Hardware accelerators for some algorithms may be a way to achieve better time and energy efficiency of computational problems. We explore some possible applications of static analysis in the design phase of constructing hardware design for algorithms targeting field-programmable gate arrays (FPGA).

Drawing inspiration from Alan Mycroft's 2007 invited talk on static analysis and subsequent articles discussing the connection between hardware evolution, language design, and static analysis, we explore the usage of static analysis as a tool to facilitate the realization of hardware accelerators for algorithms. We examine methodologies for analyzing communication and data flows within the hardware design, thereby enhancing our understanding of these aspects in the pursuit of efficient FPGA-based algorithm implementations.

Keywords: formal semantics · static analyses · hardware description language

1 Introduction

At the 2007 Static Analysis Symposium [14] Alan Mycroft outlined some of the changes modern hardware development would have on language design and static analysis. Many programming languages and program analysis techniques are based on the single processor architecture whereas the development of hardware has moved to architecture with higher levels of parallelism.

The hardware development combined with awareness of the energy consumption of IT systems has sparked interest in potential energy savings by realizing algorithms in hardware. In previous work [9,10] we have explored and measured energy saving from moving software into hardware designs for Field Programmable Gate Arrays (FPGA). Converting algorithms for traditional architectures into highly parallel circuits raises a number of interesting challenges and

To Alan Mycroft.

Ph.D. supervisor and Ph.D. supervisor's supervisor.

This work is supported by the Independent Research Fund Denmark Project no. 2102-00281B.

D. Orchard et al. (Eds.): Alan Mycroft Festschrift, LNCS 15500, pp. 151–169, 2026.
https://doi.org/10.1007/978-3-032-08187-2_8

in this paper, we will explore some ways to use classical data flow analyses in this process.

High-level synthesis (HLS) tools provide a means to create hardware solutions by converting programs written in a common programming language into hardware specifications using hardware description languages (HDLs). These specifications enable the implementation of hardware components, such as FPGA processors. Although HLS tools have made significant progress, there remains an efficiency gap compared to manual hardware design using HDLs [21]. Carefully crafted HDL designs often outperform synthesized designs, highlighting the need for further exploration of algorithmic redesign to exploit the potential of high-level parallelism fully. Furthermore, we observe that while software implementation of algorithms, such as heapsort, can be achieved with relatively short code (e.g., 30–40 lines) [17], hardware designs for the same algorithms often require a significantly larger number of lines in an HDL (e.g., 600–700 lines). [9,10,25]

Our approach is to identify a substantial subset of the HDL Chisel, well-suited for algorithm realization. The aim is to have a small and manageable language while preserving expressiveness. We exclude Chisel's support for compile-time code generation and evaluation, making it possible to write parameterized modules that can be used in different settings. Furthermore, the language will be restricted to one form of inter-module communication and one form of memory banks. The subset can be used to describe datapath architectures in which modules of finite-state machines are connected via data channels and each module has a separate memory area. States in each module may have several parallel register transfers, and multiple modules can be active in the same clock cycle. Despite the high degree of parallelism, the system's execution is deterministic.

We provide a formal semantics for the subset of Chisel and establish a framework for constructing data flow analysis of this subset. The analysis is meant to be used in the development phase to give information on possible flows and values to locate inefficiencies or unintended behaviours of the design.

This paper aims to explore parts of the agenda described by Alan Mycroft in 2007. We explore ways of moving algorithms to hardware with high levels of parallelism and explore ways to analyze the designs to obtain more efficient solutions.

1.1 Outline

In Sect. 2 we identify a subset of the hardware description language Chisel [1] and provide a formal semantics in a denotational style for the subset. In Sect. 4 we describe an interval analysis for the language and show how it can be used for analyzing the bit-width of registers, possible underflow of registers, and communication patterns for modules. We discuss other potential data flow analysis techniques that can be used in this language in section 5. In Sect. 6 we discuss some of the potential extensions to the analysis described in the paper and ways to improve the precision of the analysis. Several related works are discussed in Sect. 7. Implementations of the semantics and analyses can be found in an accompanying GitHub repository [13].

2 Core Chisel

Chisel [1] as a hardware description language provides a comprehensive set of features and constructs that enable designers to describe hardware designs at various levels of abstraction. By employing Chisel, algorithmic solutions can be translated into register transfer level (RTL) hardware designs, encompassing interconnected registers and logical gates.

Chisel, as an embedded HDL, resides within the Scala programming language, providing developers with a powerful toolset for hardware development. This integration enables the utilization of both object-oriented and functional programming paradigms in the design and can simplify the design process.

In our subset of Chisel, a hardware design contains multiple interconnected modules connected by datapath channels for communication. These modules and channels are statically allocated. Each module has registers, data banks, channel connections, and a finite state machine. Within each state, simultaneous operations such as register transfers, memory access, and channel communications can occur in parallel. The evaluation process exhibits multiple levels of parallelism, with all modules activated simultaneously, each state accommodating multiple register transfers, and each register transfer involving the evaluation of expressions and sub-expressions within the same clock cycle.

Despite the presence of substantial parallelism in the hardware circuit, the evaluation process remains deterministic, following the same sequence of states for a given initial configuration of registers and memory banks. This deterministic behavior arises from all modules and communication channels being part of the same hardware circuit and controlled by the same clock.

2.1 Datapath Communication

Inter-module communication in the hardware design is supported in Chisel as port constructors [4] which works as one-way channels, serving as outbound streams from one module and inbound streams to another. These channels are statically allocated and are synchronized. Each channel consists of three components: data storage for writing and reading between modules, along with two boolean values indicating readiness for writing and reading operations using a ready-valid protocol [7]. The synchronization allows a one-cycle transition from writing to reading on a channel, followed by an extra cycle to reset the channel for subsequent writing operations (Fig. 1).

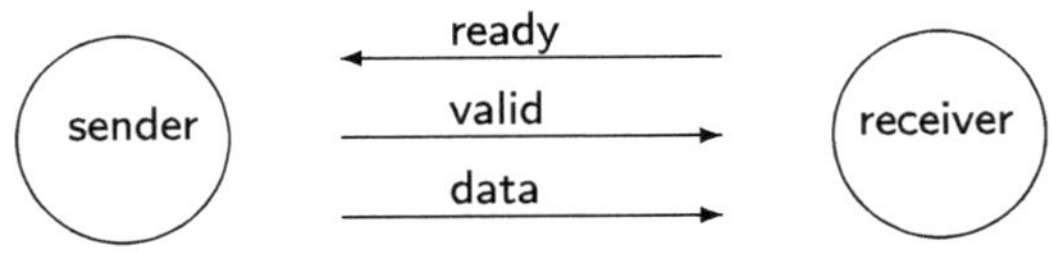

Fig. 1. Channel - consists of three "wires": ready (1 bit), valid (1 bit), and data (1 or more bits).

Writing is allowed when *ready&!valid* is satisfied. Writing will set *valid* to true. Reading from the channel requires *ready&valid* to be satisfied and will set *ready* to false. Reset happens when *ready* is false and will set *ready* to true and *valid* to false. After reset the channel can be used for writing.

2.2 Finite State Machine

The hardware design comprises multiple modules interconnected through channels. Each module contains a finite state machine with a state register. In order to enter a state involving input/output (I/O) operations, all I/O operations must be feasible, ensuring proper synchronization. State operations encompass various tasks, including simple register assignments, reading from and writing to channels, and accessing memory banks. Access to a memory bank is restricted to allow a maximum of one read and one write operation per clock cycle. A value read from a memory bank is not accessible before the end of a clock cycle and cannot be used in other expressions but must be stored in a register so that it can be used in subsequent clock cycles. Part of the register transfer operations within a clock cycle involves computing a new value for the state register. This also means that the condition in a state is evaluated using the values registers had at the start of the clock cycle and not after any updates happen in the state.

2.3 Abstract Syntax

We describe the subset of Chisel using an abstract syntax that allows for a straightforward translation to and from the actual syntax in Chisel. A hardware description in this subset has two main parts: module and channel allocation, followed by module declaration. The module allocation part enables the creation of one or more instances of the modules declared in the second part.

Declaring a stream in the abstract syntax will in the actual syntax of Chisel correspond to declaring the three connections in a datapath and an operation to reset the channel when the channel is not ready.

```
⟨program⟩    ::= ⟨module⟩+⟨connnection⟩* ⟨module-decl⟩+

⟨module⟩     ::= 'val' ⟨ident⟩ '=' 'Module' '(' ⟨ident⟩ ')'

⟨connection⟩ ::= ⟨ident⟩ '.' ⟨ident⟩ '<>' ⟨ident⟩ '.' ⟨ident⟩

⟨module-decl⟩ ::= 'module' ⟨ident⟩ ⟨declaration⟩* ⟨state⟩+

⟨declaration⟩ ::= 'int' ⟨ident⟩ [ '=' ⟨number⟩ ]
               | 'int' '[' ⟨number⟩ ']' ⟨ident⟩
               | 'instream' ⟨ident⟩
               | 'outstream' ⟨ident⟩

⟨state⟩      ::= 'state' ⟨number⟩ [ 'when' ⟨expr⟩ ] ⟨statement⟩* 'goto' ⟨gotoexp⟩

⟨statement⟩  ::= ⟨ident⟩ '=' ⟨expr⟩
               | ⟨ident⟩ '[' ⟨expr⟩ ']' '=' ⟨expr⟩
               | ⟨ident⟩ '=' ⟨ident⟩ '[' ⟨expr⟩ ']'
               | ⟨ident⟩ '.' 'write' '(' ⟨expr⟩ ')'
               | ⟨ident⟩ '=' ⟨ident⟩ '.' 'read' '(' ')'

⟨expr⟩       ::= ⟨ident⟩
               | ⟨number⟩
               | ⟨expr⟩ ⟨operation⟩ ⟨expr⟩
               | 'Mux' '(' ⟨expr⟩ ',' ⟨expr⟩ ',' ⟨expr⟩ ')'
               | ⟨ident⟩ '.' 'ready'
               | ⟨ident⟩ '.' 'valid'

⟨operation⟩  ::= '+' | '-' | '*' | '/' | '%' | '&' | '|' | '>' | '<' | '>=' | '<='| '==' | '!='

⟨gotoexp⟩    ::= ⟨number⟩
               | 'Mux' '(' ⟨expr⟩ ',' ⟨gotoexp⟩ ',' ⟨gotoexp⟩ ')'
```

The program starts with a declaration of modules and channels and the connection of channels between modules. Channels are one-way channels but two modules can be connected with two separate channels to achieve bi-directional communication. Each module contains a number of states and each state will end with an expression to find the next state. States can have a `'when'` clause which is used to check that all communication in the state is allowed. Statements are either simple register transfers or transfers to or from channels or memory banks.

2.4 Example

Below we have a small example of a hardware description with modules that communicate via a channel. The sender module will transmit three numbers along the channel and the receiver module will store the numbers in a databank. The receiver requires two states since the value read from the channel cannot be stored in a databank until the following clock cycle.

```
val sender = Module(Sender)
val receiver = Module(Receiver)
sender.out <> receiver.in

module Sender
  int x
  outstream out
state 1
  x = 0
  goto 2
state 2 when out.ready()
  out.write(x)
  x = x + 1
  goto Mux(x <= 3, 2, 3)
state 3
  goto 3

module Receiver
  int x
  int i=0
  int[4] data
  instream in
state 1 when in.valid()
  x = in.read()
  goto 2
state 2
  data[i] = x
  i = i + 1
  goto Mux(i < 3, 1, 99)
state 3
  goto 3
```

The program will send 5 values on the stream but the receiver will only read 4 so that the two modules will reach the final states with data ready to read in the channel. The sender will send until the variable '`x`' is 4 but the test is performed at the same time as the register is incremented so that its final value is 5.

2.5 Well-Formed Programs

The semantics makes several assumptions on hardware descriptions.

- Each output stream must be connected to an input stream in another module.
- All allocated modules must have a declaration.
- All registers and memory banks used in a module must be declared. Registers and memory banks can only be used in the module in which they are declared.
- The labels in the state machine for each module must be unique.

- A state can contain at most one assignment to a register and at most one read and one write operation to a memory bank.
- Reading from a memory bank should be done using a register only used for that purpose.
- The condition on states should be a check that all I/O operations in the state are feasible.

3 Semantics

We present a formal semantics of the Core Chisel subset. The denotation of a hardware description will be a mapping of an initial state environment to a final state environment. In the final state, no further state transitions can take place in the design.

State Environment. The state of the hardware description at any given time can be recorded as a state environment. This environment contains the value of all registers in all modules and the value of registers in channels We consider each module and each channel as a separate namespace. Modules are identified by the name and we give each channel a number to identify it in the environment. For memory banks, we treat each location in the bank as a separate register and in the environment reference the individual elements by a concatenation ($::$) of the name of the memory bank and the index. The domain for state environments is the set Σ.

$$r \in \mathrm{Reg} : (\mathsf{N} \cup \mathbb{A}) \times \mathbb{A}$$
$$\sigma \in \Sigma : \mathrm{Reg} \rightarrow \mathbb{Z}_{\perp}$$

The semantics has two parts. The initialization phase lays out all modules and connects modules with channels. This gives us the initial state environment of the hardware design. The second phase is the clock-step operation. This consists of a reset of channels(R) if needed, and performing state transitions in each module (T) if the conditions in **when** clauses are met. The state transition function records changes to the state environment. All changes to modules and channels are collected in parallel and then used to update the state environment.

Updating an environment with values from another environment is written as

$$\sigma_1 \oplus \sigma_2 = \lambda x.\ \mathbf{if}\ \sigma_1(x) = \perp_\Sigma\ \mathbf{then}\ \sigma_2(x)\ \mathbf{else}\ \sigma_1(x)$$

Initial Environment. The initial state environment for a program consists of initialization of all registers and memory banks in modules and connecting channels to streams in modules.

$$\begin{aligned}
&\mathbf{I}[\![mod^+ con^* mdcl^+]\!] = \mathbf{I}_c[\![con^*]\!] \oplus \mathbf{I}_m[\![mod^*]\!](\mathsf{D}[\![mdcl^*]\!])\\
&\mathbf{I}_c[\![con_1 \ldots con_n]\!] = \mathbf{I}_c[\![con_1]\!]\ 1 \oplus \cdots \mathbf{I}_c[\![con_1]\!]\ n\\
&\mathbf{I}_c[\![m_1.out_1\,\texttt{`<>'}\,m_2.in_2]\!]\ i = [(m_1.out_1) \mapsto i] \oplus [(m_2.in_2) \mapsto i] \oplus\\
&\qquad [(i, \texttt{`ready'}) \mapsto 0] \oplus [(i, \texttt{`valid'}) \mapsto 0] \oplus [(i, \texttt{`data'}) \mapsto 0] \oplus\\
&\qquad [(m_1, c_1) \mapsto i] \oplus [(m_2, c_2) \mapsto i]\\
&\mathbf{I}_m[\![mod_1 \cdots mod_n]\!]\ d = \mathbf{I}_m[\![mod_1]\!]\ d \oplus \cdots \oplus \mathbf{I}_m[\![mod_n]\!]\ d\\
&\mathbf{I}_m[\![\texttt{`val'}m\texttt{`='}\texttt{`Module'}\texttt{`('}M\texttt{`)'}]\!] d = d\ M\ m
\end{aligned}$$

The **D** function defines the declaration and initialization of registers and memory banks in modules.

$$\begin{aligned}
&\mathbf{D}[\![mdcl_1 \ldots mdcl_n]\!]\ M\ m = \mathbf{D}[\![mdcl_1]\!]\ M\ m \oplus \cdots \oplus \mathbf{D}[\![mdcl_n]\!]\ M\ m\\
&\mathbf{D}[\![\text{`}\mathtt{module}\text{'}M_1 decl\ states]\!]\ M\ m = \mathbf{if}\ M = M_1\ \mathbf{then}\ \mathbf{D}[\![decl]\!]m\ \mathbf{else} \perp_\Sigma\\
&\mathbf{D}[\![d_1 \cdots d_n]\!]\ m = \mathbf{D}[\![d_1]\!]\ m \oplus \mathbf{D}[\![d_n]\!]\ m \oplus [(m, \text{`}\mathtt{state}\text{'}) \mapsto 1]\\
&\mathbf{D}[\![\text{`}\mathtt{int}\text{'}x = n]\!]\ m = [(m, x) \mapsto n]\\
&\mathbf{D}[\![\text{`}\mathtt{int}\text{'}[n]a]\!]\ m = [(m, a::0) \mapsto n] \oplus \cdots \oplus [(m, a::(n-1))) \mapsto n]
\end{aligned}$$

Channel Reset. Reset of channels in environment σ is done in each cycle for channels where the data has been read.

$$\begin{aligned}
&\mathbf{R}[\![con_1 \cdots con_n]\!]\ \sigma = \mathbf{R}[\![con_1]\!]\ \sigma \oplus \cdots \oplus \mathbf{R}[\![con_n]\!]\ \sigma\\
&\mathbf{R}[\![m_1.out_1\text{`}\mathtt{<>}\text{'}m_2.in_2]\!]\ \sigma = \mathbf{let}\ c = \sigma(m_1, out_1)\\
&\qquad \mathbf{if}\ \sigma(c, \text{`}\mathtt{ready}\text{'}) = 0\ \mathbf{then}\ [(c, \text{`}\mathtt{ready}\text{'}) \mapsto 1, (c, \text{`}\mathtt{valid}\text{'}) \mapsto 0]\ \mathbf{else} \perp_\Sigma
\end{aligned}$$

State Transitions. The semantic functions record changes to the state environment σ for each module in each clock cycle. The function $\mathbf{T}_d$ is applied to module declarations, $\mathbf{T}_t$ to the states in modules and $\mathbf{T}_s$ to statements in states.

$$\begin{aligned}
&\mathbf{T}[\![mod^+ con^* mdcl^+]\!]\sigma = (\mathbf{T}_m[\![mod^*]\!](\mathbf{T}_d[\![mdcl^*]\!])\ \sigma) \oplus \mathbf{R}[\![con^*]\!]\sigma\\
&\mathbf{T}_m[\![mod_1 \cdots mod_n]\!]\ d\ \sigma = \mathbf{T}_m[\![mod_1]\!]\ d\ \sigma \oplus \cdots \oplus \mathbf{T}_m[\![mod_n]\!]\ d\ \sigma\\
&\mathbf{T}_m[\![\text{`}\mathtt{val}\text{'}m\text{`}\mathtt{=}\text{'}\text{`}\mathtt{Module}\text{'}\text{`}\mathtt{(}\text{'}M\text{`}\mathtt{)}\text{'}]\!]\ d\ \sigma\ m = d\ \sigma\ M\ m\\
&\mathbf{T}_d[\![mdcl_1 \cdots mdcl_n]\!]\ \sigma\ M\ m = \mathbf{T}_d[\![mdcl_1]\!]\ \sigma\ M\ m \oplus \cdots \oplus \mathbf{T}_d[\![mdcl_n]\!]\ \sigma\ M\ m\\
&\mathbf{T}_d[\![\text{`}\mathtt{module}\text{'}M_1 decl\ states]\!]\ \sigma\ M\ m = \mathbf{if}\ M = M_1\ \mathbf{then}\ \mathbf{T}_t[\![states]\!]\sigma\ m\ \mathbf{else} \perp_\Sigma
\end{aligned}$$

$$\begin{aligned}
&\mathbf{T}_t[\![state_1 \cdots state_n]\!]\ \sigma\ m = \mathbf{T}_t[\![state_1]\!]\sigma\ m \oplus \cdots \oplus \mathbf{T}_t[\![state_n]\!]\sigma\ m\\
&\mathbf{T}_t[\![\text{`}\mathtt{state}\text{'}n\text{`}\mathtt{when}\text{'}e\ s_1 \cdots s_n\text{`}\mathtt{goto}\text{'}e_g]\!]\ \sigma\ m =\\
&\qquad \mathbf{if}\ \sigma(m, \text{`}\mathtt{state}\text{'}) \neq n\ \mathbf{then} \perp_\Sigma\ \mathbf{else}\\
&\qquad \mathbf{if}\ \mathbf{E}[\![e]\!]\ \sigma\ m \neq 1\ \mathbf{then} \perp_\Sigma\ \mathbf{else}\\
&\qquad \mathbf{T}_t[\![s_1]\!]\ \sigma\ m \oplus \cdots \oplus \mathbf{T}_t[\![s_n]\!]\ \sigma\ m \oplus [(m, \text{`}\mathtt{state}\text{'} \mapsto \mathbf{E}[\![e_g]\!]\ \sigma\ m]
\end{aligned}$$

The five types of statements are simple register transfers from expressions to registers, reading and writing to channels, and reading and writing to memory banks. Values of locations in memory banks are stored in the environment under a name obtained by concatenating the name of the memory bank with the index using a concatenation operation (::).

$$\begin{aligned}
&\mathbf{T}_s[\![x\text{`}\mathtt{=}\text{'}e]\!]\ \sigma\ m = [(m, x) \mapsto \mathbf{E}[\![e]\!]\sigma m]\\
&\mathbf{T}_s[\![a[e_1]\text{`}\mathtt{=}\text{'}e_2]\!]\ \sigma\ m = [(m, a::\mathbf{E}[\![e_1]\!]\ \sigma\ m) \mapsto \mathbf{E}[\![e_2]\!]\ \sigma\ m]\\
&\mathbf{T}_s[\![x\text{`}\mathtt{=}\text{'}a[e_1]]\!]\ \sigma\ m = [(m, x) \mapsto \sigma(m, a::\mathbf{E}[\![e_1]\!]\ \sigma\ m)]\\
&\mathbf{T}_s[\![out\text{`}\mathtt{.write(}\text{'}e\text{`}\mathtt{)}\text{'}]\!]\ \sigma\ m =\\
&\qquad [(\sigma(m, out), \text{`}\mathtt{data}\text{'}) \mapsto \mathbf{E}[\![e]\!]\sigma\ m, (\sigma(m, out), \text{`}\mathtt{valid}\text{'}) \mapsto 1]\\
&\mathbf{T}_s[\![x\text{`}\mathtt{=}\text{'}in\text{`}\mathtt{.read()}\text{'}]\!]\ \sigma\ m =\\
&\qquad [(m, x) \mapsto \sigma(\sigma(m, in), \text{`}\mathtt{data}\text{'}), (\sigma(m, out), \text{`}\mathtt{ready}\text{'}) \mapsto 0]
\end{aligned}$$

Each channel is identified with a number in the state environment. When we read and write to channels we change the status bits in the channel and before reading or writing we check whether the channel is ready for reading or writing.

$\mathbf{E}[\![n]\!]\ \sigma\ m = n$
$\mathbf{E}[\![v]\!]\ \sigma\ m = \sigma(m, v)$
$\mathbf{E}[\![\texttt{'Mux('}e_1, e_2, e_3\texttt{')'}]\!]\ \sigma\ m = \mathbf{if}\ \mathbf{E}[\![e_1]\!]\ \sigma\ m = 1\ \mathbf{then}\ \mathbf{E}[\![e_2]\!]\ \sigma\ m\ \mathbf{then}\ \mathbf{E}[\![e_3]\!]\ \sigma\ m$
$\mathbf{E}[\![e_1\ op\ e_2]\!]\ \sigma\ m = op(\mathbf{E}[\![e_1]\!]\ \sigma\ m, \mathbf{E}[\![e_2]\!]\ \sigma\ m)$
$\mathbf{E}[\![in\texttt{'.ready()'}]\!]\ \sigma\ m = \sigma(\sigma(m, in), \texttt{'ready'}) = 1 \wedge \sigma(\sigma(m, in), \texttt{'valid'}) = 0$
$\mathbf{E}[\![in\texttt{'.valid()'}]\!] \sigma\ m = \sigma(\sigma(m, in), \texttt{'ready'}) = 1 \wedge \sigma(\sigma(m, in), \texttt{'valid'}) = 1$

The semantics functions can also be found in our GitHub repository [13] and can be used as an interpreter for the language. Below we use the semantics function to collect possible environments at each program point in the system.

3.1 Label Vector Graph

What corresponds to a program point for a hardware description is the vector of state numbers (or labels) for each module. We will assume we have numbering of the modules $m_1, \dots m_n$, and in an environment σ this vector of label numbers can be found as follows

$$\text{lab}(\sigma) = \langle \sigma(m_1, \texttt{'state'}), \dots, \sigma(m_n, \texttt{'state'}) \rangle$$

The set of possible label vectors will be

$$\Lambda : \{1, \dots, k\}^n$$

where k is the maximal state number in modules and n is the number of modules.

The aim of the next section (4) is to develop a safe approximation of the possible environments for each label vector during a run of the system. Here we will give the standard interpretation that collects the set of possible state environments for each program point or label vector.

Collecting the set of possible environments for each label vector has strong similarities to the minimal function graph interpretation of applicative languages by Jones and Mycroft [8]. The semantics collect environments reachable from the initial environment.

The initial environment σ_{init} can be found using the functions above.

$$\sigma_{init} = \mathbf{I}[\![mod^+ con^* mdcl^+]\!]$$

We want to construct a mapping of label vectors to sets of possible environments

$$f : \Lambda \to \wp(\Sigma)$$
$$f_0 : [\langle 1, \dots, 1 \rangle \mapsto \{\sigma_{init}\}]$$

It can be found as a fixpoint of the transition function

$$F(f) = f_0 \sqcup f \sqcup$$
$$\{[\ell' \mapsto \sigma'] \mid \ell \in \text{dom}(f) \wedge \sigma \in f(\ell) \wedge \sigma' = (\mathbf{T}[\![prg]\!]\sigma \oplus \sigma) \wedge \ell' = \text{lab}(\sigma')\}$$

For each label vector, it records the set of possible environments at the start of the states with the given state numbers. It will record all state vectors reachable from the initial environment.

An implementation of the standard semantics and the label vector graph interpretation can be found in our GitHub repository [13].

4 Abstract Interval Semantics

One of the challenges in hardware design is to economize with the allocation of logical units and allocating just the right number of bits to registers is one way to achieve that. We will here explore how to use interval analysis for this purpose. The analysis can also be used for the underflow of registers and record communication patterns to identify unwanted delays in the design. These applications will be discussed in the next section.

At the core of the analysis is a domain of intervals which will be used to describe sets of possible behaviours

$$\mathbf{I} = \{\} \cup \{[n : m] \mid n \in \mathbb{Z} \cup \{-\infty\} \wedge m \in \mathbb{Z} \cup \{\infty\} \wedge n \leq m\}$$

This domain is infinite and to secure termination we must ensure that only finite parts of he domain are used.

The widening operation is used to guarantee the termination of the analysis. One of the aspects we are interested in is the number of bits needed for each register with unsigned integers. The widening operation we will use is based on capturing the number of bits in values.

$$\begin{array}{l}
\nabla : \mathbf{I} \rightarrow \mathbf{I} \\
\nabla = \\
\nabla[n, m] = [n', m'] \quad \text{ where} \\
\quad n' = max\{k \leq n \wedge k \in \{-\infty, 0, 1, 2, 4, .., 2^{32}\}\} \\
\quad m' = min\{k \geq m \wedge k \in \{0, 1, 3, 7, 15, .., 2^{32} - 1, \infty\}\}
\end{array}$$

The widening operation can be applied at various stages of the analysis. We could insert it on all operations in the analysis so that the range of the widening function becomes the abstract domain of the analysis. We will use it sparingly to give higher precision and to guarantee termination.

The domain of intervals is similar to the domain in the analysis proposed by Kuchler et al. [12] for analysis of binaries but the widening operation [6] we use is different.

4.1 Semantic Domains

The analysis aims to construct an abstract environment of mappings of registers to intervals for each label vector that could be reached from an initial environment.

$$\begin{array}{rcl}
\tilde{\sigma} \in \tilde{\Sigma} & = & \text{Reg} \rightarrow \mathbf{I} \\
\theta \in \Theta & = & \Lambda \rightarrow \tilde{\Sigma}_{\perp}
\end{array}$$

The abstraction of the environment to abstract environments is done by elementwise mapping of integers to singleton intervals.

$$\begin{aligned}&\alpha : \Sigma \to \tilde{\Sigma}\\&\alpha(\sigma) = \lambda x.\ \textbf{if}\ \sigma(x) = \bot\ \textbf{then}\ \bot\ \textbf{else}\ [\sigma(x), \sigma(x)]\end{aligned}$$

The initial abstract environment is the abstraction of the initial environment in semantics above $\tilde{\sigma}_{init} = \alpha(\sigma_{init})$.

The initial mapping of label vectors to environments will be

$$\theta_0 : [\langle 1, \ldots, 1\rangle \mapsto \tilde{\sigma}_{init}]$$

that maps all modules being at the initial state to the initial abstract environment.

4.2 Semantic Functions

Most of the standard interpretation above can be lifted fairly directly to interpretation over intervals. At branches and checks where communication in states can take place, there can be several possible state transitions. Our analysis will use a conditional analysis [20] to restrict the environments in branches to parts that cannot be excluded. In the abstract domain, the transition function will map an environment at a given label vector into the possible successor labels and environments.

Below we will define the abstract transition function that from a label vector and abstract environment returns a new mapping of label vectors to abstract environments.

$$\tilde{\mathbf{T}}[\![prg]\!] : \Lambda \times \tilde{\Sigma} \to \Theta$$

The approximation of intervals for registers at each label vector can be found as the fixpoint of this function.

$$F(\theta) = \theta_0 \sqcup \theta \sqcup (\sqcup\{\tilde{\mathbf{T}}[\![prg]\!]\ell\ \tilde{\sigma} \mid \ell \in \mathrm{dom}(\theta) \wedge \tilde{\sigma} = \theta(\ell)\})$$

As for label vectors, we assume that we have numbering of modules $(m_1, \ldots, m_n)$ that correspond to the label vector and that we for each module have a list of states with statements.

The transition function for all modules at label vector ℓ with abstract environment $\tilde{\sigma}$ is defined as follows

$$\tilde{\mathbf{T}}[\![m_1 \cdots m_n]\!]\ \ell\ \tilde{\sigma} = \sqcup\{[\langle \ell'_1, \ldots, \ell'_n\rangle \mapsto \tilde{\sigma}_i] \mid \langle \ell'_i, \tilde{\sigma}_i\rangle \in \tilde{\mathbf{T}}_m[\![m_i]\!]\ \ell_i\ \tilde{\sigma}\ m_i\}$$

For each module, the transition function will find a set of possible next states and next environments, and combinations of these are joined for the whole program. If the next state is an unconditional jump then that will be the next state with the current environment. For conditional jumps, we want to restrict the environment to parts that can make the condition true or false.

$$
\begin{aligned}
&\tilde{\mathbf{T}}_m[\![m_i]\!] : \mathsf{N} \times \tilde{\Sigma} \times \mathbf{A} \to \wp(\mathsf{N} \times \tilde{\Sigma})\\
&\tilde{\mathbf{T}}_m[\![state_1 \cdots state_k]\!]\ j\ \tilde{\sigma}\ m = \tilde{\mathbf{T}}_t[\![state_j]\!]\ j\ \tilde{\sigma}\ m\\
&\tilde{\mathbf{T}}_t[\![\texttt{`state'}n\texttt{`when'}e\ s_1 \cdots s_n\texttt{`goto'}e_g]\!] j\ \tilde{\sigma}\ m =\\
&\quad \textbf{if } 1 \in \tilde{\mathbf{E}}[\![e]\!]\ \tilde{\sigma}\ m \textbf{ then } \langle j, \tilde{\sigma}\rangle \textbf{ else}\\
&\quad \{\langle j', \tilde{\mathbf{T}}_s[\![s_1]\!]\ \tilde{\sigma}'\ m \sqcup \cdots \sqcup \tilde{\mathbf{T}}_t[\![s_n]\!]\ \tilde{\sigma}'\ m\rangle \mid \langle j', \tilde{\sigma}'\rangle \in \tilde{\mathbf{T}}_g[\![e_g]\!]\tilde{\sigma}\ m\}
\end{aligned}
$$

The transition function for statements is similar to the standard semantic except that elements in databanks are handled amalgamated so that only one interval is used to describe all elements.

The branching will return a set of tuples of the next label and environment

$$
\begin{aligned}
&\tilde{\mathbf{T}}_g[\![j]\!]\tilde{\sigma}\ m = \{\langle j, \tilde{\sigma}\rangle\}\\
&\tilde{\mathbf{T}}_g[\![\texttt{`Mux('}e, j_1, j_2\texttt{`)'}]\!]\ \tilde{\sigma}\ m = \{\langle j_1, \tilde{\mathbf{E}}^T[\![e]\!]\tilde{\sigma}\ m\rangle, \langle j_2, \tilde{\mathbf{E}}^F[\![e]\!]\tilde{\sigma}\ m\rangle\}
\end{aligned}
$$

where $\tilde{\mathbf{E}}^T$ and $\tilde{\mathbf{E}}^F$ are functions that take an expression and environment and return a possibly more restricted environment where values that cannot make the expression true or false, respectively, are excluded.

$$
\begin{aligned}
&\tilde{\mathbf{E}}^T[\![x > n]\!]\tilde{\sigma}\ m = [(m, x) \mapsto \tilde{\sigma}(m, x) \sqcap [n+1, \infty]] \oplus \tilde{\sigma}\\
&\tilde{\mathbf{E}}^F[\![x > n]\!]\tilde{\sigma}\ m = [(m, x) \mapsto \tilde{\sigma}(m, x) \sqcap [-\infty, n]] \oplus \tilde{\sigma}
\end{aligned}
$$

The function is also defined for a range of other comparison expressions. The safe upper approximation of these functions is just to return the environment unchanged. This happens when we cannot deduce any restrictions to the environment.

The state transition function treats memory banks amalgamated so that just one interval is just to describe the range of values for all locations.

$$
\begin{aligned}
&\tilde{\mathbf{T}}_s[\![x\texttt{`='}e]\!]\ \tilde{\sigma}\ m = [x \mapsto \tilde{\mathbf{E}}[\![e]\!]\tilde{\sigma}\ m]\\
&\tilde{\mathbf{T}}_s[\![a[e_1]\texttt{`='}e_2]\!]\ \tilde{\sigma}\ m = [(m, a) \mapsto \mathbf{E}[\![e_2]\!]\ \sigma; m \sqcup \tilde{\sigma}(m, a)]\\
&\tilde{\mathbf{T}}_s[\![x\texttt{`='}a[e_1]]\!]\ \tilde{\sigma}\ m = [x \mapsto \tilde{\sigma}(m, a)]\\
&\tilde{\mathbf{T}}_s[\![out\texttt{`.write('}e\texttt{`)'}]\!]\ \tilde{\sigma}\ m =\\
&\quad [(\tilde{\sigma}(m, out), \texttt{`data'}) \mapsto \mathbf{E}[\![e]\!]\tilde{\sigma}\ m, (\tilde{\sigma}(m, out), \texttt{`valid'}) \mapsto [1, 1]]\\
&\tilde{\mathbf{T}}_s[\![x\texttt{`='}in\texttt{`.read()'}]\!]\ \sigma\ m =\\
&\quad [x \mapsto \tilde{\sigma}(\tilde{\sigma}(in, \texttt{`data'})), (\tilde{\sigma}(m, out), \texttt{`ready'}) \mapsto [0, 0]]
\end{aligned}
$$

The interval interpretation is a fairly direct extension of the standard interpretation to intervals.

$$\begin{aligned}
&\tilde{\mathbf{T}}_s[\![x\text{`='}e]\!]\ \tilde{\sigma}\ m = [x \mapsto \tilde{\mathbf{E}}[\![e]\!]\tilde{\sigma}\ m]\\
&\tilde{\mathbf{T}}_s[\![a[e_1]\text{`='}e_2]\!]\ \tilde{\sigma}\ m = [(m,a) \mapsto \mathbf{E}[\![e_2]\!]\ \sigma; m \sqcup \tilde{\sigma}(m,a)]\\
&\tilde{\mathbf{T}}_s[\![x\text{`='}a[e_1]]\!]\ \tilde{\sigma}\ m = [x \mapsto \tilde{\sigma}(m,a)]\\
&\tilde{\mathbf{T}}_s[\![out\texttt{`.write('}e\texttt{`)'}]\!]\ \tilde{\sigma}\ m =\\
&\qquad [(\tilde{\sigma}(m,out), \texttt{`data'}) \mapsto \mathbf{E}[\![e]\!]\tilde{\sigma}\ m, (\tilde{\sigma}(m,out), \texttt{`valid'}) \mapsto [1,1]]\\
&\tilde{\mathbf{T}}_s[\![x\text{`='}in\texttt{`.read()'}]\!]\ \sigma\ m =\\
&\qquad [x \mapsto \tilde{\sigma}(\tilde{\sigma}(in, \texttt{`data'})), (\tilde{\sigma}(m,out), \texttt{`ready'}) \mapsto [0,0]]
\end{aligned}$$

The functions are used in the semantic function $\tilde{\mathbf{T}}[\![prg]\!]$ to compute intervals for all label vectors reachable from the initial environment. In the next section, we will show some examples of using the analysis on some small programs.

An implementation of the interval interpretation can be found in our GitHub repository [13] as well as an analysis of some larger examples.

5 Application

5.1 Bitwidth Analysis

The following example contains a small loop that fills a memory bank with some simply computed pseudo-random numbers. We have applied the widening operation on intervals and can see that the variable 'x' requires 10 bits, the databank 'a' 7 bits, and the count 'i' 5 bits. We could have been more restrictive in the use of widening and seen that 'i' only require 4 bits since its final value will be 11. Note that the test will fail when 'i' is 10 but it will happen at the same time as it is incremented and thus end with the value 11.

```
val random = Module(Random)

module Random
  int x, i
  int[11] a
state 1
  i = 0
  goto 2
state 2
  x = (83 * i) + 52
  goto 3
state 3
  x = x % 101
  goto 4
state 4
  a[i] = x
  i = i + 1
```

```
    goto Mux(i < 10, 2, 5)
  state 5
    goto 5
```

The result of the analysis gives us these intervals at each program point when widening is used during fixpoint iteration.

```
[1]
  empty
[2]
  {rnd:a=[0:127], rnd:i=[0:15], rnd:x=[0:255]}
[3]
  {rnd:a=[0:127], rnd:i=[0:15], rnd:x=[0:1023]}
[4]
  {rnd:a=[0:127], rnd:i=[0:15], rnd:x=[0:127]}
[5]
  {rnd:a=[0:127], rnd:i=[0:31], rnd:x=[0:255]}
```

5.2 Ready-Valid Analysis

The following program contains a small producer module that sends the numbers from 0 to 5 on a channel and a receiver module that read values from the channel until it receives the value 5. The analysis will track the possible label vectors reachable from the initial environment. When sender and receiver are both in state 2 then the channel will either be ready to read or write and there will be no unnecessary delay at that stage.

```
val sender = Module(Sender)
val receiver = Module(Receiver)
sender.out <> receiver.in

module Sender
  int i
  outstream out
state 1
  i = 0
  goto 2
state 2 when out.ready()
  out.write(i)
  i = i + 1
  goto Mux(i < 5, 2, 3)
state 3
  goto 3

module Receiver
  int x, j
  instream in
state 1
```

```
  j = 0
  goto 2
state 2 when in.valid()
  x = in.read()
  goto 3
state 3
  j = j + x
  goto Mux(x < 5, 2, 4)
state 4
  goto 4

[1, 1]
  {1:data=[0:0], 1:ready=[0:0], 1:valid=[0:0]}
[2, 2]
  {1:data=[0:4], 1:ready=[1:1], 1:valid=[0:1],
  receiver:j=[0:10], receiver:x=[0:4], sender:i=[0:5]}
[2, 3]
  {1:data=[0:4], 1:ready=[0:0], 1:valid=[1:1],
  receiver:j=[0:6], receiver:x=[0:4], sender:i=[1:5]}
[3, 2]
  {1:data=[5:5], 1:ready=[1:1], 1:valid=[1:1],
  receiver:j=[10:10], receiver:x=[4:4], sender:i=[6:6]}
[3, 3]
  {1:data=[5:5], 1:ready=[0:0], 1:valid=[1:1],
  receiver:j=[10:10], receiver:x=[5:5], sender:i=[6:6]}
[3, 4]
  {1:data=[5:5], 1:ready=[1:1], 1:valid=[0:0],
  receiver:j=[15:15], receiver:x=[5:5], sender:i=[6:6]}
```

5.3 Underflow Detection

Our last example illustrates the parallel evaluation of conditions and the body of states in modules. Each state in modules contains a calculation of the next state. The calculation is done in parallel with other operations in the state using the value of registers at the start of the state and not the values computed in the state. The following program inserts some numbers into a memory bank and extra and adds them afterward even though the end condition is that 'i>0' then 'i' will reach the value -1 at the end. This is because the test is done in the same clock cycle as the decrement.

```
val range = Module(Range)

module Range
  int x
  int i
  int j
  int[6] a
state 1
```

```
    i = 0
    j = 0
    x = 0
    goto 2
  state 2
    a[i] = i
    i = i + 1
    goto Mux(i < 5, 2, 3)
  state 3
    i = i - 1
    goto 4
  state 4
    x = a[i]
    i = i - 1
    goto Mux(i > 0, 5, 6)
  state 5
    j = j + x
    goto 4
  state 6
    goto 6
```

```
[1]
  empty
[2]
  {range:a=[0:4], range:i=[0:5], range:j=[0:0], range:x=[0:0]}
[3]
  {range:a=[0:5], range:i=[6:6], range:j=[0:0], range:x=[0:0]}
[4]
  {range:a=[0:5], range:i=[0:5], range:j=[0:15], range:x=[0:5]}
[5]
  {range:a=[0:5], range:i=[0:4], range:j=[0:14], range:x=[1:5]}
[6]
  {range:a=[0:5], range:i=[-1:-1], range:j=[15:15], range:x=[0:0]}
```

6 Future Work

The analysis presented here can be extended in a number of ways and other data flow analyses can be applied to the language to extract information. Some of these extensions we have partially explored already and others we plan to examine in the near future.

The analysis we have presented works on unsigned integers and we want to identify registers where underflow may occur. In some systems, we want to have a mixture of signed and unsigned numbers and let the analysis reflect that.

One of the restrictions in the use of databanks is that simultaneous read and write operations must not be from the same location. In hardware, a read operation in the same cycle as a write operation to the same location may give the old value, the new value, or a mixture of them. In some designs, we can verify that indices to read and write are different by constructing convex hull expressions for index expressions and checking that they do not overlap.

We will normally strive to design systems where the number of clock cycles is as small as possible. An indication of where improvements are possible is if we have states that do not depend on values stored in a previous clock cycle. By making a reaching definition analysis of the system with def-use chain information we can find some states that could potentially be merged.

The subset we use has a static fixed communication pattern where operations in states can read from a channel or write to a channel. An extension would be to let the output from a state go to the first available channel and input come from the first channel with data. It is possible to extend the language with this behaviour and still preserve the deterministic evaluation of states.

Some algorithms where implementation on FPGA could be an advantage could be based on a SIMD processor array architecture [24]. It could be interesting to examine how we can extend the language with array processing features and how it will affect the analysis options.

7 Related Works

The language Chisel was initially introduced by Bachrach et al. in their work on Chisel [1], and it has gained significant popularity in both hardware design and educational environments [1,19].

Several authors have explored the formalization of semantics, analysis, and transformations for various hardware description languages. Thomson and Mycroft have investigated the applicability of partial evaluation for hardware specifications written in HarPE [23]. Additionally, they have explored the use of abstract interpretation for the same language [22]. Formalizing hardware description languages has also been explored for execution time analysis [18].

The CIRCT is an open-source infrastructure and intermediate representation for hardware description languages and can be used with Chisel [26]. As a common framework for a range of hardware description languages, it could also be used in connection with our subset of Chisel. The CIRCT framework contains tools for verification, symbolic evaluation, and hardware generation.

The way our semantics records intermediate stages and changes to an environment has many similarities to the minimal function graph interpretation of first-order functional languages [8]. The idea of constructing data flow analysis as abstractions of formal semantics goes back to Cousot and Cousot [5].

Using interval analysis to identify underflow and range analysis of variables in binary code has been studied by Küchler [12] Brauer [3] [2] and others.

8 Conclusion

In our work, we are providing a formal semantics for a subset of the hardware description language Chisel. This formal semantics serves as a foundation for conducting various analyses and transformations on hardware designs described using this subset. An interval analysis for the language is described and we show how it can be used in the design process to provide information on the bit-width of registers, possible underflow of registers, and communication patterns.

References

1. Bachrach, J., et al.: Chisel: constructing hardware in a scala embedded language. In: The 49th Annual Design Automation Conference (DAC 2012), San Francisco, CA, USA, pp. 1216–1225. ACM (2012)
2. Brauer, J., King, A., Kowalewski, S.: Range analysis of microcontroller code using bit-level congruences. In: Kowalewski, S., Roveri, M. (eds.) FMICS 2010. LNCS, vol. 6371, pp. pp. 82–98. Springer, Heidelberg (2010). https://doi.org/10.1007/978-3-642-15898-8_6
3. Brauer, J., Noll, T., Schlich, B.: Interval analysis of microcontroller code using abstract interpretation of hardware and software. In: Proceedings of the 13th International Workshop on Software & Compilers for Embedded Systems, pp. 1–10 (2010)
4. Chisel: Documentation (2024). https://www.chisel-lang.org/api/latest/index.html
5. Cousot, P., Cousot, R.: Abstract interpretation: a unified lattice model for static analysis of programs by construction or approximation of fixpoints. In: Proceedings of the 4th ACM SIGACT-SIGPLAN symposium on Principles of programming languages, pp. 238–252 (1977)
6. Cousot, P., Cousot, R.: Comparing the Galois connection and widening/narrowing approaches to abstract interpretation. In: Bruynooghe, M., Wirsing, M. (eds.) PLILP 1992. LNCS, vol. 631, pp. 269–295. Springer, Heidelberg (1992). https://doi.org/10.1007/3-540-55844-6_142
7. Dally, W.J., Harting, R.C., Aamodt, T.M.: Digital Design Using VHDL: A Systems Approach. Cambridge University Press (2016)
8. Jones, N.D., Mycroft, A.: Data flow analysis of applicative programs using minimal function graphs. In: Proceedings of the 13th ACM SIGACT-SIGPLAN Symposium on Principles of Programming Languages, pp. 296–306 (1986)
9. Kirkeby, M.H., et al.: Energy consumption and performance of heapsort in hardware and software. arXiv preprint arXiv:2204.03401 (2022)
10. Kirkeby, M.H., et al.: Energy consumption and performance of heapsort in hardware and software. In: International Conference on ICT for Sustainability, ICT4S 2022, Plovdiv, Bulgaria, June 13–17, 2022. IEEE (2022)
11. Kirkeby, M.H.: Probabilistic program analysis. Ph.D. thesis, Roskilde Universitet (2018)
12. Küchler, A., Wenning, L., Wendland, F.: Absintio: towards showing the absence of integer overflows in binaries using abstract interpretation. In: Proceedings of the 2023 ACM Asia Conference on Computer and Communications Security, pp. 247–258 (2023)
13. Rosendahl, M., Kirkeby, M.H.: Github repository: Chiselinterval (2024). https://github.com/madsrosendahl/ChiselInterval
14. Mycroft, A.: Programming language design and analysis motivated by hardware evolution. In: Nielson, H.R., Filé, G. (eds.) SAS 2007. LNCS, vol. 4634, pp. 18–33. Springer, Heidelberg (2007). https://doi.org/10.1007/978-3-540-74061-2_2

15. Mycroft, A., Rosendahl, M.: Minimal function graphs are not instrumented. WSA **92**, 60–67 (1992)
16. Rosendahl, M.: Abstract Interpretation and Attribute Gramars. Ph.D. thesis, Cambridge University (1991)
17. Rosetta Code: Sorting algorithms/heapsort (2023). https://rosettacode.org/wiki/Sorting_algorithms/Heapsort
18. Schlickling, M.: Timing model derivation: static analysis of hardware description languages. Ph.D. thesis, Universität des Saarlandes (2012)
19. Schoeberl, M.: Digital Design with Chisel. Kindle Direct Publishing (2019). https://github.com/schoeberl/chisel-book
20. Sherman, E., Dwyer, M.B.: Structurally defined conditional data-flow static analysis. In: Beyer, D., Huisman, M. (eds.) TACAS 2018, Part II. LNCS, vol. 10806, pp. 249–265. Springer, Cham (2018). https://doi.org/10.1007/978-3-319-89963-3_15
21. Sozzo, E.D., Conficconi, D., Zeni, A., Salaris, M., Sciuto, D., Santambrogio, M.D.: Pushing the level of abstraction of digital system design: A survey on how to program FPGAs. ACM Comput. Surv. **55**(5), 1–48 (2022)
22. Thompson, S., Mycroft, A.: Abstract interpretation of combinational asynchronous circuits. In: Giacobazzi, R. (ed.) SAS 2004. LNCS, vol. 3148, pp. 181–196. Springer, Heidelberg (2004). https://doi.org/10.1007/978-3-540-27864-1_15
23. Thompson, S., Mycroft, A.: Bit-level partial evaluation of synchronous circuits. In: Proceedings of the 2006 ACM SIGPLAN Symposium on Partial Evaluation and Semantics-Based Program Manipulation, pp. 29–37 (2006)
24. Walsh, D., Dudek, P.: A compact FPGA implementation of a bit-serial SIMD cellular processor array. In: 2012 13th International Workshop on Cellular Nanoscale Networks and their Applications, pp. 1–6. IEEE (2012)
25. Yousefifeshki, F., Li, H., Khomh, F.: Studying the challenges of developing hardware description language programs. Inf. Softw. Technol. **159**, 107196 (2023)
26. Zhao, J., Kang, J., Zhao, Y.: K-CIRCT: a layered, composable, and executable formal semantics for CIRCT hardware IRS. arXiv preprint arXiv:2404.18756 (2024)

Context-Aware Air Quality Analytics Using Low-Cost Sensors and First-Order Logic

Eleftheria Katsiri(✉)

Democritus University of Thrace, Kimmeria Campus, 67100 Xanthi, Greece
ekatsiri@ee.duth.gr

Abstract. Low-cost sensors changed the pollution monitoring paradigm due to their ability to measure air pollution ad hoc, close to the sources and in great spatio-temporal resolution. Our team has been engaged in the development of highly reliable air quality sensing devices, using low-cost sensors. Air quality measurements are transmitted to a scalable dynamic knowledge-base maintenance system for representing and reasoning with knowledge about Sentient Computing, extended with air quality predicates. The system functions similarly to a two-level cache: the lower layer maintains knowledge about air quality at the sensor level by continually processing a high rate of observations from the measuring devices. The higher layer maintains easily-retrievable, user-defined abstract knowledge about current and historical states of air quality along with temporal properties such as the time of occurrence of observation timeseries and their length. Our approach uses deductive systems in an unusual way: by creating a model of real-world air quality we are able to prove quality aspects of logical predicates both at the sensor level - such as the existence of outliers, stuck-at-zero values or whether a timeseries is additive or multiplicative - and at the derived predicate level - such as AQI index, a person's aggregated exposure to pollutants or analytical trends and patterns, paving the road to explainability. Furthermore, by embedding the lower layer of the architecture inside the monitoring devices we support in-network processing, lowering the number of published messages and extending the device lifetime. The preliminary results provide useful insights on both pollution level and the intensity of industrial activity in the dairy.

Keywords: low-cost sensors · air quality monitoring · internet of things · wireless sensor networks · delay tolerant networking · middleware · analytics · python · pattern detection · outliers · visual analytics

1 Introduction

Air pollution is the fourth most important risk of death in the world with a proven burden of disease that includes billions of deaths and thousands of

D. Orchard et al. (Eds.): Alan Mycroft Festschrift, LNCS 15500, pp. 170–196, 2026.
https://doi.org/10.1007/978-3-032-08187-2_9

DALYS [1–4,7]. Furthermore, 80% of the planet's urban population lives in cities that don't meet air quality standards [8–10]. Furthermore, millions of people around the world are susceptible to long term exposure to pollutants. Dairy processing is comprised of techniques and technology used to receive raw milk, transform it into a finished product, and store and package the product for sale in stores. Given the high risk of contamination, dairy processing facilities must adhere to strict regulations and meet high standards for air purity. Airborne particulate matter such as dust, is among the most important environmental pressures linked to all stages of dairy processing; it can settle on the products themselves and dairy processing equipment, reducing shelf life and leading to spoilage and serious regulatory, legal and health risks. Contamination can also affect the texture and appearance of some dairy products, which can affect the customer experience.

Low-cost sensor technology has changed the pollution monitoring paradigm [12,31–37]. These features make it possible to answer new questions about the underlying causes of poor air quality, ensure more accurate modeling and prediction at local scales [6,38], improve the ability to identify the links between air quality and human health [5,39,40] or environmental degradation [41], identify potential 'hot spots' of air pollution, improve the ability to quantify the impacts of pollutant mitigation techniques and promote savings through on-demand ventilation [11].

This paper focuses on the case of a modern dairy in Greece that produces milk, yogurt, cream, and other professional milk-based products that are sensitive to infection caused by particulate matter such as dust. Outdoor sources of pollution include a) a flour mill located south of the dairy, b) Saharan dust carried by southerly winds c) molds and wild yeasts, which can affect flavor and odor and cause dairy products to spoil and d) microbial clouds by humans. The SibaIoT PM device used in this work is capable of certified measurement as it includes pre-calibrated sensors and embedded software that is delay-tolerant, real-time and capable of in-network processing. The device measures with high reliability ambient particulate matter concentrations in ug/m^3 of three classes of particles, namely *PM1.0*, *PM2.5* and *PM10*, humidity and temperature. The device has very good accuracy, response time and sensitivity in indoor pollution levels. Fifteen Siba IoT PM devices were installed in three different production areas with varying air quality sensitivity as shown in Fig. 1. Twelve PM devices were developed indoors measuring particulate matter concentrations at *points of interest*, i.e., locations identified as critical for health and safety and three outdoors over the north, west and south entrances of the dairy. As a result, a very large volume of additional continuous measurements were collected [60]. The monitored air pollutants are determined with the analytical methods in accordance to the current regulations. In order to allow the continuous visualization of the measured data, allowing immediate intervention in case in case of exceeding the limits, a specific analytical information system has been elaborated. This system can be consulted remotely, and reports not only the raw data collected, but also some immediate elaborations, in order to promptly interpret the results,

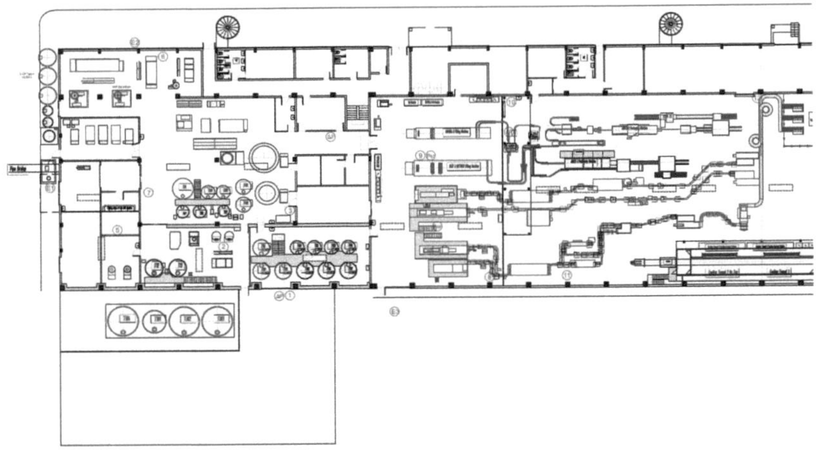

Fig. 1. Dairy sensor network.

generate knowledge about air quality with reference to all stages of dairy processing (Sect. 3). Finally, both low-level and abstract knowledge predicates are elaborated graphically using Grafana [64] dashboards.

2 Approach

A reliable air quality sensor network is structured as a set of reliable air quality micro-measuring devices placed at positions characterised in terms of x, y, z coordinates. Each device measures with high reliability a set of pollutants, humidity and temperature. The sampling rate is in the few seconds range. Each device is associated with an *atomic location*, a spherical influence zone centered around the device, defining the boundary of a micro-climate. Each micro-climate is associated with an *atomic air-quality* status that involves the measured pollutants, humidity and temperature and gives an indication of air purity at the current instant. This status may be expressed in terms of pollutant concentrations, either in the form of volumes, i.e., for gaseous pollutants, or in the form of mass, i.e., for ambient particulate matter, or even in the form of absolute numbers of particles. Each production area (room) in a dairy plant may have one or more device installed. It is a composite location, wherein atomic locations are nested. It is associated with a *regional air quality* status, i.e., is an abstraction of the atomic air-quality statuses of the micro-climates for the specific production area. This abstraction is a spatial aggregation, for example a sum or average of the atomic air qualities of the micro-climates. Furthermore, we define *an analytic* to be an abstraction of air quality at a single position over time. This abstraction is usually a temporal aggregation of atomic air-quality, for example a sum or average of atomic air qualities of a single micro-climate over 24 h. An analytic can also be a dis-aggregation of the overall air-quality as for example in the case of spatial interpolation.

3 Novelty

Sentient computing [17] is the proposition that applications can be made more responsive and useful by observing and reacting to the physical world. A dual-layer knowledge representation architecture for Sentient Computing was introduced in the author's previous work [15] that makes it possible for the user to perform easily complex computations involving spatial and temporal notions of a dynamic changing environment;

This work builds on the previous system, where Sentient Computing predicates represent*location-awareness*, extending it with first order logic predicates that represent knowledge about air quality, such as its status and its potential impact on the dairy processing environment, including its human capital. More specifically, the system reasons with temporal abstractions of measured air quality over aggregated periods such as *hour of the day, day of the week, week of the month and month of the year*, but also *8-hour shift*, *weekday, weekend.* Spatial abstractions of air quality over logical regions that represent whole or partial production areas are also computed by the system. These abstractions form the basis for reasoning with *air analytics*, i.e., knowledge on the potential risk of air quality on various stakeholders. Analytics pave the road for protecting human health.

In this view, the *Sensor Abstract Layer* knows of air quality observations at the atomic locations, at the current instant; for example, predicates at this level include:

- *PollutantConcentrationAtPosition*
- *ParticulateMatterMassAtPosition*
- *ParticulateMatterMassAtPosition*
- *ParticulateMatterNumberAtPosition*
- *TemperatureAtPosition*
- *HumidityAtPosition.*

These predicates represent the abilities of our sensing devices with low cost sensors and specifically our PM sensing device that is presented in Sect. 1.

The *Deductive Abstract Layer*, on the other hand, maintains abstract knowledge about the current status of air quality in logical regions. This is implemented using *continuous queries* such as the *running average* of a pollutant. For example, predicates at this level include:

- *AveragePollutionAtLocation*
- *AveragePollutionAtLocationAtHourOfDay*
- *mathitAveragePollutionAtLocationAtDayOfWeek*
- *AveragePollutionAtLocationAtDayOfMonth*

- *AveragePollutionAtLocationInMonthOfYear*
- *MostPollutedShift*

Furthermore, the potential impact of air quality on products and employees, including regulatory, health and legal risks is represented by predicates such as *UserAggregatedExposure* (at pollutant). Last, historical predicates are stored persistently representing more traditional *analytics* such as *AveragePollutionAtLocationHistoric*, *UserAggregatedExposureHistoric* and *MostPollutedDayOfWeekHistoric*. Using deductive reasoning on historical knowledge predicates, the overall aggregated personal exposure of an employee to all pollutants can be inferred with accuracy [62], while using AI techniques similarities among employees could be estimated creating for example *exposure groups*. Furthermore, the *popularity* of a production area can be inferred, both for a specific user, and for all users. It should be noted than in order to represent knowledge on user location, a sensing infrastructure such as an indoor location system is required, as discussed in Sect. 10.

4 Formal Specification

Sensor Abstract Layer (SAL). SAL predicates are prefixed with *L_* and have no temporal variables. They represent low-level sensor-derived knowledge for example pollutant concentrations or user positions in the last hour and are presented in Listing 1.

```
(L_AtomicLocation(uid ?user_id)(x ?x)(y ?y)(z ?z))
(L_Pollutant(polid ?polid)(polname ?polname)(value ?value)
(x ?x)(y ?y)(z ?z))
(L_PollutionAtPosition(pid ?pollutant_id)(value ?value)
(x ?x)(y ?y)(z ?z))
(L_DeviceAtPosition(uid ?user_id)(x ?x)(y ?y)(z ?z))
```

Listing 1. SAL predicates

Deductive Abstract Layer (DAL). DAL predicates are prefixed with *H_* and have temporal variables such as the start-time the predicate instance became true, the hour-of-day, day_of_month, shift etc. For each SAL predicate there is a corresponding DAL predicate that offers an abstraction over some aspect of the low-level predicate e.g., they know of regions rather than positions, aggregated values of pollutant concentrations over a period of time rather than raw values at a given timestamp. DAL predicates are formatted as follows and are presented in Listing 2:

```
(<AggregationFunction>PollutionAtLocation(<temporalAgg/tion>
(pollutant)(region))
```

```
(H_AveragePollutionAtLocation(pid ?pollutant_id)
(rid ?region_id)
(value ?value)(count ?count)(sum ?sum)(hod ?hour_of_day)
(dow ?day_of_week)(dom ?day_of_month)(moy ?month_of_year
(shift ?shift)(stime ?start_time))
(H_MostPollutedHourOfDayAtLocation(pid ?pollutant_id)
(rid ?region_id)(value ?value)(hod ?hour_of_day)
(stime ?start_time))
```

Listing 2. DAL predicates

Historical Predicates. Historical predicates are sufixed with *Historic* and have temporal variables such as the start-time and end time. Listing 3 presents such an example:

```
(H_AveragePollutionAtLocationHistoric(pid ?pollutant_id)
(rid ?region_id)(value ?value)(count ?count)(sum ?sum)
(hod ?hour_of_day)(dow ?day_of_week)(dom ?day_of_month)
(moy ?month_of_year)(shift ?shift)(stime ?start_time)
(etime ?end_time))
```

Listing 3. Historical predicates

5 Architectural Overview

A distributed reference architecture of the dual-layer knowledge base is shown in Fig. 2. Sensing devices periodically generate sensor observations, aka sensor events, that are asserted in the Sensor Abstract layer (SAL) as low-level predicate instances that represent low-level knowledge of air quality at the position where the sensing device is located, at the current instant. A new predicate instance is created every-time the sensor is sampled by the device. For each device, SAL knows of pollutant concentrations at each monitored position in the last hour. Every time an assert action is performed the SAL layer checks that each field of the new predicate instance is correctly formatted and does not contain any null or NAN values. It also matches consecutive predicate instances against patterns that indicate stuck-at-zero values or outliers and modifies these predicate instances adding a tag field that can be used to exclude them from further deduction if necessary. For example, in order to detect outliers using the z-score metric, both the standard deviation and the mean of the 1 h timeseries needs to be computed. Each predicate instance value (representing the pollutant concentration) is first compared against these value to determine the score according to Eq. 1 and is next modified adding a tag field.

$$z_i = \frac{x_i - \mu}{\sigma} \tag{1}$$

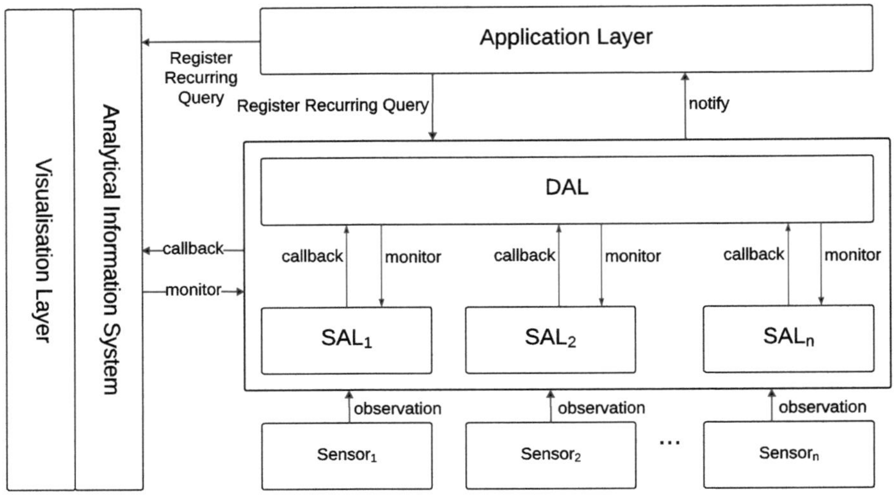

Fig. 2. System reference architecture

With respect to the Deductive Abstract Layer (DAL), users register recurring query specifications that represent high-level knowledge about air quality in the monitored area. Each query is structured as a Rete network described in Sect. 6. It monitors continually low-level predicates residing in SAL causing new instances of the DAL predicates to be asserted, using a callback mechanism. DAL predicates are available for further querying by applications and they can be composed into recurring or single queries to meet application requirements. For example, periodically, SAL time-series of predicate instances are resampled and high-level instances of aggregated values such as the 1h average are asserted into DAL. Section 7 includes a worked-out example of how the AQI air quality index is deduced using this process.

With respect to the *Analytical Information System(AIL)* it complements the knowledge base to which it is linked, by offering two services:

1. First, it offers descriptive and visual analytics over both SAL and DAL predicate instances that can not be easily deduced in clips and whose outcome is translated to an additional attribute of the underlying data. For example, as it is common knowledge that a *PM2.5* timeseries and a *PM1.0* timeseries will be strongly correlated as *PM2.5*-class particles contain *PM1.0*-class particles the results of a correlation test verifying the above assumption can be used as an additional quality attribute that the data is reliable. A scatterplot can then be produced to verify the result visually. A new DAL predicate is then asserted in the knowledge base to represents this information. However in case the underlying data does not follow the normal distribution, it contains outliers and the relationship between the two statistical variables is not linear, Spearman's rank correlation coefficient may be a better choice.

2. Second, it offers predictive analytics in order to predict future values. Similarly to before, it can be determined whether a timeseries is additive or multiplicative so that a correct forecast model respectively can be applied to a given timeseries. A new DAL predicate is then asserted in the knowledge base to represent the outcome of the prediction. Clustering is another tool for discovering similarity among the data. The whole path from the sensor observations to the prediction will be traceable in the knowledge base providing transparency and paving the road towards explainability.

As the SAL layer receives as input a high-rate of sensor events reasonable CPU and memory are required for implementing the recurring query logic. This makes SAL appropriate for distribution and edge-processing. On the other hand, the DAL layer is less frequently interrupted by callbacks, which preserves resources such as flash memory and allows for near real-time response. DAL queries are simpler than SAL ones, using only a few predicates and operators thus taking up less memory and CPU cycles. They also fire much less frequently than SAL queries making DAL appropriate for implementation on a resource constrained device or a small Virtual Machine saving costs. From the above it can be inferred that the current architecture is appropriate for sensor networks where devices are constrained in terms of battery and resources. In one embodiment of the reference architecture, the SAL layer is distributed and SAL instances are placed on the sensing devices that are capable of edge-processing while the DAL layer resides on a local gateway. The analytical system also includes the Grafana a visualisation cloud platform. Because each SAL instance only generates a low-rate of abstract events [16] that are asserted into DAL as high-level predicate instances, they are prevented from communicating too frequently with the DAL, thus saving energy, which is an additional contribution in the case of battery-based devices, which however is not necessary in this work as devices are powered by mains.

6 Technical Description

A *formal system* is an abstract structure and formalization of an axiomatic system used for deducing, using rules of inference, theorems from axioms by a set of inference rules. A formal system includes a formal language and a *deductive system* that consists of the axioms and rules of inference that can be used to derive theorems of the system. A logical system is a deductive system together with additional non-logical axioms. According to model theory, a logical system may be given interpretations which describe whether a given structure - the mapping of formulas to a particular meaning - satisfies a well-formed formula. A structure that satisfies all the axioms of the formal system is known as a model of the logical system. This work uses deductive systems in an unusual way, namely in order to check whether a structure consisting of sensor-derived observations is a model of the real world and more specifically a accurate and reliable model of ambient air quality and related concepts. Furthermore, by annotating logical predicates with concepts such as outliers and confidence levels it supports explainability of the deduced high-level predicates.

The inference is based on the *Rete algorithm*, a very efficient algorithm for matching facts against patterns in rules. It is implemented by building a network of nodes. It is designed in such a way that it saves the state of the matching process from cycle to cycle and re-computes changes only for the modified facts. The state of the matching process is updated only as facts are added and removed and the fewer they are the faster the matching will be. Each rule has an inference cycle consisting of three phases: match, select and execute. In the matching phase, the conditions of the rule are matched against the facts to determine which rules are to be executed. The rules whose conditions are met are stored in a list called agenda for firing. Form the list of rules, one of the rules is selected to execute or fire, according to a selection strategy, e.g., based on priority, recency of usage, specificity of the rule or other criteria. The rule selected from the list is executed by carrying out the actions in the right hand side of the rule. The action may be an assertion, executing a user-defined or built-in function. The main advantage of Rete is speed as it takes the advantage of structural similarity in rules. On the other hand, its main drawback is that it is memory intensive as saving pattern matches and partial matches requires considerable amounts of memory. Its space complexity is of the order of $O(RFP)$, where R is the number of rules, F is the number of asserted facts and is the average number of patterns per rule.

A *Rete network* is a direct acyclic graph that consists of nodes representing patterns in the conditions of the rules. The nodes behave like filters, testing the incoming tokens and sending on only those that pass the test. The Rete network consists of two parts: alpha network, consisting of nodes known as alpha nodes and beta network, consisting of beta nodes. Alpha nodes have one input and evaluate the conditions of the rule where beta nodes have two-inputs and define inter-element (fact) conditions. The Rete network starts with the root node. Kind nodes follow the root node and there is a kind node for each fact type. Alpha nodes are then created for each pattern and are connected to the corresponding kind note. Each alpha node is associated with an alpha memory that stores the matching facts. Alpha nodes are then joined by beta nodes that only have two inputs thus supporting partial matching. Each beta node has a memory to store joined patterns. Assertion of a fact creates a token that initially enters the root node. The network then splits a branch for each token type. Each kind node gets a copy of the token and preforms a SELECT operation to select tokens of its kind. It then passes a copy of the token to the alpha nodes. On receiving the token the alpha nodes do a PROJECT operation and extract components from the token that match the variables of the pattern, thus evaluating the pattern. Beta nodes then determine the possible cross-products of the rule. Finally, actions in the rule will be executed.

A *template* enforces checks on predicate instance fields dynamically every time an instance is asserted so that only observations that are formatted correctly are accepted. For example they either specify default values to be used for unspecified slots of a template predicates instance or specify that a value must explicitly be assigned for a slot when an assert is performed thus preventing the assertion of instances with missing values. Templates also specify slot types preventing the assertion of predicate instances with NAN or incorrect values in that field.

A custom embedded *middleware component* links the system components using a text-based interface which involves exchanging text files containing logical programs written in CLIPS via FTP thus linking the SAL and DAL layers. The gateway hosts an FTP server where the user uploads the recurring query specifications that are registered in the dual knowledge base using the middleware.

A REST-based interface between DAL and Grafana involves parsing both SAL and DAL level predicate specification files, converting them to a Grafana-compatible format (Line Protocol) and uploading them to Grafana for visualisation. Last, raw data tupples produced by the device sensors are parsed, converted to SAL predicate instances and asserted into the SAL layer. For example Device 2 that is installed at the "incubator" location produces the following raw data tupple:

$$PMData(13.56, 3.5, 1.92, 20, 32, 1729660961) \tag{2}$$

This instance of raw data corresponds to the following logical predicate where the timestamp variable is of type Epoch Unix Timestamp.

$$PMData(PM10, PM2.5, PM1.0, T(C), RH(\%), timestamp) \tag{3}$$

The operation of the overall system is next illustrated with a concrete example explaining in detail how the AQI index for air quality is derived from low-level sensor observations in the case of the dairy.

7 Air Quality Index AQI

The American EPA establishes an AQI for five major air pollutants regulated by the Clean Air Act. Each of these pollutants has a national ambient air quality standard (NAAQS) set by EPA to protect public health:

- ozone
- particulate matter
- carbon monoxide
- nitrogen dioxide
- sulfur dioxide

The AQI value of 100 generally corresponds to an ambient air concentration that equals the level of the short-term NAAQS for protection of public health. AQI values at or below 100 are generally thought of as satisfactory. When AQI values are above 100, air quality is unhealthy: at first for certain sensitive groups of people, then for everyone as AQI values get higher. The AQI is the highest value calculated for each pollutant as follows[1]:

$$I_p = \frac{I_{HI} - I_{Lo}}{BP_{HI} - BP_{Lo}}(C_p - BP_{Lo}) + I_{Lo} \tag{4}$$

where I_p = the index for pollutant p
C_p = the truncated concentration of pollutant p
BP_{HI} =the concentration break-point that is greater than or equal to Cp
BP_{Lo} = the concentration break-point that is less than or equal to Cp
I_{HI} = the AQI value corresponding to BPHi
I_{Lo}=the AQI value corresponding to BPLo
It takes a full 24 h to obtain an AQI value as 24 hourly average values are needed for *PM10*, *PM2.5* or the max 1-h or 8-h average value in a 24-h period for other pollutants. More specifically, for *PM10* & *PM2.5* first hourly averages are accumulated for a period of 24 h and then the 24-hour average is calculated from the hourly averages. As a result AQI calculation using the traditional database approach requires a server with a database, tables for each pollutant storing raw pollution data from 24 h before. Several SQL-type query are required to calculate the 24-hourly, 8-hourly and 1-hourly concentrations, the AQI for each pollutant and to select the max 1-h or 8-h values and finally the max AQI.

7.1 AQI Calculation Using the Knowledge Engine

At system setup, templates, i.e., predicate specifications for pollutant concentrations per type of pollutant and device position as well as function-predicate specifications written in clips are loaded in the knowledge base. After system initiation, each device generates logical predicate instances that represent the raw sensor data for that device. For example, Listing 4 presents low-level predicate instances that can be generated every 5 s by Device 4 that is installed at position "incubator", where the values: 30, 8 and 3.5 represent the measured concentrations for *PM10*, *PM2.5* and *PM1.0* respectively, 20 is the temperature value in Celsius, 32 is the relative humidity at the incubator while 1000 is a value associated with a Unix epoch timestamp.

```
(L_PM10AtIncubator(value 30)(timestamp 1000))
(L_PM2.5AtIncubator(value 8)(timestamp 1000))
(L_PM1.0AtIncubator(value 3.5)(timestamp 1000))
(L_TempAtIncubator(value 20)(timestamp 1000))
(L_RHAtIncubator(value 32)(timestamp 1000))
```

Listing 4. SAL predicate instances related to AQI calculation

Every hour three things happen: first, all facts that are older than 1 h are retracted from the SAL layer by a SELECT recurring query with one condition

[1] Concentration breakpoints are shown in Table 1 in the Appendix.

that matches their timestamp with the local-time; second, the value of all remaining facts is averaged by a function predicate and third instances of DAL predicates that represent hourly average values for *PM10*, *PM2.5* and *PM1.0* are asserted in the knowledge base. For example, for Device 4, the instances presented in Listing 5 can be asserted in DAL.

```
(H_AvgPM10AtIncubator(value 12)(type 1h)(start-time 4600))
(H_Avg1PM2.5AtIncubator(value 8)(type 1h)(start-time 4600))
(H_AvgPM1.0AtIncubator(value 3.5)(type 1h)(start-time 4600))
(H_AvgTempAtIncubator(value 20)(type 1h)(start-time 4600))
(H_AvgRHAtIncubator(value 32)(type 1h)(start-time 4600))
```

Listing 5. DAL predicate instances related to AQI calculation

The retraction of all facts older than 1 h is implemented by a SELECT recurring query with two conditions: predicate type e.g., *L_PM10AtIncubator* and a temporal condition: $((now - timestamp) > 3600)$. The calculation of the hourly average for *PM10* concentrations at the Incubator is triggered by a recurring query with a single temporal condition in order to fire every hour and invoke a function that calculates the average as follows:

First both the ?*sum* and ?*count* variables are initialised to 0. Next all existing SAL predicate instances are matched against a single condition that selects only facts of a given SAL predicate, e.g., *L_PM10AtIncubator*. Next, for each matching predicate instance, the pollutant concentration value is added to the value of ?*sum* and the value of ?*count* is incremented by one. This is repeated until all matching instances have been processed. Last, unless no matching predicates are found, the total ?*sum* value is divided by the ?*count* value to produce the hourly average for *L_PM10AtIncubator* represented by *H_AvgPM10AtIncubator*. Similarly the values for *H_AvgPM2.5AtIncubator* and *H_AvgPM1.0AtIncubator* are produced.

Similarly to the SAL layer, every 24 h three things happen at DAL level: first, instances of one-hour average predicates that are older than 24 h are modified using a SELECT recurring query with two conditions (predicate type and temporal condition) to become historic predicates; second, the values of all remaining instance that fall within the current 24-hour period are averaged as before asserting DAL predicate instances representing the 24-hour average value for each pollutant at a given position; third, the calculation of the per-pollutant AQI according to Eq. 4 is triggered and the respective facts are asserted in the DAL layer as shown in Listings 6. Although ultra fine particles such as smoke classified as *PM1.0* are not currently included in AQI, the authors feel it may make sense to include them in indoors case studies such as the one described in this paper as they may have significant values. Finally the overall AQI is the maximum value of all 24-hour AQI values and it is calculated by whichever of the three recurring queries has a LHS that evaluates to TRUE as shown in Listings: 7 to 9. Although the authors have experience developing sensing devices also for the rest of the AQI pollutants of Eq. 4, only PM devices were installed in the specific case study providing real time data.

```
(H_AQIPM10AtIncubator(value 26)(type 24h)(start-time 86400))
(H_AQIPM2.5AtIncubator(value 40)(type 24h)(start-time 86400))
(H_AQIPM1.0AtIncubator(value 6)(type 24h)(start-time 86400))
```

Listing 6. 24 hour AQI DAL predicate instances

```
value1 :
(H_AQIPM10AtIncubator(value ?value1)(type 24h)
(start-time 86400))∧
(not (H_AQIPM1.0AtIncubator && (value ?value2
&:(> ?value2 ?value1))(type 24h)(start-time 86400)))∧
(not (H_AQIPM2.5AtIncubator && (value ?value2
&:(> ?value2 ?value1))(type 24h)(start-time 86400)))
 ⟹
H_maxAQIPM10AtIncubator(value ?value1) (type 24h)
(start-time 86400))
```

Listing 7. Logical program inferring the final AQI from maximum PM10 AQI

```
value1 :
(H_AQIPM1.0AtIncubator(value ?value1)(type 24h)
(start-time 86400))∧
(not (H_AQIPM10AtIncubator && (value ?value2
&:(> ?value2 ?value1))(type 24h)(start-time 86400)))∧
(not (H_AQIPM2.5AtIncubator && (value ?value2
&:(> ?value2 ?value1))(type 24h)(start-time 86400)))
 ⟹
H_maxAQIPM1.0AtIncubator(value ?value1) (type 24h)
(start-time 86400))
```

Listing 8. Logical program inferring the final AQI from maximum PM1.0 AQI

```
value1 :
(H_AQIPM2.5AtIncubator(value ?value1)(type 24h)
(start-time 86400))∧
(not (H_AQIPM1.0AtIncubator && (value ?value2
&:(> ?value2 ?value1))(type 24h)(start-time 86400)))∧
(not (H_AQIPM10AtIncubator && (value ?value2
&:(> ?value2 ?value1))(type 24h)(start-time 86400)))
 ⟹
H_maxAQIPM2.5AtIncubator(value ?value1) (type 24h)
(start-time 86400))
```

Listing 9. Logical program inferring the final AQI from maximum PM2.5 AQI

8 Example Queries

The following query that indicates an unusual situation illustrates the expressiveness of the system.

The 1-h average concentration of PM10 is higher than the PM10 AQI and 1-h average concentrations of PM10 and PM2.5 are correlated and the 1-h average concentration of PM2.5 is higher than the PM2.5 AQI and the 10-min median concentration variance of PM1.0 is expected to be moderate while humidity is between 30 and 25 and there are at least 2 collocated people at each production area.

The predicates in this example are all high-level DAL predicates that are updated periodically as the low-level pollutant concentrations along with temperature and humidity change with time. More specifically the logical predicates:

- *H_PM10PM2.5Correlation*
- *H_ExpectedVarPM1.0*

are asserted in the knowledge base as a result from analytics that are calculated by the analytical information system e.g., as shown in Sect. 9. Should such a query be inserted in the SAL layer it would be significantly more complex while it would not be able to express knowledge related to either correlation or expectation derived from clustering techniques. For example, in Room 1 there are 4 different monitoring positions for all of which the predicate patterns need to apply.

```
(H_AvgPM10AtRoom1(value ?v1)(type 1h))∧
(H_AQIPM10AtRoom1(value ?v2)(type 24h))∧
(?v1 > ?v2) ∧
(H_AvgPM10AtRoom2(value ?v3)(type 1h))∧
(H_AQIPM10AtRoom2(value ?v4)(type 24h))∧
(?v3 > ?v4) ∧
(H_AvgPM10AtRoom3(value ?v5)(type 1h))∧
(H_AQIPM2.5AtRoom3(value ?v6)(type 24h))∧
(?v5 > ?v6)∧
(PM10PM2.5CorrelationAtRoom1(value ?v10)(type 1h)) ∧
(?v10 > 0.7)∧
(PM10PM2.5CorrelationAtRoom2(value ?v11)(type 1h))∧
(?v11 > 0.7)∧
(PM10PM2.5CorrelationAtRoom3(value ?v12)(type 1h))∧
(?v12 > 0.7)∧
(H_ExpectedVarPM1.0AtRoom1(value ?v7)(type 10min)
(confidence ?c1))∧
(?v7 = "Moderate")∧
(c1 < 0.5)∧
(H_ExpectedVarPM1.0AtRoom2(value ?v8)(type 10min)
(confidence ?c2)∧
(?v8 = "Moderate")∧
(c2 < 0.5)∧
(H_ExpectedVarPM1.0AtRoom3(value ?v9)(type 10min)
(confidence ?c3))∧
(?v9 = "Moderate")∧
(c3 < 0.5)∧
(H_UserCollocation(uid1, uid2,···, uidn)(rid ?region id))∧
(?regionid = "Room1")∧
(H_UserCollocation(uid1, uid2,···, uidn)(rid ?region id))∧
(?regionid = "Room2")∧
(H_UserCollocation(uid1, uid2,···, uidn)(rid ?region id))∧
(?regionid = "Room3")
⟹
(UnusualSituationAlert("Room1", "Room2", "Room3"))
```

Listing 10. Unusual situation alert

9 Results

9.1 Descriptive Analytics

This section first discusses some indicative results from the pilot application described earlier and more specifically from two indoor positions (Device 2 & Device 7). The monitoring dataset covers the period from 24/02/2020 to 01/08/2021. The dairy operates 24-by-7 in three 8-h shifts: 6 am–2 pm, 2 pm–10 pm, 10 pm–6 am [61].

1. The most polluted hour-of-day for all pollutants is 8am. 1pm, 3pm, 7pm and 2am also show increased concentrations of one of the PM classes.
2. The most polluted days of the week, on average, are Tuesdays (where increased concentrations of *PM1.0* are recorded) and Thursdays (where increased concentrations of *PM2.5*, *PM10* are recorded). Tuesday is also the hottest day-of-the-week, while Thursday is the most humid, on average.
3. Weekdays are more polluted, on average, than weekends in terms of *PM1.0* and *PM2.5* while during weekends, increased *PM10* concentrations are recorded, on average. Weekends are also more humid, on average, than weekdays, however weekdays are, on average, hotter than weekends.
4. The morning shift is more polluted, and hotter, on average, than the afternoon and evening ones, in terms of *PM1.0* and *PM2.5*. However, during the afternoon shift increased *PM10* concentrations and increased humidity are recorded, on average, followed by the evening shift.
5. The most polluted month-of-the-year for all pollutants, on average, is January (2021), followed by April (2020). Temperatures between 21°C and 23°C are more likely to be associated with good air quality (especially between 27 and 40°C humidity).

Furthermore, we can also make the following observations.

1. *PM10* seems to follow humidity often without lag (e.g., Thursdays, weekends and the afternoon and evening shifts are both most polluted by *PM10* and humid).
2. On the other hand, *PM1.0* seems to follow temperature often without lag (e.g., Tuesdays, weekdays and the morning shifts show increased values for both *PM1.0* and humidity).
3. it seems that temperature follows humidity with a lag.

The above outcomes were confirmed also by Device 8 that is installed indoors at a different production area. However the following differences occurred that most can be attributed to the different usage of the two production areas at different times.

1. The most polluted hour-of-day for *PM10* and *PM2.5* is 6pm while for *PM1.0* it is 10pm. Moreover, all pollutants show increased concentrations at 4pm.
2. The most polluted day of the week, on average, is Monday, which is also the most humid day of the week while Wednesday is the hottest.
3. The afternoon shift is more polluted, and hotter, on average in terms of *PM1.0* and *PM2.5* while for *PM10* is the evening shift. Moreover, during the afternoon shift increased temperature and humidity are recorded.
4. The most polluted month-of-the-year for all pollutants, on average, is March 2021. The most humid month of the year is August 2020 while the hottest is August 2021.

9.2 Visual Analytics

Pearson Correlation. This section discusses some results from analysing data from the pilot application described earlier. More specifically, *PM10* air quality observations were compared with humidity and temperature observations at each of two positions: indoors (Device 8) and outdoors (Device 14), at the south side of the building. The monitoring period is 4 weeks long, from 01/05/2020 to 28/05/2020. The outdoor dataset contains 3786 samples while the indoor dataset 4032. First raw data timeseries were resampled at 10 min intervals. Next, based on data timestamps, for each resampled predicate instance the mean value and variance over *daily zones* was computed: Night (00:00–06:00), Early morning (06:00–09:00), Morning (09:00–12:00), Midday (12:00–16:00), Afternoon (16:00–20:00), Evening (20:00–00:00) and similarly per *weekday*. Outdoor *PM10* variance predicate instances were next correlated with the respective temperature and humidity ones using scatter-plots as shown in Fig. 3 where night instances are shown in blue, early morning in orange, midday in red, afternoon in purple and evening in brown. The y axis portrays *PM10* variance values from 0 to 120 with a step of 20 while the x axis temperature values between 10 and 40 with a step of five. Visual inspection shows that: *if it is a weeknight except Monday and Thursday and the temperature outdoors is below 15 °C, or if it is a Saturday night and the temperature outdoors ranges between 15 °C and 20 °C, one can expect to experience PM10 variance below 10 ug/*m^3. The above outcome is indicative and further analysis is required for further reasoning.

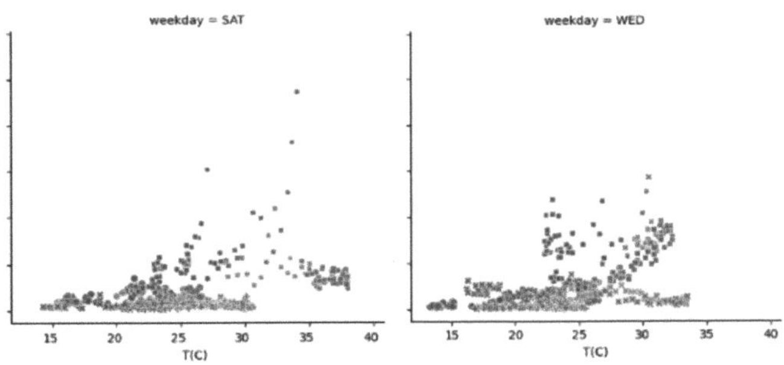

Fig. 3. Outdoor *PM10* 10-minute variance grouped per daily zone correlated with temperature and humidity.

K-Means Clustering. During a second experiment, *PM10* 10-min median concentration variance from the indoors device were mapped to custom, user-defined air quality statuses according to the following cases:

- Good: concentration lower than the timeseries median value
- Fair: concentration lower than the timeseries mean value

- Poor: concentration lower than the timeseries mean value and lower than the sum of the timeseries mean value and standard deviation
- Very Poor: concentration higher than the sum of the mean value and standard deviation

The statuses where next used to tag the *PM10* 10-min median timeseries with the air quality status. The resulting predicate instances for *PM10* where merged with temperature and humidity so that they could be clustered by the k-means algorithm producing the results shown in Fig. 4. Visual inspection shows that: *PM10*concentration variance values can be expected to correspond to good air quality, as defined earlier, with some confidence, when they occur at temperature between 21 °C and 22 °C. Further analysis is required for further reasoning.

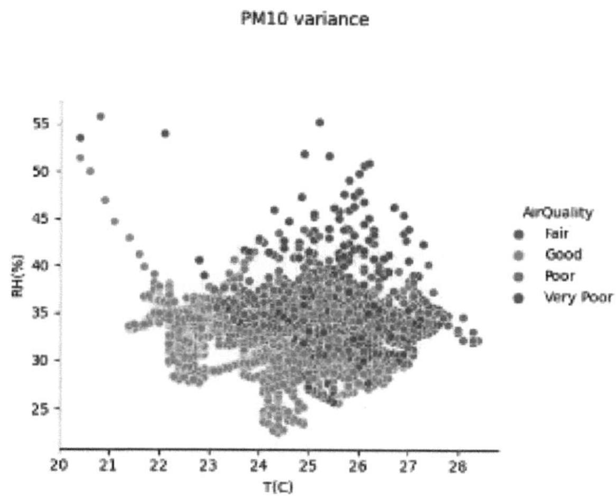

Fig. 4. *PM10* 10-min median concentration variance clusters. PM data are tagged with daily zone and air quality status, merged with temperature and humidity.

10 Related Work

Although some work has investigated dust in barns and kettle farms [13,14] the impact of particulate matter on dairy processing has not been sufficiently investigated. As a result, there is very little air quality data available for modern dairies, thus making it difficult to identify the best plan protection actions or intervention strategies. Multiple sensors can be used for detecting the human presence in indoor environments, including passive infrared (PIR) sensors [19], video cameras [20,21], infrared cameras, light beams placed in door frames and device-free localization that is based on radio signals [22]. The stream reasoning research area remains vastly unexplored, both from a theoretical point of view and also from the perspective of systems and tools supporting it. Notably, the implementations often are done before having a sound theoretical foundation. The most consolidated group of research findings on semantic stream processing and reasoning includes contributions from RSP engines and stream reasoners. These contributions aim at enabling the semantic integration of heterogeneous stream data sources with (large) static datasets stored in relational databases or triple stores through declarative continuous queries based on RDF and SPARQL. By adding window operators to SPARQL and extending the RDF model to capture temporal aspects of stream elements, RSP engines such as C-SPARQL [23] CQELS [24,25], and SPARQLstream [26] integrate the features of data stream management systems (DSMSs) and SPARQL engines. Despite a significant amount of work dedicated to modeling stream data in RDF- and SPARQL-like continuous query languages in the last 10 years, none of them can provide a comprehensive, clean, and sound theoretical foundation along with a robust implementation. IoT and smart cities have an extremely wide application range where the ideas of semantic sensor Web [29] and semantic sensor stream [30] can be applicable for various applications. InfluxQL [75], is an SQL-like query language for working with data in InfluxDB databases. InfluxQL and the most recent Flux both support continuous queries.

A Formal Specification Examples

The following queries aim to illustrate the expressiveness of the implemented system. Listing 11 presents some air quality logical predicates introduced in this work while Listing 12 presents the original Sentient Computing logical predicates. Furthermore, Listings 13, 14, 15 and 16 present recurring queries that infer knowledge on the number of collocated users on most polluted days of the week, on whether the current pollution value has exceeded the annual day of the week average, on generating a pollution alert, and on estimating a person's aggregated exposure to pollutants respectively.

```
(H_MaxPollutionAtLocation (pid ?pollutant_id)(rid ?region_id)
(value ?value)(count ?count)(sum ?sum)(hod ?hour_of_day)
(dow ?day_of_week)(dom ?day_of_month)(moy ?month_of_year)
(shift ?shift)(stime ?start_time))
(H_MinPollutionAtLocation (pid ?pollutant_id)(rid ?region_id)
(value ?value)(count ?count)(sum ?sum)(hod ?hour_of_day)
(dow ?day_of_week)(dom ?day_of_month)(moy ?month_of_year)
(shift ?shift)(stime ?start_time))
(H_StDevPollutionAtLocation (pid ?pollutant_id)
(rid ?region_id)(value ?value)(count ?count)(sum ?sum)
(hod ?hour_of_day)(dow ?day_of_week)(dom ?day_of_month)
(moy ?month_of_year)(shift ?shift)(stime ?start_time))
(H_MostPollutedHourOfDayAtLocation(pid ?pollutant_id)
(rid ?region_id)(value ?value)(hod ?hour_of_day)
(stime ?start_time))
(H_MostPollutedDayOfWeekAtLocation(pid ?pollutant_id)
(rid ?region_id)(value ?value)(dow ?day_of_week)
(stime ?start_time))
(H_MostPollutedDayOfMonthAtLocation(pid ?pollutant_id)
(rid ?region_id)(value ?value)(dom ?day_of_month)
(stime ?start_time))
(H_MostPollutedDayOfYearAtLocation(pid ?pollutant_id)
(rid ?region_id)(value ?value)(doy ?day_of_year)
(stime ?start_time))
(H_MostPollutedMonthOfYearAtLocation(pid ?pollutant_id)
(rid ?region_id)(value ?value)(moy ?month_of_year)
(stime ?start_time))
(H_MostPollutedShiftAtLocation(pid ?pollutant_id)
(rid ?region_id)(value ?value)(shift ?shift)
(stime ?start_time))
```

Listing 11. Air quality logical predicates

```
(L_UserAtPosition (uid ?user_id)(x ?x)(y ?y)(z ?z))
(L_AtomicLocation(rid ?region_id)(polyhedron))
(H_UserAtLocation(uid ?user_id) (rid ?region_id
(stime ?start_time))
(H_UserCollocation(uid_1, uid_2, ···, uid_n)(rid ?region_id)
(stime ?start_time))
```

Listing 12. Sentient Computing logical predicates

```
n:
(H_MostPollutedDayOfWeekAtLocation(pid ?pollutant_id)
(rid ?region_id)(value ?value)(dow ?day_of_week)
(stime ?start_time))∧
(H_UserCollocation(uid_1,uid_2,··· ,uid_n)
(rid ?region_id)(dow ?day_of_week)(stime ?start_time))
⟹
(H_MostPollutedDayOfWeekAtLocationWithCollocatedUsers
(pid ?pollutant_id)
(rid ?region_id)(value ?value)(uid_1,uid_2,··· ,uid_n)
(dow ?day_of_week)(stime ?start_time))
```

Listing 13. Number of collocated users on most polluted day of the week

```
(H_PollutionAtLocation(pid ?pollutant_id)(rid ?region_id)
(value ?value)(hod ?hour_of_day)(stime ?start_time))∧
(H_AveragePollutionAtLocation(pid ?pollutant_id)
(rid ?region_id)(value ?value)(count ?count)
(sum ?sum)(hod ?hour_of_day)(stime ?start_time))
⟹
(H_PollutionAtLocationGreaterThanHourOfDayAverage
(pid ?pollutant_id)(rid ?region_id)(value ?value)
(hod ?hour_of_day)(stime ?start_time))
```

Listing 14. Current pollution exceeded annual day of the week average

```
(H_PollutionAtLocationGreaterThanHourOfDayAverage
(pid ?pollutant_id)(rid ?region_id)(value ?value)
(hod ?hour_of_day)(stime ?start_time))
⟹
(H_Alert(uid ?uid)
("Current_pollution_value_over_annual_dow_average")
(stime ?stime))
```

Listing 15. Pollution alert creation

```
(H_UserAtLocationHistoric(uid ?user_id)(rid ?region_id)
(hod ?hour_of_day)(dow ?day_of_week)(dom ?day_of_month)
(moy ?month_of_year)(shift ?shift)(stime ?start_time)
(etime ?end_time))∧
(H_AveragePollutionAtLocationHistoric(pid ?pollutant_id)
(rid ?region_id)(value ?value)(count ?count)(sum?sum)
(hod ?hour_of_day)(dow ?day_of_week)(dom ?day_of_month)
(moy ?month_of_year)(shift ?shift)(stime ?start_time)
(etime ?end_time)
⟹
(H_UserAggregatedExposureHistoric(uid ?user_id)
(rid ?region_id)(value ?value)(hod ?hod)(dow ?day_of_week)
(dom ?day_of_month)(moy ?month_of_year)(shift ?shift)
(stime ?start_time)(etime ?end_time)
```

Listing 16. Personal aggregated exposure estimation

References

1. Krzyzanowski, M., Martin, R.V., Van Dingenen, R., van Donkelaar, A., Thurston, G.D.: Exposure assessment for estimation of the global burden of disease attributable to outdoor air pollution. Environ. Sci. Technol. **46**, 652–660 (2012)
2. Review of evidence on health aspects of air pollution – REVIHAAP project. Technical report, WHO-Regional office for Europe (2013)
3. Health effects of particulate matter: Policy implications for countries in eastern Europe. Caucasus and central Asia. Technical report, WHO-Regional office for Europe (2013)
4. Samet, J.M., Dominici, F., Curriero, F.C., Coursac, I., Zeger, S.L.: Fine particulate air pollution and mortality in 20 U.S. Cities, 1987–1994. N Engl. J. Med. **43**, 1742–1749 (2000)
5. Bano, N.: Assessment of indoor environmental impacts on human health (Case study: Glass city, Firozabad (India). Pollution **3**(2), 175–183 (2017)
6. Setton, E., et al.: The impact of daily mobility on exposure to traffic-related air pollution and health effect estimates. J. Eposure Sci. Environ. Epidemiol. **21**(1), 42–48 (2011)
7. Stanek, L.W., Brown, J.S.: Air pollution: sources, regulation, and health effects, reference module in biomedical sciences. In: Philip Wexler Encyclopedia of Toxicology. Elsevier, Amsterdam, Holland (2019)
8. Kousis, I., Pigliautile, I., Pisello, A.L.: Intra-urban microclimate investigation in urban heat island through a novel mobile monitoring system. Sci. Rep. **11**(1), 9732 (2021)
9. World health organization, WHO global air quality guidelines: particulate matter (*PM2.5* and *PM10*), ozone, nitrogen dioxide, sulfur dioxide and carbon monoxide, World Health Organization. https://apps.who.int/iris/handle/10665/345329. Accessed 24 Nov 2024
10. Edwards, L., Wilkinson, P., Rutter, G., Milojevic, A.: Health effects in people relocating between environments of differing ambient air pollution concentrations: a literature review. Environ. Pollut. **292**(Part A), 118314 (2022)

11. Kumar, P., et al.: Indoor air quality and energy management through real–time sensing in commercial buildings. Energy Build. **111**, 145–153 (2016)
12. Mahajan, S., Kumar, P.: Evaluation of low-cost sensors for quantitative personal exposure monitoring. Sustain. Cities Soc. **57**, 102076 (2020)
13. Nieckarz, Z., Pawlak, K., Baran, A., et al.: The concentration of particulate matter in the barn air and its influence on the content of heavy metals in milk. Sci. Rep. **13**, 10626 (2023)
14. Kic, P.: Influence of technological housing conditions on the concentration of airborne dust in dairy farms in the summer: a case study. Animals **13**(14), 2322 (2023)
15. Katsiri, E., Mycroft, A.: Knowledge-representation and scalable abstract reasoning for sentient computing using first-order logic. In: Proceedings of Workshop on Challenges and Novel Applications of Automated Reasoning (CADE-19) (2003)
16. Katsiri, E., Bacon, J., Mycroft, A.: An extended publish/subscribe protocol for transparent subscriptions to distributed abstract state in sensor-driven systems using abstract events. In: 26th International Conference on Software Engineering - W18L Workshop International Workshop on Distributed Event-based Systems (DEBS 2004), pp. 68–73 (2004)
17. Hopper, A.: The Clifford Paterson lecture, sentient computing. Phil. Trans. R. Soc. **358**(1773), 3582349–2358 (2000)
18. Harter, A., Hopper, A., Steggles, P., Ward, A., Webster, P.: The anatomy of a context-aware application. In: Proceedings of the Fifth Annual ACM/IEEE International Conference on Mobile Computing and Networking, pp. 59–60. ACM, Seattle, Washington, USA (1999)
19. Dodier, R.H., Henze, G.P., Tiller, D.K., Guo, X.: Building occupancy detection through sensor belief networks. Energy Build. **38**(9), 1033–1043 (2006)
20. Di Lascio, R., Foggia, P., Percannella, G., Saggese, A., Vento, M.: A real time algorithm for people tracking using contextual reasoning. Comput. Vis. Image Underst. **117**(8), 892–908 (2013)
21. Yoshinaga, S., Shimada, A., Taniguchi, R.: Real-time people counting using blob descriptor. Procedia. Soc. Behav. Sci. **2**(1), 143–152 (2010)
22. Vance, P., Prasad, G., Harkin, J., Kevin, C.: Analysis of device-free localisation (DFL) techniques for indoor environments. In: The 21st Irish Signals and Systems Conference (ISSC 2010), pp. 76–81. Cork, Ireland (2010)
23. Barbieri, D.F., Braga, D., Ceri, S., Grossniklaus, M.: An execution environment for C-SPARQL queries. In: Proceedings of the 13th International Conference on Extending Database Technology (EDBT 2010), pp. 441–452. ACM, Lausanne, Switzerland (2010)
24. Le-Phuoc, D., Dao-Tran, M., Xavier Parreira, J., Hauswirth, M.: A native and adaptive approach for unified processing of linked streams and linked data. In: Aroyo, L., et al. (eds.) ISWC 2011. LNCS, vol. 7031, pp. 370–388. Springer, Heidelberg (2011). https://doi.org/10.1007/978-3-642-25073-6_24
25. Le-Phuoc, D., Eiter, T., Le-Tuan, A.: A scalable reasoning and learning approach for neural-symbolic stream fusion. In: Proceedings of the AAAI Conference on Artificial Intelligence (AAAI 2021), vol. 35, no. 6, pp. 4996–5005. AAAI Press, virtual (2021). https://doi.org/10.1609/aaai.v35i6.16633
26. Calbimonte, J.-P., Corcho, O., Gray, A.J.G.: Enabling ontology-based access to streaming data sources. In: Patel-Schneider, P.F. (ed.) ISWC 2010. LNCS, vol. 6496, pp. 96–111. Springer, Heidelberg (2010). https://doi.org/10.1007/978-3-642-17746-0_7

27. Komazec, S., Cerri, D., Fensel, D., Sparkwave: continuous schema-enhanced pattern matching over RDF data streams. In: Proceedings of the 6th ACM International Conference on Distributed Event-Based Systems (DEBS 2012), pp. 58–68. ACM, Berlin, Germany (2012). https://doi.org/10.1145/2335484.2335491
28. Rinne, M., Solanki, M., Nuutila, E.: Rfid-based logistics monitoring with semantics-driven event processing. In: Proceedings of the 10th ACM International Conference on Distributed and Event-Based Systems (DEBS 2016), pp. 238–245. ACM, Irvine, California (2016). https://doi.org/10.1145/2933267.2933300
29. Sheth, A.P., Henson, C.A, Sahoo S.S.: Semantic sensor web. IEEE Internet Comput. **12**(4), 78–83
30. Barnaghi, P., Wang, W., Dong, L., Wang, C.: A linked-data model for semantic sensor streams. In: 2013 IEEE International Conference on Green Computing and Communications and IEEE Internet of Things and IEEE Cyber, Physical and Social Computing, pp. 468–475. IEEE Computer Society (2013). https://doi.org/10.1109/GreenCom-iThings-CPSCom.2013.95
31. Kumar, P., Morawska, L., Martani, C., Biskos, G., Neophytou, M., Di Sabatino, S., et al.: The rise of low-cost sensing for managing air pollution in cities. Environ. Int. **75**, 199–205 (2015)
32. Morawska, L., et al.: Applications of low-cost sensing technologies for air quality monitoring and exposure assessment: how far have they gone? Environ. Int. **116**, 286–299 (2018)
33. Snyder, E.G., et al.: Applications of low-cost sensing technologies for air quality monitoring and exposure assessment: how far have they gone? Environ. Sci. Technol. **47**, 11369–11377 (2013)
34. Anjomshoaa, A., Duarte, F., Rennings, D., Matarazzo, T.J., deSouza, P., Ratti, C.: City scanner: building and scheduling a mobile sensing platform for smart city services. IEEE Internet Things J. **5**, 4567–4579 (2018)
35. DeSouza, P., Anjomshoaa, A., Duarte, F., Kahn, R., Kumar, P., Ratti, C.: Air quality monitoring using mobile low-cost sensors mounted on trash-trucks: methods development and lessons learned. Sustain. Cities Soc. **60**, 102239 (2020)
36. Elen, B., et al.: The aeroflex: a bicycle for mobile air quality measurements. Sensors **13**, 221–240 (2013)
37. Dutta, P., et al..: Common sense: participatory urban sensing using a network of handheld air quality monitors. In: Proceedings of the 7th ACM Conference on Embedded Networked Sensor Systems, pp. 349–350. ACM. New York, NY, USA, Berkeley, CA, USA (2009). https://doi.org/10.1145/1644038.1644095
38. Hasenfratz, D., Saukh, O., Sturzenegger, S., Thiele, L.: Participatory air pollution monitoring using smartphones. Mob. Sens. **1**, 1–5 (2012)
39. deSouza, P., Kahn, A.R., Limbacher, A.J., Marais, A.E., Duarte, F., Ratti, C.: Combining low-cost, surface-based aerosol monitors with size-resolved satellite data for air quality applications. Atmos. Meas. Tech. **13**(10), 5319–5334 (2020)
40. Koukouli, M.E., et al.: Sudden changes in nitrogen dioxide emissions over Greece due to lockdown after the outbreak of COVID-19. Atmos. Chem. Phys. **21**, 1759–1774 (2020)
41. Postolache, O.A., Pereira, J.M.D., Girao, P.M.B.S.: Smart sensors network for air quality monitoring applications. IEEE Trans. Instrum. Meas. **58**, 3253–3262 (2009)
42. Hagan, D.H., et al.: Inferring aerosol sources from low-cost air quality sensor measurements: a case study in Delhi. India. Environ. Sci. Technol. Lett. **6**(8), 467–472 (2019)

43. Yazdi, M.N., Arhami, N., Delavarrafiee, M., Ketabchy, M.: Developing air exchange rate models by evaluating vehicle in-cabin air pollutant exposures in a highway and tunnel setting: case study of Tehran. Iran. Environ. Sci. Pollut. Res Int. **26**(1), 501–513 (2019)
44. Bukowiecki, N., Dommen J., Prévôt, A.S.H., Richter, R., Weingartner, E., Baltensperger U.: A mobile pollutant measurement laboratory—measuring gas phase and aerosol ambient concentrations with high spatial and temporal resolution. Atmos. Environ. **36**, 5569–5579 (2002)
45. Apte, J.S., et al.: High-resolution air pollution mapping with google street view cars: exploiting big data. Environ. Sci. Technol. **51**, 6999–7008 (2017)
46. Capezzuto, L., et al.: A maker friendly mobile and social sensing approach to urban air quality monitoring. In: Proceedings of the 2014 IEEE on SENSORS, pp. 12–16. Valencia, Spain (2014). https://doi.org/10.1109/ICSENS.2014.6984920
47. Murty, R.N., et al. Citysense: an urban-scale wireless sensor network and testbed. In: Proceedings of the 2008 IEEE Conference on Technologies for Homeland Security, pp. 583–588, Waltham, MA, USA (2008). https://doi.org/10.1109/THS.2008.4534518
48. Kadri, A., Yaacoub, E., Mushtaha, M., Abu-Dayya, A.: Wireless sensor network for real-time air pollution monitoring. In: Proceedings of the 2013 1st International Conference on Communications, Signal Processing, and their applications (ICCSPA), pp. 1–5, Sharjah, United Arab Emirates (2013). https://doi.org/10.1109/ICCSPA.2013.6487323
49. Jiang, Y., et al.: MAQS: a personalized mobile sensing system for indoor air quality monitoring. In: Proceedings of the 13th International Conference on Ubiquitous Computing, pp. 271–280. ACM, Beijing, New York, NY, USA, China (2011). https://doi.org/10.1145/2030112.2030150
50. Jelicic, V., Magno, M., Brunelli, D., Paci, G., Benini, L.: Context-adaptive multimodal wireless sensor network for energy-efficient gas monitoring. IEEE Sens. J. **13**, 328–338 (2013)
51. Mansour, S., Nasser, N., Karim, L., Ali, A.: Wireless sensor network-based air quality monitoring system. In: Proceedings of the 2014 International Conference on Computing, Networking and Communications (ICNC), pp. 545–550, Honolulu, HI, USA (2014). https://doi.org/10.1109/ICCNC.2014.6785394
52. Sun, L., et al.: Development and application of a next generation air sensor network for the Hong Kong marathon 2015 air quality monitoring. Sensors **16**(2), 211 (2016). https://doi.org/10.3390/s16020211
53. Honicky, R., Brewer, E.A., Paulos, E., White, R.: N-smarts: networked suite of mobile atmospheric real-time sensors. In: Proceedings of the Second ACM SIGCOMM Workshop on Networked Systems for Developing Regions, pp. 25–30. ACM, New York, NY, USA, Seattle, WA, USA (2008). https://doi.org/10.1145/1397705.139771
54. Lane, N.D., Miluzzo, E., Lu, H., Peebles, D., Choudhury, T., Campbell, A.T.: A survey of mobile phone sensing. IEEE Commun. Mag. **48**, 140–150 (2010)
55. Helbig, C., Bauer, H.-S., Rink, K., Wulfmeyer, V., Frank, M., Kolditz, O.: Concept and workflow for 3D visualization of atmospheric data in a virtual reality environment for analytical approaches. Environ. Earth Sci. **72**(10), 3767–3780 (2014). https://doi.org/10.1007/s12665-014-3136-6
56. Setti, L., et al.: Evaluation of the potential relationship between particulate matter (PM) pollution and COVID-19 infection spread in Italy: first observational study based on initial epidemic diffusion. BMJ Open **10**(9) (2020)

57. Wu, X., Nethery, R.C., Sabath, M.B., Braun, D., Dominici, F.: Air pollution and COVID-19 mortality in the United States: strengths and limitations of an ecological regression analysis. Sci. Adv. **6**(45) (2020)
58. Saadat, S., Rawtani, D., Hussain, C.M.: Environmental perspective of COVID-19. Sci. Total Environ. **728**, 138870 (2020)
59. Le Quéré, C., et al.: Temporary reduction in daily global CO2 emissions during the COVID-19 forced confinement. Nat. Clim. Chang. **10**, 647–653 (2020)
60. Katsiri, E.: Sensor networks with edge intelligence for reliable air quality monitoring in the COVID-19 Era. In: Daimi, K., et al. (eds.) ICR 2022. AISC, vol. 1431, pp. 383–396. Springer, Cham (2020). https://doi.org/10.1007/978-3-031-14054-9_36
61. Katsiri, E.: Industrial air quality sensor analytics. In: Daimi, K., et al. (eds.) ICR 2023. LNNS, vol. 721, pp. 369–380. Springer, Cham (2023). https://doi.org/10.1007/978-3-031-35308-6_31
62. Katsiri, E.: Air-19: reliable monitoring of air quality and microorganisms in post pandemic municipality building. In: Proceedings of the 18th International Conference on Environmental Science and Technology (CEST2023), Athens, Greece (2023)
63. Katsiri, E.: Developing reliable air quality monitoring devices with low cost sensors: method and lessons learned. Int. J. Environ. Sci. **6**, 425–444 (2020)
64. Grafana: the open observability platform. https://grafana.com. Accessed 24 Nov 2024
65. Fadhel, M., Sekerinski, E., Yao, S.: A comparison of time series databases for storing water quality data. In: Auer, M.E., Tsiatsos, T. (eds.) IMCL 2018. AISC, vol. 909, pp. 302–313. Springer, Cham (2019). https://doi.org/10.1007/978-3-030-11434-3_33
66. Buelvas, J., Múnera, D., Tobón V.D.P., et al.: Data quality in IoT-based air quality monitoring systems: a systematic mapping study. Water Air Soil Pollut. **234**(248) (2023)
67. Sharifi, R., Langari, R.: Nonlinear sensor fault diagnosis using mixture of probabilistic PCA models. Mech. Syst. Sig. Process. **85**, 638–650 (2017)
68. Wang, R.Y., Strong, D.M.: Beyond accuracy: what data quality means to data consumers. J. Manag. Inform Syst. **12**(4), 5–33 (1996)
69. Li, Y., Parker, L.E.: Nearest neighbor imputation using spatial-temporal correlations in wireless sensor networks. Inform. Fusion. **15**, 64–79 (2014)
70. Aggarwal, C.C.: An Introduction to Outlier Analysis, pp. 1–40. Outlier analysis. Springer, New York (2013)
71. Ahmad, N.F., Hoang D.B., Phung M.H.: Robust preprocessing for health care monitoring framework. In: 2009 11th International Conference on e-Health Networking, Applications and Services (Healthcom), pp. 169–74 (2009). https://doi.org/10.1109/HEALTH.2009.5406196
72. Anderson, R.L.: Distribution of the serial correlation coefficient. Ann. Math. Stat. **13**(1), 1–13 (1942)
73. Bosman, H.H., Iacca, G., Tejada, A., Wörtche, H.J., Liotta, A.: Spatial anomaly detection in sensor networks using neighborhood information. Inform. Fusion **33**, 41–56 (2017)
74. Moursi, A.S., El-Fishawy, N., Djahel, S., Shouman, M.A.: An IoT enabled system for enhanced air quality monitoring and prediction on the edge. Compl. Intell. Syst. **7**(6), 2923–2947 (2021). https://doi.org/10.1007/s40747-021-00476-w
75. InfluxDB line protocol reference. https://docs.influxdata.com/influxdb/v1.8/write_protocols/line_protocol_reference/. Accessed 24 Nov 2024

76. Glantz, S.A., Slinker, B.K., Neilands, T.B.: Primer of Applied Regression & Analysis of Variance, 3rd edn. McGraw Hill, New York (2016)
77. Aho, K.A.: Foundational and Applied Statistics for Biologists, 1st edn. Chapman & Hall/CRC Press (2014)
78. Bartlett, M.S.: On the theoretical specification and sampling properties of autocorrelated time-series. Suppl. J. Roy. Stat. Soc. **8**(1), 27–41 (1946). JSTOR
79. Quenouille, M.H.: The joint distribution of serial correlation coefficients. Ann. Math. Stat. **20**(4), 561–571 (1949)
80. Author, F.: Article title. Journal **2**(5), 99–110 (2016)
81. Author, F., Author, S.: Title of a proceedings paper. In: Editor, F., Editor, S. (eds.) CONFERENCE 2016, LNCS, vol. 9999, pp. 1–13. Springer, Heidelberg (2016). https://doi.org/10.10007/1234567890
82. Author, F., Author, S., Author, T.: Book title, 2nd edn. Publisher, Location (1999)
83. Author, A.-B.: Contribution title. In: 9th International Proceedings on Proceedings, pp. 1–2. Publisher, Location (2010)
84. LNCS homepage. http://www.springer.com/lncs, Accessed 25 Oct 2023

Software

Sustainable Software Development: New Challenges for Programming, Language Design and Analysis

Bent Thomsen(✉), Lone Leth Thomsen, and Thomas Bøgholm

Aalborg University, Aalborg, Denmark
{bt,lone,boegholm}@cs.aau.dk

Abstract. Energy consumption and the associated CO_2 footprint of Information and Communication Technology (ICT) has become a major concern. Some estimates suggest that 4–6% of global electricity consumption in 2020 was spent on ICT and, although the ICT industry is very good at using green energy, CO_2 emissions from ICT are at par with or has overtaken CO_2 emissions from aviation. Pessimistic forecasts suggest that electricity consumption from ICT may rise to 20% in 2030.

Clearly software does not emit CO_2, but software is executed on hardware, and hardware consumes energy when executing software. In recent years there has been a huge effort in understanding the relationship between software and energy consumption of the underlying hardware. There is now evidence that the structure of the software, the program constructs used in the software and even the programming languages and compilers used for developing the software influence the energy consumption when the software is executed. There is a huge global effort on raising awareness of sustainable software development and there is a growing body of knowledge of many aspects.

However, the literature on how programming language design and analysis can impact energy consumption of the underlying hardware is sparse.

In a seminal presentation at SAS'07 Alan gave an overview of the changes going on in hardware and outlined his view on the implications of this on programming language design and analysis research. In this paper we follow in Alan's footsteps and outline our view on the implications of energy consumption on programming language design and analysis research.

1 Introduction

The World Economic Forum estimates that digital technologies can reduce global CO_2 emissions by 15% in sectors such as energy, manufacturing, agriculture, construction and transport [6,19]. Despite the fact that ICT often is able to exploit green energy, CO_2 emissions from ICT are at par with or has overtaken CO_2 emissions from aviation [9]. Some pessimistic forecasts suggest that ICT in 2030 may consume as much as 20% of the global electricity production [26]. [35]

D. Orchard et al. (Eds.): Alan Mycroft Festschrift, LNCS 15500, pp. 199–214, 2026.
https://doi.org/10.1007/978-3-032-08187-2_10

reports that in Ireland Data Center electricity use accounted for more than 21% of total metered electricity consumption in 2023.

Developers of ICT systems have a strong desire to help reduce global CO_2 emissions in general and from ICT systems in particular. Tremendous advances in hardware technology have to a large extent kept a lid on an explosion of energy consumption from ICT despite a rise in demand for computations. Considering the bleak forecast in [26] it seems that the energy consumption from the worlds data centers has been kept at around 2% despite at six fold rise in throughput since 2010.

The impressive achievements of hardware engineers have, however, not been matched by software engineers, who to a large degree, are unaware of the opportunities and possibilities that they have regarding reducing energy consumption caused by ICT. Software engineers are not entirely to blame for this situation as they have been shielded from the development in hardware that still, as Alan pointed out in his SAS'07 talk, tries to give the software engineers the illusion that hardware operates according to a computational model aligned more or less with the i486 from 1985. Even when software engineers understand that hardware has changed dramatically they often lack the tools to help them even address the issue [31].

From a research perspective, there has been a huge effort in understanding the relationship between software and energy consumption of the underlying hardware. There is now evidence that the structure of the software, program constructs used in the software and even the programming languages and compilers used for developing the software influence the energy consumption when the software is executed. There are various tools able to identify energy hungry program patterns and replace these with less energy demanding patterns. There are also recommendations that software engineers integrate an energy testing practice into their software development process to identify energy hotspots as early as possible.

In this paper we will follow in Alan's footsteps and first outline changes in technology, then discuss programming implications (for programmers and for languages) and finally outline opportunities for static analysis and type systems, before listing our conclusions.

2 Changes in Technology

As Alan explained in his SAS'07 talk [36], hardware has been on a tremendous journey from the invention of the integrated circuit in 1958 where a few transistors could be placed together to a situation today in 2023 where over 100 billion transistors can be fitted on a chip. Early CPU's had a few thousand transistors, e.g. in 1971 the Intel 4004 chip had 2300 transistors, in 2007 the Intel Itanium 2 dual core processors had more than 1.7 billion transistors, and in 2023 the Intel Core i9-11900K has 17 billion transistors and the Apple M1 Ultra has 114 billion transistors. The development has followed Moore's law: doubling the number of transistors per unit area in an integrated circuit every 18 months (or every two years), although a slight slowdown seems to have materialized in recent years since we have not quite reached the 256 billion transistors on a chip that Alan predicted!

2.1 The Single-Core Era

The huge number of available transistors has implications for the architecture of CPUs. In the early years, the seventies to mid-eighties, more and more complex CPUs with more and more advanced instructions were constructed, however in the late seventies and early eighties the x86 instruction set emerged as a dominant player in the PC market. With shrinking feature size it was possible to increase clock speed and thus speed up execution time, leading to the misquoted version of Moore's law that processor speed doubles every 18 months.

Although feature size has gone down uniformly, the speed of circuits has not developed uniformly. In the early years there was a 1-1 relationship between execution of instructions on the CPU and memory access to RAM. However, from the mid-eighties this correspondence started to drift with RAM becoming relatively slower and slower. A large part of the increased number of transistors was in the period from 1985 to 2005 used to hide this fact by introducing on-chip caches, pipelines and super scalar processing, thus hiding the fact that the relative speed between CPU and RAM by 2005 was a factor 1–200. With the shrinking feature size comes an additional challenge, namely that accessing on chip memory is also getting slower as a round trip on a chip may take as much as 75 clock cycles. Therefore several layers of caches, referred to as L1, L2, L3 etc., were introduced - this means that a large part of the chip is used for memory.

Koomey's law, which states that the number of computations per joule of energy dissipated doubles about every 1.57 years, indicates that hardware is getting more energy efficient in general. However, this is a very broad trend with huge variations.

Already before the turn of the millennium it had become clear that the increase in processor speed comes with a higher energy cost. As reported in [21] the reason for the increase in power is that the design techniques used in the desktop microprocessors tended to result in much more energy being expended per instruction due to the higher capacitance toggled to process each instruction. [21] reports that the Pentium Pro processor was 1.8 times faster than the Pentium processor but consumed 3.3 times the power. The increase in speed was entirely a result of the deeper pipeline on the Pentium Pro processor since the process technology was the same for both.

[21] compares energy per instruction (EPI) for a number of intel processors. Although the processors are manufactured using different feature sizes, have different clock frequencies and different voltage, normalized to the i486 the EPI reported are: 10 nJ for the i486, 14 nJ for the Pentium, 24 nJ for the Pentium Pro, 38 nJ for the Pentium 4 Willamette, 48 nJ for the Pentium 4 Cedarmill, 15 nJ for the Pentium M and 11 nJ for the Core Duo (benchmarked using a single core).

The energy efficiency of the mobile processors, Pentium M and the Core Duo, is a result of more modest pipeline depths, moderately-sized out-of-order structures, aggressive clock gating, and micro-op fusion. The Pentium M and Core Duo processors deliver higher performance by performing more useful work in each clock cycle. Similarly in 2020 AMD reported that, since 2014, the company has managed to improve the efficiency of its mobile processors by a factor of 31.7. Thus with the advent of mobile computing came a new focus on energy efficiency, which later proliferated to desktop and server hardware.

A simple way of saving energy is to reduce the voltage supplied to the CPU and as higher frequencies require higher voltage the concept of dynamic voltage and frequency scaling (DVFS) has been introduced, sometimes referred to as overvolting and undervolting or turbo boosting. With these techniques the CPU energy consumption, and heating, can be controlled to some extent from software by throttling down when e.g. conservation of battery is important or boosting when high demand jobs are executing.

2.2 The Multi-Core Era

One problem with the shrinking feature size is that the heat produced as a consequence of switching circuits gets concentrated on a smaller and smaller area. This puts a limit on how much the clock speed can be raised and as a consequence clock speeds since 2005 have been kept relatively stable around 2.5–3.5 GHz. Instead of a faster single core CPU a development towards multi-core architectures, starting with dual core CPUs in commercial use from 2005 onward, has been pursued. Extrapolating based on Moore's law we should by now have chips with more than a thousand cores and indeed there are experimental 1000 core CPUs and even commercial CPUs like the Arm-based CPU "Ampere Altra/Altra Max" with up to 256 cores.

However, mainstream computing has stopped at 4 to 12 cores on consumer platforms, with a few high-end server processors with 40 or more cores. Instead of adding more cores the focus has been on integrating the GPU and providing cores with different energy consumption characteristics.

With the advent of multicore architectures another power saving method has been introduced, where some cores are "turn off" or at least put into reduced power state when not needed. Power management states, P-states and C-states, are mechanisms used in modern processors to control and optimize power consumption. P-states are also known as performance states. P-states were introduced in Intel Skylake in 2015 and AMD Zen2 from 2019. These are different operating states or frequency/voltage pairs that a processor can switch between to balance performance and power consumption. At higher P-states, the processor runs at higher clock frequencies and voltages, providing better performance but consuming more power. Lower P-states involve lower clock frequencies and voltages, reducing power consumption at the cost of lower processing performance. The operating system and the processor work together to adjust the processor's P-state dynamically based on the current workload. This allows the system to save power during periods of low activity and ramp up performance when needed. C-states are idle or sleep states that a processor enters when there is little to no computational load. These states help reduce power consumption when the CPU is not actively processing tasks. Each C-state corresponds to a different level of idle activity, with higher-numbered C-states indicating deeper levels of sleep and lower power usage. When a processor enters a C-state, it effectively powers down parts of its core or cores to minimize power usage. This can involve halting the clock or even turning off parts of the processor until activity resumes. As soon as the processor detects activity, it exits the C-state and returns to an active state to resume processing tasks. The combination of P-states and C-states allows modern processors to adapt their power usage in real-time to match the system's workload, optimizing power efficiency while still providing adequate performance when required. This is crucial for laptops and mobile devices to extend battery life and for data centers to reduce energy consumption while maintaining responsiveness.

With modern multi-core processors determining the EPI is more difficult. [44] presents an instruction-level energy model for the Intel Xeon Phi processor, identifying how energy per instruction scales with the number of cores, the number of active threads per core, and instruction types and modes of data operand access. Compared to [21] it is now clear that instructions have different energy costs. For example [44] reports that scalar operations with operands in registers cost 0.45 nJ, whereas scalar operations on data in L1, L2 or in memory costs; 0.88 nJ, 7.72 nJ, 52.14 nJ (with prefetch) and 232.62 nJ (without prefetch). For vector instructions the EPI with register operands is 1.00 nJ while the EPI of moving data from memory to the ALU without prefetching is 233.17 nJ.

2.3 The Heterogeneous-Core Era

Another power saving approach was introduced in Intel's Alder Lake chips which come with two sets of CPU cores: P-cores and E-cores. P cores are designed for high-performance tasks. They typically have a higher clock speed and are optimized for single-threaded performance, making them well-suited for tasks that do not benefit from multiple cores. P cores use a more advanced process node and often have a higher power consumption compared to E cores. E cores are designed for power efficiency and less demanding tasks. They have a lower power consumption and are optimized for tasks that can benefit from multi-threading. E cores are typically used for background tasks, lightweight applications, and power-saving scenarios to extend battery life in laptops or reduce power consumption in desktops. Alder Lake processors use a combination of P and E cores to achieve a balance between high performance and power efficiency. This architecture is sometimes referred to as a "big.LITTLE" design introduced by ARM in 2011 and by Intel in 2021 in the Alder Lake architecture, with P cores acting as the "big" high-performance cores and E cores serving as the "LITTLE" power-efficient cores. The operating system and software are responsible for scheduling tasks to run on the appropriate core based on their resource requirements.

Although P and E cores in consumer PCs are mainly used for running different applications with different execution speed needs, it also makes sense to have different sized processors in a many-core architecture to improve parallel speedup by reducing the time it takes to run the less parallel code. As described in [7] an implication of Amdahl's law is that the less parallel portion of a program can limit performance on a parallel computer. Therefore it makes sense to execute the inherent sequential code of an application on a faster processor with larger caches, a bigger multiplier, deeper pipelines, even if this also implies more power consumption. [7] presents the following argument:

"For example, assume 10% of the time a program gets no speedup on a 100-processor computer. Suppose to run the sequential code twice as fast, a single processor would need 10 times as many resources as a simple core, the comparative speedups of a homogeneous 100 simple processor design and a heterogeneous 91 processor design relative to a single simple processor are: Speedup Homogeneous = 1/(0.1 0.9/100) = 9.2 times faster. Speedup Heterogeneous = 1/(0.1/2 0.9/90) = 16.7 times faster. In this example, even if a single larger processor needed 10 times as many resources to run twice as fast, it would be much more valuable than 10 smaller processors it replaces."

Some modern processors facilitate simultaneous multi-threading (SMT), called hyper threading on Intel processors. SMT allows a single physical processor core to simulate two or more logical cores. If a core encounters a stall or waits for data, it can switch to another thread that is ready to execute, thereby reducing idle time and improving overall CPU utilization.

Another parallelisation strategy is Single Instruction, Multiple Data (SIMD), sometimes refered to as vector operations or Streaming SIMD Extensions (SSE) instructions. SSE was first introduced with the Intel Pentium II processor, but they are now found on all modern x86 processors, and are the default floating point interface in 64-bit mode.

To make use of SIMD instructions, software developers often rely on compilers to automatically vectorize their code. The compiler identifies opportunities to apply SIMD instructions and generates the appropriate machine code to take advantage of parallelism. Proper data alignment is crucial when using SIMD instructions. Data elements in SIMD vectors must be aligned to fit the specified width of the SIMD registers. Misaligned data can result in performance penalties.

SIMD instructions were partially introduced to support game programming. Another trend coming from game programming is the General-Purpose Graphics Processing Unit (GPGPU) using the graphics processing units (GPUs) for computational tasks beyond traditional graphics rendering. While GPUs were originally developed to handle graphics-related calculations (such as rendering images, videos, and 3D graphics), their highly parallel architecture has proven valuable for a wide range of general-purpose computational tasks. Modern GPUs are highly parallel processors with hundreds or thousands of cores compared to the relatively fewer cores in CPUs. GPUs are optimized for handling large amounts of data and performing computations on this data quickly due to their high memory bandwidth and parallel processing capabilities. For certain workloads, GPGPUs can be more energy-efficient than CPUs, as they can perform a large number of computations in parallel, potentially saving time and power.

Moving data to the GPU can take significant time, but co-locating the GPU and the CPU can significantly reduce this time. Some chip manufacturers have even started to replace the GPU with specialized designs for AI computations. An example of this is Apple's Neural Engine, a group of specialized cores functioning as a neural processing unit (NPU) dedicated to the acceleration of AI that require far less power to execute the same processes as a GPU at comparable speeds.

It is too early to say what effect the heterogeneous-core era will have on EPI in mainstream computing, except that it probably will be even more difficult determining the EPI than in the multi-core era. Hopefully trends observed over the period from 2012 to 2022 across super-computing systems and specialized architectures for AI/ML accelerators reported in [43] will be indicative. Although [43] concludes: "The energy efficiency at the bit-level does not translate into efficiency at the instruction-level, or at the system level for a variety of systems, especially for large-scale AI/ML accelerators or supercomputers". [43] also observes that newer systems tend to be more energy efficient.

3 Programming Implications (for Programmers and for Languages)

In his SAS'07 talk Alan identified several implications of the change in hardware for programmers and programming languages. First and foremost he identified that the programmers view of memory and computations being in a 1-1 relationship was no longer accurate. Therefore programmers should write code that as far as possible uses local data or consider re-computing as "Wires are no longer free, and local re-computation is far better than sharing computation with a distant place". Alan points out that on a 15 mm chip running at 2.5 GHz, a cross-chip round-trip takes nearly 30 ns or 75 clock cycles. Off chip-access to external memory will of course be far worse.

The implication of this is that the programming model underpinning imperative programming languages like C is no longer accurate and Alan calls for research on programming languages to support non-uniform memory and designs which de-emphasise shared RAM and serialised access.

Alan suggested that "Pointers (should be) considered harmful", at least unrestricted pointers as known from C, Java or ML, because pointer copying is more expensive than integer copying and because pointer copying creates aliasing. Alan also suggested that OO-languages (C++ and Java) should be "considered harmful". He highlights the problem with various parameter mechanisms, by value and by reference, whereby the programmer at an early stage of development is forced to freeze constraints about whether a function shares a data address space with its caller. Another concern with OO is that proper OO design fosters a memory layout of data where it is very difficult to achieve locality - just think of how many pointers have to be followed to random places in memory when traversing an AST in a compiler designed following best OO practice.

Clearly functional languages are safe(r) because the compiler can choose to copy or alias data in pure functional languages. But ML has references that cannot be copied and Haskell's laziness may imply that copying becomes rework! Even pure data poses the question of when to distribute and when not?

If we look at what happened in programming language evolution since 2007, functional languages, especially Haskell, but also ML (especially the OCaml variant) had a surge in popularity, in particular in the FinTech industry. However, these languages are still not in widespread use. Instead the major OO languages (C++, C# and Java) were extended with first class functions, also known as lambdas, albeit with various restrictions. The introduction of lambdas exposed mainstream programmers to functional programming concepts such as higher order functions and immutable data. A new breed of functional OO languages, like Scala, F#, Kotlin and Swift, have also emerged. However, none of these languages have eliminated the "pointer" problem, although they encourage a value oriented functional programming style. In particular Scala has been popular in Big Data analytics due to its adoption in Spark/Hadoop, which is based on the map/reduce functional idiom.

Multi-core chips bring the possibility of parallel programming into mainstream. However, as Alan predicted, the new model (in 2007) of shared memory multi-core computing would scale to 2, 4 and maybe 8 cores, but questioned that it would scale to 1024. This is simply because shared memory would become a bottleneck and with shared memory comes the need for locking mechanisms, and as Alan said "Locks considered harmful" and needs to be discouraged along with programming mechanisms which stress it without user awareness. E.g. synchronized objects in Java.

Around 2010 the idea of software transactional memory (STM) became a hot topic and it was seen as a solution to the problem of getting mainstream programmers to deal with parallel execution and locking on shared memory architectures. Languages like Haskell and Scala were extended with STM libraries and the emergence of the Clojure language, a LISP variant, designed around STM. However, it turns out that programmers find STM just as difficult as locking. It also turns out that STM performance degrades with the number of cores, as the likelihood of conflicting transactions increases with the number of truly parallel tasks executing.

Instead of a shared memory parallel programming model, Alan suggests a move to a message-passing programming model, as the Actor model has disjoint memory spaces per process. He reminds us of the Needham-Lauer "Duality of operating structures" which showed that shared memory and message-passing are duals and observes that message passing and shared memory are directly equivalent with linear uses of buffers.

Alan mentions the Occam language which has a message passing model based on the CSP calculus. The Occam programming model was designed to be very close to the system architecture of the Transputer which, according to [4], "was the first general purpose microprocessor designed specifically to be used in parallel computing systems". In recent years the Erlang language, based on the

Actor model, has risen in popularity, in part due to its use in the popular WhatsApp, and also the Go system programming language from Google has a message passing model based on CSP. Another representative of this category is the XC language designed for the XMOS xCORE embedded microcontroller and heavily influenced by the occam programming language. The XC language is explicitly designed with energy efficient software development in mind [18].

In 2004 [10] Microsoft Research presented Polyphonic C# with synchronous and asynchronous methods, based on ideas from the join-calculus. A restricted version of asynchronous methods was adopted in the F# language and later in the C# language leading to a concurrent programming style based on futures and promises. This programming style is now in widespread use in many modern programming languages [1], replacing the need for explicit programming with threads and locks.

The rise of the GPGPU led to a flurry of extensions and libraries in high level languages, like Scala, but these extensions were not widely adopted. Also a number of high level GPU programming languages, such as Futhark [24] and Bend [2] have been put forward. However, the proprietary language CUDA from NVIDIA and the OpenMP API dominate GPGPU programming. Comparisons of energy efficiency of CUDA versus OpenMP show no clear winner [33]. The rise of AI is to a large extent powered by GPGPU, but the programming is mainly reserved for specialist programmers writing powerful libraries in C/C++ and CUDA/OpenMP with such libraries being accessed by mainstream programmers through the use of Python libraries such as TensorFlow, NumPy and SciPy. Studies show significant energy savings through this approach [25,42].

So we are still lacking a programming model and programming languages supporting such a model that align better with modern hardware architectures.

Equally challenging, or perhaps closely related, is the lack of programming and programming language support for programmers wishing to write software that minimizes energy consumption by the underlying hardware (but still achieve needed functional and performance goals).

There is a growing number of studies of program structures, program patterns, program constructs and even the programming language and compiler used for developing the software showing how these subjects influence the energy consumption when the software is executed. The majority of these studies are experimental measuring energy consumption of computers while running benchmarks illuminating a given subject. There are basically two ways of measuring energy consumption from running software, either by an external device, often referred to as wall-plug measurements, or through on chip sensors using the Running Average Power Limit (RAPL) interface, supported on Intel processors, for reporting the accumulated energy consumption of various power domains (for example, PP01 or Package). Wall-plug measurements are usually sampled once every second, whereas RAPL updates the energy counters approximately once every millisecond. Studies show that wall-plug measurements and RAPL measurements are well aligned [27].

An example of such a study is [28] which for Java code shows (not surprisingly) that primitive data types are more energy-efficient than wrapper classes, static variables (somewhat surprisingly) causing a 50% increase in energy consumption compared to local variables, static variables causing 60% increase in execution time compared to local variables. The study also shows that short circuit operators have better energy efficiency if the first case is the most common one, string concatenation being more energy efficient than StringBuilder and StringBuffer append methods, method calls in statements like for loops do not always have increased overhead, try-catch blocks have no cost if no exceptions are thrown. Another study, [15], showed that inheritance proved to be more energy efficient than delegation, with a reduction in run time of 77% and a reduction in average power consumption of 4%. [41] presents at tool to analyse Java collections and replace collections by others with a positive impact on the energy consumption as well as on the execution time. Using jStanley [41] shows energy gains between 2% and 17%, and a reduction in execution time between 2% and 13%. There are similar studies for constructs in C++, C# and Haskell. There are studies that compare various compilers and compiler options, studies comparing various implementations of the JVM and studies comparing concurrency constructs.

Studies show that it can be of great importance in which programming language code is written, i.e. the same logic, with the same workload, can be more or less power-intensive [16,40]. Overall, these studies show that code written in C is the most energy efficient, that code in Java is approximately 2 times and code written in C# is more than 3 times more power intensive than C. Code written in Ruby is 45 times more power intensive than C. At the same time, some of these studies show that there is not always a correlation between speed and power consumption, i.e. sometimes fast code is more power consuming than slow code. The results reported in [16,40] have been used to argue that in the future all code should be written in the Rust programming language [34] and that code written in Python "is Destroying the Planet" [8]. Before drawing such dire conclusions one should consider that the benchmarks used in [16,40] are all rather small, micro benchmark like, and often well suited for compiled C-like languages.

The majority of studies are not looking into the causes of their results. One notable exception is [44] which show that on Linpack, across different input sizes, around 10% of the energy is spent on redundant software prefetch operations that fetch data already in the target cache.

It should be noted that although RAPL updates the energy counter roughly every millisecond, this implies that 2.5 million cycles are executed on a 2.5 Ghz processor in between each update. [23] shows that there can be a fluctuation of up to 50.000 cycles between updates. This means that measuring short code paths is not feasible or rather has to be wrapped in a loop executing the short code path thousands of times. Many studies attempt to reduce jitter by pinning execution to a single core, turning turbo boost and hyper-threading off and executing the benchmark in a minimal OS environment where as many background processes as possible are turned off. One may of course ponder if results from such experiments are transferable to real-life production environments. [44] observes that for both scalar and vector instructions, the EPI is 67% higher when running in a single thread configuration compared to running in a configuration with two threads.

All in all the current state of sustainable software development is characterized by a growing number of experiments illuminating various aspects of programming and programming languages suggesting that programmers should be careful in their programming practice and integrate energy consumption testing in the continuous integration practice.

There are few, if any, suggestions to align programming practice or programming languages more closely to the hardware.

One possible exception is the emerging new programming paradigm: data oriented programming (DOP), which is an approach to software development that prioritizes the efficient organization and manipulation of data to improve performance and scalability [45]. It focuses on structuring and processing data in a way that maximizes system throughput and minimizes memory access bottlenecks. DOP emphasizes designing software around how data is accessed and manipulated rather than focusing solely on object-oriented or procedural programming paradigms. It aims to optimize data layout and processing to improve performance. In DOP specialized data structures and layouts that enhance memory access patterns, minimize cache misses, and facilitate efficient processing of large volumes of data, are used. Often parallel processing capabilities (multithreading) and Single Instruction, Multiple Data (SIMD) operations are used to leverage the full potential of modern hardware architectures. DOP is commonly associated with game development due to the need for real-time performance. However, its principles are also applicable to various high-performance computing scenarios, such as scientific simulations, data processing, and more. DOP is now being promoted in mainstream languages like Python, C# and Java. According to [3], DOP in Python entails separating code from Data (in a functional style) and representing data with generic data structures (such as pandas). Separating code from data usually leads to a performance gain and reduced energy consumption, mainly due to using static method calls. However, as a study of OOP versus DOP in C# shows, a significant reduction in energy consumption can be achieved, but no reduction in cache misses was observed [29], probably due to the generic data structures not aligning with modern hardware. The Zig language [5] is promoting DOP through enhanced memory access patterns, for example its MultiArrayList stores the data of a list of structs in struct of arrays (SoA) rather than an array of structs (AoS).

An alternative to adopting explicit DOP is spreadsheet programming. In [12] it has been shown that execution of large spreadsheets scales almost linearly in the number of cores. The spreadsheet model is well aligned with DOP and with the extension of lambdas in Excel or more generally, sheet defined functions [11, 32], spreadsheet programming is now Turing-complete and accessible to millions of non-programmers.

4 Opportunities for Static Analysis and Type Systems

Although Alan in his SAS'07 talk mainly focused on programming language design and type systems, there may be some interesting work to be done on programming analysis for energy efficiency. Most compiler optimizations are targeting speed-up and clearly there is a correlation between speed and energy consumption. However, as shown in [44], there may be up to 10% energy savings by removing prefetch instructions inserted to gain speed. Also, as Alan pointed out, it may be cheaper to recompute some expressions rather that fetch their results from RAM, thus eliminating the need for the common sub-expression elimination optimization found in many compilers. [40] shows that often the most energy efficient implementation is not the fastest implementation. Hence there is a need for tools that can help find the best compromise between speed and energy.

In general there is a lack of tools to (statically) analyse programs in high level languages regarding their potential energy consumption. A few tools are based on linter principles, identifying syntactic patterns and suggesting replacements. [38] shows that recommendations for exchange of Java collections are very hardware dependent. Another study shows that sometimes two energy optimizations may counteract each other and therefore lead to higher energy consumption [17].

In his SAS'07 talk Alan presented ideas for "Structured programming for pointers". His idea of introducing a call-by-either-value-or-reference parameter mechanism and checking if a function can tell the difference is essentially linear or quasi-linear types. He also suggested that ownership types from the OO community may be useful. He suggested that pointers are extended to know which memory region they apply to, essentially regions as introduced by Tofte and Talpin [48]. However, Alan also questioned whether such mechanisms will be lightweight enough for ordinary programmers.

An attempt to introduce regions in a C like language was presented in the Cyclone language [22]. Unfortunately, the development of Cyclone has been discontinued. The idea of ownership types has to some extent been introduced in the Rust programming language with its focus on reference lifetimes and borrowing. Quasi-linear types have been applied in attempts to formalize the Rust type system [39]. It seems that (some) programmers actually find these types understandable enough.

[14] introduces a type system for energy management based on the observation that energy management is often based on discrete phases and modes. A phase characterizes a distinct pattern of program workload, and a mode represents an energy state the program is expected to execute in. This is akin to modes in real-time systems [46] which has been used to handle energy management programmatically in the Safety Critical Java profile allowing the program to manage DFVS [30]. To take the dynamic behaviour of the program including parallel tasks into account, it may be worth revisiting [37,47] which extend region types with processes describing the dynamic communication behaviour of the underlying CML, respectively Facile, programs. Akin to this work, a huge body of work on behavioural types exists [20]. We imagine that our joint work

with Alan on schedulability abstractions [13] could be extended to take energy consumption into account using priced timed-automata. One could even imagine such energy abstractions be used to inform the OS and hardware in advance so schedules for e.g. migration of tasks could be planned to minimize heat from a particular core or movement to a location able to utilize green electricity.

5 Conclusion

The development of processor architectures towards more energy efficient computing is impressive. However, the development has not been matched by developments in software, although software engineers are keen to play their part in reducing energy consumption, and thereby CO_2 emission, from the global ICT infrastructure. Huge potentials are being demonstrated by a growing list of experiments showing examples of how energy consumption can be reduced by changing the structure of software, e.g. more or less energy demanding program patterns, by choosing the most energy efficient data structures and algorithms, by using the most energy efficient program constructs and even by choosing the most energy efficient programming languages and compilers. However, inspired by Alan's thoughts there are ample opportunities to make these efforts easier and more accessible to software engineers by designing new programming languages to better reflect new hardware, new type systems and new programming analyses taking the complex hardware infrastructure more into account. Clearly it would also be interesting to see innovative hardware ways to use all the extra transistors to make programming closer to the hardware easier for software developers. We may, just as Alan did in his SAS'07 talk, conclude that "what is a computer" is now changing quite quickly and this gives opportunities for new research areas.

References

1. Asyncawait. https://en.wikipedia.org/wiki/Async/await
2. Bend. https://github.com/HigherOrderCO/Bend
3. Data-oriented programming in python. https://www.javatpoint.com/data-oriented-programming-in-python
4. Transputer. https://en.wikipedia.org/wiki/Transputer
5. Zig. https://ziglang.org/
6. kommisionen 4.0, S.: Digitalisering af klimakampen. https://ida.dk/om-ida/siri-kommissionen/digitalisering-af-klimakampen
7. Asanovic, K., et al.: The landscape of parallel computing research: a view from Berkeley (2006)
8. Ayar, M.: Python is destroying the planet. https://levelup.gitconnected.com/python-is-destroying-the-planet-951e83f22748
9. Ayers, S., Ballan, S., Gray, V., McDonald, R.: Measuring the emissions and energy footprint of the ICT sector: implications for climate action (2023)
10. Benton, N., Cardelli, L., Fournet, C.: Modern concurrency abstractions for C#. ACM Trans. Program. Lang. Syst. (TOPLAS) **26**(5), 769–804 (2004)

11. Bock, A.A., Bøgholm, T., Sestoft, P., Thomsen, B., Thomsen, L.L.: On the semantics for spreadsheets with sheet-defined functions. J. Comput. Lang. **57**, 100960 (2020)
12. Bøgholm, T., Larsen, K.G., Muniz, M., Thomsen, B., Thomsen, L.L.: Analyzing spreadsheets for parallel execution via model checking. Models, Mindsets, Meta: The What, the How, and the Why Not? Essays Dedicated to Bernhard Steffen on the Occasion of His 60th Birthday, pp. 27–35 (2019)
13. Bogholm, T., Thomsen, B., Larsen, K.G., Mycroft, A.: Schedulability analysis abstractions for safety critical java. In: 2012 IEEE 15th International Symposium on Object/Component/Service-Oriented Real-Time Distributed Computing, pp. 71–78. IEEE (2012)
14. Cohen, M., Zhu, H.S., Senem, E.E., Liu, Y.D.: Energy types. In: Proceedings of the ACM International Conference on Object Oriented Programming Systems Languages and Applications, pp. 831–850 (2012)
15. Connolly Bree, D., Cinnéide, M.Ó.: Inheritance versus delegation: which is more energy efficient? In: Proceedings of the IEEE/ACM 42nd International Conference on Software Engineering Workshops, pp. 323–329 (2020)
16. Couto, M., Pereira, R., Ribeiro, F., Rua, R., Saraiva, J.: Towards a green ranking for programming languages. In: Proceedings of the 21st Brazilian Symposium on Programming Languages, pp. 1–8 (2017)
17. Couto, M., Saraiva, J., Fernandes, J.P.: Energy refactorings for android in the large and in the wild. In: 2020 IEEE 27th International Conference on Software Analysis, Evolution and Reengineering (SANER), pp. 217–228. IEEE (2020)
18. Eder, K., et al.: Entra: whole-systems energy transparency. Microprocess. Microsyst. **47**, 278–286 (2016)
19. Forum, W.E.: Digital technology can cut global emissions by 15. https://www.weforum.org/agenda/2019/01/why-digitalization-is-the-key-to-exponential-climate-action/
20. Gay, S., Vasconcelos, V.T., Wadler, P., Yoshida, N.: Theory and applications of behavioural types (dagstuhl seminar 17051). In: Dagstuhl Reports, vol. 7. Schloss Dagstuhl-Leibniz-Zentrum fuer Informatik (2017)
21. Grochowski, E., Annavaram, M.: Energy per instruction trends in intel microprocessors. Technol. Intel Mag. **4**(3), 1–8 (2006)
22. Grossman, D., Morrisett, G., Jim, T., Hicks, M., Wang, Y., Cheney, J.: Region-based memory management in cyclone. In: Proceedings of the ACM SIGPLAN 2002 Conference on Programming Language Design and Implementation, pp. 282–293 (2002)
23. Hähnel, M., Döbel, B., Völp, M., Härtig, H.: Measuring energy consumption for short code paths using RAPL. ACM SIGMETRICS Perform. Eval. Rev. **40**(3), 13–17 (2012)
24. Henriksen, T., Serup, N.G., Elsman, M., Henglein, F., Oancea, C.E.: Futhark: purely functional GPU-programming with nested parallelism and in-place array updates. In: Proceedings of the 38th ACM SIGPLAN Conference on Programming Language Design and Implementation, pp. 556–571 (2017)
25. Holm, H.H., Brodtkorb, A.R., Sætra, M.L.: Performance and energy efficiency of CUDA and OpenCL for GPU computing using python. In: Parallel Computing: Technology Trends, pp. 593–604. IOS Press (2020)
26. Jones, N., et al.: How to stop data centres from gobbling up the world's electricity. Nature **561**(7722), 163–166 (2018)

27. Khan, K.N., Hirki, M., Niemi, T., Nurminen, J.K., Ou, Z.: RAPL in action: experiences in using RAPL for power measurements. ACM Trans. Model. Perform. Eval. Comput. Syst. (TOMPECS) **3**(2), 1–26 (2018)
28. Kumar, M., Li, Y., Shi, W.: Energy consumption in java: an early experience. In: 2017 Eighth International Green and Sustainable Computing Conference (IGSC), pp. 1–8. IEEE (2017)
29. Lauri Leemet, Magnus Bindesbøl Starup, M.B.I.: Comparing impacts of data and object oriented programming on energy consumption in c# (2024)
30. Luckow, K.S., Bøgholm, T., Thomsen, B.: Supporting development of energy-optimised java real-time systems using tetasarts (2013)
31. Manotas, I., et al.: An empirical study of practitioners' perspectives on green software engineering. In: Proceedings of the 38th International Conference on Software Engineering, pp. 237–248 (2016)
32. Mccutchen, M., Borghouts, J., Gordon, A.D., Jones, S.P., Sarkar, A.: Elastic sheet-defined functions: generalising spreadsheet functions to variable-size input arrays. J. Funct. Program. **30**, e26 (2020)
33. Memeti, S., Li, L., Pllana, S., Kołodziej, J., Kessler, C.: Benchmarking OpenCL, OpenACC, OpenMP, and CUDA: programming productivity, performance, and energy consumption. In: Proceedings of the 2017 Workshop on Adaptive Resource Management and Scheduling for Cloud Computing, pp. 1–6 (2017)
34. Miller, S., Lerche, C.: Sustainability with rust. https://aws.amazon.com/cn/blogs/opensource/sustainability-with-rust/
35. Moss, S.: Irish data centers used more than 21 percent of nation's total metered electricity. https://www.datacenterdynamics.com/en/news/irish-data-centers-used-more-than-21-percent-of-nations-total-metered-electricity/
36. Mycroft, A.: Programming language design and analysis motivated by hardware evolution: (invited presentation). In: International Static Analysis Symposium, pp. 18–33. Springer (2007)
37. Nielson, F., Nielson, H.R.: From cml to process algebras. In: International Conference on Concurrency Theory, pp. 493–508. Springer (1993)
38. Oliveira, W., Oliveira, R., Castor, F., Pinto, G., Fernandes, J.P.: Improving energy-efficiency by recommending java collections. Empir. Softw. Eng. **26**, 1–45 (2021)
39. Pearce, D.J.: A lightweight formalism for reference lifetimes and borrowing in rust. ACM Trans. Program. Lang. Syst. (TOPLAS) **43**(1), 1–73 (2021)
40. Pereira, R., et al.: Ranking programming languages by energy efficiency. Sci. Comput. Program. **205**, 102609 (2021)
41. Pereira, R., Simão, P., Cunha, J., Saraiva, J.: jstanley: placing a green thumb on java collections. In: Proceedings of the 33rd ACM/IEEE International Conference on Automated Software Engineering, pp. 856–859 (2018)
42. Reya, N.F., Ahmed, A., Islam, T.: Greenpy: evaluating application-level energy efficiency in python for green computing. Ann. Emerg. Technol. Comput. (AETiC) **7**(3), 93–110 (2023)
43. Shankar, S., Reuther, A.: Trends in energy estimates for computing in AI/machine learning accelerators, supercomputers, and compute-intensive applications. In: 2022 IEEE High Performance Extreme Computing Conference (HPEC), pp. 1–8. IEEE (2022)
44. Shao, Y.S., Brooks, D.: Energy characterization and instruction-level energy model of intel's xeon phi processor. In: International Symposium on Low Power Electronics and Design (ISLPED), pp. 389–394. IEEE (2013)
45. Sharvit, Y.: Data-oriented Programming: Reduce Software Complexity. Simon and Schuster (2022)

46. Søndergaard, H., Ravn, A.P., Thomsen, B., Scoeberl, M.: A practical approach to mode change in real-time systems. Technical Report 08-001, Department of Computer Science, Aalborg University (2008)
47. Thomsen, B.: Polymorphic sorts and types for concurrent functional programs. Technical Report ECRC-93-10 (1993)
48. Tofte, M., Talpin, J.P.: Region-based memory management. Inf. Comput. **132**(2), 109–176 (1997)

On the Limits of Making Programming Easy

Tomas Petricek[1(✉)] and Joel Jakubovic[1,2]

[1] Charles University, Prague, Czechia
tomas@tomasp.net, joel.jakubovic@cantab.net
[2] University of Kent, Canterbury, UK

Abstract. A lot of programming research shares the same basic motivation: how can we make programming easier? Alas, this problem is difficult to tackle directly. Programming is a tangle of conceptual models, programming languages, user interfaces and more and we cannot advance all of these at the same time. Moreover, we have no good metric for measuring whether programming is easy. As a result, we usually give up on the original motivation and pursue narrow tractable research for which there is a rigorous methodology.

In this paper, we investigate the limits of making programming easy. We use a dialectic method to circumscribe the design space within which easier programming systems may exist. In doing so, we not only bring together ideas on open-source software, self-sustainable systems, visual programming languages, but also the analysis of limits by Fred Brooks in his classic "No Silver Bullet" essay. We sketch a possible path towards easier programming of the future, but more importantly, we argue for the importance of proto-theories as a method for tackling the original motivating basic research question.

Keywords: Programming systems · complexity · technical dimensions

1 Introduction

A cold winter morning, 1st December 2023, outside the Cambridge Computer Laboratory; two computer scientists arrive in the area known as The Street in front of the lecture theaters; they came to attend the MycroftFest symposium: Tomas Petricek—a former PhD student of Alan—and Joel Jakubovic, Tomas' PhD student. The elder and younger researchers discuss threads of programming study as different from each other as The Street and the Cambridge Computer Laboratory are from Trinity Street and Peterhouse.

Let's eavesdrop.

2 Programming Systems

TOMAS: I hope you are ready for your PhD defense next week, Joel! The examiners will surely ask you to give a brief summary of your work, so you'll need

D. Orchard et al. (Eds.): Alan Mycroft Festschrift, LNCS 15500, pp. 215–233, 2026.
https://doi.org/10.1007/978-3-032-08187-2_11

a good answer for that. Have you figured out how to summarize what your PhD work is about?

JOEL: I always like to introduce it as making programming "suck less!" I suppose I will need something that sounds more formal than that. Of course, I mean it in a very focused and specific way that is small enough to fit into a PhD.

TOMAS: My PhD was about making programming easier too. I worked on client-server web programming before [35] and found it tricky to keep track of the right context on the two sites. Some code requires resources that are only available on the server (e.g. a database), while some requires resources only available in the web browser (e.g. the user's location).

JOEL: So what did you do to make client-server web programming easier?

TOMAS: I tried to fix this by designing a context-aware programming language that would track the context requirements, or *coeffects*, in the type system [34]. With coeffects (Fig. 1a), the type would tell you not just what your functions take and return, but also what resources they require. Coeffects would tell you that some part of your code can run only on some of the sites.

JOEL: I thought coeffects were about tracking how programs use variables. The two examples I saw involved dataflow and liveness. There was no mention of client-server web programming!

TOMAS: Well, yes, there is some irony in the fact that the original motivation did not actually fit all that well with the formal model that we developed. Dataflow and liveness were much better examples.

JOEL: And did coeffects make programming easier in the end?

TOMAS: I only ever built a prototype implementation of a language with coeffect support,[1] but if someone implemented a proper language based on the theory, then it would make programming client-server web applications easier...

JOEL: Oh dear... so your work was only concerned with improving programming *languages*.

TOMAS: Of course. Programming languages are the medium through which you program. But you make it sound like you have something else in mind.

JOEL: We both say that we are interested in making *programming* easier. Programming is about much more than programming languages and their formal properties. We should be thinking about programming *systems* more generally, not just about languages (see Fig. 1).

TOMAS: What is the difference? What is a programming system?

JOEL: A programming *language* is an abstract formal entity. A programming *system* is a running, interactive and stateful collection of software. A system may implement a language (or multiple languages). It includes a runtime and a

[1] The prototype can be found, in the form of an interactive essay, at https://tomasp.net.

$$(var)\ \frac{x : \tau \in \Gamma}{C^{\mathsf{e}}\Gamma \vdash x : \tau} \qquad (app)\ \frac{C^{r}\Gamma \vdash e_1 : C^{t}\tau_1 \rightarrow \tau_2 \qquad C^{s}\Gamma \vdash e_2 : \tau_1}{C^{r \vee (s \oplus t)}\Gamma \vdash e_1\, e_2 : \tau_2}$$

$$(sub)\ \frac{C^{s}\Gamma \vdash e : \tau}{C^{r}\Gamma \vdash e : \tau}\ (s \leq r) \qquad (abs)\ \frac{C^{r \wedge s}(\Gamma, x : \tau_1) \vdash e : \tau_2}{C^{r}\Gamma \vdash \lambda x.e : C^{s}\tau_1 \rightarrow \tau_2}$$

(a) Type and coeffect system for tracking context requirements [34].

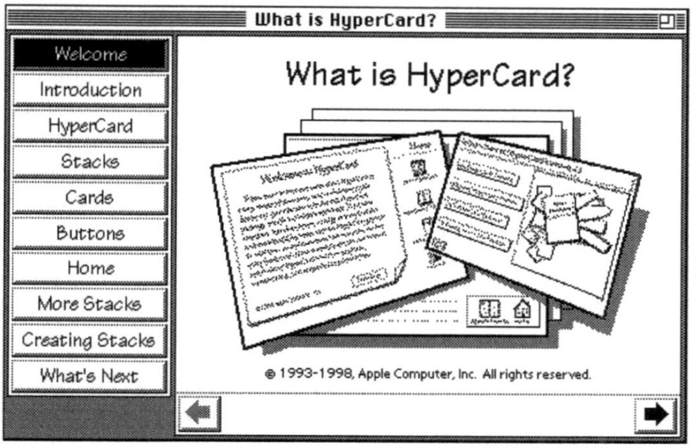

(b) A screenshot of Hypercard, an early hypertext system that allowed users to easily create their own interactive "decks".

Fig. 1. The contrast between programming languages and programming systems. We know how to study *languages* (a), but not how to study *systems* (b).

compiler or an interpreter, but it also consists of graphical interfaces used to edit code, debug code and so on.

TOMAS: I'm still not convinced. Of course you need to write your code and invoke the compiler in some way. That's why you also have a terminal and Emacs to do programming.

JOEL: You are still thinking about the problem through the lens of the *languages* paradigm. The point is that the *systems* paradigm gives you a different perspective, different problems and different research methods. Gabriel wrote about this in his "Structure of a Programming Language Revolution" [16], where he points out that there was a paradigm shift through the 1990s from thinking about systems to thinking about languages.

JOEL: The paradigm shift encouraged more formal academic work on programming, but Gabriel also explains how some good ideas about programming became unthinkable because of this shift.

TOMAS: Does he say unthinkable, or unpublishable in OOPSLA?

JOEL: The latter, but in practice, the two co-evolve and end up being the same thing! What can be published tends to shape people's research agendas and their way of thinking about problems...

TOMAS: You can say that a programming language plus all the extra things it needs is a programming system, but what other good ideas about programming does this view enable?

JOEL: First, the different view lets us consider ways to make programming easier which are hard to think about as languages. For example, visual programming, block-based editing [37] or systems like Flash [2] and Hypercard. These are programming systems we should learn from. Second, the view lets us talk about interactivity and self-sustainable systems that can be modified from within themselves [20,21]. It would be useful to understand highly malleable programming systems like Lisp and Smalltalk, because they can in principle be used to make their *own* programming easier.

TOMAS: But Lisp and Smalltalk are languages ... ah, I see what you're going to say. Smalltalk-the-system *contains* Smalltalk-the-language, but a lot of other important things like its interface! And similarly for systems built on Lisp...

JOEL: Exactly, and there is much more than the interface. When you think about Smalltalk-the-system or Lisp-the-system, you also need to consider all the libraries that are readily available to you as parts of the system.

TOMAS: Those are very good points. I'm starting to believe that this programming systems view is actually useful. But let's return to it later, because I wanted to return to one more point you made...

3 Essential Complexity

TOMAS: You said that the goal of your work was to make programming easier. I can see how thinking about programming systems rather than programming languages is a better way to approach the problem. Yet, I worry that this may not be as much help as you hope. Didn't Fred Brooks show that you cannot make programming an order of magnitude easier?

JOEL: Interesting, why did he think that?

TOMAS: Brooks [7] analysed the different kinds of complexity involved in building software. The *essential complexity* is the inherent complexity of the concepts that software works with. It arises from the data sets, interconnections, algorithms and operations that the software is to perform. The *accidental complexity* comes from imperfection in our tools and languages.

JOEL: This would make more sense to me if the essential complexity came from the fact that our software has to encode the many (perhaps ad-hoc) rules of the human world. Algorithms and data structures sound less essential to me.

TOMAS: I like your interpretation, but maybe the algorithms and data structures that Brooks talks about are reflections of the real world? In any case, Brooks argues that we can reduce the accidental complexity through better tools, but the essential complexity will remain. He then points out that we will not be able to get an order of magnitude improvement in overall complexity of software unless the accidental complexity in software today is more than 10x that of the essential complexity.

JOEL: This assumes that you have to tackle the essential complexity all at once, but that is only the case if you are designing a system from scratch. Did Brooks say anything about open source that was emerging at the time and avoids this problem by letting anyone use and adapt software as they wish?

TOMAS: No, Brooks does not mention open source. He talks about buying off-the-shelf packages as an alternative to building software. Even with open source, I think Brooks' basic idea still holds. No matter if you use open source or replace the Waterfall of the 1980s with Agile methodologies of the 2020s, you still have to put together the entire system with all its essential complexity.

JOEL: Well, I know you like to relate software development to architecture [32], so perhaps that can help me explain what I'm thinking.

TOMAS: Architecture needs upfront planning even more than software. You first have to resolve all the design problems that the design of the house involves. There are different ways of doing this. You can rely on modernist analysis or the traditional "unselfconscious" way of building that the Christopher Alexander favoured in his early work [1], but you still need a detailed plan before you start building (Fig. 2).

JOEL: I think you can look at the problem very differently though. As argued by Stewart Brand [5], buildings also evolve. Old power stations become galleries, a garage becomes a co-working space, while a formal city plaza suddenly gains new use as an ice-skating rink [8]. Even when the spaces are not designed for their future use, they often end up fitting it remarkably well.

TOMAS: You are probably right. Buildings seem like the most static things, yet they evolve. Software, being structured information, ought to be much more malleable than the rigid materials of buildings; accordingly, it evolves much faster. But how can this solve the problem of software complexity?

JOEL: Like buildings, I think we often build software by gradual adaptation. We may not always think about it that way, but we should embrace this view. Very often, you have software that does *almost* what you want, but not quite.

TOMAS: I guess systems that you can buy and configure, like SAP that was slowly rising to prominence when Brooks was writing his paper [27], would be an interesting example of that. Contemporary no-code and low-code systems go even further in that they blur the distinction between code and configuration.

JOEL: This is not quite what I had in mind, but fair enough! My point is that we can sidestep Brooks' "doom prophecy" by focusing on how software is built by

Fig. 2. MIT Building 20 was a temporary timber building, erected for radar research during the World War II. It continued to exist for over 50 years and was highly popular for its infinite adaptability [5] (photo: MIT Museum).

making small changes to existing software. To make software development easy, we should make it easy to make *changes!*

TOMAS: Wait a second! Aren't we getting back to open source and the free software movement? The free software manifesto says you should have "The freedom to study how the program works, and *change it so it does your computing as you wish.*" [14] This sounds very much like building software through a sequence of small adaptations.

JOEL: In theory, yes, but does access to source code really give you the freedom to change a program as you wish for any moderately complex open-source software today?

TOMAS: I think you are right. The complexity of most software that we are dealing with today means that, even as a hacker myself, I cannot hope to understand and modify software with a reasonable amount of effort, even if I do have the source code.

JOEL: In fact, the freedom to change a program as you wish probably worked in the 1980s when the GNU utilities were a manageable size and all the users were hackers who could modify and compile the code!

TOMAS: The kind of sofware we need today is just more complex, because computers get used for more complex problems. We are facing Brooks' essential complexity again. To make a small change to a large piece of software, you may not need to understand all of it, but you need to understand a significant part of it and even that is prohibitive.

4 Programming that Scales

JOEL: Isn't it inevitable that static source code simply doesn't scale for understanding complex dynamic systems? The change we want to make is to the dynamic behaviour, but we have to trace the causality backwards and figure out which change to the *initial* state will produce it. At today's scales, this is like being a surgeon forced to operate on the DNA and then regrow the entire patient. Who would expect this to work?

TOMAS: Isn't the whole point of programming to tackle this kind of complexity through abstractions? Going back to my own PhD, a key idea in it was that you can hide multiple fairly complex specific instances of context-dependence behind a simple unified mathematical structure.

JOEL: Many computer scientists like to see programming as a formal mathematical activity, but this is just a metaphor and it has its limits. De Millo, Lipton and Perlis pointed this out in 1979 [9]! They believed that formal verification of software is bound to fail, because the complexity of the formal entities *computer scientists* work with is different than the complexity of the formal entities *mathematicians* work with. A mathematical proof is probably correct because mathematicians excitedly go over it on a whiteboard with their colleagues, but no such social process accompanies formal proofs of software.[2]

TOMAS: If seeing programs as formal mathematical entities is not the right perspective, then what is the alternative?

JOEL: In the early 2000s, the Software Engineering Institute at Carnegie Mellon University asked this very question as part of their project on Ultra-large-scale systems [13] They said that we need to shift how we think about problems we face and that new perspectives will by inspired by work looking at disciplines such as microeconomics, biology, city planning, and anthropology.

TOMAS: I do like the city planning metaphor for thinking about software. If you look how people understand a city, as documented in the classic book "The Image of the City" [28], I think much of that applies to source code. If you want to get from one place to another in a city, you do not need to understand the whole city. There are paths through the city that take you there like, for example, the metro line. Is this what you are thinking about?

JOEL: You can surely alleviate some of the scaling problems with source code by organising it better, but it is still wrong to have to search through the source code and look for names that sound like the right thing, in order to find the relevant code for the change we want to achieve.

TOMAS: What do you imagine, then?

JOEL: Well, a programming system should model the chain of cause to effect in programs that you create. Then, when you want to make a change to

[2] For a detailed and a refined account of the debate that followed the publication of the paper, as well as the historical context, see the book written by MacKenzie [29].

something that you can see, or to something that produces visible outputs or effects on the screen, it can point you back to the code that you need to change. Bret Victor demonstrated what this could look like [39], but I'm unaware of any follow-up work to realise his vision—which raises the question of how he himself got his demo to work, something that does occasionally keep me up at night.

TOMAS: I think I can imagine the technical characteristics such a system would need to work: it would need to record information about its execution and make it acessible. Basman [3] refers to this idea as "materialized execution" and traces it to the 1980s Boxer project [11]. We used a similar idea recently to automatically link data visualizations by analysing code used to produce them [31].

JOEL: This is useful technical background, but we should also look to interesting *real* programming systems—not just demos—for inspiration about interfaces that would make such program editing accessible.

TOMAS: Perhaps the various live and exploratory programming systems [36] may be relevant here?

JOEL: Yes, those tools give you rapid feedback. Perhaps a surprisingly good example here is Excel, which also, to some extent, keeps track of the chain of cause to effect in that you can view the source of the formula and see which other cells were used to compute the result. You do have to backtrace the causal chain manually by looking up the cells one by one. But it is the best example I can think of.

TOMAS: Excel has surprisingly good backtracing support these days! But regardless of whether you trace manually or with the system's help, this only works with the relatively simple formula language. If you want to achieve some more complicated behaviour, you have to do that with VBA macros and give up this traceability.

5 Programming Substrates and Notations

JOEL: True, so let's stop to think about notations for a bit. We can understand them better by charting the scope of change that can be achieved through a particular notation against the difficulty of using the notation. Figure 3a shows this for a hypothetical accounting system and a spreadsheet system.

TOMAS: I see. For an accounting system, you have the graphical interface that provides a notation for using the system and a notation (say, Java or C++) with which the system is implemented. For a spreadsheet, you have tables where you enter your data, formulas, VBA macros and then the notation used to implement Excel itself.

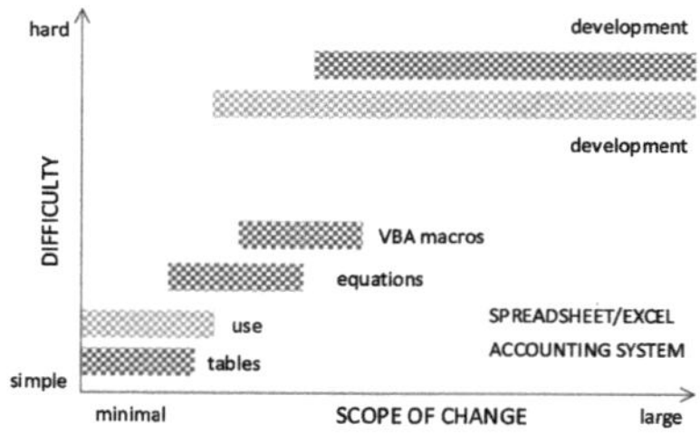

(a) Excel offers multiple but disconnected substrates (data entry, formulas, macros).

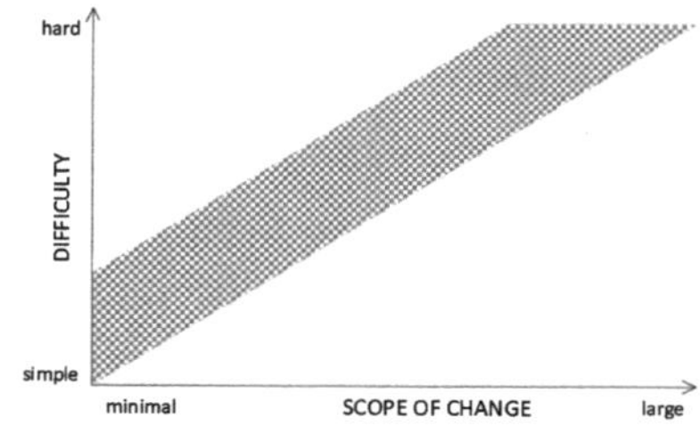

(b) An ideal system would have one adaptable substrate that makes minimal changes simple, but allows harder larger chages.

Fig. 3. Scope of change vs. difficulty of use of multiple programming substrates.

JOEL: Right. This is already better than regular software, because there are appropriate notations for changes at multiple difficulty levels, but it is not a perfect system of notations yet...

TOMAS: There is perhaps a nice characterization of the ideal notational continuum that we are looking for in the work of Pierre Depaz [10, p.123] on aesthetics of code. He says that *"simplicity is found in source code when the syntax and the ontologies used are an exact fit to the problem: simple code is code that is neither too precise, nor too generic, displaying an understanding of and a focus on the problem domain, rather than the applied tools."*

JOEL: I think this really boils down to two things. First, to be able to use the right tools for different jobs, you need to be free from a restriction to just one notation. Second, you should also be free from a restriction to plain text; non-textual notations should be on the menu, because those are sometimes the most appropriate fit for a problem.

TOMAS: Hmm, but wouldn't such a "notational pluralism" be impractical? In Excel, you may use multiple disjoint notations such as tables, formulas and macros—yet this also means that there is no gradual progression between them. If you learn how to use formulas, it does not help you at all with learning how to write macros (or even become a C++ developer working on Excel at Microsoft...).

JOEL: Yes, the right approach seems to be to have an adaptable substrate. Something that has a basic form, but can be adapted in various ways to suit particular domain-specific problems. See the illustration in Fig. 3b where the same (adaptable) substrate can be used for both small and simple changes, but also large and (inevitably) difficult changes.

TOMAS: This reminds me of a brief research programme focused on "extensible programming languages" in the late 1960s [33], which tried to solve the problem of designing a universal programming language by having a base language that can be extended by the user. I'm still trying to figure out what happened to this idea...

JOEL: Ah, but you are talking about languages again, rather than systems!

TOMAS: But how would this work? You would need a substrate where an end-user can make a small change and gradually progress. The starting point then has to be something they are already familiar with. To take a spreadsheet as an example, do you think the substrate could somehow "grow" from filling numbers in a table to modifying some simple aspects of the system that users may care about, like making the interface color scheme colour blind friendly or making the wording of menu items clearer?

JOEL: Something like this could work in spreadsheets. I can think of some parts of Excel-the-application that transfer well to a portion of a spreadsheet. One could press a button to "reflect" the key/value pairs in the preferences menu into two columns of cells. When edited, these cells would update Excel's internal preferences that you normally edit in a dialog box. At a stretch, perhaps other parts of such a dialog could also be reflected—say, the list of options in a drop-down box. And then you could, for example, have your preferences computed with formulas!

TOMAS: Hmm, are you getting at some general principle with this idea?

JOEL: The notation for development should resemble the notation for use!

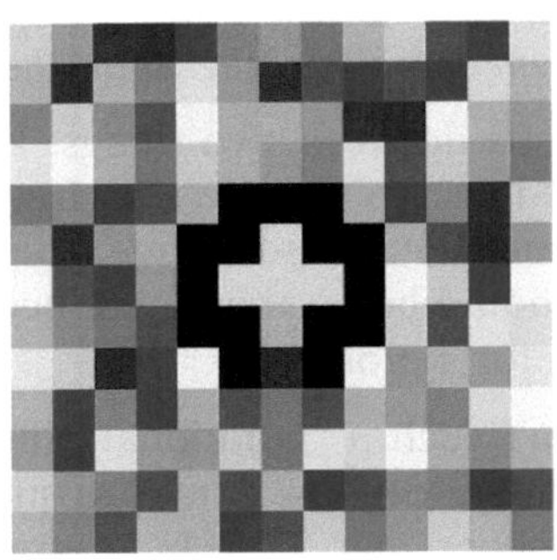

Fig. 4. "Hello world" program in the esoteric programming language Piet. The program instructions are encoded as colours and are executed as a pointer moves over the individual colour regions of the bitmap.

TOMAS: Well, this is a heavy constraint on the notations we can use for development! What would justify such an idea?

JOEL: I admit, it's about as restrictive as one could get! The motivation is that the user is already familiar with the "notation for use" in the software—so to the extent that "development" can be massaged to use the same notation, they are able to adapt the software by re-using the same skills. They no longer have to invest in learning a completely different notation (like a programming language) before they can do that.

TOMAS: So, to take this idea to its limits, you're saying that Microsoft Paint should be written in the Piet esolang that we can see in Fig. 4?!

JOEL: Fair enough. I wouldn't go so far; *given that* the use-notation in Paint is what it is, there aren't many changes to Paint that fit sensibly within it. That being said—the program's tool icons could be "reflected" in its canvas and re-drawn that way, but that's the only straw I can think to grasp!

JOEL: The principle will break down with absurd examples if you commit to it fully, but that doesn't mean we shouldn't explore its domain of validity. It is still promising, but you need to think about what is the essence of the substrate through which most people interact with computers. It is not pixels...

TOMAS: Do you mean buttons, tabs, tables, lists, forms and such?

JOEL: I believe there is a more fundamental substrate behind all of those. You can model a lot of user interface widgets as rigid bodies that exist in some space, connected with rods and springs and perhaps forces such as attraction and repulsion between particular entities.

TOMAS: How do you imagine this would provide a programming substrate?

JOEL: I do not have a perfect answer to this question, but you can think of the basic substrate as a sort of "user interface physics" within which specific visual notations for particular problems could be defined.[3] Such a substrate could even be the result of taking a 2D physics engine [15], stripping it of concepts like mass and rotations, and optimising it for this simpler domain.

JOEL: If we had that, then I think we would make a step towards the ideal substrate for programming. And the substrate would need to live within an actual running materialized system, rather than a static blueprint like a program in source code today.

6 Research Methodologies

TOMAS: You certainly have some very interesting ideas about the future of programming here, but let me ask an annoying practical question. How do you turn this into a realistic research project? Is there something you can analyse formally or measure about a prototype? To make this into a research agenda, there needs to be some scientific methodology behind it!

[3] Constraint-based systems for specifying user interfaces, such as Cassowary [4], can be seen as related to this idea, although they focus more on rendering the layout for the end-user than on developing a foundational underlying substrate. Additionally, individual constraints are too low-level for a human-friendly UI substrate, although they could well be what such a substrate "compiles" to in order to run. This was the subject of much research in the 1990s [30].

JOEL: Tomas, remind me, didn't you run into a problem in your thesis with the intersection of provable and interesting things?

TOMAS: You remember correctly. There was a point in my PhD when I realized that all the things I could prove about my programming language were not that interesting, and all the things that I found interesting about programming were not particularly formalizable. I guess I was getting increasingly interested in what people sometimes call "programming experience" research.[4] The experience also made me think much more about research methodology and led me to interest in history and philosophy of science.

JOEL: Does that shed any light on why programming language researchers are so focused on formalization and proofs?

TOMAS: For one thing, there is a bias for theory over experiment in all branches of science. Ian Hacking [19] pointed this out in the case of physics, as did Hossenfelder [22], and the same applies to computer science. Finding a suitable methodology for programming experience research is an open problem that does not have a definite answer. It may need a range of qualitative and quantitative methods, including formalisms, empirical evaluation, but also system descriptions, user studies and perhaps even interactive artifacts [12].

JOEL: I do not understand how you are supposed to make general and unifying claims if you do not first start by looking at the concrete and specific!

TOMAS: Fair enough, and there are two examples to support your perspective. For most of its history, particle physics consisted of two sub-cultures that Peter Galison refers to as the "image" and "logic" traditions [17]. While the latter focused on statistical analysis of observations, the former attempted to capture "golden events" that show the decay of a single particle. These concrete traces went on to be hugely influential in shaping the theory of particle physics. And in the case of city planning, Jane Jacobs made a similar argument [23] in favor of looking at specific cases, which she calls "unaverage clues". An example is a chain of bookshops that always remain open until late, except for one branch in Brooklyn. The clue tells you something significant about that part of the city.

JOEL: OK, but on reflection, we need something in between. In order to do any formalisation or a user study, you need conceptual clarity on what you're studying and what you're trying to find out. I don't think we have any such clarity on many interesting aspects of programming systems.

TOMAS: But what kind of knowledge structure can give you such conceptual clarity, without being as detailed as a formal model?

JOEL: You made a reference to Fred Brooks earlier. I think his other essay "The Mythical Man-Month" [6] is a good example. In the essay, Brooks explains why adding more workforce to a delayed project only makes the delay worse.

[4] The topic is the subject of the Programming Experience workshop (https://programming-experience.org) that has been running since 2016.

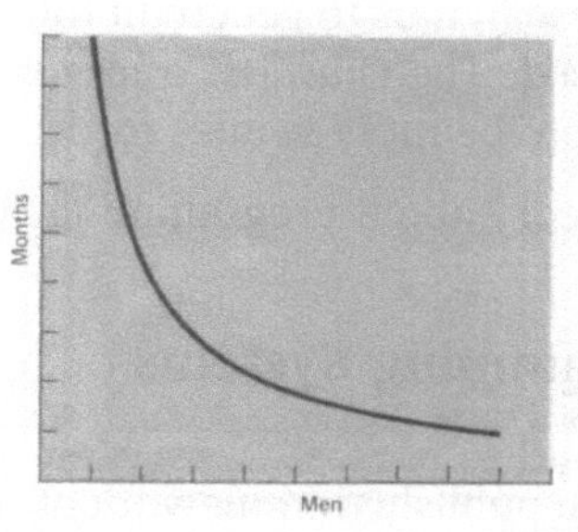

(a) Time versus number of workers:
Perfectly partionable task

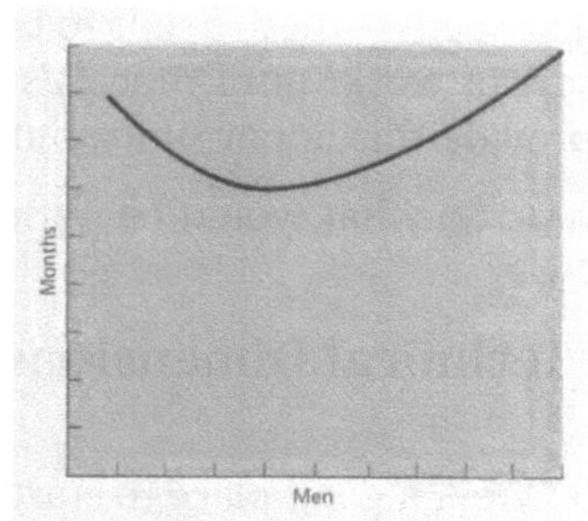

(b) Time vs. number of workers:
Task with complex inter-relationships

Fig. 5. Two illustrations by Brooks showing how communication overhead means that adding workforce to a delayed project makes things worse (from [6])

The argument is based on analysing the amount of communication that needs to happen (Fig. 5). For a perfectly partitionable programming task, adding people helps. But if the work requires communication, the overhead of the communication grows exponentially as people are added, eventually overtaking the gain you get from the linear growth of people who can do the programming. Brooks illustrates this with charts and equations. He does not have formal proofs or specific numbers, but the model provides a good theory that provides conceptual clarity.

TOMAS: Interesting, this kind of reasoning seems to be quite common in software engineering. I can think of another example from a book about the history of anti-ballistic missile systems [38]. One of the arguments for why such systems cannot be reliably built was based on comparing the rate of change in the environment and the rate of change of the system. The idea was that the US cannot build a reliable defence system, because changing the software takes more work than changing some of the characteristics of the Soviet missiles. Ergo, their defences won't be able to keep pace with Soviet innovations in offensive capability. Again, this is a somewhat mathematical argument that provides conceptual clarity.

JOEL: Right. I think we can refer to such models that provide conceptual clarity *proto-theories*. I would say that we need more thinking like this! They can be later refined to more formal models, but not prematurely. I would also add that mathematical formulations like those above are not the only kinds of proto-theories we should be creating.

TOMAS: Well, I would have loved to pursue proto-theories during my PhD—but I fear I would not have been able to defend it!

JOEL: Exactly—there needs to be a way for researchers to get credit for doing this sort of work; until then, it's disincentivised. The *Onward!* tracks at SPLASH provide this opportunity, but there ought to be more venues for it.

TOMAS: So what would be a useful proto-theory about programming systems?

7 Technical Dimensions of Programming Systems

JOEL: Well, a good place to start would be the published framework of "technical dimensions" [25] which break down programming systems into narrower properties of which they can have more or less.

TOMAS: Dimensions? That rings a bell...

JOEL: You're thinking of the Cognitive Dimensions of Notations [18] which was the main inspiration. However, the Technical Dimensions are concerned with the programming system as a whole, not just its notation.

TOMAS: I can see how you capture various properties of notations. They can be more or less dense, more or less consistent, more or less easy to modify etc. But what kind of properties can you capture as dimensions about programming systems in general?

JOEL: The list is quite long and I do not think it is complete. but it includes some of the characteristics of programming systems that we have talked about already. For example, *modes of interaction* captures whether you do everything in a single environment or whether "using" is distinct from "programming"; *notational structure* captures whether there is just a single adaptable notation or a range of different ones; *self-sustainability* captures the degree to which the system can be modified from within itself and so on.

TOMAS: Just to get back to our original question, how does such a framework contribute to making programming easier?

JOEL: Remember Fig. 1, which illustrated that we know how to study programming languages, but not how to study programming systems? Well, many people came up with interesting programming systems that make programming easier in some way. But because we lacked a good way for talking about them, the ideas were never clearly described and nobody was able to adopt them and develop them further.

TOMAS: This is the incommensurability that Gabriel [16] warns us about! He would chuckle and reminisce about the glory days of Lisp systems in the 1980s, before shift to the mathematical paradigm made all the programming systems work incomprehensible.

JOEL: Alas, we cannot travel in time back to the 1980s! We should take time *today* to set up a framework for programming languages people to understand and appreciate work on programming systems.

TOMAS: I guess what you are saying is that technical dimensions of programming systems gives us a set of common points of reference that allow for apples-to-apples comparison of widely different programming systems? But is this meant to supersede the existing programming language research methods?

JOEL: Not at all. Since many programming systems contain a programming language, all existing programming language research is applicable to their syntax, semantics, types, paradigms, and so on. The technical dimensions simply establish the analogues of those concepts for the other parts of those systems.

TOMAS: Didn't you link the change from thinking about programming languages to thinking about programming systems to the idea of Kuhnian scientific revolution before?

JOEL: Yes, it would be a corrective to the shift that Gabriel observed in the opposite direction [16]; not by *fighting* PL research, but by simply making space to do the more general thing. To truly establish a new paradigm, the return to thinking about systems would put more emphasis on research methods that can talk about them in their full complexity. It would not *invalidate* programming language theory, but it could make it more of a speciality instead of the default. However, we are quite far from what Kuhn called "normal science". It is still early days for programming systems research!

TOMAS: What do you think still needs to be done? I have to say that, compared to established programming language research methods, the work on technical dimensions seems quite informal!

JOEL: Right. The full realisation of the aims of the framework is a long-term research program. What we have already is the seed to start it off. We have a set of dimensions that come with qualitative descriptions. Future work, as set out towards the end of my dissertation [24], involves making these descriptions more precise and possibly even quantifiable.

TOMAS: Quantifiable? Does this risk the problem we mentioned about focusing on what is formalizable rather than on what is interesting?

JOEL: That spectre is always hanging over it, yes. But the solution is to refine the framework slowly and carefully, with input and critique from the research community. This is why the dimensions were published in their qualitative state; better to grit our teeth and endure the informality, than to prematurely formalise before we know what we're doing! Just the fact that we're breaking down programming systems into a common vocabulary of properties to focus on, helps to analyse programming systems and compare them with each other. It also means we can map the design space of possible systems and spot combinations of properties that haven't been tried yet.

TOMAS: It is funny to hear us discussing the theoretical framework of programming systems, after we complained about the scientific bias in favour of theoretical work! You have just outlined the future work for interested "theoreticians", but the future work for "experimentalists" should be at least as important. I guess the experimental work should be filling the database of how different systems fit into the framework.

JOEL: That is certainly one task for the experimentalists. But they can also explore the design space to find new designs. To get back to our original motivation of making programming easier, my thesis explores programming systems that have three properties: *notational freedom*, which would give you the kind of adaptable substrate we talked about, *explicit structure*, which is a pre-condition for building such a substrate, and *self-sustainability*, which would make it possible to evolve the system from within itself, enabling a virtuous cycle of self-improvement.

TOMAS: So your thesis not only proposes a proto-theory, but it also showcases an application of it. Is that something that you'll be able to defend?

JOEL: Let's hope so! I do feel prepared to defend it; we'll find out for sure in one week's time![5]

8 Conclusions

ALAN (*arrives in his festive Christmas jumper*): HO HO HO! It is nice to see you! What have you two been chatting about here?

TOMAS: Joel was practicing the elevator pitch for his PhD thesis, but we got a bit distracted. We ended up talking about whether it is possible for programming to be easier, whether there are any fundamental limits to that, and also what kind of research methodology can get us there!

ALAN: And what did you conclude?

JOEL: On a more general level, we agreed that we need more thinking about interactive, stateful programming systems and their characteristics. Programming can only become easier if we start thinking about how programming systems are used. In other words, think more about *programming systems* than about *programming languages*. Today, this is tricky, because we lack the right vocabulary for talking about programming systems, but the technical dimensions are a useful *proto-theory* that serves as the starting point!

ALAN: And on the more specific level?

JOEL: We do not have a concrete system yet, but we believe it will have a number of general properties. It needs to be built around a programming substrate that can grow with the user. It should make it easy to make small changes to the system, but also allow making more complex and difficult changes. We also need to think about programming as gradual adaptation, to overcome Brooks' "doom prophecy" of essential complexity. But I remain optimistic.

TOMAS: My tongue-in-cheek suggestion is that your *Concepts in Programming Languages* module, which I very much enjoyed supervising back in the day,

[5] It turned out such a thing did work out after all.

should become *Concepts in Programming Systems*! We need a new generation of researchers who will adopt the programming systems perspective and come up with great new theories and experimental systems!

ALAN: So, what do you think the next generation of Computer Lab programming systems PhD students should be doing?

JOEL: I would love to see more research that looks at how programming languages are embedded in broader stateful interactive systems. This is something where we are lacking both theory and new interesting design ideas. I also think programming researchers should look at things that we do not really see as programming languages. What is it that makes systems like Excel, but also Flash, Hypercard or game engines work well as programming tools? We also need to be more fearless in looking at problems that are interesting, but informal. If we are to study informal properties that are not simply true or false, we will also need more focus on finding consensus among researchers working on programming tools, such as agreeing on the right proto-theories on which to further advance our work.[6]

Acknowledgments. The events portrayed in this essay are entirely fictional. Any resemblance to actual persons, living or dead, is purely coincidental. But we are grateful to the non-fictional people who participated in a lively discussion at Mycroftfest and helped to shape this essay, as well as to the anonymous reviewers who may find some of their suggestions embedded in the dialogue.

The authors were supported by the Charles University grant "Type systems for data-centric programming" (PRIMUS24/SCI/021) and the first author also beneifted from the support of the Charles University-funded research centre "Language, Image, and Gesture: Forms of Discursivity" (UNCE24/SSH/026).

References

1. Alexander, C.: Notes on the synthesis of form. Harvard University Press
2. Ankerson, M.S.: Dot-com design: the rise of a usable, social, commercial web, vol. 15. NYU Press (2018)
3. Basman, A.: Boxer and the tradition of materialised programming. Presented at Boxer Salon, Porto (2022)
4. Borning, A., Marriott, K., Stuckey, P., Xiao, Y.: Solving linear arithmetic constraints for user interface applications. In: Proceedings of the 10th Annual ACM Symposium on User Interface Software and Technology, UIST 1997, pp. 87–96. Association for Computing Machinery, New York (1997). https://doi.org/10.1145/263407.263518
5. Brand, S.: How Buildings Learn: What Happens After They're Built. Viking (1994)
6. Brooks, F.P.: The Mythical Man-Month: Essays on Software Engineering. Addison-Wesley Professional (1975)

[6] A recent seminar focused on the problem of developing new "theories of programming" [26]. However, we believe that a theory needs to start as an informal proto-theory and that *premature* scientific framing in terms of hypotheses may inhibit progress.

7. Brooks, F.P.: No silver bullet: essence and accidents of software engineering. Computer **20**(4), 10–19 (1987). https://doi.org/10.1109/MC.1987.1663532
8. Cohen, S.: Physical context/cultural context: including it all. Oppositions **2**, 1–40 (1974)
9. De Millo, R.A., Lipton, R.J., Perlis, A.J.: Social processes and proofs of theorems and programs. Commun. ACM **22**(5), 271–280 (1979). https://doi.org/10.1145/359104.359106
10. Depaz, P.: The role of aesthetics in understanding source code. Ph.D. thesis, Université Sorbonne Nouvelle, ED120 - THALIM (2023)
11. diSessa, A.A., Abelson, H.: Boxer: a reconstructible computational medium. Commun. ACM **29**(9), 859–868 (1986). https://doi.org/10.1145/6592.6595
12. Edwards, J., Kell, S., Petricek, T., Church, L.: Evaluating programming systems design. In: Marasoiu, M., Church, L., Marshall, L. (eds.) Proceedings of the 30th Annual Workshop of the Psychology of Programming Interest Group (PPIG 2019). Newcastle University, UK (2019)
13. Feiler, P., et al.: Ultra-Large-Scale Systems: The Software Challenge of the Future (2006). https://insights.sei.cmu.edu/library/ultra-large-scale-systems-the-software-challenge-of-the-future/. Accessed 5 Feb 2024
14. Free Software Foundation: What is free software (version 1.1) (2001). https://www.gnu.org/philosophy/free-sw.en.html. Accessed 5 Feb 2024
15. Gabriel, R.P.: Exploratory research proposal: Virtual-world-inspired programming language design. https://www.dreamsongs.com/Files/VirtualWorldsForCodeProposalPure.pdf
16. Gabriel, R.P.: The structure of a programming language revolution. In: Proceedings of the ACM International Symposium on New Ideas, New Paradigms, and Reflections on Programming and Software, Onward! 2012, pp. 195–214. Association for Computing Machinery, New York (2012). https://doi.org/10.1145/2384592.2384611
17. Galison, P.: Image and Logic: A Material Culture of Microphysics. University of Chicago Press (1997)
18. Green, T.R.G.: Cognitive dimensions of notations. In: Proceedings of the Fifth Conference of the British Computer Society, Human-Computer Interaction Specialist Group on People and Computers V, pp. 443–460. Cambridge University Press, USA (1990)
19. Hacking, I.: Representing and Intervening: Introductory Topics in the Philosophy of Natural Science. Cambridge University Press, Cambridge (1983)
20. Hirschfeld, R., Masuhara, H., Rose, K. (eds.): Workshop on Self-Sustaining Systems, S3 2010, Tokyo, Japan, 27–28 September 2010. ACM (2010). https://doi.org/10.1145/1942793
21. Hirschfeld, R., Rose, K. (eds.): Self-Sustaining Systems, First Workshop, S3 2008, Potsdam, Germany, 15–16 May 2008, Revised Selected Papers, Lecture Notes in Computer Science, vol. 5146. Springer (2008). https://doi.org/10.1007/978-3-540-89275-5
22. Hossenfelder, S.: Lost in Math: How Beauty Leads Physics Astray. Basic Books (2018)
23. Jacobs, J.: The Death and Life of Great American Cities. Random House (1961)
24. Jakubovic, J.: Achieving Self-Sustainability in Interactive Graphical Programming Systems. Ph.D. thesis, University of Kent (2024). https://kar.kent.ac.uk/105537/
25. Jakubovic, J., Edwards, J., Petricek, T.: Technical dimensions of programming systems. Art Sci. Eng. Program. **7**(3), 13-1 (2023)
26. LaToza, T.D., Ko, A., Shepherd, D.C., Sjøberg, D., Xie, B.: Theories of programming (dagstuhl seminar 22231). In: Dagstuhl Reports, vol. 12. Schloss Dagstuhl-Leibniz-Zentrum für Informatik (2023)

27. Leimbach, T.: The sap story: evolution of sap within the German software industry. IEEE Ann. Hist. Comput. **30**(4), 60–76 (2008). https://doi.org/10.1109/MAHC.2008.75
28. Lynch, K.: The Image of the City. MIT Press, Cambridge (1960)
29. MacKenzie, D.: Mechanizing Proof: Computing, Risk, and Trust. The MIT Press (2001). https://doi.org/10.7551/mitpress/4529.001.0001
30. Myers, B.A. (ed.): Languages for developing user interfaces. A. K. Peters Ltd, USA (1992)
31. Perera, R., Nguyen, M., Petricek, T., Wang, M.: Linked visualisations via galois dependencies. Proc. ACM Program. Lang. **6**(POPL) (2022). https://doi.org/10.1145/3498668
32. Petricek, T.: Programming as architecture, design, and urban planning. In: Proceedings of the 2021 ACM SIGPLAN International Symposium on New Ideas, New Paradigms, and Reflections on Programming and Software, Onward! 2021, pp. 114–124. Association for Computing Machinery, New York (2021). https://doi.org/10.1145/3486607.3486770
33. Petricek, T.: The rise and fall of extensible programming languages (2023). https://tomasp.net/academic/drafts/extensible-rise/hapoc-2023.pdf. Presented at HaPoP
34. Petricek, T., Orchard, D., Mycroft, A.: Coeffects: unified static analysis of context-dependence. In: Fomin, F.V., Freivalds, R., Kwiatkowska, M., Peleg, D. (eds.) ICALP 2013. LNCS, vol. 7966, pp. 385–397. Springer, Heidelberg (2013). https://doi.org/10.1007/978-3-642-39212-2_35
35. Petricek, T., Syme, D.: F# Web Tools: Rich client/server web applications in F#. Unpublished draft. https://tomasp.net/academic/articles/fswebtools/fswebtools-ml.pdf
36. Rein, P., Ramson, S., Lincke, J., Hirschfeld, R., Pape, T.: Exploratory and live, programming and coding. Art Sci. Eng. Program. **3**(1) (2018)
37. Resnick, M., et al.: Scratch: programming for all. Commun. ACM **52**(11), 60–67 (2009). https://doi.org/10.1145/1592761.1592779
38. Slayton, R.: Arguments that Count: Physics, Computing, and Missile Defense, 1949–2012. MIT Press (2013). https://doi.org/10.7551/mitpress/9234.001.0001
39. Victor, B.: Learnable programming: Designing a programming system for understanding programs (2012). http://worrydream.com/LearnableProgramming

Triemaps that Match

Simon Peyton Jones[1] and Sebastian Graf[2(✉)]

[1] Epic Games, Cary, USA
[2] Karlsruhe Institute of Technology, Karlsruhe, Germany
sgraf1337@gmail.com

Abstract. The *trie* data structure is a good choice for finite maps whose keys are data structures (trees) rather than atomic values. But what if we want the keys to be *patterns*, each of which matches many lookup keys? Efficient matching of this kind is well studied in the theorem prover community, but much less so in the context of statically typed functional programming. Doing so yields an interesting new viewpoint—and a practically useful design pattern, with good runtime performance.

1 Introduction

Many functional languages provide *finite maps* either as a built-in data type, or as a mature, well-optimised library. Generally the keys of such a map will be small: an integer, a string, or perhaps a pair of integers. But in some applications the key is large: an entire tree structure. For example, consider the Haskell expression

let $x = a + b$ **in** ... (**let** $y = a + b$ **in** $x + y$) ....

We might hope that the compiler will recognise the repeated sub-expression $(a + b)$ and transform to

let $x = a + b$ **in** ... $(x + x)$ ....

An easy way to do so is to build a finite map that maps the expression $(a + b)$ to x. Then, when encountering the inner **let**, we can look up the right hand side in the map, and replace y by x. All we need is a *finite map keyed by syntax trees.*

Another similar challenge is this: we often want a finite map keyed by *patterns* rather than expressions. GHC (a Haskell compiler) supports user-written rewrite rules. For example:

{-# **RULES** "map/map" $\forall f\ g\ xs.\ map\ f\ (map\ g\ xs) = map\ (f \circ g)\ xs$ #-}

Given a target expression to optimise, the compiler must decide if any rewrite rule matches the target, after intantiating the forall-bound variables of the rule. Another application, which also appears in GHC, is type class instance lookup. In both cases we need a fast way to see if a target expression matches one of the patterns in a set of $(pattern, rhs)$ pairs. We could do this by testing the patterns

D. Orchard et al. (Eds.): Alan Mycroft Festschrift, LNCS 15500, pp. 234–261, 2026.
https://doi.org/10.1007/978-3-032-08187-2_12

one by one, but if there are many patterns it would be much better to consult some kind of efficient *finite map keyed by patterns.*

When the key is a perhaps-large data structure, traditional finite-map implementations can behave badly, because they are often based on balanced trees and make the assumption that comparing two keys is a fast, constant-time operation. That assumption is false when the key is large. For the lookup task, a good solution is well known: use a *trie* (e.g. [10]). The matching task is also well studied but, surprisingly, only in the automated reasoning community: they use so-called *discrimination trees*, as we discuss in Sect. 7.1. In this paper we apply these trie-based ideas in the context of a statically-typed functional programming language, Haskell. This shift of context is surprisingly fruitful, and we make the following contributions:

- Following [10], we develop a standard pattern for a *statically-typed triemap* for an arbitrary algebraic data type (Sect. 3.2). In contrast, most of the literature describes untyped tries for a fixed, generic tree type. In particular:
  - Supported by type classes, we can make good use of polymorphism to build triemaps for polymorphic data types, such as lists (Sect. 3.6).
  - We cover the full range of operations expected for finite maps: not only *insert*ion and *lookup*, but *alter*, *union*, *foldr*, *map* and *filter* (Sect. 3.2).
  - We develop a generic optimisation for singleton maps that compresses leaf paths. Intriguingly, the resulting triemap *transformer* can be easily mixed into arbitrary triemap definitions (Sect. 3.7).
- We show how to make our triemaps insensitive to *α-renamings* in keys that include binding forms (Sect. 4). Accounting for α-equivalence is not hard, but it is crucial for the applications in compilers.
- We extend our triemaps to support *matching* lookups (Sect. 5). This is an important step, because the only readily-available alternative is linear lookup. Our main contribution is to extend the established idea of tries keyed by arbitrary data types, so that it can handle matching too.
- We present measurements that compare the performance of our triemaps (ignoring their matching capability) with traditional finite-map implementations in Haskell (Sect. 6).

All the code in this paper is available online ancillary to the extended version of this paper [15] or in the accompanying GitHub repository [16]. It is written in Haskell and makes crucial use of some distinctive features of Haskell, including type classes, associated types, higher kinded type variables, and polymorphic recursion.

We discuss related work in Sect. 7. Our contribution is not so much a clever new idea as an exposition of some old ideas in a new context. Nevertheless, we found it surprisingly tricky to develop the "right" abstractions, such as the *TrieMap* and *Matchable* classes, the singleton-and-empty map data type, and the combinators we use in our instances. These abstractions have been through *many* iterations, and we hope that by laying them out here we may shorten the path for others.

2 The Problem We Address

Our general task is as follows: *implement an efficient finite mapping from keys to values, in which the key is a tree.* Semantically, such a finite map is just a set of *(key,value)* pairs; we query the map by looking up a *target.*

2.1 Expressions as Keys

As a concrete example of the general problem, suppose a compiler is manipulating syntax trees representing expressions in the language being compiled. An expression might be defined like this:

```
type Var = String
data Expr = App Expr Expr | Lam Var Expr | Var Var
```

Here the type *Var* represents variables; these can be compared for equality and used as the key of a finite map. The definition of *Var* is not important for this paper, but for the sake of concreteness we have defined *Var* to be *String*. In a real compiler, a variable would have a unique identifier (a number, say) that supports constant-time comparison, so despite the *String* we will assume that variables can be compared in constant time.

The data type *Expr* is capable of representing expressions like *add x y* and $\lambda x \rightarrow add\ x\ y$. We will use this data type throughout the paper, because it has all the features that occur in real expression data types: free variables like *add*, represented by a *Var* node; lambdas which can bind variables (*Lam*), and occurrences of those bound variables (*Var*); and nodes with multiple children (*App*). A real-world expression type would have many more constructors, including literals, let-expressions and suchlike.

2.2 Alpha-Renaming

In the context of a compiler, where the keys are expressions or types, the keys may contain internal *binders*, such as the binder x in $\lambda x \rightarrow x$. If so, we would expect insertion and lookup to be insensitive to α-renaming, so we could, for example, insert with key $\lambda x \rightarrow x$ and look up with key $\lambda y \rightarrow y$, to find the inserted value.

2.3 Lookup Modulo Matching

Beyond just the basic finite maps we have described, our practical setting in GHC demands more: we want to do a lookup that does *matching*. As mentioned above, GHC supports so-called *rewrite rules* [17], which the user can specify in their source program, like this:

```
{-# RULES "map/map" ∀f g xs. map f (map g xs) = map (f ∘ g) xs #-}
```

This rule asks the compiler to rewrite any target expression that matches the shape of the left-hand side (LHS) of the rule into the right-hand side (RHS). We use the term *pattern* to describe the LHS, and *target* to describe the expression we are looking up in the map. The pattern is explicitly quantified over the *pattern variables* (here f, g, and xs) that can be bound during the matching process. In other words, we seek a substitution for the pattern variables that makes the pattern equal to the target expression. For example, if the program we are compiling contains the target expression $map\ double\ (map\ square\ nums)$, we would like to produce a substitution $[f \mapsto double, g \mapsto square, xs \mapsto nums]$ so that the substituted RHS becomes $map\ (double \circ square)\ nums$; we would replace the former expression with the latter in the code under consideration.

Of course, the pattern might itself have bound variables, and we would like to be insensitive to α-conversion for those. For example:

{-# **RULES** "map/id" $map\ (\lambda x \rightarrow x) = \lambda y \rightarrow y$ #-}

We want to find a successful match if we see a call $map\ (\lambda z \rightarrow z)$, even though the bound variable has a different name.

A similar application is GHC's lookup for type class and type family instances. Suppose we have

instance $C\ [a]\ Int$ **where** ...
instance $C\ Bool\ (Maybe\ b)$ **where** ...
... *and so on*

When solving an instance constraint $C\ [Char]\ Int$, say, GHC must look through all the type class instances to find one that matches. In this case, the first instance matches, by binding $[a \mapsto Char]$.

There may occasionally be thousands of rules, or thousands of type class or type family instances. We would like to find a matching candidate more efficiently than by linear search.

2.4 Non-solutions

At first sight, our task can be done easily: define a total order on *Expr* and use a standard finite map library. Indeed that works, but it can be terribly slow. A finite map is implemented as a binary search tree; at every node of this tree, we compare the key (an *Expr*, remember) with the key stored at the node; if it is smaller, go left; if larger, go right. Each lookup thus must perform a (logarithmic) number of potentially-full-depth comparisons of two expressions.

Another possibility might be to hash the *Expr* and use the hash-code as the lookup key. That would make lookup much faster, but it requires at least two full traversals of the key for every lookup: one to compute its hash code for every lookup, and a full equality comparison on a "hit" because hash-codes can collide.

But the killer is this: *neither binary search trees nor hashing is compatible with matching lookup.* For our purposes they are non-starters.

What other standard solutions to matching lookup are there, apart from linear search? The theorem proving and automated reasoning community has been working with huge sets of rewrite rules, just as we describe, for many years. They have developed term indexing techniques for the job [18, Chapter 26], which attack the same problem from a rather different angle, as we discuss in Sect. 7.1.

3 Tries

A standard approach to a finite map in which the key has internal structure is to use a *trie* [12]. Generalising tries to handle an arbitrary algebraic data type as the key is a well established, albeit under-used, idea [4,10]. We review these ideas in this section. Let us consider a simplified form of expression:

```
data Expr = Var Var | App Expr Expr
```

We omit lambdas for now, so that all *Var* nodes represent free variables, which are treated as constants. We will return to lambdas in Sect. 4.

```
type TF v = Maybe v → Maybe v
data Map k v = ...   -- Keys k, values v
Map.empty     :: Map k v
Map.insert    :: Ord k ⇒ k → v → Map k v → Map k v
Map.lookup    :: Ord k ⇒ k → Map k v → Maybe v
Map.alter     :: Ord k ⇒ TF v → k
                   → Map k v → Map k v
Map.foldr     :: (v → r → r) → r → Map k v → r
Map.map       :: (v → w) → Map k v → Map k w
Map.unionWith :: Ord k ⇒ (v → v → v)
                   → Map k v → Map k v → Map k v
Map.size      :: Map k v → Int
Map.compose   :: Ord b ⇒ Map b c → Map a b → Map a c
infixr 1 >=>             -- Kleisli composition
(>=>) :: Monad m ⇒ (a → m b) → (b → m c)
                  → a → m c
infixr 1 >>>             -- Forward composition
(>>>) :: (a → b) → (b → c) → a → c
infixr 0 ▷               -- Reverse function application
(▷) :: a → (a → b) → b
```

Fig. 1. API for various library functions used in this work.

3.1 The Interface of a Finite Map

Building on the design of widely used functions in Haskell (see Fig. 1), we seek these basic operations:

```
emptyEM :: ExprMap v
lkEM    :: Expr → ExprMap v → Maybe v
atEM    :: Expr → TF v → ExprMap v → ExprMap v
```

The lookup function *lkEM*[1] has a type that is familiar from every finite map. The update function *atEM*, typically called *alter* in Haskell libraries, changes the value stored at a particular key. The caller provides a *value transformation function TF v*, an abbreviation for *Maybe v → Maybe v* (see Fig. 1). This function transforms the existing value associated with the key, if any (hence the input *Maybe*), to a new value, if any (hence the output *Maybe*). We can easily define *insertEM* and *deleteEM* from *atEM*:

```
insertEM :: Expr → v → ExprMap v → ExprMap v
insertEM e v = atEM e (\_ → Just v)

deleteEM :: Expr → ExprMap v → ExprMap v
deleteEM e = atEM e (\_ → Nothing)
```

You might wonder whether, for the purposes of this paper, we could just define *insertEM*, leaving *atEM* to the supplemental material of the extended version of this paper [15,16], but as we will see in Sect. 3.3, our approach using tries requires the generality of *atEM*.

We also support other standard operations on finite maps, with types analogous to those in Fig. 1, including *unionEM*, *mapEM*, and *foldrEM*.

3.2 Tries: The Basic Idea

Here is a trie-based implementation for *Expr*:

```
data ExprMap v
  = EM {em_var :: Map Var v, em_app :: ExprMap (ExprMap v)}
```

Here *Map Var v* is any standard finite map (e.g. in *containers*[2]) keyed by *Var*, with values *v*. One way to understand this slightly odd data type is to study its lookup function:

```
lkEM :: Expr → ExprMap v → Maybe v
lkEM e (EM {em_var = var, em_app = app}) = case e of
  Var x       → Map.lookup x var
  App e1 e2 → case lkEM e1 app of
    Nothing → Nothing
    Just m1 → lkEM e2 m1
```

This function pattern-matches on the target *e*. The *Var* alternative says that to look up a variable occurrence, just look that variable up in the *em_var* field. But if the expression is an *App* e_1 e_2 node, we first look up e_1 in the *em_app*

[1] We use short names *lkEM* and *atEM* consistently in this paper for compact code listings.

[2] https://hackage.haskell.org/package/containers.

field, *which returns an* *ExprMap*. We then look up e_2 in that map. Each distinct e_1 yields a different *ExprMap* in which to look up e_2.

We can substantially abbreviate this code, at the expense of making it more cryptic, thus:

```
lkEM (Var x)     = em_var ⋙ Map.lookup x
lkEM (App e1 e2) = em_app ⋙ lkEM e1 >=> lkEM e2
```

The function $em\_var :: ExprMap\ v \rightarrow Map\ Var\ v$ is the auto-generated selector that picks the *em_var* field from an *EM* record, and similarly *em_app*. The functions ($>=>$) and ($\ggg$) are right-associative forward composition operators, respectively monadic and non-monadic, that chain the individual operations together (see Fig. 1). Finally, we have η-reduced the definition, by omitting the *m* parameter. These abbreviations become quite worthwhile when we add more constructors, each with more fields, to the key data type.

Notice that in contrast to the approach of Sect. 2.4, *we never compare two expressions for equality or ordering*. We simply walk down the *ExprMap* structure, guided at each step by the next node in the target.

This definition is extremely short and natural. But it embodies a hidden complexity: *it requires polymorphic recursion* [13]. The recursive call to $lkEM\ e_1$ instantiates *v* to a different type than the parent function definition. Haskell supports polymorphic recursion readily, provided you give a type signature to *lkEM*, but not all languages do.

3.3 Modifying Tries

It is not enough to look up in a trie – we need to *build* them too. First, we need an empty trie. Here is one way to define it:

```
emptyEM :: ExprMap v
emptyEM = EM {em_var = Map.empty, em_app = emptyEM}
```

It is interesting to note that *emptyEM* is an infinite, recursive structure: the *em_app* field refers back to *emptyEM*. We will change this definition in Sect. 3.5, but it works perfectly well for now. Next, we need to *alter* a triemap *at* some key, implemented as *atEM*:[3]

```
atEM :: Expr → TF v → ExprMap v → ExprMap v
atEM e tf m@(EM {em_var = var, em_app = app}) = case e of
  Var x     → m {em_var = Map.alter tf x var}
  App e1 e2 → m {em_app = atEM e1 (liftTF (atEM e2 tf)) app}
liftTF :: (ExprMap v → ExprMap v) → TF (ExprMap v)
liftTF f Nothing  = Just (f emptyEM)
liftTF f (Just m) = Just (f m)
```

[3] The name *atEM* is borrowed from the *At* type class of the *lens*[4] package. Indeed, *ExprMap* could have an *At* instance if *atEM* were generalised to an applicative traversal.

In the *Var* case, we must just update the map stored in the *em_var* field, using the *Map.alter* function from Fig. 1. In the *App* case we look up e_1 in *app*; we should find a *ExprMap* there, which we want to alter with *tf*. We can do that with a recursive call to *atEM*, using *liftTF* for impedance-matching.

The *App* case shows why we need the generality of *atEM*. Suppose we attempted to define an apparently-simpler *insertEM* operation. Its equation for (*App* e_1 e_2) would look up e_1—and would then need to alter that entry (an *ExprMap*, remember) with the result of inserting (e_2, v). So we are forced to define *atEM* anyway.

We can abbreviate the code for *atEM* using combinators, as we did in the case of lookup, and doing so pays dividends when the key is a data type with many constructors, each with many fields. However, the details are fiddly and not illuminating, so we omit them here. Indeed, for the same reason, in the rest of this paper we will typically omit the code for *atEM*, though the full code is available in the supplement [15,16].

3.4 Unions of Maps

A common operation on finite maps is to take their union:

```
unionEM :: ExprMap v → ExprMap v → ExprMap v
```

In tree-based implementations of finite maps, such union operations can be tricky. The two trees, which have been built independently, might not have the same left-subtree/right-subtree structure, so some careful rebalancing may be required. But for tries there are no such worries – their structure is identical, and we can simply zip them together. There is one wrinkle: just as we had to generalise *insertEM* to *atEM*, to accommodate the nested map in *em_app*, so we need to generalise *unionEM* to *unionWithEM*:

```
unionWithEM :: (v → v → v)
            → ExprMap v → ExprMap v → ExprMap v
```

When a key appears on both maps, the combining function is used to combine the two corresponding values. With that generalisation, the code is as follows:

```
unionWithEM f (EM {em_var = var₁, em_app = app₁})
              (EM {em_var = var₂, em_app = app₂})
  = EM {em_var = Map.unionWith f var₁ var₂
       , em_app = unionWithEM (unionWithEM f) app₁ app₂}
```

It could hardly be simpler.

3.5 Folds and the Empty Map

The strange, infinite definition of *emptyEM* given in Sect. 3.3 works fine (in a lazy language at least) for lookup, alteration, and union, but it fails fundamentally when we want to *iterate* over the elements of the trie. For example, suppose we wanted to count the number of elements in the finite map; in *containers* this is the function *Map.size* (Fig. 1). We might attempt:

```
sizeEM :: ExprMap v → Int
sizeEM (EM {em_var = var, em_app = app})
  = Map.size var + ???
```

We seem stuck because the size of the *app* map is not what we want: rather, we want to add up the sizes of its *elements*, and we don't have a way to do that yet. The right thing to do is to generalise to a fold:

```
foldrEM :: ∀v. (v → r → r) → r → ExprMap v → r
foldrEM k z (EM {em_var = var, em_app = app})
  = Map.foldr k z1 var
  where
    z1 = foldrEM kapp z (app :: ExprMap (ExprMap v))
    kapp m1 r = foldrEM k r m1
```

In the binding for z_1 we fold over *app*, using *kapp* to combine the map we find with the accumulator, by again folding over the map with *foldrEM*.

But alas, *foldrEM* will never terminate! It always invokes itself immediately (in z_1) on *app*; but that invocation will again recursively invoke *foldrEM*; and so on forever. The solution is simple: we just need an explicit representation of the empty map. Here is one way to do it (we will see another in Sect. 3.7): The right thing to do is to generalise to a fold:

```
data ExprMap v = EmptyEM | EM {em_var :: ..., em_app :: ...}

emptyEM :: ExprMap v
emptyEM = EmptyEM

foldrEM :: (v → r → r) → r → ExprMap v → r
foldrEM k z EmptyEM = z
foldrEM k z (EM {em_var = var, em_app = app})
  = Map.foldr k z1 var
  where
    z1 = foldrEM kapp z app
    kapp m1 r = foldrEM k r m1
```

Equipped with a fold, we can easily define the size function, and another that returns the range of the map: The right thing to do is to generalise to a fold:

```
sizeEM :: ExprMap v → Int
sizeEM = foldrEM (λ_ n → n + 1) 0

elemsEM :: ExprMap v → [v]
elemsEM = foldrEM (:) []
```

3.6 A Type Class for Triemaps

Since all our triemaps share a common interface, it is useful to define a type class for them: The right thing to do is to generalise to a fold:

```
class Eq (Key tm) ⇒ TrieMap tm where
  type Key tm :: Type
  emptyTM      :: tm a
  lkTM         :: Key tm → tm a → Maybe a
  atTM         :: Key tm → TF a → tm a → tm a
  foldrTM      :: (a → b → b) → tm a → b → b
  unionWithTM :: (a → a → a) → tm a → tm a → tm a
  ...
```

The class constraint *TrieMap tm* says that the type *tm* is a triemap, with operations *emptyTM*, *lkTM* etc. The class has an *associated type* [3], *Key tm*, a type-level function that transforms the type of the triemap into the type of *keys* of that triemap.

Now we can witness the fact that *ExprMap* is a *TrieMap*, like this: The right thing to do is to generalise to a fold:

```
instance TrieMap ExprMap where
  type Key ExprMap = Expr
  emptyTM = emptyEM
  lkTM    = lkEM
  atTM    = atEM
  ...
```

Having a class allows us to write helper functions that work for any triemap implementation, such as The right thing to do is to generalise to a fold:

```
insertTM :: TrieMap tm ⇒ Key tm → v → tm v → tm v
insertTM k v = atTM k (\_ → Just v)

deleteTM :: TrieMap tm ⇒ Key tm → tm v → tm v
deleteTM k = atTM k (\_ → Nothing)
```

But that is not all. Suppose our expressions had multi-argument apply nodes, *AppV*, thus

```
data Expr = ... | AppV Expr [Expr]
```

Then we would need to build a trie keyed by a *list* of *Expr*. A list is just another algebraic data type, built with nil and cons, so we *could* use exactly the same approach, thus

```
lkLEM :: [Expr] → ListExprMap v → Maybe v
```

But rather than define a *ListExprMap* for keys of type [*Expr*], and a *ListDeclMap* for keys of type [*Decl*], etc., we would obviously prefer to build a trie for lists of *any type*, like this [10]:

```
instance TrieMap tm ⇒ TrieMap (ListMap tm) where
  type Key (ListMap tm) = [Key tm]
  emptyTM = emptyLM
  lkTM    = lkLM
  ...

data ListMap tm v = LM { lm_nil :: Maybe v
                       , lm_cons :: tm (ListMap tm v) }

emptyLM :: TrieMap tm ⇒ ListMap tm
emptyLM = LM { lm_nil = Nothing, lm_cons = emptyTM }

lkLM :: TrieMap tm ⇒ [Key tm] → ListMap tm v → Maybe v
lkLM []       = lm_nil
lkLM (k : ks) = lm_cons >>> lkTM k >=> lkLM ks
```

The code for *atLM* and *foldrLM* is routine. Notice that all of these functions are polymorphic in *tm*, the triemap for the list elements.

3.7 Singleton Maps, and Empty Maps Revisited

Suppose we start with an empty map, and insert a value with a key (an *Expr*) such as

```
App (App (Var "f") (Var "x")) (Var "y")
```

Looking at the code for *atEM* in Sect. 3.3, you can see that because there is an *App* at the root, we will build an *EM* record with an empty *em_var*, and an *em_app* field that is... another *EM* record. Again the *em_var* field will contain an empty map, while the *em_app* field is a further *EM* record.

In effect, the key is linearised into a chain of *EM* records. This is great when there are a lot of keys with shared structure, but once we are in a sub-tree that represents a *single* key-value pair it is a rather inefficient way to represent the key. So a simple idea is this: when an *ExprMap* represents a single key-value pair, represent it directly as a key-value pair, like this:

```
data ExprMap v = EmptyEM
               | SingleEM Expr v   -- A single key/value pair
               | EM { em_var :: ..., em_app :: ... }
```

But in the triemap for each new data type *X*, we will have to tiresomely repeat these extra data constructors, *EmptyX* and *SingleX*. For example we would have to add *EmptyList* and *SingleList* to the *ListMap* data type of Sect. 3.6. It is better instead to abstract over the enclosed triemap, as follows:[5]

```
data SEMap tm v = EmptySEM
                | SingleSEM (Key tm) v
                | MultiSEM (tm v)
```

[5] *SEMap* stands for "singleton or empty map".

```
instance TrieMap tm ⇒ TrieMap (SEMap tm) where
  type Key (SEMap tm) = Key tm
  emptyTM = EmptySEM
  lkTM    = lkSEM
  atTM    = atSEM
  ...
```

The code for lookup practically writes itself. We abstract over *Maybe* with some *MonadPlus* combinators to enjoy forward compatibility to Sect. 5:

```
lkSEM :: TrieMap tm ⇒ Key tm → SEMap tm v → Maybe v
lkSEM k m = case m of
  EmptySEM       → mzero
  SingleSEM pk v → guard (k == pk) ≫ pure v
  MultiSEM m     → lkTM k m
```

Where *mzero* means *Nothing* and *pure* means *Just*. The *guard* expression in the *SingleSEM* will return *Nothing* when the key expression *k* doesn't equate to the pattern expression *pk*. To test for said equality we require an *Eq* (*Key tm*) instance, hence it is a superclass of *TrieMap tm* in the **class** declaration in Sect. 3.6.

The code for alter is more interesting, because it governs the shift from *EmptySEM* to *SingleSEM* and thence to *MultiSEM*:

```
atSEM :: TrieMap tm
      ⇒ Key tm → TF v → SEMap tm v → SEMap tm v
atSEM k tf EmptySEM = case tf Nothing of Nothing → EmptySEM
                                         Just v  → SingleSEM k v
atSEM k1 tf (SingleSEM k2 v2) = if k1 == k2
  then case tf (Just v2) of
    Nothing → EmptySEM
    Just v' → SingleSEM k2 v'
  else case tf Nothing of
    Nothing → SingleSEM k2 v2
    Just v1 → MultiSEM (insertTM k1 v1 (insertTM k2 v2 emptyTM))
atSEM k tf (MultiSEM tm) = MultiSEM (atTM k tf tm)
```

Adding a new item to a triemap can turn *EmptySEM* into *SingleSEM* and *SingleSEM* into *MultiSEM*; and deleting an item from a *SingleSEM* turns it back into *EmptySEM*. You might wonder whether we can shrink a *MultiSEM* back to a *SingleSEM* when it has only one remaining element? Yes we can, but it takes quite a bit of code, and it is far from clear that it is worth doing so.

Finally, we need to re-define *ExprMap* and *ListMap* using *SEMap*:

```
type ExprMap    = SEMap ExprMap'
data ExprMap' v = EM {em_var :: ..., em_app :: ExprMap (ExprMap v)}
type ListMap       = SEMap ListMap'
data ListMap' tm v = LM {lm_nil :: ..., lm_cons :: tm (ListMap tm v)}
```

The auxiliary data types *ExprMap'* and *ListMap'* have only a single constructor, because the empty and singleton cases are dealt with by *SEMap*. We reserve the original, un-primed, names for the user-visible *ExprMap* and *ListMap* constructors.

3.8 Generic Programming

We have not described a triemap *library*; rather we have described a *design pattern*. More precisely, given a new algebraic data type X, we have described a systematic way of defining a triemap, *XMap*, keyed by values of type X. Such a triemap is represented by a record:

- Each *constructor* K of X becomes a *field* *x_k* in *XMap*.
- Each *field* of a constructor K becomes a *nested triemap* in the type of the field *x_k*.
- If X is polymorphic then *XMap* becomes a triemap transformer, like *ListMap* above.

Actually writing out all this boilerplate code is tiresome, and it can of course be automated. One way to do so would be to use generic or polytypic programming, and Hinze describes precisely this [10]. Another approach would be to use Template Haskell.

We do not develop either of these approaches here, because our focus is only the functionality and expressiveness of the triemaps. However, everything we do is compatible with an automated approach to generating boilerplate code.

```
type DBNum = Int
data DBEnv = DBE {dbe_next :: DBNum, dbe_env :: Map Var DBNum}
emptyDBE :: DBEnv
emptyDBE = DBE {dbe_next = 1, dbe_env = Map.empty}
extendDBE :: Var → DBEnv → DBEnv
extendDBE v (DBE {dbe_next = n, dbe_env = dbe})
   = DBE {dbe_next = n + 1, dbe_env = Map.insert v n dbe}
lookupDBE :: Var → DBEnv → Maybe DBNum
lookupDBE v (DBE {dbe_env = dbe}) = Map.lookup v dbe
```

Fig. 2. De Bruijn leveling

4 Keys with Binders

If our keys are expressions (in a compiler, say) they may contain binders, and we want insert and lookup to be insensitive to α-renaming. That is the challenge we address next. Here is our data type *Expr* from Sect. 2.2, which brings back binding semantics through the *Lam* constructor:

```
data Expr = App Expr Expr | Lam Var Expr | Var Var
```

The key idea is simple: we perform de Bruijn numbering on the fly, renaming each binder to a natural number, from outside in. So, when inserting or looking up a key $(\lambda x.\, foo\ (\lambda y.\, x + y))$ we behave as if the key was $(\lambda.\, foo\ (\lambda.\#_1 + \#_2))$, where each $\#_i$ stands for an occurrence of the variable bound by the i'th lambda, counting from the root of the expression. In effect, then, we behave as if the data type was like this:

```
data Expr' = App Expr Expr | Lam Expr | FVar Var | BVar BoundKey
```

Notice (a) the *Lam* node no longer has a binder and (b) there are two sorts of *Var* nodes, one for free variables and one for bound variables, carrying a *BoundKey* (see below). We will not actually build a value of type *Expr'* and look that up in a trie keyed by *Expr'*; rather, we are going to *behave as if we did.* Here is the code (which uses Fig. 2):

```
data ModAlpha a = A DBEnv a
type AlphaExpr = ModAlpha Expr
instance Eq AlphaExpr where ...

type BoundKey = DBNum
type ExprMap = SEMap ExprMap'
data ExprMap' v
  = EM { em_fvar :: Map Var v             -- Free vars
       , em_bvar :: Map BoundKey v        -- Lambda-bound vars
       , em_app  :: ExprMap (ExprMap v)
       , em_lam  :: ExprMap v }

instance TrieMap ExprMap' where
  type Key ExprMap' = AlphaExpr
  lkTM = lkEM
  ...

lkEM :: AlphaExpr → ExprMap' v → Maybe v
lkEM (A bve e) = case e of
  Var v → case lookupDBE v bve of
    Nothing → em_fvar >>> Map.lookup v
    Just bv → em_bvar >>> Map.lookup bv
  App e1 e2 → em_app >>> lkTM (A bve e1) >=> lkTM (A bve e2)
  Lam v e   → em_lam >>> lkTM (A (extendDBE v bve) e)

lookupClosedExpr :: Expr → ExprMap v → Maybe v
lookupClosedExpr e = lkEM (A emptyDBE e)
```

We maintain a *DBEnv* (cf. Fig. 2) that maps each lambda-bound variable to its de Bruijn level [5],[6] its *BoundKey*. The expression we look up—the first argument of *lkEM*—becomes an *AlphaExpr*, which is a pair of a *DBEnv* and an *Expr*. At a

[6] The de Bruijn *index* of the occurrence of a variable v counts the number of lambdas between the occurrence of v and its binding site. The de Bruijn *level* of v counts the number of lambdas between the root of the expression and v's binding site. It is convenient for us to use *levels*.

Lam node we extend the *DBEnv*. At a *Var* node we look up the variable in the *DBEnv* to decide whether it is lambda-bound or free, and behave appropriately.[7]

The construction of Sect. 3.7, to handle empty and singleton maps, applies without difficulty to this generalised map. To use it we must define an instance *Eq AlphaExpr* to satisfy the *Eq* super class constraint on the trie key, so that we can instantiate *TrieMap ExprMap'*. That *Eq AlphaExpr* instance simply equates two α-equivalent expressions in the standard way. The code for *atEM* and *foldrEM* holds no new surprises either.

And that is really all there is to it: it is remarkably easy to extend the basic trie idea to be insensitive to α-conversion and even mix in trie transformers such as *SEMap* at no cost other than writing two instance declarations.

5 Tries that Match

A key advantage of tries over hash-maps and balanced trees is that we can support *matching* (Sect. 2.3).

5.1 What "Matching" Means

Semantically, a matching trie can be thought of as a set of (pattern, value) pairs. What is a pattern? It is a pair (vs, p) where

- vs is a set of *pattern variables*, such as $[a, b, c]$.
- p is a *pattern expression*, such as $f\,a\,(g\,b\,c)$.

A pattern may of course contain free variables (not bound by the pattern), such as f and g in the above example, which are regarded as constants by the algorithm. A pattern (vs, p) *matches* a target expression e iff there is a unique substitution S whose domain is vs, such that $S(p) = e$.

We allow the same variable to occur more than once in the pattern. For example, the pattern $([x], f\ x\ x)$ should match targets like $(f\ 1\ 1)$ or $(f\ (g\ v)\ (g\ v))$, but not $(f\ 1\ (g\ v))$. This ability is important if we are to use matching tries to implement class or type family lookup in GHC.

5.2 Matching Expressions

Our matching trie is founded on a function *matchE* that matches a target *AlphaExpr* against a *single* pattern:

```
matchE :: PatExpr → AlphaExpr → MatchME ()
```

Here *matchE* takes a *pattern* of type *PatExpr*, and a *target* key of type *AlphaExpr*. It sees whether the pattern matches the target, and returns a value

[7] The implementation in the supplement [15,16] uses more efficient *IntMaps* for mapping *BoundKey*. *IntMap* is itself a trie data structure, so it could have made for a nice "Tries all the way down" argument. But we found it distracting to present here, hence regular ordered *Map*.

of type *MatchME* () to say whether or not it matched, and if so with what substitution of the pattern variables. But what exactly are *PatExpr* and *MatchME*? We look at each in turn.

Patterns. A pattern *PatExpr* over *AlphaExpr* can be defined like this:

```
data PatExpr = P PatKeys AlphaExpr
type PatKeys = Map PatVar PatKey
type PatVar  = Var
type PatKey = DBNum
```

A pattern *PatExpr* is a pair of an *AlphaExpr* and a *PatKeys* that maps each of the quantified pattern variables to a canonical de Bruijn *PatKey*. Just as in Sect. 4, *PatKeys* make the pattern insensitive to the particular names, and order of quantification, of the pattern variables. We canonicalise the quantified pattern variables before starting a lookup, numbering pattern variables in the order they appear in the expression in a left-to-right scan. For example

Original pattern	Canonical *PatExpr*
$([a, b], f\ a\ b\ a)$	$P\ [a \mapsto 1, b \mapsto 2]\ (f\ a\ b\ a)$
$([x, g], f\ (g\ x))$	$P\ [x \mapsto 2, g \mapsto 1]\ (f\ (g\ x))$

The Matching Monad. Since matching must accommodate failure, it turns out to be convenient for the result of matching, *MatchME*, to be a monad.[8] Here is one possible implementation, defining *MatchME* as a state transformer over lists:

```
type MatchME v = StateT SubstE [ ] v
type SubstE = Map PatKey Expr
```

More concretely, *MatchME v* is a function taking a substitution (of type *SubstE*) for pattern variables, and yielding a possibly-empty list of values (of type *v*), each paired with an extended *SubstE*. Notice that:

- the *domain* of the substitution *SubstE* is the canonical pattern keys *PatKey*, not *PatVar*.
- the *range* of the substitution is *Expr*, not *AlphaExpr*, because the pattern variables cannot mention lambda-bound variables within the target expression.

Type *MatchME* comes with some auxiliary functions that we will need later:

```
runMatchExpr :: MatchME v → [(SubstE, v)]
liftMaybe    :: Maybe v → MatchME v
refineMatch :: (SubstE → Maybe SubstE) → MatchME ()
```

[8] "*MatchME*" connotes a monadic matcher *MatchM* on expressions, hence the "*E*".

Their semantics should be apparent from their types. For example, *runMatchExpr* runs a *MatchME* computation, starting with an empty *SubstE*, and returning a list of all the successful (*SubstE*, *v*) matches. The function *refineMatch f* extends the current substitution by applying *f* to it; if the result is *Nothing* the match fails; otherwise it turns a single match with the new substitution.

Matching Summary. The implementation of *matchE* is entirely straightforward, using simultaneous recursive descent over the pattern and target. The code is given in the supplement [15, 16].

The key point is this: nothing in this section is concerned with tries. Here we are simply concerned with the mechanics of matching, and its underlying monad. There is ample room for flexibility. For example, if the key terms had two kinds of variables (say type variables and term variables) we could easily define *MatchME* to carry two substitutions; or *MatchME* could return just the first result rather than a list of all of them; and so on.

5.3 Matching Tries for *AlphaExpr*

Next, we show how to implement a matching triemap for our running example, *AlphaExpr*. The data type follows the pattern we developed for *ExprMap* (Sect. 3 4):[9]

```
data MExprMap v
  = EmptyMEM
  | SingleMEM PatExpr v
  | MultiMEM { mm_fvar :: Map Var v          -- Free var
             , mm_bvar :: Map BoundKey v     -- Bound var
             , mm_pvar :: Map PatKey v       -- Pattern var
             , mm_app  :: MExprMap (MExprMap v)
             , mm_lam  :: MExprMap v }
```

The main new feature is that we add an extra field *mm_pvar* to *MExprMap*, for occurrences of a pattern variable. You can see how this field is used in the lookup code:

```
lookupPatMM :: ∀v. AlphaExpr → MExprMap v → MatchME v
lookupPatMM ae@(A bve e) EmptyMEM
  = mzero
lookupPatMM ae@(A bve e) (SingleSEM pat val)
  = matchE pat ae ≫ pure val
lookupPatMM ae@(A bve e) (MultiMEM {..})
  = rigid `mplus` flexi
```

[9] To avoid clutter we have, for now, added empty and singleton maps directly to *MExprMap*, via *EmptyMEM* and *SingleMEM*, much as in Sect. 3.5. In Sect. 5.5 we show how to use the type classes to share the empty/singleton case as we did in Sect. 3.7.

```
where
  rigid = case e of
    Var x       → case lookupDBE x bve of
      Just bv   → mm_bvar ▹ liftMaybe ∘ Map.lookup bv
      Nothing   → mm_fvar ▹ liftMaybe ∘ Map.lookup x
    App e1 e2   → mm_app  ▹ lkMTM (A bve e1)
                          >=> lkMTM (A bve e2)
    Lam x e     → mm_lam  ▹ lkMTM (A (extendDBE x bve) e)
  flexi = mm_pvar ▹ IntMap.toList ▹ map match_one ▹ msum
  match_one :: (PatVar, v) → MatchME v
  match_one (pv, v) = matchPatVarE pv ae ≫ pure v
```

Matching lookup on a trie matches the target expression against *all patterns the trie represents*. The *rigid* case is no different from exact lookup; compare the code for *lkEM* in Sect. 4. The only difference is that we need *liftMaybe* (from Sect. 5.2) to take the *Maybe* returned by *Map.lookup* and lift it into the *MatchME* monad.

The *flexi* case handles the triemap entries whose pattern is simply one of the quantified pattern variables; these entries are stored in the new *mm_pvar* field. We enumerate these entries with *toList*, to get a list of (*PatVar*, *v*) pairs, match each such pair against the target with *match_one*, and finally accumulate all the results with *msum*. In turn *match_one* uses *matchParVarE* to match the pattern variable with the target and, if successful, returns the corresponding value *v*.

The *matchPatVarE* function does the heavy lifting, using some simple auxiliary functions whose types are given below:

```
matchPatVarE :: PatKey → AlphaExpr → MatchME ()
matchPatVarE pv (A bve e) = refineMatch $ λms →
  case Map.lookup pv ms of
    Nothing  -- pv is not bound
      | noCaptured bve e → Just (Map.insert pv e ms)
      | otherwise        → Nothing
    Just sol  -- pv is already bound
      | noCaptured bve e
      , eqExpr e sol     → Just ms
      | otherwise        → Nothing
eqExpr     :: Expr → Expr → Bool
noCaptured :: DBEnv → Expr → Bool
```

To match a pattern variable *pv* against an expression (*A bve e*), we first look up *pv* in the current substitution (obtained from the *MatchME* monad). If *pv* is not bound we simply extend the substitution.

But wait! Consider matching the pattern $([p], \lambda x \to p)$ against the target $(\lambda y \to 3)$. That's fine: we should succeed, binding *p* to 3. But suppose we match that same pattern against target $(\lambda y \to y)$. It would be nonsense to "succeed" binding *p* to *y*, because *y* is locally bound within the target. Hence the *noCaptured* test, which returns *True* iff the expression does not mention any of the locally-bound variables.

If *pv* is already bound in the substitution, we have a repeated pattern variable (see Sect. 5.1), and we must check that the target expression is equal (using *eqExpr*) to the one already bound to *pv*. Once again, however, we must check that the target does not contain any locally-bound variables, hence the *noCaptured* check.

It turns out that *lookupPatMM*, described above, is the trickiest case. The code for *alterPatMM*, and the other operations of the class, is very straightforward, and is given in the supplement [15,16].

5.4 The External API

The matching tries we have described so far use canonical pattern keys, a matching monad, and other machinery that should be hidden from the client. We seek an external API more like this:

```
type PatMap :: Type → Type
alterPM   :: ([Var], Expr) → TF v → PatMap v → PatMap v
lookupPM :: Expr → PatMap v → [(PatSubst, v)]
type PatSubst = [(Var, Expr)]
```

When altering a *PatMap*, we supply a client-side pattern, which is just a pair ([*Var*], *Expr*) of the quantified pattern variables and the pattern. When looking up in a *PatMap*, we supply a target expression, and get back a list of matches, each of which is a pair of the value and the substitution for those original pattern variables that made the pattern equal to the target.

So *alterPM* must canonicalise the client-side pattern variables before altering the trie; that is easy enough. But how can *lookupPM* recover the client-side *PatSubst*? Somehow we must remember the canonicalisation used when *inserting* so that we can invert it when *matching*. For example, suppose we insert the two (pattern, value pairs)

$$(([p], f\ p\ True), v_1) \quad \text{and} \quad (([q], f\ q\ False), v_2)$$

Both patterns will canonicalise their (sole) pattern variable to the de Bruin level 1. So if we look up the target ($f\ e\ True$) the *MatchME* monad will produce a final *Subst* that maps $[1 \mapsto e]$, paired with the value v_1. But we want to return $([("p", e)], v_1)$ to the client, a *PatSubst* that uses the client variable "p", not the internal index 1.

The solution is simple enough: *we store the mapping in the triemap's domain*, along with the values, thus:

```
type PatMap v = MExprMap (PatKeys, v)
```

Now the code writes itself. Here is *alterPM*:

```
alterPM :: ∀v. ([Var], Expr) → TF v → PatMap v → PatMap v
alterPM (pvars, e) tf pm = atMTM pat ptf pm
  where
```

```
    pks :: PatKeys = canonPatKeys pvars e
    pat :: PatExpr = P pks (A emptyDBE e)
    ptf :: TF (PatKeys, v)
    ptf Nothing      = fmap (λv → (pks, v)) (tf Nothing)
    ptf (Just (_, v)) = fmap (λv → (pks, v)) (tf (Just v))
canonPatKeys :: [Var] → Expr → PatKeys
```

The auxiliary function *canonPatKeys* takes the client-side pattern (*pvars*, *e*), and returns a *PatKeys* (Sect. 5.2) that maps each pattern variable to its canonical de Bruijn index. *canonPatKeys* is entirely straightforward: it simply walks the expression, numbering off the pattern variables in left-to-right order.

Then we can simply call the internal *atMTM* function, passing it a canonical *pat* :: *PatExpr* and a transformer *ptf* :: *TF* (*PatKeys*, *v*) that will pair the *PatKeys* with the value supplied by the user via *tf* :: *TF v*. Lookup is equally easy:

```
lookupPM :: Expr → PatMap v → [(PatSubst, v)]
lookupPM e pm
  = [(Map.toList (subst `Map.compose` pks), x)
    | (subst, (pks, x)) ← runMatchExpr $
                            lkMTM (A emptyDBE e) pm]
```

We use *runMatchExpr* to get a list of successful matches, and then pre-compose (see Fig. 1) the internal *Subst* with the *PatKeys* mapping that is part of the match result. We turn that into a list to get the client-side *PatSubst*. The only tricky point is what to do with pattern variables that are not substituted. For example, suppose we insert the pattern ([*p*, *q*], *f p*). No lookup will bind *q*, because *q* simply does not appear in the pattern. One could reject this on insertion, but here we simply return a *PatSubst* with no binding for *q*.

5.5 Adding Type Classes

All of this has been specific to matching tries keyed by *AlphaExpr*, but as before we can profitably define a type class of such matching tries, like this:

```
class Matchable (MKey tm) ⇒ MTrieMap tm where
  type MKey tm :: Type
  emptyMTM :: tm v
  lkMTM    :: MKey tm → tm v → MatchM (MKey tm) v
  atMTM    :: Pat (MKey tm) → TF v → tm v → tm v
class Eq (Pat k) ⇒ Matchable k where
  type Pat k :: Type
  type Subst k :: Type
  match :: Pat k → k → MatchM k ()
newtype MatchM k v = M (Subst k → [(Subst k, v)])
```

The following points are worth noting:

- The old *TrieMap* class, in Sect. 3.6, required the keys to be comparable for *equality*. Unsurprisingly the new *MTrieMap* class instead requires the keys to be *Matchable*. What does it mean to be *Matchable*? As you can see from the *Matchable* class, it just means that we must provide a *match* function, like *matchE* defined in Sect. 5.2.
- The *match* function returns *MatchM*, a slight generalisation of *MatchME*. Specifically, *MatchM* carries a substitution whose type *Subst k* depends on the key type *k*. *Subst* is an associated type of the *Matchable* class.
- The lookup function takes a key of type *MKey tm*, but it returns something in the *MatchM* monad, rather than the *Maybe* monad (as was the case in Sect. 3.6).
- The *atMTM* takes a *pattern* (rather than just a key), of type *Pat* (*MKey tm*), and alters the trie's value at that pattern.[10]

Now we can write instances for these two classes to make them work for *AlphaExpr* keys:

```
instance MTrieMap MExprMap where
  type MKey MExprMap = AlphaExpr
  emptyMTM = EmptyMEM
  lkMTM = lookupPatMM
  ..
instance Matchable AlphaExpr where
  type Pat   AlphaExpr = PatExpr
  type Subst AlphaExpr = SubstE
  match = matchE
```

We can also generalise *SEMap* (Sect. 3.7) in a similar way:

```
data MSEMap tm v = EmptyMSEM
                 | SingleMSEM (Pat (MKey tm)) v
                 | MultiMSEM (tm v)
instance MTrieMap tm ⇒ MTrieMap (MSEMap tm) where
  type MKey (MSEMap tm) = MKey tm
  emptyMTM = EmptyMSEM
  lkMTM    = lkMSEM
  atMTM    = atMSEM
```

Notice that *SingleMSEM* contains a *pattern*, not merely a *key*, unlike *SingleSEM* in Sect. 3.7. The code for *lkMSEM* and *atMSEM* is straightforward; we give the former here, leaving the latter for the supplement [15,16]

```
lkMSEM :: MTrieMap tm ⇒ MKey tm → MSEMap tm a
                       → Match (MKey tm) a
lkMSEM k EmptyMSEM            = mzero
lkMSEM k (MultiMSEM m)        = lkMTM k m
lkMSEM k (SingleMSEM pat v) = match pat k ≫ pure v
```

[10] Remember, a matching trie represents a set of (pattern,value) pairs.

Notice the call to *mzero* to make the lookup fail if the map is empty; and, in the *SingleMSEM* case, the call *match* to match the pattern against the key.

5.6 Most-Specific Match and Unification

It is tempting to ask: can we build a lookup that returns only the *most specific* matches? And can we build a lookup that returns all values whose patterns *unify* with the target. Both would have useful applications, in GHC at least.

However, both seem difficult to achieve. All our attempts became mired in complexity, and we leave this for further work, and as a challenge for the reader. We outline some of the difficulties of unifying lookup in Appendix B of the extended version of this paper [15].

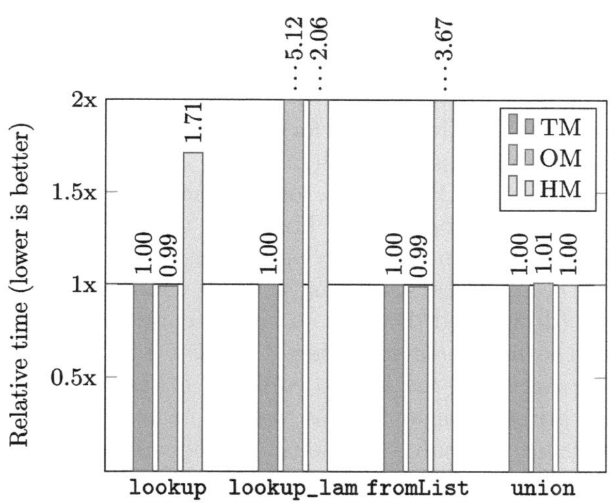

Fig. 3. Benchmarks comparing our trie map (TM) to ordered maps (OM) and hash maps (HM).

6 Evaluation

So far, we have seen that trie maps offer a significant advantage over other kinds of maps like ordered maps or hash maps: the ability to do a matching lookup (in Sect. 5). In this section, we will see that query performance is another advantage. Our implementation of trie maps in Haskell can generally compete in performance with other map data structures, while significantly outperforming traditional map implementations on some operations. Not bad for a data structure that we can also extend to support matching lookup!

We took runtime measurements of the (non-matching) *ExprMap* data structure on a selection of workloads, conducted using the *criterion*[11] benchmarking library.[12] Fig. 3 presents a quick overview of the results.

Appendix A of the extended version of this paper [15] featurs a more in-depth analysis and finer runtime as well as space measurements and indicators for statistical significance.

Setup. All benchmarks except `fromList` are handed a pre-built map containing 10000 expressions, each consisting of roughly 100 *Expr* data constructors drawn from a pseudo-random source with a fixed (and thus deterministic) seed.

We compare three different non-matching map implementations, simply because we were not aware of other map data structures with matching lookup modulo α-equivalence and we wanted to compare apples to apples. The *ExprMap* forms the baseline. Asymptotics are given with respect to map size n and key expression size k:

- *ExprMap* (designated "TM" in Fig. 3) is the trie map implementation from this paper. Insertion and lookup perform at most one full traversal of the key, so performance should scale with $O(k)$.
- *Map Expr* (designated "OM") is the ordered map implementation from the mature, well-optimised *containers*[13] library. It uses size balanced trees under the hood [1]. Thus, lookup and insert operations incur an additional log factor in the map size n, for a total of $O(k \log n)$ factor compared to both other maps.
- *HashMap Expr* (designated "HM") is an implementation of hash array mapped tries [2] from the *unordered-containers*[14] library. Like *ExprMap*, map access incurs a full traversal of the key to compute a hash and then a $O(\log_{32} n)$ lookup in the array mapped trie, as well as an expected constant number of key comparisons to resolve collisions. Consequently, lookup and insert are both in $O(k + \log_{32} n)$, where the log summand can effectively be treated like a constant for all intents and purposes.

Some clarification as to what our benchmarks measure:

- The `lookup` benchmark looks up every expression that is part of the map. So for a map of size 10000, we perform 10000 lookups of expressions each of which have approximately size 100.
- `lookup_lam` is like `lookup`, but wraps a shared prefix of 100 layers of (*Lam* `"$"`) around each expression.

---

11 https://hackage.haskell.org/package/criterion.

12 The benchmark machine runs Ubuntu 18.04 on an Intel Core i5-8500 with 16GB RAM. All programs were compiled on GHC 9.0.2 with `-O2 -fproc-alignment=64` to eliminate code layout flukes and run with `+RTS -A128M -RTS` for 128MB space in generation 0 in order to prevent major GCs from skewing the results.

13 https://hackage.haskell.org/package/containers.

14 https://hackage.haskell.org/package/unordered-containers.

- `fromList` benchmarks a naïve *fromList* implementation on *ExprMap* against the tuned *fromList* implementations of the other maps, measuring map creation performance from batches.

Querying. The results suggest that *ExprMap* is about as fast as *Map Expr* for completely random expressions in `lookup`. But in a more realistic scenario, at least some expressions share a common prefix, which is what `lookup_lam` embodies. There we can see that *ExprMap* wins against *Map Expr* by a huge margin: *ExprMap* looks at the shared prefix exactly once on lookup, while *Map* has to traverse the shared prefix of length $O(k)$ on each of its $O(\log n)$ comparisons.

Although *HashMap* loses on most benchmarks compared to *ExprMap* and *Map*, most measurements were consistently at most a factor of two slower than *ExprMap*. We believe that is due to the fact that it is enough to traverse the *Expr* twice during lookup barring any collisions (hash and then equate with the match), thus it is expected to scale similarly as *ExprMap*. Thus, both *ExprMap* and *HashMap* perform much more consistently than *Map*.

Modification. While *ExprMap* consistently wins in query performance, the edge is melting into insignificance for `fromList` and `union`. One reason is the uniform distribution of expressions in these benchmarks, which favors *Map*. Still, it is a surprise that the naïve *fromList* implementations of *ExprMap* and *Map* as list folds beat the one of *HashMap*, although the latter has a tricky, performance-optimised implementation using transient mutability.

What would a non-naïve version of *fromList* for *ExprMap* look like? Perhaps the process could be sped up considerably by partitioning the input list according to the different fields of *ExprMap* and then calling the *fromList* implementations of the individual fields in turn. The process would be very similar to discrimination sort [9], which is a generalisation of radix sort to tree-like data and very close to tries. Indeed, the *discrimination*[15] library provides such an optimised $O(n)$ *toMap* implementation for *Map*.

7 Related Work

7.1 Matching Triemaps in Automated Reasoning

Matching triemaps have been used in the automated reasoning community for decades, where they are recognised as a kind of *term index* [18], a data structure that allows efficient lookup and matching of terms such as logic formulas or program expressions. An automated reasoning system has hundreds or thousands of axioms, each of which is quantified over some variables (just like the RULEs described in Sect. 2.3). Each of these axioms might apply at any sub-tree of the term under consideration, so efficient matching of many axioms is absolutely central to the performance of these systems.

[15] https://hackage.haskell.org/package/discrimination.

This led to a great deal of work on so-called *discrimination trees*, starting in the late 1980's, which is beautifully surveyed in the Handbook of Automated Reasoning [18, Chapter 26]. All of this work typically assumes a single, fixed, data type of "first order terms" like this[16]

```
data MKey = Node Fun [MKey]
```

where *Fun* is a function symbol, and each such function symbol has a fixed arity. Discrimination trees are described by imagining a pre-order traversal that (uniquely, since function symbols have fixed arity) converts the *MKey* to a list of type [*Fun*], and treating that as the key. The map is implemented like this:

```
data DTree v = DVal v | DNode (Map Fun DTree)
lookupDT :: [Fun] → DTree v → Maybe v
lookupDT []       (DVal v)  = Just v
lookupDT (f : fs) (DNode m) = case Map.lookup f m of
  Just dt → lookupDT fs dt
  Nothing → Nothing
lookupDT _        _         = Nothing
```

Each layer of the tree branches on the first *Fun*, and looks up the rest of the [*Fun*] in the appropriate child. Extending this basic setup with matching is done by some kind of backtracking.

Discrimination trees are heavily used by theorem provers, such as Coq, Isabelle, and Lean. Moreover, discrimination trees have been further developed in a number of ways. Vampire uses *code trees* which are a compiled form of discrimination tree that stores abstract machine instructions, rather than a data structure at each node of the tree [19]. Spass [20] uses *substitution trees* [8], a refinement of discrimination trees that can share common *sub-trees* not just common *prefixes*. (It is not clear whether the extra complexity of substitution trees pays its way.) Z3 uses *E-matching code trees*, which solve for matching modulo an ever-growing equality relation, useful in saturation-based theorem provers. All of these techniques except E-matching are surveyed in [18].

If we applied our ideas to *MKey* we would get a single-field triemap which (just like *lookupDT*) would initially branch on *Fun*, and then go though a chain of *ListMap* constructors (which correspond to the *DNode* above). You have to squint pretty hard—for example, we do the pre-order traversal on the fly—but the net result is very similar, although it is arrived at by entirely different thought process.

Many of the insights of the term indexing world re-appear, in different guise, in our triemaps. For example, when a variable is repeated in a pattern we can eagerly check for equality during the match, or instead gather an equality constraint and check those constraints at the end [18, Section 26.14].

[16] Binders in terms do not seem to be important in these works, although they could be handled fairly easily by a de Bruijn pre-pass.

A related application of matching tries appear in [14, Section 2.2], where *eliminators* express both parameter-binding and pattern-matching in a single Core language construct, with a semantics not unlike GHC's own `-XLambdaCase` extension. They realise that their big-step interpreter implements eliminators via special generalised tries that can express variable matching – which corresponds to our triemaps applied to linear patterns.

7.2 Haskell Triemaps

Trie data structures have found their way into numerous Haskell packages over time. There are trie data structures that are specific to *String*, like the *StringMap*[17] package, or polymorphically, requiring just a type class for trie key extraction, like the *TrieMap*[18] package. None of these libraries describe how to index on expression data structures modulo α-equivalence or how to perform matching lookup.

Memoisation has been a prominent application of tries in Haskell [6,7,11]. Given a function f, the idea is to build an *infinite*, lazily-evaluated trie, that maps every possible argument x to (a thunk for) $(f\ x)$. Now, a function call becomes a lookup in the trie. These ideas are implemented in the *MemoTrie*[19] library, and have been generalised to representable functors in the *representable-tries*[20] library. For memo tries, operations like alter, insert, union, and fold are all irrelevant: the infinite trie is built once, and then used only for lookup.

A second strand of work concerns data type generic, or polytypic, approaches to generating tries, which nicely complements the design-pattern approach of this paper (Sect. 3.8). [10] describes the polytypic approach, for possibly parameterised and nested data types in some detail, including the realisation that we need *atEM* and *unionWithEM* in order to define *insertEM* and *unionEM*. The aforementioned *MemoTrie*, *representable-tries* and *generic-trie*[21] libraries generate trie implementations polytypically. For our approach to do the same, we would need to find a good way to specify binding structure (as in *Lam*) in a polytypic setting, which thus far has been elusive.

The *twee-lib*[22] library defines a simple term index data structure based on discrimination trees for the *twee* equation theorem prover. We would arrive at a similar data structure in this paper had we started from an expression data type

data *Expr* = *App Con* [*Expr*] | *Var Var*

In contrast to our *ExprMap*, *twee*'s *Index* does path compression not only for paths ending in leaves (as we do) but also for internal paths, as is common for radix trees.

---

[17] https://hackage.haskell.org/package/StringMap.
[18] https://hackage.haskell.org/package/TrieMap.
[19] https://hackage.haskell.org/package/MemoTrie.
[20] https://hackage.haskell.org/package/representable-tries.
[21] https://hackage.haskell.org/package/generic-trie.
[22] https://hackage.haskell.org/package/twee-lib.

It is however unclear how to extend *twee*'s *Index* to support α-equivalence, hence we did not consider it for our benchmarks in Sect. 6.

8 Conclusion

We presented trie maps as an efficient data structure for representing a set of expressions modulo α-equivalence, re-discovering polytypic deriving mechanisms described by [10]. Subsequently, we showed how to extend this data structure to make it aware of pattern variables in order to interpret stored expressions as patterns. The key innovation is that the resulting trie map allows efficient matching lookup of a target expression against stored patterns. This pattern store is quite close to discrimination trees [18], drawing a nice connection to term indexing problems in the automated theorem proving community.

Acknowledgments. We warmly thank Leonardo de Moura and Edward Yang for their very helpful feedback.

References

1. Adams, S.: Functional pearls efficient sets—a balancing act. J. Funct. Program. **3**(4), 553–561 (1993). https://doi.org/10.1017/S0956796800000885
2. Bagwell, P.: Ideal hash trees. Technical report, Infoscience Department, École Polytechnique Fédérale de Lausanne (2001)
3. Chakravarty, M.M.T., Keller, G., Peyton Jones, S.: Associated type synonyms. In: Proceedings of the Tenth ACM SIGPLAN International Conference on Functional Programming, ICFP 2005, pp. 241–253. Association for Computing Machinery, New York (2005). https://doi.org/10.1145/1086365.1086397
4. Connelly, R., Morris, F.L.: A generalization of the trie data structure. Math. Struct. Comput. Sci. **5**, 381–418 (1995)
5. de Bruijn, N.: Lambda calculus notation with nameless dummies, a tool for automatic formula manipulation, with application to the church-rosser theorem. Indagationes Mathematicae (Proceedings) **75**(5), 381–392 (1972). https://doi.org/10.1016/1385-7258(72)90034-0
6. Elliott, C.: Composing memo tries (2008). http://conal.net/blog/posts/composing-memo-tries
7. Elliott, C.: Elegant memoization with functional memo tries (2008). http://conal.net/blog/posts/elegant-memoization-with-functional-memo-tries
8. Graf, P., Meyer, C.: Advanced indexing operations on substitution trees. In: McRobbie, M.A., Slaney, J.K. (eds.) CADE 1996. LNCS, vol. 1104, pp. 553–567. Springer, Heidelberg (1996). https://doi.org/10.1007/3-540-61511-3_113
9. Henglein, F.: Generic discrimination: sorting and paritioning unshared data in linear time. SIGPLAN Not. **43**(9), 91–102 (2008). https://doi.org/10.1145/1411203.1411220
10. Hinze, R.: Generalizing generalized tries. J. Funct. Program. **10**(4), 327–351 (2000). http://journals.cambridge.org/action/displayAbstract?aid=59745
11. Hinze, R.: Memo functions, polytypically! In: Proceedings of the 2nd Workshop on Generic Programming, Lima, Portugal, pp. 17–32 (2000)

12. Knuth, D.E.: The Art of Computer Programming, Volume III: Sorting and Searching. Addison-Wesley (1973)
13. Mycroft, A.: Polymorphic type schemes and recursive definitions. In: Paul, M., Robinet, B. (eds.) Programming 1984. LNCS, vol. 167, pp. 217–228. Springer, Heidelberg (1984). https://doi.org/10.1007/3-540-12925-1_41
14. Perera, R., Nguyen, M., Petricek, T., Wang, M.: Linked visualisations via galois dependencies. Proc. ACM Program. Lang. **6**(POPL) (2022). https://doi.org/10.1145/3498668
15. Peyton Jones, S., Graf, S.: Triemaps that match (2023). https://arxiv.org/abs/2302.08775
16. Peyton Jones, S., Graf, S.: Supplemental github repository (2024). https://github.com/simonpj/triemap-paper
17. Peyton Jones, S., Tolmach, A., Hoare, T.: Playing by the rules: rewriting as a practical optimisation technique in GHC. In: 2001 Haskell Workshop. ACM SIGPLAN. ACM (2001). https://www.microsoft.com/en-us/research/publication/playing-by-the-rules-rewriting-as-a-practical-optimisation-technique-in-ghc/
18. Sekar, R., Ramakrishnan, I., Voronkov, A.: Handbook of Automated Reasoning, vol. 2. Elsevier (2001)
19. Voronkov, A.: The anatomy of vampire: Implementing bottom-up procedures with code trees. J. Autom. Reason. **15**, 237–265 (1995)
20. Weidenbach, C., Dimova, D., Fietzke, A., Kumar, R., Suda, M., Wischnewski, P.: SPASS version 3.5. In: Schmidt, R.A. (ed.) CADE 2009. LNCS (LNAI), vol. 5663, pp. 140–145. Springer, Heidelberg (2009). https://doi.org/10.1007/978-3-642-02959-2_10

Author Index

D. Orchard et al. (Eds.): Alan Mycroft Festschrift, LNCS 15500, p. 263, 2026.
https://doi.org/10.1007/978-3-032-08187-2

MIX
Papier aus verantwortungsvollen Quellen
Paper from responsible sources
FSC® C105338

If you have any concerns about our products,
you can contact us on
ProductSafety@springernature.com

In case Publisher is established outside the EU,
the EU authorized representative is:
Springer Nature Customer Service Center GmbH
Europaplatz 3, 69115 Heidelberg, Germany

Printed by Libri Plureos GmbH
in Hamburg, Germany